JOURNAL FOR THE STUDY OF THE OLD TESTAMENT SUPPLEMENT SERIES
364

Editors
David J.A. Clines
Philip R. Davies

Executive Editor
Andrew Mein

Editorial Board
Richard J. Coggins, Alan Cooper, J. Cheryl Exum, John Goldingay,
Robert P. Gordon, Norman K. Gottwald, John Jarick,
Andrew D.H. Mayes, Carol Meyers, Patrick D. Miller

Sheffield Academic Press
A Continuum imprint

The Shekhinah Departs

The Signs of Sin

Seriousness of Offence
in Biblical Law

Jonathan P. Burnside

Journal for the Study of the Old Testament
Supplement Series 364

For my parents, with love and gratitude

Copyright © 2003 Sheffield Academic Press
A Continuum imprint

Published by Sheffield Academic Press Ltd
The Tower Building, 11 York Road, London SE1 7NX
370 Lexington Avenue, New York NY 10017-6550

www.continuumbooks.com

All rights reserved. No part of this publication may be reproduced or transmitted in any form or by any means, electronic or mechanical, including photocopying, recording or any information storage or retrieval system, without permission in writing from the publishers.

British Library Cataloguing-in-Publication Data

A catalogue record for this book is available from the British Library

Typeset by Sheffield Academic Press
Printed on acid-free paper in Great Britain by Bookcraft Ltd, Midsomer Norton, Bath.

ISBN 0-8264-6218-9

CONTENTS

List of Figures   viii
Foreword   ix
Acknowledgments   xii
Abbreviations   xiv

Introduction   1

Chapter 1
DETERMINING SERIOUSNESS OF OFFENCE IN BIBLICAL LAW   10
   1.1   'Mind the Gap!': Modern and Biblical Legal Praxis   10
   1.2   Semantic versus Narrative Readings of Biblical Law   15
   1.3   Identifying the Values of Biblical Law   20
   1.4   A Rationalist Approach to Seriousness of Offence   21
   1.5   A Semiotic Approach to Seriousness of Offence   24
   1.6   Literary Presentation and Seriousness   29
   1.7   Identifying the Texts   32

Chapter 2
THE WRATH OF GOD ON THE SONS OF DISOBEDIENCE:
SERIOUSNESS OF OFFENCE AND DEUTERONOMY 21.18-21   37
   2.1   Offence Description   38
   2.2   Building the Identikit   40
   2.3   Identifying the Paradigm Case   45
   2.4   The Rebellious Son as a 'Son of Belial'   55
   2.5   Seriousness of Offence   59
   2.6   Different Jurisdictions, Different Forms of Proof   68
   2.7   Disinheritance: A Further Dimension of Seriousness?   71
   2.8   Conclusion   78

Chapter 3
LINEAGE, TITLE AND THE BAREFOOT MAN:
SERIOUSNESS OF OFFENCE AND DEUTERONOMY 25.5-10   79
   3.1   Offence Description   84
   3.2   The Paradigm Case   90
   3.3   Seriousness of Offence   102
   3.4   Seriousness of Punishment   105
   3.5   Conclusion   119

Chapter 4
PROSTITUTION AND THE JEALOUSY OF GOD AND MAN:
SERIOUSNESS OF OFFENCE IN LEVITICUS 21.9 AND
DEUTERONOMY 22.20-21   121
   4.1   Performative Registers in Leviticus 21.9   122
   4.2   Descriptive Registers in Leviticus 21.9   126
   4.3   Offence Description (Leviticus 21.9)   128
   4.4   Seriousness of Offence   134
   4.5   Performative Registers in Deuteronomy 22.20-21   135
   4.6   Descriptive Registers in Deuteronomy 22.20-21   136
   4.7   Offence Description (Deuteronomy 22.20-21)   137
   4.8   Seriousness of Offence   155
   4.9   Conclusion   155

Chapter 5
SIN, STATUS AND SACRIFICE:
SERIOUSNESS OF OFFENCE AND LEVITICUS 4:1-35   157
   5.1   Leviticus 4.1-35 as a Text for Seriousness   157
   5.2   Registers of Seriousness   160
   5.3   Offence Description   161
   5.4   Offender Status   166
   5.5   Registers of Seriousness in Leviticus 4   174
   5.6   Conclusion   185

Chapter 6
THE SHEKHINAH DEPARTS:
SERIOUSNESS OF OFFENCE AND EZEKIEL 8.1-18   186
   6.1   Performative Registers of Seriousness   186
   6.2   Descriptive Registers of Seriousness   189
   6.3   Offence Description   190

6.4	The Seriousness of Idolatry		198
6.5	Social Status as an Element of Seriousness of Offence		206
6.6	Location as an Element of Seriousness		210
6.7	Conclusion		223

Chapter 7
SERIOUSNESS OF OFFENCE IN BIBLICAL LAW   225

7.1	The Praxis of Seriousness of Offence	225
7.2	Values	227
7.3	Elements of Seriousness	228
7.4	Performative registers	229
7.5	Descriptive Registers	232
7.6	Communicating Legal Values	233
7.7	Harmfulness and Wrongfulness	239
7.8	Character	245
7.9	Semiotic Groups	247

Chapter 8
CONCLUSION   253

Bibliography   254
Index of References   268
Index of Authors   000

LIST OF FIGURES

Figure 1.	Summary of cases presented in Deuteronomy 22.13-29	138
Figure 2.	Registers of seriousness according to status of offender in Leviticus 4	174
Figure 3.	Aerial view of Sanctuary showing grades of holiness	178
Figure 4.	Degree of pollution caused by the sin of the המשיח הכהן and the כל־עדת ישראל	180
Figure 5.	Degree of pollution caused by the sin of the נשיא and the member of the עם הארץ	181
Figure 6.	A semiotic square showing the seriousness of idolatry	200
Figure 7.	Map of the prophet's movements according to Ezekiel 8	219

Foreword

'Seriousness of offence' is a subject that lies at the crossroads of law, criminology and theology and one that shows the need for dialogue between these disciplines. The subject of what makes an offence serious, or one crime worse than another, is not just a question of criminal law, or of social hygiene but of morality. The morality of seriousness is arguably seen most clearly in biblical law. This is because, in any given society, elements of seriousness and the justificatory theory of criminal law that validates their selection is the object of social struggle. By contrast, matters are different in a theocracy such as ancient Israel where law is normative. Here, the elements of seriousness stand in sharper relief.

Exploring seriousness of offence in biblical law is (almost by definition) to explore the dark side of life which has lost contact with God. It is to become reacquainted with the seamy underbelly of human nature. Here, we will encounter a zoo of lusts, a bedlam of ambitions, a nursery of fear and a harem of fondled hatreds.[1] It will be familiar territory, not least to a twenty-first century society whose state of moral promiscuity and passive receptivity has made us tolerant consumers, if not connoisseurs, of vice and weirdness. We readily identify with the second-century Roman playwright Terence who wrote: *'homo sum; humani nil a me alienum puto'* ('I am a man, I count nothing human foreign to me').[2] But biblical law moves us on from the acceptance of iniquity ('nothing human is foreign to me') to the recognition that human dysfunction and brutality is not what it means to bear the image of God ('nothing *foreign* is *human* to me'). Naming the beastly and subhuman is a prelude to recognising the truly human. As Emile Durkheim noted in another context, crime is both a crisis and an opportunity.

Biblical law takes the opportunity, when punishing an offender, to express something of the nature of the offence. This is expressed by means

---

1. C.S. Lewis, *Surprised by Joy* (London: Geoffrey Bles, 1955), p. 181.
2. Terence, *Heauton Timorumenos* in *The Comedies* (trans. Betty Radice; London: Penguin Books, 1965), l. 77.

of signs because punishment in biblical law has, among other things, an educative purpose. It may be painful, but it is always meaningful. It communicates to the offender and to wider society in ways that everyone can understand precisely what it is about the offence that makes it serious. To coin a phrase, it has semiotic valence. It communicates its message effectively and on many different levels. To this extent, it may be contrasted with the reductionist approach to punishment in the modern penal system. We rely far too much upon imprisonment as a primary form of punishment. It is as limiting as a golfer playing a round of golf with only one club. Such a system is restricted in the range of censure it can express and it suffers from a corresponding lack of semiotic power. This deficiency is part of the reason why it was said, at the end of the last century, 'There is a serious void at the centre of the criminal justice system. There is no clearly understood set of purposes which it is meant to achieve or principles which it is meant to observe'.[3] The descent into penal pragmatism bodes ill, and not only for those who are punished.

There is a great need today to repair the moral foundations of punishment and to respond to wrongdoing appropriately. This makes the apposite nature of the penalties in biblical law one of their most striking features. It is this aspect that partly justifies the stress on semiotics in this book and its title, *The Signs of Sin*. As Dostoevsky saw in *The House of the Dead*, 'if one wanted…to annihilate a man utterly, to inflict on him the most terrible of punishments…one need only give him work of an absolutely, completely useless and irrational character'.[4] Even hard, but purposeful, labour is rational; there is sense and meaning in such a punishment. But if one has 'to move a heap of earth from one place to another and back again—I believe the convict would hang himself in a few days…preferring rather to die than endure such humiliation, shame and torture'.[5] Even in punishment—or *especially* in punishment—we cannot escape the need for meaning. Punishment without meaning is punishment without value. Suffering without meaning destroys, but punishment with justice has the potential to transfigure. This is the true purpose of the criminal law.

Our study of crime and punishment in the Hebrew Bible posits a moral universe in which human beings are held accountable to God as responsible creatures. It presents penalties that are intelligible, constructive and most of all legitimate. It is a vision of punishment with justice.

3. D. Faulkner, 'All flaws and Disorder', *The Guardian*, 11 November 1993.
4. F. Dostoevsky, *The House of the Dead* (New York: MacMillan, 1982), p. 28.
5. Dostoevsky, *House of the Dead*, p. 28.

That said, there is much about this book that remains dark. The case studies will remind us of our capacity to choose not only what is hurtful to God and to society, but what is damaging to oneself. Salvation is deliverance from that which will destroy us. The message of Ezekiel, which forms the climax of the case studies in this book, is that crime and deviance, the spawn of idolatry, force the *Shekhinah*, the glory of God, to depart. What is left behind is evil, horror, waste and emptiness. The punishment of God is experienced in abandonment. For the Christian, the full extent of this abandonment is heard in Jesus' cry of dereliction from the cross, 'My God, my God, why hast thou forsaken me?' (Mt. 27.46). In the New Testament, this is the moment when the Shekhinah departs. Jesus the Temple is destroyed when God abandons him. It is this traumatic event, the ultimate dissociation, that illustrates the gravity of seriousness. The statement in 2 Corinthians that Christ 'became' sin (2 Cor. 5.21) means that the crucifixion is the ultimate 'sign of sin'. For Christians, law, criminology and theology meet at the cross for this is the place where the seriousness of every offence is given its true weight.

ACKNOWLEDGMENTS

It is a pleasure to record with deep thanks all who supported the writing of this book.

The Signs of Sin is a slightly modified version of a doctoral thesis submitted to the Faculty of Law, University of Liverpool. Accordingly, my first and most profound debt of gratitude is to my supervisor, Prof. Bernard Jackson. His unique combination of rationality and imagination has been a constant source of inspiration. His rationality helped to keep me honest to the text and his imagination turned every problem into an opportunity. His support and example is beyond praise.

I am greatly indebted to the coalition of charities, both Jewish and Christian, who gave financial support during that period, including: the Goldberg Family Trust; the P. H. Holt Charitable Trust; the Oxford Centre for Hebrew and Jewish Studies; the Relationships Foundation; the Saint Luke's College Foundation; and the Whitefield Institute.

I also wish to thank Prof. K. A. Kitchen and Prof. A. R. Millard of the School of Archaeology, Classics and Oriental Studies, who gave timely advice and assistance throughout the period of research.

Dr. Michael Schluter launched this odyssey over breakfast in a Scottish bed and breakfast establishment in 1994 and provided key support ever since. I am grateful to the Minnaar family who allowed me to share their home whilst both thesis and book were completed; and especially to Kees and Doris, who also enabled me to spend a memorable summer at the Hebrew University of Jerusalem. The Bible was never the same again.

A special debt is due to the President, staff and community of the Oxford Centre for Hebrew and Jewish Studies for making my stay as a David Paterson Junior Visiting Fellow in Jewish Law in 1997 so profitable and memorable. I also want to thank those in Oxford who gave of their time during this period, especially Dr. Paul Joyce and Professors John Barton, John Finnis, Oliver O'Donovan and Hugh Williamson. Remaining defects, of course, belong to none of the above persons, but to myself alone.

Acknowledgments

I am grateful to Cecil Grant, Hilary Jolly, Irene Lancaster and Penelope Lee who kindly read and commented on earlier drafts of the manuscript. Finally, my thanks to Hannelie Grobler for providing the diagrams and frontispiece art.

'Wherefore the law is holy, and the commandment holy, and just, and good' (Rom. 7.12, KJV).

Jonathan P. Burnside
Bristol
November 2001

ABBREVIATIONS

AA	*American Anthropologist*
AASOR	Annual of the American Schools of Oriental Research
AB	Anchor Bible
ABD	David Noel Freedman (ed.), *The Anchor Bible Dictionary* (New York: Doubleday, 1992)
AJS	*American Journal of Sociology*
ANET	James B. Pritchard (ed.), *Ancient Near Eastern Texts Relating to the Old Testament* (Princeton: Princeton University Press, 1950)
BA	*Biblical Archaeologist*
BASOR	*Bulletin of the American Schools of Oriental Research*
BB	*Biblebhashyam*
BBE	The English Bible in Basic English
BDB	Francis Brown, S.R. Driver and Charles A. Briggs, *A Hebrew and English Lexicon of the Old Testament* (Oxford: Clarendon Press, 1907)
Bib	*Biblica*
BibInt	*Biblical Interpretation: A Journal of Contemporary Approaches*
BJC	British Journal of Criminology
BJRL	*Bulletin of the John Rylands University Library of Manchester*
BR	*Bible Review*
BT	*The Bible Translator*
BTB	*Biblical Theology Bulletin*
CBQ	*Catholic Biblical Quarterly*
CE	Codex Eshnunna
Cod.	Justinian's *Code*
Coll.	*Collatio Legum Mosaicarum et Romanarum*
Dig.	Justinian's *Digest*
EncJud	*Encyclopaedia Judaica*
FLR	Family Law Reports
GTJ	*Grace Theological Journal*
HBT	*Horizons in Biblical Theology*
HTR	*Harvard Theological Review*
HUCA	*Hebrew Union College Annual*
IBD	J.D. Douglas *et al.* (eds.), *Illustrated Bible Dictionary* (3 vols.; Leicester: InterVarsity Press, 1994)

ICC	International Critical Commentary
IDB	George Arthur Buttrick (ed.), *The Interpreter's Dictionary of the Bible* (4 vols.; Nashville: Abingdon Press, 1962)
ILR	*Israel Law Review*
Int	*Interpretation*
JAAR	*Journal of the American Academy of Religion*
JANESCU	*Journal of the Ancient Near Eastern Society of Columbia University*
JAOS	*Journal of the American Oriental Society*
JBL	*Journal of Biblical Literature*
JBS	*Journal of the Behavioural Sciences*
JJS	*Journal of Jewish Studies*
JLA	*Jewish Law Annual*
JNES	*Journal of Near Eastern Studies*
JPS	Tanakh. The Holy Scriptures
JQR	*Jewish Quarterly Review*
JSNT	*Journal for the Study of the New Testament*
JSNTSup	*Journal for the Study of the New Testament*, Supplement Series
JSOT	*Journal for the Study of the Old Testament*
JSOTSup	*Journal for the Study of the Old Testament*, Supplement Series
JSQ	*Jewish Studies Quarterly*
JSS	*Journal of Semitic Studies*
JTS	*Journal of Theological Studies*
KJV	King James Version
LE	Laws of Eshnunna
LH	Laws of Hammurabi
NBD	J.D. Douglas *et al.* (eds.), *New Bible Dictionary* (London: Inter-Varsity Press, 1996)
NCBC	New Century Bible Commentary
NEB	New English Bible
NIBC	New International Biblical Commentary
NICOT	New International Commentary on the Old Testament
NIDOTE	Willem A. VanGemeren (ed.), *New International Dictionary of Old Testament Theology and Exegesis* (5 vols.; Grand Rapids: Zondervan, 1997)
NIV	New International Version
NKJ	New King James Version
NRSV	New Revised Standard Version
NTS	*New Testament Studies*
OCHJS	Oxford Centre for Hebrew and Jewish Studies
RB	*Revue biblique*
ResQ	*Restoration Quarterly*
RSV	Revised Standard Version
SBL	Society of Biblical Literature

SBLDS	SBL Dissertation Series
SBLMS	SBL Monograph Series
TA	*Transactional Analysis*
TDNT	Gerhard Kittel and Gerhard Friedrich (eds.), *Theological Dictionary of the New Testament* (trans. Geoffrey W. Bromiley; 10 vols.; Grand Rapids: Eerdmans, 1964–)
TDOT	G.J. Botterweck and H. Ringgren (eds.), *Theological Dictionary of the Old Testament*
ThWAT	G.J. Botterweck and H. Ringgren (eds.), *Theologisches Wörterbuch zum Alten Testament* (Stuttgart: W. Kohlhammer, 1970–)
TNTC	Tyndale New Testament Commentaries
TynBul	*Tyndale Bulletin*
TZ	*Theologische Zeitschrift*
VE	*Vox Evangelica*
VT	*Vetus Testamentum*
VTSup	*Vetus Testamentum*, Supplements
WBC	Word Biblical Commentary
ZAW	*Zeitschrift für die alttestamentliche Wissenschaft*

Translations of biblical passages are from the Revised Standard Version, unless otherwise noted.

INTRODUCTION

What makes one crime worse than another, and why? This is not an academic question. In fact, the issue cuts to the heart of criminal justice policy. Under section 1(2)(a) of the Criminal Justice Act 1991, seriousness of offence is the primary ground, in practice, for determining who is sent to prison.[1] As a result, defining seriousness has huge practical implications because imprisonment is the worst thing that the State is legally allowed to do to another human being. Other reasons for sending people to prison lie close at hand (e.g. deterrence, rehabilitation and risk to the public). But since 1992 (when the Criminal Justice Act 1991 came into force), the primary ground has been that of seriousness. On average, 375 people are committed to prison in England and Wales *every day*,[2] usually because it is thought that their offence is so serious that only prison will do.

Seriousness of offence embodies the maxim that it is 'absurd…to apply the same punishment to crimes of different malignity'.[3] As Montaigne wrote, 'Vices are all alike as they are vices…but though they are equally vices, yet they are not equal vices'.[4] Seriousness assumes, by definition, that offences vary in their degree of moral turpitude. Of course, attempts have been made to define 'seriousness' without recourse to morality. One pragmatic definition of seriousness is found in the Home Office's decision, in the early 1980s, to develop a blueprint on 'seriousness' based on a statistical analysis of current court practice. 'Seriousness' was defined in

---

1. Other, less prevalent, grounds for justifying a custodial sentence are found in §1(2)(b) (where the offence is of a sexual or violent nature) and §1(3) (where the offender has refused to agree to a community service order that requires his or her consent).
2. Prison Population and Accommodation Briefing (June 2001), H.M. Prison Service.
3. S. Mendelsohn, *The Criminal Jurisprudence of the Jews* (New York: Sepher-Hermon Press, 1991 [1890]), pp. 37-38.
4. M. de Montaigne, *Essais livre second* (Paris: Fernand Rockes, 1931 [1613]), chapter 2, p. 2.

terms of the *status quo*. There was nothing normative about this definition of seriousness. It was simply a matter of 'what the courts do'. Needless to say, such definitions do not satisfy because they do not provide the criminal justice process with a 'general justifying aim'[5] in regard to punishment.

Seriousness of offence means deciding that one form of behaviour is more morally repugnant than another. These judgments are based on a set of values; a value being 'an idea which serves as a ground for choosing between possibilities'.[6] By telling us what penalties are appropriate for offending, seriousness of offence is a touchstone for what society sees as most threatening to its survival.

In a great many cases it is not difficult to determine the relative seriousness of an offence. We can all agree that murder is worse than stealing a library book. But on the other hand, there are many cases where the needle of our moral compass hovers uncertainly between life and property. Which is worse: pouring paint over someone else's car or killing a suspected burglar in your home? In America, where surveys of crime seriousness can influence the scaling of punishment, respondents averred that pouring paint over someone else's car was more serious than killing a suspected burglar.[7] Another American survey (in fact, the largest of its kind ever conducted) found that robbing a victim of $1,000 at gunpoint was equal to walking into a public museum and stealing a painting worth $1,000.[8] For these American respondents, the salient factor seems to be the amount of money involved.

Such responses indicate that a society's views of seriousness are ultimately shaped by its underlying values. If a society's underlying values are chiefly material, then there is no difference between robbery at gunpoint and art theft. But if the starting-point is the primacy of human life, the conclusion will be very different.

People have differing (and often bitterly contested) perceptions of seriousness: for example the current debate in the UK regarding legalizing

---

5. The term 'general justifying aim' is taken from H.L.A. Hart, 'Prolegomenon to the Principles of Punishment', in *Punishment and Responsibility* (Oxford: Clarendon Press, 1968), pp. 1-27.

6. P.J. Allott, *Eunomia* (Oxford: Oxford University Press, 1990), p. 48.

7. F.T. Cullen *et al.*, 'The Seriousness of Crime Revisited', *Criminology* 20 (1982), pp. 83-102 (91).

8. P.B. Hoffman and P.L. Hardyman, 'Crime Seriousness Scales: Public Perception and Feedback to Criminal Justice Policymakers', *Journal of Criminal Justice* 14 (1986), pp. 413-31 (422).

cannabis and lowering the age of consent for anal intercourse. Like justice (inevitably), seriousness of offence is an essentially contested concept. This means that in any discussion of seriousness of offence we must ask: whose ideas of seriousness are we talking about? And more particularly, who, in law, decides what is a serious offence?

According to the Court of Appeal in *Baverstock* ([1993] 14 Cr. App. R. [S.], 477) and *Cox* ([1993] 14 Cr. App. R. [S.], 481) seriousness of offence refers to 'the kind of offence which when committed...would make all right thinking members of the public, knowing all the facts, feel that justice had not been done by the passing of any sentence other than a custodial one'. This is, of course, a very convenient formula for the sentencer. As Ashworth rightly observes: 'Who are these people, if not the judges and magistrates themselves?'[9] The problem with this definition of seriousness is that sentencers can effectively keep the content of the test under wraps.[10] Instead of treating seriousness as a normative question that should be answered systematically,[11] the Court of Appeal has turned what should be a moral question into an exercise in judicial discretion that is either unreviewable, or which can only be reviewed on an unprincipled basis.[12] The long and the short of it is that we have no way of knowing whether the Act is being correctly applied. Unfortunately, there is no formula or set of sentencing guidelines that will do away with the quandary. This is because the problem of seriousness reflects the wider difficulty of how to secure moral agreement in a pluralist culture. It is the dilemma of a postmodern legal culture that has no reference point beyond itself.

Perhaps we may begin to progress towards firmer criteria in sentencing by addressing directly the problem that seriousness poses for liberal jurisprudence. This stems from the fact that a formative influence upon modern liberalism was the Enlightenment contention that truth could be attained by rational method, which could in turn appeal to principles undeniable by any fully reflective, rational person.[13] On this view, reason alone would

---

9. A. Ashworth, *Sentencing in the 80's and 90's: The Struggle for Power* (Eighth Eve Saville Memorial Lecture, 21 May 1997; London: Institute for the Study and Treatment of Delinquency), p. 7.

10. A. Ashworth and M. Hough, 'Sentencing and the Climate of Opinion', *Criminal Law Review* (1996), pp. 776-87 (784).

11. A. Ashworth and A. von Hirsch, 'Recognising Elephants: The Problem of the Custody Threshold', *Criminal Law Review* (1997), pp. 187-99 (189).

12. Ashworth and von Hirsch, 'Recognising Elephants', p. 196.

13. See generally H.J. Laski, *The Rise of European Liberalism* (London: Unwin Books, 1962).

enable us to work out the elements of seriousness. Today, however, there is less confidence, particularly among post-Enlightenment relativists and perspectivists, that such optimism can be sustained. Alasdair MacIntyre is an example of one modern philosopher who traces the shortcomings of liberal thought back to its abandonment of a conception of rational enquiry as embodied in a tradition: what he terms a tradition of enquiry.[14] Enlightenment and post-Enlightenment theories of justice that seek to apply to all societies everywhere are rejected in favour of those theories that are derived from historical traditions of enquiry. Justice is a concept with a history, and since there are diverse traditions of enquiry, with histories, there are justices rather than justice. For this reason justice is not abstract; it finds its meaning within the context of a particular living, historic and geographic community. Consequently, it is not possible to ask and answer questions about justice from a standpoint external to all traditions.[15]

A tradition is defined as an argument extended through time, from which standards of rational justification emerge as part of a history. Different traditions embody different visions of what is just and since there is a diversity of traditions of enquiry with histories, there are rationalit*ies* rather than rationality and justic*es* rather than justice. MacIntyre concludes that:

> there is no other way to engage in formulation, elaboration, rational justification, and criticism of accounts of...justice except from within some one particular tradition... There is no standing ground, no place for enquiry, no way to engage in the practices of advancing, evaluating and rejecting reasoned argument apart from that which is provided by some particular tradition or other.[16]

The postmodern task, as identified by MacIntyre, is to engage in debate within the context of a tradition of enquiry. It is an approach that runs counter to the liberal assumption that it is possible to assess and justify a particular moral tradition from a neutral vantage-point. Rather, it is only from within traditions that anyone is able to acquire the standing-ground or the vocabulary from which to reject or defend particular ethical practices. The one who stands outside all traditions is a mute. The completely 'impartial' person has no possible basis on which to make a valuative judgment. As Moore writes:

---

14. A. MacIntyre, *Whose Justice? Which Rationality?* (Trowbridge: Duckworth, 1988), p. 7.
15. MacIntyre, *Whose Justice?*, p. 369.
16. MacIntyre, *Whose Justice?*, p. 350.

> It is an illusion to suppose that there is some neutral vantage-point from which to assess and justify a particular moral tradition... The person who stands outside all practices is...rendered speechless with no grounds for rejecting or defending any particular ethical conception.[17]

One approach to the problem of seriousness might therefore be to draw on the tradition of justice represented by biblical law. There are several reasons for choosing biblical law. Firstly, it provides excellent resources for evaluating the problem. Insofar as 'seriousness' is properly regarded as a moral issue, it is advantageous to examine seriousness of offence in a legal system that draws no distinction between law and morality. This is the case in biblical law. Secondly, this tradition provides continuity with the past. Law is an organic structure and so, in seeking answers to contemporary problems, it is important to have some continuity with the past.[18] Law takes society from the past to the future. It is a means of transforming society in accordance with its values and it tends to make the future of that society into what society has determined in the past that its future should be.[19] To the extent that Judaeo-Christian thought has had a major influence upon individual and social consciousness, it is fair to claim that this tradition is an integral part of the dynamism of law. Thanks to the influence of Christianity,[20] biblical law has had a significant influence on the English criminal justice system.[21]

However, some might doubt whether biblical law has anything to say about seriousness. Is it not the case that in the Bible *all* transgressions are called sin, irrespective of the magnitude of the particular deed? As R. Abba b. Kahana puts it: 'The Scripture has made the lightest command in

---

17. M. Moore, *Foundations of Liberalism* (Oxford: Clarendon Press, 1993), p. 171
18. Cf. Sir J.G. Frazer, *Folk-lore in the Old Testament: Studies in Comparative Religion, Legend and Law* (London: Macmillan, 1923), p. 351: 'Only a law which in some measure answers to a people's past has any power to mould that people's future'.
19. Allott 1990, pp. 84-85.
20. D.M. Walker, *The Oxford Companion to Law* (Oxford: Clarendon Press, 1980), pp. 57, 213, 664, 724.
21. See, variously, S.J. Bailey 'Hebrew Law and its Influence on the Law of England', *Law Quarterly Review* 47 (1931), pp. 533-35; D.S. Davies, *The Bible in English Law* (London: Jewish Historical Society of England, 1954); B.S. Jackson, 'Liability for Animals in Scottish Legal Literature', *The Irish Jurist* 10 (1975), pp. 334-51; 'Susanna and the Singular History of Singular Witnesses', in W. de Vos *et al.* (eds.), *Acta Juridica: Studies in Honour of Ben Beinart* (Cape Town: Juta & Co., 1977), II, pp. 37-54; 'Travels and Travails of the Goring Ox', in Y. Avishur and J. Blau (eds.), *Studies in Bible and the Ancient Near East* (Jerusalem: Rubinstein, 1978), pp. 41-56.

the *Torah* equal to the heaviest command'.[22] Surely such an approach does not encourage us to weigh the relative seriousness of one offence against another?

However, whilst it is true that 'sin is sin is sin', the punishment for sin varies. This is enough to tell us that biblical law discriminates between the gravity of different offences. In addition biblical law, like the concept of seriousness, bids recognition of relative rank, significance and primacy in its individual commandments. As the quote by R. Abba b. Kahana itself indicates, the Rabbis constantly mention and discuss the distinction between light and heavy and small and great commandments.[23] The problem of seriousness demonstrates precisely what the prophets[24] and Jesus taught:[25] namely, there are priorities to be observed in responding to God's law. For these reasons it is appropriate to examine the problem of seriousness of offence from the perspective of biblical law.

Others, however, may not be convinced of the need for the present study. Why does it matter whether seriousness of offence is couched in a tradition of enquiry, or not? Why not let it be a purely pragmatic exercise, to be applied by judges as they see fit? The reason is that any attempt to define seriousness without reference to moral values leaves the question of who is sent to prison extremely vulnerable to political pressure. In recent years, we have seen how political statements by successive British Home Secretaries to the effect that 'prison works' have redefined the meaning of seriousness. The result is that seriousness has quickly become equated with how many people the Prison Service can (or ought) to hold. This is ironic because the motive for putting seriousness at the heart of the criminal justice process was to reduce the prison population. That was the stated policy behind the Criminal Justice Act 1991.[26] Before the Criminal Justice Act 1991 was implemented in 1992, the prison population in England and

---

22. *Qid.* 1.27d.

23. Walter C. Kaiser Jr, 'The Weightier and Lighter Matters of the Law: Moses, Jesus and Paul', in Gerald F. Hawthorne (ed.), *Current Issues in Biblical and Patristic Interpretation* (Grand Rapids: Eerdmans, 1975), pp. 180-83.

24. Mic. 6.6-8; Amos 5.21-24; Hos. 6.6; Isa. 1.11-17; 43.22-24; Ps. 51.16-19; 1 Sam. 15.22.

25. E.g. Mk 12.28-34. Jesus instructs the Pharisees to go home and reflect on Hos. 6.6 if they want to understand the requirements of the law of Moses (cf. Mt. 9.13 and 12.7).

26. Home Office, *Crime, Justice and Protecting the Public* (Cm. 965, London: HMSO, 1990).

Wales stood at 45,800. Now it stands at 66,026 (as of 1 June 2001),[27] an increase of over 40 per cent. Why? Is it because more people are committing serious crimes? No. In fact, the number of convictions for indictable offences has actually *fallen* during this period.[28] What has happened is that judges and magistrates are sending more people to prison for crimes that would not have attracted a prison sentence ten years ago. This development is most probably a response to the 1993 'law and order counter-reformation' in which politicians promoted the use of imprisonment as a form of punishment. Judges, it would seem, are sending more people to prison for less serious offences rather than risk being pilloried for handing down what might be seen as a soft sentence. If so, then it means that the size of the prison population has become a question of political choice—not of justice, nor of seriousness. For this reason, modern law and the problem of seriousness underline the need for transcendent values in the sentencing process. Take them away and all that is left is a programme of social exclusion and social engineering. That truly is a serious offence.

Crime-seriousness has gained importance in recent years, thanks to the rise of 'just-desert' orientated conceptions of sentencing which demand that the punishment should be proportionate to the gravity of the offence.[29] Yet, surprisingly, 'the jurisprudence of crime seriousness is a topic that has scarcely been touched'.[30] Von Hirsch, the leading desert theorist, and Jareborg write: 'The gravity of the crime has such obvious relevance to the sanction...[one] would think that judges and legal scholars surely must have been theorising about it for years. Yet that has not been the case.'[31] The purpose of this book is to examine the problem of seriousness of offence from a comparative perspective, that of biblical law. My hope is that the 'depleted discourse' of 'seriousness of offence' will benefit from an interdisciplinary conversation between law and theology.

---

27. National Association for the Care and Rehabilitation of Offenders.
28. I. Dunbar and A. Langdon, *Tough on Justice: Sentencing and Penal Policies in the 1990s* (London: Blackstone, 1998), p. 144.
29. See A. Von Hirsch, 'Proportionality in the Philosophy of Punishment: From "Why Punish?" to "How Much?"', *Criminal Law Forum* 1 (2) (1990), pp. 259-90 and 'The Politics of "Just Deserts"', *Canadian Journal of Criminology* 32 (1990), pp. 397-413.
30. A. Von Hirsch and N. Jareborg, 'Gauging Criminal Harm: A Living-Standard Analysis', *Oxford Journal of Legal Studies* 11 (1991), pp. 1-38 (2).
31. Von Hirsch and Jareborg, 'Gauging Criminal Harm', p. 2.

The use of the phrase 'seriousness of offence' in relation to biblical law presupposes an etic perspective to the text.[32] I am conscious that throughout this book I shall step between the 'emic' and the 'etic'. We are, however, justified in using the term 'seriousness of offence' in relation to biblical law. Every modern reading of a text brings certain categories to a text in order to understand it. 'Seriousness of offence' is one such category. It reflects the concerns of a modern reader without doing violence to the ancient text. Indeed, it can be argued that the link between the ancient and the modern world is primarily one of values.[33]

The aim is to identify some of the key elements and registers of seriousness of offence in biblical law by means of a series of case-studies. The conceptual distinction between elements and registers of seriousness is one that I shall draw throughout the book. Elements, or components, of seriousness refer to those factors that contribute to our assessment of the seriousness of an offence. They may include, for example, the identity of the offender, the identity of the victim, the location of the offence and so on. Registers of seriousness refer to the different semiotic forms in which values can be expressed. These can be either linguistic or non-linguistic.[34] We can distinguish between registers that are primarily descriptive and those that are primarily performative. Descriptive registers are those registers that relate to the language of the text. The language of the text often characterizes the offence in a certain way (e.g. describing the offence as 'evil' or as an 'abomination'). It also describes what ought to happen in a given case (e.g. what ought to be done to the offender). Performative registers, on the other hand, are concerned with the acts of those people who perform what is in the description (e.g. the performance of a sacrificial ritual).

In outlining these aspects of seriousness of offence in biblical law I do not assume that values of seriousness remain constant throughout the

---

32. Cf. J.W. Rogerson, *Anthropology and the Old Testament* (Oxford: Basil Blackwell, 1978) and R.E. Clements (ed.), *The World of Ancient Israel: Sociological, Anthropological and Political Perspectives* (Cambridge: Cambridge University Press, 1989).

33. See, e.g., V.H. Matthews and D.C. Benjamin, *Social World of Ancient Israel, 1250–586 BCE* (Peabody, MA: Hendrickson, 1993).

34. I am therefore using the word 'register' in a modified sense to that of modern linguists for whom 'registers' describe linguistically distinct activities related to particular occupations, see e.g. D. Crystal, *The Cambridge Encyclopaedia of Language* (Cambridge: Cambridge University Press, 1991), p. 52.

biblical period, nor that different writers of the same period necessarily share the same values. To the extent that the final version of the biblical text reflects the values of its final editors, I shall be examining seriousness of offence in terms of how it is understood at the end of the redaction process. The claim is not being made that the elements of seriousness of offence to which I draw attention are representative of every period of biblical law. Nonetheless, it is hoped that our thematic exploration will shed new light on certain aspects of biblical law and inform reflection on the modern search for seriousness.

Chapter 1

DETERMINING SERIOUSNESS OF OFFENCE IN BIBLICAL LAW

> 'The enterprise is exploration into God.'
> Christopher Fry, *A Sleep of Prisoners*

How are we to determine the values that underlie seriousness of offence in biblical law? This is not a straightforward issue. We must start by recognizing that our understanding of law depends, to a large degree, on the use to which it is put. For this reason, my approach to the question of legal values begins with an analysis of legal praxis.

1.1. *'Mind the Gap!': Modern and Biblical Legal Praxis*

There appears to be a sharp contrast between the assumptions that underlie modern and biblical legal praxis. Modern legal praxis is based on the Rule of Law, that is, the belief that adjudication should be governed by laws and not by people.[1] This legislative model of law, based upon the application of statutes in court, holds that general normative propositions laid down in advance are normally sufficient to deal with every human situation that may arise. The role of the judge is to apply general rules laid down by a higher authority, whether the legislature itself or superior courts in a system of precedents.

Jackson argues that this Western conception of law is culturally-contingent and does not reflect biblical legal praxis.[2] In other words, the idea that judges should see their role as the application of general rules laid down by authority was not the dominant conception of the relationship between

---

1. An assumption that is, arguably, far removed from the reality of the judicial process, B.S. Jackson, 'Ideas of Law and Legal Administration: A Semiotic Approach', in R.E. Clements (ed.), *The World of Ancient Israel: Sociological, Anthropological and Political Perspectives* (Cambridge: Cambridge University Press, 1989), pp. 185-202 (258).
2. Jackson, 'Ideas of Law', pp. 185-86.

1. *Determining Seriousness of Offence*

legislator and judge in biblical law. It is true that written *Torah* existed in the pre-exilic period.[3] However, a number of sources seem to indicate that its function was not the provision of statutory rules to be applied as such by the judges. In other words, the rules were not regarded as authoritative in their linguistic form as well as their content.[4] There are a number of reasons for this.

1.1.1. *Deuteronomy 17.18-20*
In Deut. 17.18-20, the written legal text (the ספר תורה, 'Book of the Law') is intended for the king. It is for his instruction, and its primary purpose is to make him wise. In contrast to the legislative model of law, the law in Deut. 17.18-20 has, primarily, a sapiential function.[5]

1.1.2. *Deuteronomy 16.18-20*
According to Deut. 16.18-20, the newly appointed judges (שפטים) are charged in entirely general terms. They are not asked to follow any particular rules, rather, they are told simply to act justly and to avoid corruption. Of course, this does not mean that the שפטים have *carte blanche*. But the connotations of wisdom that are implied in Deut. 16.18-20 suggest that the judge's sense of justice is to be informed by the conventional norms of practical wisdom.[6] Only when local wisdom proves insufficient, do the local judges need to consult the central authorities (Deut. 17.8-13). Again there is no reference to any authoritative set of rules that the priests have to apply.[7]

1.1.3. *2 Chronicles 19.4-11*
This pattern is reinforced by Jehoshaphat's charge to his newly appointed judges:

> Consider what you do, for you judge not for man but for the LORD; he is with you in giving judgement. Now then, let the fear of the LORD be upon you; take heed what you do, for there is no perversion of justice with the LORD our God, or partiality, or taking bribes (2 Chron. 19.6-7).

---

3. Hos. 8.12; F. Crüsemann, *The Torah: Theology and Social History of Old Testament Law* (trans. A.W. Mahnke; Edinburgh: T. & T. Clark, 1996), pp. 17-26.
4. Jackson, 'Ideas of Law', p. 245.
5. Jackson, 'Ideas of Law', pp. 246-47.
6. Jackson, 'Ideas of Law', p. 245.
7. The verb דרש suggests that an oracular consultation is used to resolve the matter; Jackson, 'Ideas of Law', p. 246.

Verse 6 implies that the judges' intuition will be divinely directed. Executing justice is primarily a matter of exercising Solomonic wisdom, not the application of legal rules.[8] This is confirmed by the injunction 'let the fear of the LORD be upon you'. The fear of the LORD is, of course, the beginning of wisdom (e.g. Prov. 1.7).[9] The judges are to be careful in what they do and are warned against injustice, partiality and bribery (cf. Deut. 16.18-20). Nothing is said about any set of laws written in a ספר ('book') nor is there even any mention of *Torah*. This does not mean that the judges lacked access to the divine law which was, after all, supposed to make them wise in the first place. What it means is that the mere possession of divine rules was not sufficient to secure justice. Biblical law required, in addition, inspiration. Judges came to decisions in accordance with divinely inspired intuition, to produce a just result in terms of a specific case. Nor are the local judges subjected, as *per* the legislative approach, to general rules passed on from on high. Rather, they are given a *general* authority to judge according to divinely inspired intuitions of justice.[10]

Jehoshaphat's appointment of judges for Jerusalem follows a similar pattern. Again no substantive rules of divine law are commended to them and the charge to these judges is entirely general in character (2 Chron. 19.9-11).[11] The stress is again on charisma ('you must serve faithfully and wholeheartedly') and wisdom ('in the fear of the LORD') (2 Chron. 19.9). The fact that the Jerusalem judges have to report to the chief priest 'for every matter concerning the LORD' suggests that the priests were the real source of the law to be applied by the judges. But even here, as in Deut.

---

8. 1 Kgs 3.9 records Solomon's prayer thus, 'Give thy servant therefore an understanding mind to govern thy people, that I may discern between good and evil'. This is followed by an example of Solomon's wise ruling which causes 'all Israel...[to stand] in awe of the king, because they perceived that the wisdom of God was in him, to render justice' (1 Kgs 3.28).

9. 2 Chron. 19.7 uses פחד־יהוה instead of the phrase יראת יהוה common to Proverbs. But this does not matter. The phrase יראת יהוה appears in 2 Chron. 19.9 where Jehoshaphat charges the Jerusalemite judges in similar terms to those of 2 Chron. 19.6-7: פחד־יהוה is simply a stylistic variant.

10. Jackson, 'Ideas of Law', p. 247.

11. Jackson, 'Ideas of Law', p. 247. Cf. the NIV which imports the 'legislative' model into the text, 'Jehoshaphat appointed...[them] *to administer the law of the LORD*' (my italics), 2 Chron. 19.8. But the text simply says למשפט יהוה ('to give judgment for the LORD'). For the meaning of משפט, see e.g. Herntrich, 'The Old Testament Term משפט', in *TDNT*, III, pp. 923-33.

1. Determining Seriousness of Offence

17.8-13, there is no reference to a binding set of rules that even these ultimate authorities must apply.[12]

1.1.4. *2 Chronicles 17.7-9*

As part of the same judicial reform, the king orders his officers to take copies of 'the book of the law of the LORD' (ספר תורת יהוה) around the country and to teach it to the people by oral proclamation (2 Chron. 17.7-9).[13] The audience is the people, not legal experts. This further undermines the legislative model. Nor is there any suggestion that the officers leave the written law with their audience for private study.[14]

1.1.5. *Self-Executing Rules*

A further indication that at least some of the rules of biblical law are directed to the general public and not to experts may be found in the somewhat arbitrary character of several laws of the Covenant Code. For example, the law in Exod. 21.36 is not concerned with whether the substitute ox is of equal value to the one that has been killed.[15] The relative values of the oxen is 'arbitrary' in the sense that, rather than delay matters by technical or legal arguments that require adjudication, the parties are encouraged to put the matter behind them as quickly as possible. Similar concerns may underlie Exod. 22.3 [H 22.2] which offers no guarantee that the value of the thief, or of his labour for the period involved, will coincide with the value of the stolen animal.[16] Likewise the remedy in Exod. 22.5 [H 22.4] does not state that the quantum or the quality of the produce from the tortfeasor's field must be identical to the produce which his animal has wrongfully consumed.[17] Jackson characterizes such cases as

---

12. Jackson, 'Ideas of Law', p. 247.

13. Cf. the practice of the Assyrian kings in sending royal officers to each town to exercise a teaching function with regard to the law; M. Weinfeld, *Deuteronomy and the Deuteronomic School* (Oxford: Clarendon Press, 1972), p. 163.

14. B.S. Jackson, 'Some Semiotic Questions for Biblical Law', in A.M. Fuss (ed.), *Jewish Law Association Studies III: The Oxford Conference Volume* (Atlanta: Scholars Press, 1987), pp. 1-25 (14).

15. B.S. Jackson, 'An Aye for an I?: The Semiotics of Lex Talionis in the Bible', in W. Pencak and J. Ralph Lindgren (eds.), *Semiotics and the Human Sciences: New Directions—Essays in Honor of Roberta Kevelson* (New York and Bern: Peter Lang, 1997), pp. 127-49 (138-40).

16. B.S. Jackson, *Studies in the Semiotics of Biblical Law* (JSOTSup, 314; Sheffield: Sheffield Academic Press, 2000), pp. 86-87.

17. Jackson, 'An Aye for an I?', pp. 138-40.

'self-executing laws', viz. rules so formulated as to reduce the need for third-party adjudication.[18] This is possible through the use of evidentiary tests and dispute-resolving mechanisms that are easy to administer. For example, Exod. 22.2-3 [H 22.1-2] states that it is justifiable to kill by night and not by day. This 'self-executing rule' means that the kin of a deceased thief would know, without an adjudication, whether the killing had been justified or not. In the next verse (Exod. 22.4 [H 22.3]) theft is proved by the simple evidentiary test of 'hot possession'. Such 'arbitrary' rules make proof of an offence easier and provide remedies that can be readily implemented by the parties without the need for institutional adjudication. The possibility of resolving the dispute without the need for a formal adjudication may have been a necessity but it is itself a benefit. It avoids the transaction costs of adjudication and the potential for shame (cf. Prov. 25.7-10).[19] Finally, such self-executing rules presuppose a system of self-help. They reflect the practical value of having norms that are capable of execution by the people themselves, without the need for specialist intervention. The use of arbitrary tests is consistent with a pre-institutionalised legal process where the norms are directed to the people as a form of teaching, and to be implemented by them directly.

1.1.6. *ANE Legal Praxis*
This picture is consistent with what is known of legal praxis elsewhere in the ANE. According to Eichler, the literary structure of the Laws of Eshnunna (c. 1800 BCE) suggests that this text was the product of scholastic activity rather than litigation proceedings.[20] In particular, the use of polar cases with maximal variation is thought to confirm the sapiential function of the Laws of Eshnunna. They seem designed to provoke thought and discussion, especially on the range of real life cases that are found between the polarity.[21] Within this large grey area, judges must use their discretion.

---

18. B.S. Jackson, 'Practical Wisdom and Literary Artifice in the Covenant Code', in B.S. Jackson and S.M. Passamaneck (eds.), *Jewish Law Association Studies VI: The Jerusalem 1990 Conference Volume* (Atlanta: Scholars Press, 1992), pp. 65-92 (70).

19. Jackson, 'Ideas of Law, pp. 197-98.

20. B.L. Eichler, 'Literary Structure in the Laws of Eshnunna', in F. Rochberg-Halton (ed.), *Language, Literature and History: Philological and Historical Studies Presented to Erica Reiner* (New Haven: American Oriental Society, 1987), pp. 71-84 (84).

21. LE §23 and §24, §25 and §26, §29 and §30, §33 and §34/35, Eichler, 'Literary Structure', pp. 77, 76, 75, 79 respectively.

1. Determining Seriousness of Offence

A similar use of polar cases may also be found in the Laws of Hammurabi (c. 1700 BCE).[22]

Further evidence of a 'gap' between law and legal procedure in Mesopotamia may be found in the fact that neither the prologue nor the epilogue of LH commends them to the use of the judges.[23] Indeed, of the large corpus of judicial decisions from Old Babylonia to which we have access, there is only one quotation from LH and not even this is of a substantive legal provision.[24] Sometimes the rulings of the courts conform to the code, but frequently they do not.

For these reasons, neither LE nor LH bear out any expectation that the codes were applied in the courts like modern statutes.[25] Jackson notes that biblical law is arguably even further removed from the model of modern legislation than the ANE codes because of the complex literary and narrative framework in which it has been transmitted.[26]

1.1.7. Summary

The modern idea of law, based upon the application of statutes in court, is not applicable to ancient Israel. In both Deuteronomy and 2 Chronicles written law has a didactic rather than a legislative function. It is given in order to teach, not to turn its recipients into legal experts. Nor is it the sole basis of adjudication: a right attitude towards YHWH is prerequisite.

1.2. Semantic versus Narrative Readings of Biblical Law

1.2.1. Semantic Readings

The legislative model necessarily gives rise to a semantic view of law. A legal statute is seen as a text whose very words, as opposed to its meaning, are thought to be authoritative. Because every word in modern legislation is regarded as of binding character, the technical rules of statutory interpretation are primarily semantic. Judges must take into account all of the canonical words of legislation and cannot substitute as their primary source of authority words from any other source. Nor can they extrapolate from the words some main point or principle.[27] A semantic reading sees the law

---

22. LH §129 and §130, Eichler, 'Literary Structure', p. 82.
23. *ANET*, pp. 164-65, 177-80.
24. Jackson, 'Ideas of Law', p. 248.
25. Eichler, 'Literary Structure', p. 81, cf. Jackson 'Ideas of Law', pp. 248-49.
26. Jackson, 'Ideas of Law', p. 186.
27. Jackson, 'Ideas of Law', p. 187.

in question as comprising a set of words whose meaning needs to be elucidated. The question 'what does this law mean?' becomes 'what is the meaning of words *x* in the statute?' The answer to the latter question requires a paraphrase and results in one verbal proposition being replaced by another. The law then applies to all cases falling within the semantic meaning of the words.

Biblical law is frequently read in semantic terms. However, to the extent that the legislative model itself is inapplicable to ancient Israel (see 1.1.7 above), we should perhaps question the value of taking a semantic approach to biblical law. For example, Deut. 21.18-21 deals with the case of the 'stubborn and rebellious' son who is denounced by his parents for being a 'glutton and a drunkard'. Brichto asks, what would be the case if the son was 'stubborn, rebellious and gluttonous' but not a 'drunkard'.[28] This is a good example of a semantic approach and it misses the point. We shall argue in Chapter 2 that a better approach is to read Deut. 21.18-21 in narrative terms.

1.2.2 *Narrative Readings*

Jackson argues that a narrative as opposed to a semantic approach to the meaning of language is more consistent with the biblical legal praxis outlined in 1.1.1–1.1.5 above. He contends that the task of making sense of biblical law needs to be based on some conception of sense-making in general.[29] A semiotically inspired approach to legal philosophy, in which law is read narratively in terms of narrative rules or paradigm cases, sees the law as evoking narrative typifications of action.[30] That is, on a narrative reading, words are not purely linguistic signifiers but the signifiers of life-bound images. They differ from modern statutory language in the sense that they are more concrete than legislative rules. By contrast, legislative rules are more abstract and conceptual.[31] Interpreting legislative texts requires levels of generality and abstraction that concrete, picture-oriented formulations of narrative rules usually lack.

---

28. H.C. Brichto, 'Kin, Cult, Land and Afterlife—A Biblical Complex', *HUCA* 44 (1973), pp. 1-54 (32).

29. Jackson, 'An Aye for an I?', p. 133.

30. For the relationship between 'narrative typification' and the general semiotic theory of B.S. Greimas see B.S. Jackson, *Making Sense in Law* (Liverpool: Deborah Charles Publications, 1995), pp. 140-63.

31. Paradigm cases are only the first step in the process of abstraction. They abstract from a total situation those features that are regarded as particularly significant.

1. *Determining Seriousness of Offence* 17

Critically, the assumptions that underpin legislative and narrative readings of a text are quite different. A legislative approach sees the text as covering all cases that may be subsumed under it. A narrative approach, on the other hand, suggests that the paradigm may sometimes extend beyond what is covered by the semantic reading. This is the difference between regarding the text as containing paradigms (or narrative-rules) and viewing it as imposing a legislative stipulation.[32]

Decisions that are based on paradigm cases or narrative rules proceed differently from decisions based on legislative texts. A narrative approach proceeds from judgments of relative similarity between the case in hand and the narrative typification of action or narrative stereotype.[33] It is not based on the semantic analysis and application of the words in which the narrative rule is expressed. Thus, if a case arises that is different from the typical case or narrative rule, the question is not the semantic one that is associated with legislative texts, viz., 'Do the words of the rule "cover" the case?' Rather, the question is: 'How similar is this case to the one in the narrative rule?'[34] It is an important difference, because questions of relative similarity evoke intuitive judgments of justice to a greater degree than semantic questions. This is because the question 'how similar?' is not merely a descriptive question, it is also an evaluative question ('How justifiable is it to treat these cases as similar?'). By contrast, semantic questions are more concerned with the meaning of the words.[35]

It should be noted that the 'typical' case does not mean simply 'frequency of occurrence'. A case can be 'paradigmatic' in two different senses: (1) because it 'happens all the time' or (2) in the sense that although it does not happen all the time there is a stock of social knowledge of what ought to happen (or usually does happen) in such circumstances.

1.2.3. *Narrative Rules and Biblical Law*
Biblical law, in common with other legal collections of antiquity, is far from comprehensive in terms of the range of cases that it deals with.[36]

---

32. B.S. Jackson, *Law, Fact and Narrative Coherence* (Liverpool: Deborah Charles Publications, 1988), pp. 101-10.
33. Cf. D. Sudnow, 'Normal Crimes: Sociological Features of the Penal Code in a Public Defender Office', *Social Problems* 12 (1965), pp. 255-76.
34. B.S. Jackson, *Making Sense in Jurisprudence* (Liverpool: Deborah Charles Publications, 1996), pp. 240-41.
35. Jackson, *Making Sense in Jurisprudence*, pp. 240-41.
36. R. Yaron, 'Biblical Law: Prolegomena', in B.S. Jackson (ed.), *Jewish Law in*

Even if we assume, for the sake of argument, that biblical society possessed a more complete body of divine law than has survived in our sources, it is still likely that a great many cases lacked specific guidance. In such circumstances, where the case in hand is not one of the paradigm cases for which specific solutions are provided, Deuteronomy and 2 Chronicles suggest that it is for the judges, applying their intuitive and divinely guided sense of justice, to decide which of the known paradigms the case most resembles (see 1.1.1–1.1.4, above). The laws give rise to discussion at a popular level. This debate would be concerned, not with linguistic questions comparable to our methods of statutory interpretation, but rather substantive analogies. This in turn would generate, at a deeper level, some consideration of values.[37]

The case for reading biblical law in narrative, rather than semantic, terms is strengthened when we consider that the law has a didactic rather than a statutory purpose (see 1.1.1–1.1.4, above). If the purpose of the law is to teach, it is likely that such teaching is directed, particularly in its non-scholastic form, to central issues and situations rather than to peripheral ones.[38] This creates a working presumption that the law is mainly concerned with typical cases. This, however, is only a presumption and I propose to test it on a case-by-case basis (Chapters 2 to 6).[39]

In determining whether the law is mainly concerned with typical cases, social context is a key factor. If the social context is one in which a certain law is the typical case then the assumption is strong that this is the meaning of the teaching. We should not therefore assume that the same rule applies in non-typical cases, even though these cases might fall within the semantic meaning of the words. A narrative approach may thus yield very different results from a semantic approach. For example, we should not

Legal History and the Modern World (Jewish Law Annual Supplement 2; Leiden: E.J. Brill, 1980), pp. 27-44 (37).

37. B.S. Jackson, 'Practical Wisdom', p. 92.

38. B.S. Jackson, 'Legalism and Spirituality', in Edwin B. Firmage, Bernard G. Weiss and John W. Welch (eds.), *Religion and Law: Biblical-Judaic and Islamic Perspectives* (Winona Lake, IN: Eisenbrauns, 1990), pp. 243-61 (257-58).

39. Jackson's thesis has been developed in the context of the *Mishpatim*. Here, it may well be claimed that the norms of that particular legal collection make best sense as a collection of 'paradigm cases' or 'wisdom-laws'. Indeed, the nearest one gets to a slightly unusual case is Exod. 21.22 but even here one might claim that since women were pregnant much of the time even this case is not particularly unusual. However, the question whether this approach can be usefully extended to cases found outside the Covenant Code must be asked separately of each particular document and legal text.

assume that the talionic formula is intended to apply to a one-eyed man who put out one of the eyes of a two-eyed man.

1.2.4 *Narrative Stereotypes and Biblical Law*
A narrative approach to biblical law presupposes stereotypical social knowledge on the part of its audience. Stereotypes are the form in which social knowledge is acquired and stored. Stereotypical knowledge varies from one society to the next, depending on what the prevailing stereotypes are. Each society has its own stock of substantive narratives or typifications of action. These represent typical human behaviour patterns that are known and understood within that society or social group.[40] They provide the framework for understanding the meaning of particular laws. Some typifications are relative to particular semiotic groups.

The presence of narrative stereotypes in a text is important for our understanding of seriousness of offence. This is because narrative stereotypes or typifications of action are not neutral descriptions of typical action. They include a tacit social evaluation.[41] They express an aesthetic judgment that may often include evaluations of seriousness. For example, the collective image of acting like a 'stubborn and rebellious' son who is 'a glutton and a drunkard' does not merely describe a general lifestyle of which such behaviour is a part. It also includes the social evaluation that such a person is intolerable (see Chapter 2). The same applies to the narrative typification of 'playing the harlot' (see Chapter 5). Other stereotypes we shall encounter include the greedy 'rotter' who cares more about his inheritance than he does about his dead brother's name (see Chapter 3) and the idolater (see Chapter 6).

Again, we should not treat collective images as if they were statutory definitions. The collective image represents the core of the message. The further one departs from that collective image the less sure one can be that the same message is intended to apply, or that it would be regarded as applicable by the audience.[42] Or, to put it another way, the further one departs from the paradigm, the less 'gravitational force'[43] the paradigm will exert; whether on the parties seeking to negotiate their own solution, or on a court searching for the just solution.

---

40. B.S. Jackson, 'Anchored Narratives and the Interface of Law, Psychology and Semiotics', *Legal and Criminological Psychology* 1 (1996), pp. 17-45 (20).
41. Jackson, 'Anchored Narratives', p. 33.
42. Jackson, *Semiotics of Biblical Law*.
43. R. Dworkin, *Taking Rights Seriously* (London: Duckworth, 1978), p. 111.

1.2.5. Summary

To sum up, the legal praxis of biblical law is far removed from that of a modern statute which stipulates rules through verbal definitions. Unlike the modern law-book, biblical law is not a permanent record of the authoritative wording of the rules, to be consulted when needed by the law's subjects and its administrators.[44] Rather, the sources indicate that biblical law is sapiential in nature. Its primary purpose is to educate its hearers via a series of paradigm cases that in turn draw on stereotypical social knowledge.

1.3. Identifying the Values of Biblical Law

1.3.1. Law and Values

Every society legislates in accordance with its values. Accordingly, all societies embody values within their legal systems. This is especially true of a construct like 'seriousness of offence' which signposts what society holds dear. The difficulty is that these values often reside at an implicit rather than an explicit level. Like the foundations of a house, values are vital, but invisible. The meaning of a given rule is dependent on the moral values of the society in which the rule operates. Take for example the common rule found in Underground stations that 'Dogs must be carried on the escalator'. This rule is not as self-evident as it appears because it presupposes social knowledge about the relationship between dogs and escalators. Escalators contain cracks and dogs have small feet and there is danger that the animal could be mangled. In addition the rule assumes a shared social concern for canine welfare. Dogs must be carried in your arms and not on the escalator. However, the meaning of the rule would be radically different if the underlying social values were to change. If we lived in a sadistic society that thrived on animal cruelty and wanted to see dogs mangled, the rule would mean: 'Dogs must be carried *on* the escalator'. It would be inconceivable to carry a dog in your arms. At the other extreme, we could imagine a canine-obsessed society in which dog-carrying was elevated to a national sport. With these social values, the rule would mean it is compulsory to carry a dog on an escalator ('Dogs *must* be carried on the escalator') and non-dog lovers would have to take the stairs.

Suffice it to say, the meaning of a rule in a given society depends on shared agreement of society's moral values. The same applies to biblical law. Biblical law is characterized by brevity and an allusive style which

---

44. Jackson, 'Ideas of Law', p. 195.

presupposes knowledge of context and background (literary as well as social) which is not possessed by the typical twenty-first-century Westerner. One must be prepared to look beyond the words on the page to understand the world of values and implicit social knowledge that made the texts meaningful to their original audience.

Of course there are temporal and spatial limits to the confidence we can have in understanding the original meaning of biblical law. However, I shall assume that a reading which takes cultural assumptions explicitly into account will be a more plausible interpretation of the seriousness of an offence and its significance to an ancient audience than an interpretation that reads the texts from the perspective of modern Western moral and cultural norms.

1.3.2. *Extracting Legal Values*

We have noted that values in modern and biblical law often reside at an implicit, rather than an explicit level. How do we extract legal values from the text? Jurists have conducted their search for underlying legal values in a number of different ways. These methods reflect different conceptions of the nature of legal values and of the way in which they operate. Following Jackson, I distinguish between two models of determining legal values; the rationalist (see 1.4 below) and the semiotic (see 1.5 below).[45] I shall then examine the shortcomings of a rationalist approach to seriousness (see 1.4 below) and the advantages of adopting a semiotic approach to seriousness of offence (see 1.5 below).

1.4. *A Rationalist Approach to Seriousness of Offence*

A rationalist approach seeks underlying principles of law in explicit legal statements and as such it is primarily attached to the surface level of the text. It treats individual rules as bases for the inference of more general principles. The rationalist approach to biblical legal values is exemplified by Greenberg[46] and Finkelstein.[47]

---

45. Jackson, 'Semiotic Questions', p. 16.
46. M. Greenberg, 'Some Postulates of Biblical Criminal Law', in Menahem Haran (ed.), *Yehezkel Kaufmann Jubilee Volume* (Jerusalem: Magnes Press, 1960), pp. 5-28.
47. J.J. Finkelstein, 'The Ox That Gored', *Transactions of the American Philosophical Society* 71 (1981), pp. 3-89.

1.4.1. *Greenberg's Inner Postulates*

Greenberg argues that biblical law is an expression of 'underlying postulates or values of culture'[48] which means that particular laws can only be interpreted in the light of certain key concepts and value judgments.[49] Greenberg's rationalist approach to explicating jural postulates relies, first, on explicit value statements in the texts.[50] But because biblical law rarely provides express statements of values or principles (see 1.3.2 above) Greenberg is forced to draw on rationalist reconstructions of the supposed reasons for individual laws. He does this by assuming that particular cases are instances of more general values and that it is possible to infer by abstraction what these general values are. Concretely expressed rules regarding murder are taken in combination with concretely expressed rules regarding theft to derive *general* propositions about the value of life compared to the value of property. Thus on Greenberg's approach Exod. 21.30, for example, yields the postulate that human life and property are incommensurable.[51] It is a rationalist approach in the sense that it seeks to infer general rules by a process of abstraction. A rationalist approach to seriousness would assume that the concept of seriousness of offence reflected the inner postulates of biblical law. It would try to make explicit certain principles of seriousness that are thought to be implicit, perhaps by generalizing from a small number of concretely expressed laws.

However, this approach is fraught with methodological difficulties. Firstly, Greenberg's approach is criticized by Jackson[52] who argues that while biblical law may contain certain values or principles (for example, such maxims as 'a life for a life': Exod. 21.23; Lev. 24.18) we must be cautious about making explicit certain postulates that are only implicit. '[It is only when principles] assume an explicit form that we can be confident (a) that they exist; (b) that they were consciously articulated; (c) that a certain minimum value, sufficient for their inclusion, was placed upon them; (d) that their range can be determined within reasonable limits'. [53] Otherwise the search for values falls prey to the scholar's own subjective preconceptions.[54]

---

48. Greenberg, 'Postulates', p. 8.
49. Greenberg, 'Postulates', p. 8.
50. E.g. Gen. 9.6; Greenberg 'Postulates', p. 15.
51. Greenberg, 'Postulates', p. 8.
52. B.S. Jackson, 'Reflections on Biblical Criminal Law', *JJS* 24 (1973), pp. 29-37.
53. Jackson, 'Reflections', p. 13.
54. Jackson, 'Reflections', pp. 12-13.

Secondly, Greenberg's assumption that the law must be interpreted in the light of a total system of values underestimates the fragmentary nature of biblical law. Like other ancient legal systems, biblical law is far from comprehensive.[55]

Thirdly, a rationalist approach to seriousness would assume that basic differences in the evaluation of offences can be ascertained solely in terms of the penalties imposed.[56] But in many cases the same punishment is imposed for a variety of offences. This does not take us very far in understanding seriousness of offence because the imposition of the same penalty for different offences does not necessarily imply the same value judgments of those offences.[57] For example, some offences are punishable with the death penalty. But this does not mean that all such offences are equal in the degree to which they offend against the values of society. This is because there are different *forms* of the death penalty. We shall see in Chapter 4, for example, that the priest's daughter is burnt for 'playing the harlot' whilst the commoner's daughter is stoned for her 'harlotry'. The fact that both are executed for similar offences does not imply that their offences are equally serious. 'Burning' and 'stoning' are significantly different penalties because, within the social and cultural matrix of first millennial Israel, burning is a more severe penalty than stoning. A semiotic approach reminds us that there is significance in the form of the execution because it asks, what did this penalty *mean*? What is communicated by the choice of one form of capital punishment over another and what underlying values are thereby expressed?

Finally, it is unlikely that people in the biblical period would have used the law to abstract general concepts such as value of life, value of property and incommensurability. This is because the abstract concept is not found in biblical law at all. In cognitive terms, it is more likely that the kind of sense that biblical people would have made of these concrete rules would have been to attach tacit social evaluations to them and to compare them with one another in their literary structure. The rationalist approach assumes the justifiability of proceeding from concrete cases to abstract concepts without considering whether this kind of sense-making was appropriate to people in ancient Israel. To the extent, then, that this approach is *not* appropriate, the rationalist approach is anachronistic. To conclude, the rationalist approach

---

55. Jackson, 'Reflections', p. 12.
56. Greenberg, 'Postulates', p. 19, cf. Jackson, 'Reflections', p. 16.
57. Jackson, 'Reflections', p. 16.

adopted by Greenberg to the question of values in biblical law does not constitute a reliable methodology for determining seriousness of offence.

1.4.2. *Finkelstein's Cosmological Order*

Finkelstein's cosmological approach seeks to interpret the norms of biblical law against the views held in that society of the relationship between humankind and the natural world.[58] Finkelstein's approach is similar to that of Greenberg insofar as he, too, argues that one should seek the general characteristics that underlie concrete laws.[59] Seriousness, from this perspective, could be cast in terms of violating cosmological norms. Indeed Finkelstein sees the category of offences for which stoning is a penalty as 'crimes of the most serious kind for they are revolts against God, or the world order which is ordained by the divine word'.[60] Finkelstein's approach may even be taken to suggest some relationship between seriousness of offence and certain conceptions of natural law.

However, Finkelstein's criterion is so broad that it is difficult to find any offences proscribed by the Bible which are *not* insurrections against the cosmic order.[61] At a deeper level Finkelstein, like Greenberg, underestimates the possibility that a modern, Western rationalist methodology may be anachronistic when applied to biblical law.[62] Both impose a system on biblical texts which do not seem to be sufficiently integrated as a system. They also exclude the possibility of pluralist views of seriousness. An alternative, and more historically sensitive, approach to determining legal values is therefore required.

1.5. *A Semiotic Approach to Seriousness of Offence*

An alternative to the rationalist approach is the semiotic model of legal values. Like the rationalist approach, a semiotic approach also claims that it is possible to access popular values. However, a semiotic approach infers these values differently, contending that legal values reside primarily at the level of the popular unconscious.[63] They manifest themselves at the

58. Finkelstein, 'Ox That Gored', pp. 7-8 and 46.
59. Finkelstein, 'Ox That Gored', p. 5, 'In scrutinising the institutions of any civilisation we must first be sure that we know the conceptual postulates of the society under consideration, its system of values'.
60. Finkelstein, 'Ox That Gored', p. 28.
61. Jackson, *Semiotics of Biblical Law*, pp. 188-89.
62. Jackson, *Narrative Coherence*, p. 239.
63. Jackson, 'Semiotic Questions', p. 17.

level of both language and social reality by the total experience (especially in ancient societies) of legal symbolic acts.

This means that the issue of the communication of biblical values can be examined at two levels. The first level (language) concerns *how the act is described*. At this level, we shall examine the operation of descriptive registers (i.e. those registers that relate to the language of the text, such as descriptions of the offence). This of course includes the description of legal symbolic acts. The second level (social reality) concerns *how the act is performed*. At this level we shall be concerned with the operation of performative registers (i.e. acts performed by people in the texts, such as sacrificial rituals). These deal with the more visual and immediate experience of the act. The latter supposition that values are communicated at the level of the social reality of the text is based on the assumption that the biblical text is not a purely literary construction but that it also describes real social practice (contrary, for example, to Carmichael).[64] I am assuming that when an audience hears, or is taught, the biblical text, the audience relates the text to the performance of an act and can imagine the performance of the act.

To sum up: unlike the rationalist approach which finds popular values by raising the level of abstraction, a semiotic approach locates these values at the level of language and legal symbolic acts. Whereas the rationalist approach strips away the detail of the case to arrive at an abstract proposition, the semiotic approach pays close attention to the detail expressed in the act and its description.

A semiotic approach also distinguishes between linguistic meaning and aesthetic meaning. The performance of an act such as a punishment or a ritual evokes feelings. These feelings are aesthetic and they involve aesthetic judgments. Aesthetic meaning is a crucial component of seriousness of offence in biblical law because seriousness evokes feelings. We must therefore consider how these acts are experienced if we want to determine what meaning is attached to certain acts in the minds of the people.

---

64. E.g. C.M. Carmichael, *The Laws of Deuteronomy* (London: Cornell University Press, 1974); *Women, Law and the Genesis Traditions* (Edinburgh: Edinburgh University Press, 1979); 'Uncovering a Major Source of Mosaic Law: The Evidence of Deut. 21.15-22.5', *JBL* 101 (1982), pp. 505-20; 'Laws of Leviticus 19', *HTR* 87 (1994), pp. 239-50 and 'Forbidden mixtures in Deuteronomy 22.9-11 and Leviticus 19.19', *VT* 45 (1995), pp. 433-48. For criticism of Carmichael's approach see B.M. Levinson, 'Calum M. Carmichael's approach to the laws of Deuteronomy', *HTR* 83 (1990), pp. 227-57.

1.5.1. *Semiotics and Symbolism*

Semiotics is concerned with how meaning is constructed and conveyed and specifically with the study of sign structures and sign processes. It is relevant to the study of legal values because the peoples of the ANE often express legal values in symbolic acts.[65] Semiotics is also relevant because law is an aspect of sense-construction that involves acts of communication between sender and receiver. If we want to understand seriousness of offence in biblical law, therefore, we must examine how beliefs about seriousness are conveyed and signified. This means locating the meaning of punishment in the socio-cultural context where the performance is said to take place. Relevant questions include: 'What aspects of the content of the laws makes them intelligible to the biblical audience, even without conscious rationalization?' and 'What makes these penalties meaningful?' That is to say, why do they strike the community as natural or appropriate?[66]

1.5.2 *Advantages of a Semiotic Approach*

A semiotic approach has a number of advantages over a rationalist approach. Firstly, it provides a way of understanding what certain social acts and patterns of behaviour mean. It shows increased sensitivity to how ideas were constructed in their historical context and it reduces the possibility of anachronism.

Secondly, it allows us to differentiate between offences that are punished in similar ways. A semiotic approach foregrounds questions of communication. It is hence better placed than a rationalist approach to explicate the relative seriousness of, for example, offences that are all capital. This is an important advantage given that diverse offences in biblical law are punishable by the death penalty. A semiotic approach allows us to distinguish between different forms of capital punishment (e.g. burning instead of stoning, Chapter 4). It even allows us to distinguish between different *locations* for the same type of execution (e.g. stoning at the door of the father's house instead of stoning at the city gate, Chapter 4). The same advantage applies to more informal social sanctions that are also capable of a range of

---

65. E.g. P.A. Kruger, 'Symbolic Acts relating to Old Testament Treaties and Relationships', *Journal for Semitics* 2 (1990), pp. 156-70 (156); A. Viberg, *Symbols of Law* (Stockholm: Almquist & Wiksell, 1992).

66. Jackson, 'Semiotic Questions', p. 24.

modalities. Shame, for example, has a distinct semiotic matrix of its own.[67] A semiotic approach allows us to explore exactly what is being communicated by a particular shaming ritual (Chapter 3). The exploration of the meaning of an act includes the meaning of speech-acts. We will see this also in Chapter 3 where the widow's declaration in respect of the levir (Deut. 25.10) can be seen as a speech-act of humiliation and disgrace.

Thirdly, a semiotic approach allows us to draw on a greater range of registers of seriousness. Whereas a rationalist approach is largely restricted to the type of penalty imposed, a semiotic approach can draw on other registers. These include the way in which a punishment is carried out, the language used to describe the offence (Chapter 6) and its literary context (Chapter 2).

Fourthly, a semiotic approach places more emphasis on relationships between people than a rationalist approach which tends to emphasize relationships between concepts. A semiotic approach looks at what is being communicated between the sender and the receiver in the context of a specific relationship. By contrast, the rationalist approach considers the relationship between, say, the value of life and the value of property. In this respect, too, a semiotic approach is preferred against a rationalist approach. This is because the question of justice in biblical law, to which the problem of seriousness is intimately related, is cast in relational rather than abstract terms. Like justice, the problem of seriousness must be set in the context of particular relationships if it is to be seen in proper relief. We cannot approach seriousness of offence in biblical law as though we were trying to construct a global scale of values that can be applied across the board to all offences, irrespective of the nature of the crime or its context. Instead, we must approach each case in terms of the relationships involved.

Finally, a semiotic approach to biblical law highlights the different media of communication: who says what, to whom and what does it mean in a given context? It also recognizes that texts can operate on different levels, and may be addressed to particular semiotic groups. It encourages us to read the texts as sensitively as possible for the messages they convey, and to assess what relationship this may have to underlying realities. In doing so, a semiotic approach helps us to attend to the irreducible particularity of the individual legal case.

How does one prevent a semiotic approach from falling prey to the same 'preconceptions' to which, we noted, the rationalist approach is

---

67. See S.M. Olyan, 'Honour, Shame and Covenant Relations in Ancient Israel and its Environment', *JBL* 115 (1996), pp. 201-18.

susceptible? There is, of course, no guarantee that a semiotic approach will be free of subjectivity and were any pledge offered it would be rightly rejected as spurious. Intellectual honesty demands the recognition that total neutrality is impossible.[68] My response is, rather, that a semiotic approach is better suited to avoiding anachronisms by recognizing that different societies operate with different worldviews and social norms. There are more methodological controls on a semiotic approach than a rationalist one because the former locates the meaning of biblical law within the social culture of first-millennial Israel and pays due attention to literary presentation. It works against the tendency to abstract crime and punishment from other elements of the cultural matrix from which the biblical texts emerged and insists on seeing them in terms of their connections to other aspects of the social world as well as to the meanings presupposed by those texts. It is a suitable approach for texts produced in a 'high-context' society[69] such as ancient Israel where a rich common culture is assumed by all its members. In such a society, where members of the society are socialized into shared ways of perceiving and acting, texts tend to contain relatively little descriptive detail. Authors assume that their readers share a common culture and worldview and therefore do not need to convey much in the way of detail and exposition.[70] A semiotic approach helps to unlock the symbolic worlds of meaning that would simply have been assumed at the time the laws and narratives were written and on which the biblical writers, like all writers, depended to communicate their message.

The greater plausibility in this context of the semiotic as opposed to the rationalist approach derives from widespread evidence that the biblical writers used a range of semiotic markers to convey meaning. Style, grammar, narrative context, literary arrangement, choice of language, emphasis, inclusion and omission are all relevant to the construction of a semiotic model of legal values. This contrasts with the manifest absence of the kind of high-level abstract concepts on which the rationalist approach relies. I shall, therefore, adopt a semiotic approach to seriousness of offence in biblical law.

---

68. See e.g. N.T. Wright, *The New Testament and the People of God: Christian Origins and the Question of God: Volume 1* (London: SPCK, 2nd edn. 1993), Part II.

69. R. Simkins, *Creator and Creation: Nature in the Worldview of Ancient Israel* (Peabody, MA: Hendrickson, 1994), p. 41.

70. Simkins, *Creator and Creation*, pp. 41-42.

1.5.3 Adopting a Semiotic Approach

In the case-studies which follow (Chapters 2–6) I shall consider the semiotic significance of different registers of seriousness. These include different forms of execution (Chapters 2 and 3), the location of the execution site (Chapter 4), a shaming ceremony (Chapter 3), a sacrificial ritual (Chapter 5) and the departure of the *Shekhinah* from the Temple of Jerusalem (Chapter 6). Following Viberg, I shall assume that common symbols in biblical law have a conventional character within the culture, in other words, their meanings are commonly agreed upon. This is likely to be the case for the following registers of seriousness: the penalty of stoning (Chapter 2 and Chapter 4), the penalty of burning (Chapter 4), the sacrificial ritual described in Leviticus 4 (Chapter 5) and the departure of the *Shekhinah* (Chapter 6).

However, we may not assume that all symbols are conventional in character. Some may be non-conventional, in which case it is left to the performance of the particular act to communicate its symbolic meaning. In such cases the conventional agreement and its socio-cultural context is less important. This may be the case with the חליצה ('sandal-removal') ceremony (Chapter 3).

Finally, we are not restricted to the symbolic importance of sanctions alone. Even matters of process are value-laden.[71] Thus I shall pay careful attention to the semiotics of legal procedure and how this develops our understanding of seriousness. It is relevant to defining the seriousness of the protagonists' behaviour in Chapters 2, 3, 4 and 6.

1.6. *Literary Presentation and Seriousness*

Literary presentation is important to our understanding of seriousness of offence for several reasons. Firstly, I argued in 1.5 above that a semiotic approach to seriousness of offence attempts to understand the significance of the punishment in terms of its own contextual, conventional assumptions. However, since these assumptions are primarily available for study in literary form it follows that the world of seriousness is accessible only through the world of the text. Contextual literary interpretation is thus an important element of determining seriousness of offence in biblical law.

Our emphasis upon the final literary form of the text means that source-critical questions have less to contribute to an understanding of seriousness of offence in biblical law. Our approach identifies the key issue as the

---

71. B.S. Jackson, 'The Literary Presentation of Multiculturalism in Early Biblical Law', *International Journal for the Semiotics of Law* 23 (1995), pp. 181-206 (204).

semiotic significance of a particular punishment and how it functions in the world presented by the texts. This means that the attempt to create a hypothetical text through the use of source-critical methodologies leads to the creation of a hypothetical context for the punishment, that is, another textual world and possibly a new hypothetical meaning for the punishment. We shall rely on the understanding of the final editors of the texts since their appreciation of how these punishments functioned in their socio-cultural context is likely to be more reliable than a hypothetical context reconstructed by a modern scholar.

Secondly, a semiotic approach to the problem of seriousness considers how the modes in which seriousness of offence are displayed help us to understand the nature of the biblical conception of their difference. This emphasis upon the semiotics, rather than the pragmatics, of biblical law (i.e., the content of the law rather than its actual use) requires close attention to literary presentation.

Thirdly, a semiotic approach to seriousness of offence distinguishes between the performance of a sanction and its use in a literary context. In semiotic terms it is the difference between doing and telling. It distinguishes between the act of performing the punishment (i.e. its social reality) and the telling of the story of the punishment (i.e. its literary construction). This semiotic approach sees story-telling as a form of behaviour. Certain decisions and choices are made depending on what the narrator seeks to achieve by the act of telling the story. Narrative techniques are therefore important. Literary phenomena convey part of the message of the text in its final form. Semiotic choices made in the final editing of the text are thus an important aspect of sense-construction. We shall consider what these are in 1.6.1–1.6.4 below.

The assumption is made that the text is evidence of the social reality of the ancient world. But at the same time it is plausible to suggest that there is some disjuncture between social reality and biblical ideology. This is especially likely if the text is composed in a society that is pluralistic in its attitudes and beliefs. For this reason, Jackson thinks it necessary to distinguish between 'biblical law' and the 'law of biblical society'.[72] However, we do not know to what extent the biblical laws were intended to be descriptive and, if so, whether they described 'common practice' or 'best practice'. My position in this book is that although the laws of the Hebrew

---

72. B.S. Jackson, 'The Ceremonial and the Judicial: Biblical Law as Sign and Symbol', *JSOT* 30 (1984), pp. 25-50 (29).

Bible give only a partial view of the norms of ancient Israel, they are nevertheless a primary source for reconstructing the ideals and practices of that society. The texts are literary constructions that represent, to a greater or lesser extent, the law as actually practised.[73] But it goes too far to claim that the laws were purely literary creations. For example, some would argue that the law in Deut. 21.18-21 and Deut. 22.13-21 was never applied in practice, nor even intended to have been applied. I shall argue against this view by demonstrating that the law in both cases is eminently practicable (see Chapters 2 and 4). Indeed, it can be argued that the more unusual the ritual (e.g. the חלצה ceremony of Deut. 25.5-10, see Chapter 3), the less likely it is to be concocted and the more likely it is to have some form of historical reality. However, demonstrating the historicity of particular legal procedures and sanctions lies beyond the scope of this book.

Areas of semiotic choice that affect our understanding of seriousness include the following: terminology; literary arrangement; binary oppositional categories; and links to the wider narrative. These are set out briefly in 1.6.1–1.6.4. below.

1.6.1. *Terminology*

The use of particular words such as 'stubborn and rebellious' (סורר ומורה) and 'a glutton and a drunkard' (זולל וסבא; see Chapter 2), 'wanton' (נבלה; see Chapter 4) and 'abomination' (תועבה; see Chapter 6) is an important aspect of semiotic choice. I shall consider how the connotations and narrative evocations of such vocabulary contribute to our understanding of seriousness.

1.6.2 *Literary Arrangement*

Biblical law is more than the mere sum of the specifically legal contents of individual paragraphs. The meaning of an individual rule often goes beyond the meanings of individual sentences to depend on discursive relationships between sentences and whole groups of provisions.[74] Thus I shall look at how our understanding of seriousness is affected by the underlying interrelationships between different legal rules, particularly those which appear to be related from their literary positioning (see Chapter 2).

---

73. Jackson, 'Reflections', p. 29.
74. Jackson, 'Ideas of Law', p. 197.

1.6.3. *Binary Oppositional Categories*

An important structural feature is the correlation of normally associated binary oppositions; viz. a pair of terms that are conventionally regarded as opposites.[75] Binary oppositional categories are important to a semiotic account of seriousness because they help us to explain why classifications appear natural or intelligible. Examples in biblical law include the depasturation law of Exod. 22.5 [H 22.4]. This deals with a domesticated (as opposed to a wild) animal, acting in a non-hostile (as opposed to a hostile) fashion, in a certain cultural context, namely, having been put there to graze (as opposed to seeking new grass).[76] I shall show that conceptions of seriousness are also structured around binary oppositions, such as 'leaders' and 'followers', 'sacred' and 'non-sacred' (Chapter 5), as well as location, that is, 'east' versus 'north' and 'inside' versus 'outside' (see Chapter 6).

1.6.4. *Wider Narrative*

Unlike other ANE laws, biblical law is preserved in the form of a historical narrative. This means that to a large extent its character is best understood in terms of the literary and narrative relationships it bears with the surrounding material. Close attention is therefore paid to the position of biblical law within the overall narrative structure. For example, the charge of being 'stubborn and rebellious' and 'a glutton and a drunkard' has particular resonance in view of the wilderness narrative (see Chapter 2).

1.7. *Identifying the Texts*

In keeping with my methodology, my procedure is informed by a basic theoretical claim from semiotics, namely, the distinction between linguistic meaning and aesthetic meaning. Semiotics claims that the latter is as much a part of sense-construction as the former and, that being so, I looked for texts that involved the use of symbolic acts whose non-linguistic meaning could then be explored. This yielded a range of texts from which I have selected five. These five are carefully chosen to maximize diversity and to refract, to the fullest possible extent, the spectrum of seriousness of offence in biblical law.

Firstly, I want to discover whether there is an inner coherence to seriousness of offence. This means juxtaposing cases that deal with similar themes, for example, the rebellious son of Deut. 21.18-21 (see Chapter 2)

---

75. For a discussion see Jackson, *Making Sense in Law*, pp. 22-24.
76. Jackson, *Semiotics of Biblical Law*, p. 193.

and the rebellious daughter of Deut. 22.13-21 (see Chapter 4), the concern for the Land in Deut. 21.18-21 (see Chapter 2) and Deut. 25.5-10 (see Chapter 3), offences against YHWH alone in Leviticus 4 (see Chapter 5) and Ezekiel 8 (see Chapter 6), as well as the theme of social status in Lev. 21.9, Deut. 22.13-21, Leviticus 4 and Ezekiel 8 (see Chapters 4, 5 and 6).

Secondly, I want to cover a range of punitive acts. These include different forms of capital punishment (stoning and burning, see Chapters 2 and 4), different ways of carrying out the same mode of capital punishment (stoning an offender in one place rather than another, see Chapter 4), informal methods of punishment such as shaming (again, with different modalities involved, see Chapter 3), not to mention the role of the sacrificial system as a possible register (see Chapter 5). I also want to include an example of an extraordinary act of divine punishment upon corporate Israel (divine temple abandonment, see Chapter 6).

Thirdly, I want to include cases that involve some judgment as to relative seriousness. This occurs where there are different evaluations of seriousness attached to the performance of the same offence by different people, or by the same people in different ways. This allows us to draw firm conclusions about relative seriousness because the offence is held constant throughout. Any variation in the evaluation of seriousness must therefore be due to some other factor. For this reason too we shall look at Lev. 21.9, Deut. 22.13-21 and Leviticus 4 where the social status of the parties is relevant (see Chapters 4 and 5) and Ezekiel 8 where both the social status of the parties and the location of the offence is important (see Chapter 6).

Fourthly, I want to draw the case-studies from different literary genres. I therefore include narrative[77] (such as Ezekiel 8, see Chapter 6) as well as law and legal texts from different legal corpora (Lev. 4; 21.9; Deut. 21.18-21; 22.13-21 and 25.5-10, see Chapters 2 to 5). This allows us to explore the different audiences to whom the text is addressed and to see whether seriousness of offence varies according to different semiotic groups.

A narrative approach to 'seriousness of offence' in biblical law involves taking a pluralist rather than a reductionist approach to the question of punishment. It recognizes that a wide range of penal strategies is required in responding to proscribed behaviour. This closes the gap between biblical law and the contemporary quest for 'seriousness'. Even in modern law and penal philosophy there is no single answer to the problem of

77. For the importance of narrative in ethical enquiry, see J. Barton, *Ethics and the Old Testament* (London: SCM Press, 1998), pp. 19-36.

punishment. There is a constant tension between the ideals of 'rehabilitation', 'retributivism', 'utilitarianism' and 'eclecticism'.[78] We should not be surprised at the plurality of 'seriousness' in ancient Israel when we ourselves are far from systematic, or precise, in expressing our rationale for various punishments. Moreover, as in biblical society (see 7.9.1), the rationale behind the concept of any form of punishment can be conceived very differently by different elements in a single society. Liberals might speak of the rehabilitative function of punishment, whilst a conservative will tend to favour the punitive aspect. Others might speak of the necessity to detain prisoners as a protective device. Yet it is possible to argue that all these factors are involved in varying degrees in any given punishment.[79] A comparative approach suggests that it is probably unrealistic to expect a modern conception of 'seriousness' to take the form of an ethical 'system'. Rather, the most that can be aspired to is a conception of seriousness that displays an inner coherence.

A narrative approach militates against a systematic account of 'seriousness of offence' in biblical law. This is because there is a tension between the idea of a 'paradigm case' (which is concrete, narrative and contextual) and the notion of a 'system' (which involves abstraction). If the praxis of biblical law is the popular use of paradigm cases, we may query to what extent ideas of seriousness were systematized in ancient Israel.

Again, strangely enough, this narrows rather than widens the gap between biblical ideas of seriousness and the modern search for seriousness. This is because contemporary models of legal systems are based on the idea of precedent, and precedents, too, offer 'paradigm cases'. The key difference, of course, between the use of precedents under a 'legislative' model of law and the use of paradigm cases under a 'charismatic' model, is that, under the former, each case is only authoritative within the scope of each *ratio decidendi*.[80] Nonetheless, whilst one may try to abstract from these cases something that we may call 'family law' or 'law of torts', the fact remains that we are dealing with a variety of stories and 'paradigms' that do not always fit together coherently in a logical fashion. Thus, as with ancient Israel, we may query whether, under contemporary English law,

78. See e.g. N. Walker, *Why Punish?* (Oxford: Oxford University Press, 1991).

79. D. Garland, *Punishment and Modern Society: A Study in Social Theory* (Chicago: University of Chicago Press, 1990).

80. *Ratio decidendi* (very roughly translated 'the reason for the decision') is central to the Anglo-American doctrine of judicial precedents and refers to the legal principle on which judgment in a particular case is based.

we have any 'systematic' approach to seriousness of offence. Indeed, we may even question whether such a 'system' is desirable (see Chapter 8).

1.7.1. Presenting the Case-Studies

This book accordingly takes the form of a series of case-studies. To reiterate, my procedure reflects my methodology. A semiotic as opposed to a rationalist approach to biblical law has no prior reason for supposing that seriousness of offence fits into a system. This book, therefore, makes no attempt to unlock a hitherto concealed system (even assuming that such a system exists). It is of course possible that the acts that we shall examine do fit together, rather imperfectly, into some sort of system. But this is not essential. The structure of the book as a series of case-studies is thus perfectly authentic to the pre-systematic way in which people in the biblical period appear to have constructed the meaning of seriousness.

The result is a study that is illustrative of seriousness of offence in biblical law, rather than exhaustive. Again, this is appropriate. Biblical law makes no claim to be exhaustive in terms of the range of cases it covers. This means we are not entitled to regard its presentation of seriousness as comprehensive, either. The cases that deal with seriousness of offence in biblical law are themselves particular and not comprehensive and to this extent, the structure of this book reflects the presentation of seriousness of offence in biblical law itself.

The five case-studies are as follows. Chapter 2 examines the case of the rebellious son (Deut. 21.18-21), whilst Chapter 3 considers the case of the levir who refuses to sire an heir for his dead brother (Deut. 25.5-10). Chapter 4 contrasts the offence committed by the priest's daughter in Lev. 21.9 with that of the commoner's daughter in Deut. 22.13-21, whilst Chapter 5 examines inadvertent offending in Leviticus 4. Finally, Chapter 6 explores the seriousness of Temple-idolatry in Ezekiel 8.

1.7.2. Identifying the Paradigm Case

We saw that the praxis of biblical law, so far as we are able to establish, militates against the legislative model and in favour of a narrative approach that understands the law in terms of a paradigm case. My procedure will therefore be to reconstruct the paradigm expectation in each case and to comment on those features that have significance for our understanding of seriousness. In each case-study, I will start with the descriptive questions because unless the descriptive features of the case are clearly identified we are in no position to state the nature of the offence, let alone to evaluate its seriousness. Having identified the actual nature of the offence, I then consider the form of the punishment and why this was appropriate. Here I shall consider the historical and cultural links that connect the execution of the punishment to its semiotic meaning. The picture of seriousness in biblical law will be composed and developed as we move through each of the case-studies. We shall see that biblical law contains a sophisticated understanding of seriousness. I shall identify some of the different elements that make up the biblical conception of seriousness and the various means by which this understanding is synthesized and communicated. Finally, I shall conclude with a discussion in Chapter 8 in which I assess the relevance of the biblical conception of seriousness of offence to the modern search for seriousness.

Chapter 2

THE WRATH OF GOD ON THE SONS OF DISOBEDIENCE:
SERIOUSNESS OF OFFENCE AND DEUTERONOMY 21.18-21

> 'Good wombs have borne bad sons.'
> William Shakespeare, *The Tempest* (Act I, sc. II)

The seriousness of being a 'bad son' is set out in Deut. 21.18-21. The elements of seriousness in Deut. 21.18-21 are described as follows: the son is 'stubborn and rebellious', he does not heed his parents' voice, he is incorrigible (Deut. 21.18) and he is a 'glutton and a drunkard' (Deut. 21.20). We explore the seriousness of this offence in 2.1–2.9, below. Deut 21.18-21 contains a number of registers of seriousness; viz. different semiotic forms in which the values of seriousness can be expressed. Performative registers (i.e. acts performed by people in the text) are as follows. Firstly, the act of bringing the son before the elders ('his father and his mother shall take hold of him and bring him out to the elders of his city at the gate of the place where he lives', Deut. 21.19). The case is too serious to be dealt with by the parents alone. It must come before the jurisdiction of the elders who, unlike the parents, are legally competent to impose the death penalty. A second register is the speech-act of accusation, 'and they shall say to the elders of his city' (Deut. 21.20). Thirdly, there is the act of punishment, which is death by stoning ('Then all the men of his city shall stone him to death with stones', Deut. 21.21). In addition to describing these performative registers, the text also contains the following descriptive registers of seriousness. These include the expiatory purpose of the sanction ('so you shall purge [ובערת] the evil from your midst', 21.21). The basic idea is the rejection of the evildoer to purify the tribal or national community.[1] This statement of purpose reflects the law's own understanding of the seriousness of the offence.[2] A further descriptive register is

---

1. H. Ringgren, בער, in *TDOT*, II, pp. 201-205 (203-204).
2. Cf. Deut. 17.12; 19.13; 22.21, 22; 24 and 24.7.

found in the use of the public-example formula, 'and all Israel will hear and fear' (21.21).[3]

2.1. *Offence Description*

2.1.1. *A Narrative Reading*

We begin our analysis of seriousness by examining the description of the offence as it is given in Deut. 21.18 and 20. Comparison between vv. 18 and 20 reveals an imperfect repetition: viz. the precise terminology of the law in v. 18 differs from the parents' plea in v. 20. Verse 18 reads: 'If a man has a stubborn and rebellious son, who will not obey the voice of his father or the voice of his mother, and, though they chastise him, will not give heed to them'. Verse 20, however, is slightly different. The parents allege, 'This our son is stubborn and rebellious, he will not obey our voice; he is a glutton and a drunkard'. Verse 20 repeats the charge of being 'stubborn and rebellious' and of failing to heed his parents' voice. However, there is no repetition in v. 20 of the claim in v. 18 that he is incorrigible ('though they chastise him he will not give heed to them'; Deut. 21.18). Instead, they allege that he is 'a glutton and a drunkard' (Deut. 21.20). This imperfect repetition might suggest that the phrase 'a glutton and a drunkard' is an interpolation. However, my approach to seriousness of offence in Deut. 21.18-21 militates against this view. I shall argue, instead, that Deut. 21.18-21 presents us with a narrative typification of action in which vv. 18 and 20 refer to the typical behaviour associated with the social stereotype of the rebellious son. This is in contrast to the semantic approach favoured by other writers, such as Brichto, who wonders what would happen to the 'abstemious' rebellious son who was 'stubborn' and a 'glutton' but not a 'drunkard' (see 2.5).[4]

I shall argue that the typical behaviour associated with the social stereotype includes being 'stubborn and rebellious', not obeying the parents' voice, being incorrigible and being 'a glutton and a drunkard'. My approach means that there is no question of regarding these behaviour

---

3. This formula is also used in Deut. 13.11 [H 13.12], 17.13 and 19.20. As with Deut. 21.21, each offence is described in terms of a single culprit whose fate is then spelt out. This emphasis on the individual offender and his offence rather than the category of offenders and what their offences have in common increases the 'deterrent' effect, Carmichael, *Laws of Deuteronomy*, p. 45.

4. Brichto, 'Kin, Cult, Land', p. 32.

patterns as discrete offences as per Brichto, Bellefontaine[5] and Benjamin.[6] Rather, they are all part of the same substantive narrative or typification of action. Viewing the phrase 'he is a glutton and a drunkard' as a narrative typification of action suggests that the phrase is integral to the original text and is not an interpolation. Verse 18 presents us with three typical behaviour patterns of the narrative stereotype thus, 'If a man has [1] a stubborn and rebellious son, [2] who will not obey the voice of his father or the voice of his mother, and, [3] though they chastise him, will not give heed to them'. Verse 20 does the same: 'This our son is [1] stubborn and rebellious, [2] he will not obey our voice; [3] he is a glutton and a drunkard'. Both verses explicate the same stereotype (cf. 2.2–2.6, below). Consequently, the phrase 'a glutton and a drunkard' is integral because it is part of an overall, threefold, narrative typification of the rebellious son. Why, then, is there an imperfect repetition in v. 20? I shall argue at 2.8 below

5. Contra, for example, E. Bellefontaine, 'Deuteronomy 21.18-21: Reviewing the Case of the Rebellious Son', *JSOT* 13 (1979), pp. 13-31 (20-21) who sees the phrase 'a glutton and a drunkard' as the remains of an originally independent tribal customary law whose purpose was to destroy thoroughly corrupt members of the tribe or clan.

6. D.C. Benjamin, *Deuteronomy and City Life* (New York: University Press of America, 1983), p. 212 argues that the offence of being a 'a glutton and a drunkard' in v. 20 is a separate offence, comparable to that of being 'incorrigible' in v. 18. Benjamin argues that v. 18 contains two offences, not just one (viz. 'if a man has [1] *a stubborn and rebellious son, who will not obey the voice of his father or the voice of his mother*, and, [2] *though they chastise him, will not give heed to them*'; my italics). The son is not 'stubborn and rebellious' because his parents have chastised him and he has refused to listen. Rather, he is 'stubborn and rebellious' (one offence) and he continues to disobey after he has been chastised (a second offence). Benjamin proposes that vv. 18 and 20 both consist of two separate offences. He contends that two distinct offences have to be committed before the son can be brought before the elders (viz. [1] 'being stubborn + rebellious + refusing to listen to his parents' voice' and [2] 'being incorrigible'). Likewise, he must be accused of two serious offences before he can be executed (viz. [1] 'being stubborn + rebellious + refusing to listen to his parents' voice' and [2] 'being a glutton and a drunkard').

However, Benjamin's approach cannot be supported grammatically. There is no conjunction (ו) before the phrase 'he is a glutton and a drunkard'. Grammatically, the phrase 'he is a glutton and a drunkard' simply explicates his 'refusal to heed'. This is reflected in many translations of the Bible by the use of a semi-colon ('…; he is a glutton and a drunkard'). The sense is 'This our son is stubborn and rebellious, he will not obey our voice [*namely*, or *in other words*] he is a glutton and a drunkard'. The charge 'he is a glutton and a drunkard' is not a separate offence. It is simply part of the 'narrative stereotype'.

that the reference to 'a glutton and a drunkard' may surely reflect the need for publicly observable evidence when the son is brought before the elders. We should also bear in mind that concern about imperfect repetition reflects a modern demand for consistency that may not have applied in antiquity.

2.1.2. *Literary Context*

Deut. 21.18-21 is presented as part of the speech given by Moses at the entrance to the Promised Land (Deut. 1.1-2) and this setting is Deut. 21.18-21's most natural *Sitz im Leben*. Moses' speech is a borderline speech, both geographically and temporally, that marks the end of the desert wanderings and the beginnings of a new, settled, way of life. For the Israelites gathered on the plains of Moab (1.5) there is a contrast between scratching by in the wilderness and life in Canaan, 'a land oozing with milk and honey' (6.3). A transition had to be made from the enforced asceticism of the desert to Canaan's bounty. Understandably, not everyone would negotiate that change successfully. Some could easily fall into food abuse. Against this backdrop, Deut. 21.18-21 is a warning against behaving in a particular way at the very moment when the temptation to do just that is greatest. Of course, it is proper that Israel should enjoy all the fruits of whatever the land produces (e.g. Deut. 14.26). This enjoyment is one of YHWH's blessings (Deut. 28.4-5, 8) and its absence is one of YHWH's curses (Deut. 28.17-18, 39). But they are not to go overboard (e.g. 6.10-12). They are to limit their indulgence. The warning against food abuse in Deut. 21.18-21 is consistent with the concern throughout Deuteronomy as a whole to treat the land properly. It is, after all, YHWH's gift (e.g. Deut. 9.6). For what else is food abuse but, ultimately, an abuse of the land?

2.2. *Building the Identikit*

The rebellious son has been variously characterized in ancient and modern times. Without attempting to provide a history of interpretation, it is worth surveying briefly some of these different approaches. Rabbinic, Puritan, anthropological and psychiatric approaches have all yielded different answers to the questions: who is the rebellious son and why is he executed? Each has sought to emphasize different aspects of the typology. However, none, in my view, presents a sharp likeness. The pictures that emerge of the rebellious son tend to be either blurred or ahistorical (see 2.2.1–2.2.4). I advance a different typification of the rebellious son and the seriousness

2. *The Wrath of God on the Sons of the Disobedience*

of his offence in 2.3 and 2.4 that flows from a semiotic reading of the text. It is hoped that this typification will give a more rigorous historical shape to the identikit and a more satisfactory solution to the puzzle.

2.2.1. *A Rabbinic Approach*

As far as the Rabbis were concerned, the literal meaning of Deut. 21.18-21 was clear. In spite (or rather, because) of this, Halakhic exegesis subjected the text to an extremely narrow reading. The lawgiver's typification of a rebellious son was made so detailed that it could hardly ever be carried out. For example, the parents were not supposed to have any physical handicap (i.e. be blind, dumb, deaf or crippled)[7] nor could they be physically dissimilar (e.g. be of different heights or even have a different timbre of voice).[8] As a result the Babylonian Talmud claimed that 'there never was such a thing as a stubborn and rebellious son',[9] viz. the legal requirements for conviction were so great that no one was ever executed.

By the time of the Targum, it was believed that the Law was given in order to teach. Following an interpretation in the Gemara,[10] Hirsch claims that Deut. 21.18-21 deals with 'a problem which…in the whole of the past and in all future time was and will remain only a theoretical problem…'[11] Deut. 21.18-21 merely became a 'rich source of pedagogic truths and teachings…[that would] repay parents for their business of bringing up children'.[12]

However, although the Rabbis did their best to ensure that the penalty was never applied, it is not inconceivable that the punishment was enforced in biblical times. We have no record from the biblical period of

---

7. The *Mishnah* states, 'If one of them [his father or his mother] had a hand or fingers cut off, or was lame, dumb, blind or deaf, he does not become a "stubborn and rebellious son", because it is written, "then shall his father and his mother lay hold on him"—this excludes those with hands or fingers cut off, "and bring him out", excluding lame parents, "and they shall say", excluding the dumb, "this our son", excluding the blind, "he will not obey our voice", excluding the deaf', *Sanh.* 71a.

8. 'Why so?—The Writ saith, *he will not obey our voice* and since they must be alike in voice, they must be also in appearance and stature', R. Judah, *Sanh.* 71a.

9. 'It never happened and never will happen', R. Judah, *Sanh.* 71a.

10. *Sanh.* 71a.

11. S.R. Hirsch, *The Pentateuch Volume 5: Deuteronomy* (trans. Isaac Levy, Gateshead: Judaica Press, 1989 [1837]), p. 416.

12. Hirsch, *Deuteronomy*, p. 416. Cf. more recently A.C. Hagedorn, 'Guarding the Parents' Honour—Deuteronomy 21.18-21', *JSOT* 88 (2000), pp. 101-21 (107), 'the law is a mere literary fiction'.

the execution of a rebellious son. However, absence of evidence is not evidence of absence. Deuteronomy repeatedly presents Israel as YHWH's mutinous 'son' whose rebellion is punished by his 'father' (see 2.7.3.1, below). The analogy favours the social reality of Deut. 21.18-21. Are we to say that a punishment with which YHWH could threaten Israel could never be potentially administered by an Israelite father upon his own son? This is implausible, especially in view of the wilderness experience. The entire Exodus generation (bar two) died in the wilderness and failed to inherit the Promised Land (Num. 14.1-45) because they were 'rebellious'. This implies that the punishment was part of Israel's experience, at least on a corporate level. Of course, this does not mean that the 'wilderness experience' should be seen as evidence of successful legal procedure. Israel's corporate punishment by YHWH does not have to rely on an individual Israelite father killing his son. It may even be that the similarity between the two forms of punishment is no more than a Wittgensteinian 'family resemblance'. But nonetheless, as Hamilton writes, 'Few laws in Deuteronomy have as striking parabolic application to Israel as does this one'.[13] The social reality of the punishment in later times is suggested by a Talmudic counter-opinion[14] as well as by the New Testament (see 2.5.2.3, below). It is ahistorical to insist that Deut. 21.18-21 is hyperbole.

Some might argue that Deut. 21.18-21 was never intended to have enactment force but was, rather, passed *in terrorem* ('in terror'). Such laws are not unknown even in modern times. The UK Parliament may privately think that certain laws are unenforceable but they are on the statute book anyway. It is pointless to ask whether they are 'actually enforced' because, in theory at least, it is acceptable for a law to have didactic force only. In a similar way it might be argued that the law of the 'rebellious son' has little practical application in terms of social control but it nonetheless acted as an important 'marker' of social values.

This is not a wholly convincing line of argument, however. Even if the law was only passed *in terrorem*, it can equally be argued that the only way in which a law can have didactic force is through enforcement. Authority derives from the exercise of power and legal authority is derived from coercive power. For the legal positivist, a law which the legislator has no intention of enforcing is useless.

---

13. V.P. Hamilton, *Handbook on the Pentateuch* (Grand Rapids: Baker Book House, 1982), p. 439.

14. Rabbi Jonathan avers 'I saw him [a 'rebellious son'] and sat on his grave', B.T. *Sanh.* 71a.

Either way we are driven to ask why prophets such as Hosea, Zechariah, Isaiah, Jeremiah, Ezekiel, Zephaniah and Nehemiah used this charge to drive home their message regarding Israel (see Hos. 4.16, Zech. 7.11, Isa. 65.2, Jer. 6.28, Ezek. 20.21, Zeph. 3.1-2, Jer. 5.23, Neh. 9.26, 9.29, see further 2.3.1). Had it been social knowledge not only that the law had never been applied, but was never *intended* to be applied their warning would have rung hollow.

Crucial to the Rabbinic identikit of the rebellious son was his incorrigible character. 'We know from our sages that he is executed because of his future.'[15] According to Cohn 'the rebellious son is executed, not because of what he has actually done, but because of what he was foreseen to be prone to do were he allowed to live'.[16] The glutton and a drunkard was a portend of worse to come. The Rabbis thought that the 'rebellious son' would feed his habits by dissipating his father's wealth. Unchecked, it was thought that his escalating behaviour would ruin his parents[17] and end with his becoming a robber and a murderer. 'Therefore the Torah said, "Let him die while yet innocent and let him not die guilty". For the death of the wicked benefits themselves and the world.'[18] On this view, capital punishment is advocated as a *preventive* measure.

2.2.2. *A Puritan Approach*

The Puritans understood the law as referring to capital punishment for filial disrespect. In 1646, the General Court of Massachusetts issued the Law of the Incorrigible Child which stipulated that if parents were unable

---

15. R. Kolshec (1540–1660), cited in M. Rotenberg and B.L. Diamond, 'The Biblical Conception of Psychopathy: The Law of the Stubborn and Rebellious Son', *JBS* 7 (1971), p. 36 n. 39. Cf. *Sanh* 8.5, 'A stubborn and rebellious son is condemned because of [what he may become in] the end'.

16. H.H. Cohn, 'Rebellious Son', in *Enc. Jud.* (Jerusalem: Keter), XIII, p. 1604.

17. *Sanh. Gem.* 72a, cf. Wright's view that the son is not executed for gluttony and drunkenness in themselves, but for 'incorrigible flouting of the fifth commandment in ways that were squandering and endangering the family's substance [i.e. the inheritance]' C.J.H. Wright, *Deuteronomy* (Peabody, MA: Hendrickson, 1996), p. 237). The case of 19-year-old Christopher Trussler who sold his mother's car whilst she was in hospital and then spent the proceeds swigging champagne in Bruges may be a modern example of what the sages had in mind. Trussler sold her car for £6,000 and spent the proceeds by staying in a £600-a-night hotel suite for a week. 'It's amazing how quickly you can spend £6,000... I just drank Bollinger and Dom Perignon...' ('Son sold family car to pay for mad binge', *Daily Express*, 31 July 1997).

18. R. Jose, *Sanh.* 72a.

to deal with a recalcitrant child, he could be summoned before the court by any magistrate to account for his behaviour. If found guilty, the magistrate was empowered to 'sentence him to endure...corporal punishment by whipping...not exceeding ten stripes for one offense [sic]'.[19] If the child continued to be unruly, the parents were instructed to produce him before the magistrate again, if necessary by force. This time, if the case was proved against him, the child could be sentenced to death by hanging. Rushdoony notes that no executions were necessary: the law apparently 'kept children in line'.[20]

This draconian approach to juvenile delinquency is, on the face of it, stricter than the biblical legislation. In Deut. 21.18-21 the son has to be found guilty of two separate charges. These are (1) being stubborn and rebellious and refusing to heed his parents' voice and (2) being 'a glutton and a drunkard' (see 2.6 below). In the Puritan legislation, there is only one formal charge, that of incorrigibility. Of course, proving this charge doubtless drew on public as well as private testimony (see 2.6 below). But the absence of any formal division between the two sorts of testimony makes it appear as though the 1646 Order had a lower standard for conviction than Deut. 21.18-21. In this sense too the Puritan approach does not do justice to the biblical legislation.

2.2.3. *An Anthropological Approach*

Bellefontaine draws on the insights of several anthropologists in her diagnosis of the rebellious son.[21] Firstly, she draws on Radcliffe-Brown's observation that (so-called) simple societies include among their crimes the offence of being 'a bad lot, that is, habitually failing to observe the customs of the community'.[22] Secondly, Bellefontaine cites the work of Llewellyn and Hoebel who have documented how a tribe member may reach the status of the 'finally intolerable'.[23] The rebellious son, she argues, reaches the limits of tribal toleration in a similar way and must be destroyed. His excessive eating and drinking suggests the stereotype of the 'non-productive, non-contributing parasite'[24] who, being 'undisciplined

---

19. A.I. Katsh, *The Biblical Heritage of American Democracy* (New York: Ktav, 1977), pp. 105-106.

20. R.J. Rushdoony, *The Institutes of Biblical Law* (Craig Press: Presbyterian and Reformed Publishing Co., 1973), p. 236.

21. Bellefontaine, 'Deuteronomy 21.18-21'.

22. Radcliffe-Brown, cited in Bellefontaine, 'Deuteronomy 21.18-21', p. 21.

23. Bellefontaine, 'Deuteronomy 21.18-21', p. 21.

24. Bellefontaine, 'Deuteronomy 21.18-21', p. 21.

2. The Wrath of God on the Sons of the Disobedience

and unpredictable...would be untrustworthy in time of crises such as war'.[25] Even during peacetime, his undisciplined and unpredictable behaviour had potential to strain inter-family and inter-clan relationships, risking retaliation or a feud against himself, his family and his community. It is hard to disagree with this analysis. But this is precisely its weakness: it draws only the most general conclusions. Bellefontaine sees the 'glutton and a drunkard' as an obvious example of the 'generally disordered and dissolute life'[26] that causes one to be judged 'a bad lot'. This is true. But it does not help us to identify its specific nature or explain, in more precise terms, why this offence was capital.

2.2.4 *A Psychiatric Approach*
Rotenberg and Diamond argue that Deut. 21.18-21 is an example of an ancient personality profile.[27] On this view the terms 'stubborn' and 'rebellious' and 'a glutton and a drunkard' function as a kind of diagnostic category roughly corresponding to our modern psychopathic personality.[28] Rotenberg and Diamond aver that 'the stubborn and rebellious son and the psychiatric concept of the sociopath appear to be basically the same'.[29] The rebellious son is someone who exhibits 'the most severe behavioural symptoms of a potential criminal type',[30] hence the severe penalty. The drawback with this approach is that it risks projecting back onto the screen of ancient Israel trendy ideas about psychological profiles that are probably anachronistic.

2.3 *Identifying the Paradigm Case*

A semiotic approach to seriousness of offence in Deut. 21.18-21 would start by interpreting the description of the rebellious son narratively, rather than semantically (see 1.2.1). In other words, the verses present us, not with a linguistic definition of the rebellious son but a social stereotype.

---

25. Bellefontaine, 'Deuteronomy 21.18-21', p. 21.
26. Bellefontaine, 'Deuteronomy 21.18-21', p. 23.
27. Rotenberg and Diamond, 'Biblical Conception of Psychopathy'.
28. The psychopathic or antisocial personality type is used to describe individuals who, whilst lacking the classic outward manifestations of insanity, demonstrate pronounced behavioural abnormalities such as cruelty, delinquency, sexual perversion, alcoholism, drug addiction, irresponsibility and immorality (Rotenberg and Diamond, 'Biblical Conception of Psychopathy', p. 37).
29. Rotenberg and Diamond, 'Biblical Conception of Psychopathy', p. 37.
30. Rotenberg and Diamond, 'Biblical Conception of Psychopathy', p. 37.

Deut. 21.18-21 summons to the mind's eye a particular type of person and a corresponding sort of behaviour. There is nothing extraordinary about this. When a group of squaddies from a nearby army camp are charged with being drunk and disorderly, we all know what sort of behaviour that implies. We do not have to be specific about how many milligrams of alcohol were in the blood, or what degree of rowdiness was involved. Likewise, in the social world of ancient Israel, the stereotype of the stubborn and rebellious son conjures up a particular narrative image and connotes a particular sort of behaviour. Unpacking the significance of this stereotype, in its historical and narrative context, is central to understanding seriousness of offence in Deut. 21.18-21. Of course, we shall see that there is a lot more to the charge of being a stubborn and rebellious son than a wild night on the town. The stubborn and rebellious son is not a mere delinquent but someone who rejects, and whose continuing presence threatens, the traditions of the covenant community. His offence is essentially apostasy.

We begin with the typification expressed in v. 20 (the parents' charge before the elders). This is because, of the two typifications presented (in vv. 18 and 20), it is this charge that, if upheld, justifies the offender's execution. Three behaviour patterns are described in v. 20, being stubborn and rebellious, not obeying his parents' voice and being a 'glutton and a drunkard'. The precise significance of each of these behaviours depends on social knowledge and so we must begin by examining some of the contexts in which these behaviours are described, bearing in mind the usual caveats about the semantics of biblical language.[31] We shall pay special attention to associated imagery, since reception of the paradigm case (whether heard or read) may be designed to trigger visual images.[32]

---

31. Classically expressed by J. Barr, *The Semantics of Biblical Language* (Oxford: Oxford University Press, 1978 [1961]).

32. My approach is contrary to that taken recently by Hagedorn, 'Guarding the Parents' Honour', pp. 104-105 who claims that since 'details' are never given of the offence 'the practicability or use of the law in Deut. 21.18-21 as a manual for lawsuits [is] highly questionable'. This is a prime example of the fallacy of reading a biblical legal text as though it was a modern statute. Hagedorn presupposes the semantic and legislative approach rejected in Chapter 1 (1.2.1, above) and on this basis concludes that Deut. 21.18-21 is 'another utopian law'. But whether an ancient law was ever implemented or not cannot be determined on the basis of whether it conforms to a modern statute. Instead, we must adopt a semiotic approach that seeks to understand the text in terms of its own contextual, covenantal assumptions, its links to implicit social knowledge and the semiotic significance of the son's behaviour (see 1.2.2-1.2.4

2. The Wrath of God on the Sons of the Disobedience

2.3.1. *'This Our Son is Stubborn and Rebellious' (Deuteronomy 21.20a)*
The key words here are סורר (stubborn) and מורה (rebellious). Occasionally, as in Deut. 21.20a, the words appear together in the phrase סורר ומורה (stubborn and rebellious).[33] We shall consider each, as follows.

2.3.1.1. סורר. A concrete description of סורר is found in Hos. 4.16, 'Like a stubborn (סררה) heifer, Israel is stubborn (סרר)'. The picture is of the baulky or intractable cow who either refuses to move[34] or who cannot keep to a directed path.[35] The image has overtones of wilfulness, obstinacy and perversity. The word is frequently used in a more abstract sense to describe Israel's refusal to walk in the way of the LORD. Zech. 7.11 is typical in relating how the people 'refused to hearken [to the word of the LORD] and turned a stubborn shoulder (כתף סוררת) and stopped their ears that they might not hear'. Turning a 'stubborn shoulder' also evokes the image of the obstinate cow who this time lifts up her shoulders because she does not want the yoke around her neck. Exactly the same motifs occur in Deut. 21.18-21 (refusing to pay heed, stubborn behaviour and not listening to the parents' voice).

Stubborn behaviour is a feature of how Israel behaves towards YHWH in that 'son–father' relationship (see further 2.5.1.2, below). Israel's stubborn behaviour is said to be directed against YHWH himself ('I [YHWH] constantly spread out my hands to a disloyal people [עם סורר]', [Isa. 65.2]) whilst Jeremiah charges the people with being 'stubbornly defiant' (סרי סוררים) towards YHWH (Jer. 6.28). This behaviour is a personal affront to YHWH, 'Although I braced, I strengthened their arms, And they

---

above). In doing so we will find not only ample descriptive detail but also an indication that the law was practicable.

33. It may be argued that the prophetic uses of these words and the phrase סורר ומורה in relation to Israel are secondary allusions to the earlier legal text. However, it is not claimed that these examples provide independent evidence of what סורר ומורה originally meant. It suffices for the argument to adduce non-independent evidence; viz. to show the consistent meaning that is given to סורר ומורה within a particular tradition in the Bible. A similar objection could also be raised in purely literary terms: a later author, writing in the fashion of a 'historical novel', realized the appropriateness of presenting this law as part of Moses' valedictory speech on the point of entry to the Land. However, there is no evidence that the ancient peoples knew the concept of the historical novel. The burden of proving that Deuteronomy belongs to this literary genre lies with those who wish to establish it.

34. Ruppert, סרר, in *ThWAT*, V, pp. 957-63 (958).
35. Hirsch, *Deuteronomy*, p. 417.

plot evil (יסורו) against me!' (Hos. 7.15, JPS). Woe is promised to the 'disloyal sons' (בנים סוררים) of Israel who, in Isa. 30.1, make a treaty with Egypt, swapping the protection of one overlord for another. Again, the charge of being a stubborn or disloyal son echoes that of Deut. 21.18-21.

2.3.1.2. *מורה*. The word מורה is a parallel word to סורר and belongs to the same semantic field as being 'stiff-necked' and 'obstinate'.[36] It refers to a hardened attitude that (perhaps like the cow) will not budge. Its binary opposite is שמע ('to listen' or 'to obey'). 'Rebellion' against YHWH is thematically typified by the wilderness generation. The psalmist recalls: 'Our forefathers in Egypt did not perceive your wonders; they did not remember your abundant love, but rebelled (וימרו) at the sea, at the Sea of Reeds' (Ps. 106.7). Elsewhere in the Psalms, wilderness behaviour is seen as a paradigm of rebellion. 'How often they rebelled (ימרוהו) against him in the wilderness and grieved him in the desert' (Ps. 78.40). It is also echoed by the prophets, such as Ezekiel: 'And I said to their children in the wilderness, "Do not walk in the statutes of your fathers, nor observe their ordinances". But the children rebelled (ימרוהו) against me; they did not walk in my statutes and were not careful to observe my ordinances' (Ezek. 20.18, 21). Isa. 30.9 juxtaposes 'rebellious people (עם מרי)' with 'faithless children (בנים כחשים) who refused to heed the instructions of the LORD'. As with סורר, Israel's rebellion is personally wounding to YHWH, 'they rebelled (מרו) and grieved his holy Spirit, therefore he turned to be their enemy' (Isa. 63.10). Jerusalem's rebellion provides further examples, including Zephaniah's lament, 'Woe to her that is rebellious (מראה) and defiled, the oppressing city! She listens to no voice, she accepts no correction (מוסר)'[37] (Zeph. 3.1-2). As in Deut. 21.18-21, מראה is identified with a refusal to listen and to learn from chastisement.

2.3.1.3. *סורר ומורה*. The words סורר and מורה also appear together in the form סורר ומורה. This phrase is used several times to describe corporate Israel. In drawing a comparison between the use of סורר ומורה in Deut. 21.18-21 and its application in regard to corporate Israel, we acknowledge that there may, in theory, be a difference between the meaning of סורר ומורה when applied to a specific individual and its meaning when applied

---

36. Ruppert, סרר, p. 958.
37. Cf. ויסרו, Deut. 21.18. Both Zeph. 3.2 and Deut. 21.18 use the same root, יסר (to chastise).

2. *The Wrath of God on the Sons of the Disobedience*   49

to a corporate body. The epitome of the stubborn and rebellious son is the nation of Israel, especially the wilderness generation. The psalmist laments the 'stubborn and rebellious generation (סורר ומרה)...whose heart was not steadfast, whose spirit was not faithful to YHWH' (Ps. 78.8). Jeremiah charges 'the house of Jacob' with 'a stubborn and rebellious (סורר ומורה) heart' (Jer. 5.20, 23) whilst Nehemiah's damning résumé of Israel's forefathers includes the charge, 'they were disobedient and rebelled (וימרו וימרדו) against thee [YHWH], and cast thy law behind their back' (Neh. 9.26). A couple of verses later it is said that 'they [Israel's forefathers] acted presumptuously...and turned a stubborn shoulder (כתף סוררת), and stiffened their neck and would not obey' (Neh. 9.29). In Neh. 9.26-29, the roots סרר and מרה do not appear together, but they are sufficiently close to suggest a parallel with Deut. 21.18-21, although it might be queried whether these texts are an allusion to Deut. 21.18-21 or vice versa.

Wright sees סורר ומורה as a term for the 'serious and persistent rejection of authority'.[38] Benjamin goes further, claiming that סורר ומורה refers to 'measurable and public'[39] apostasy. Israel's stubbornness (the opposite of obedience) is the reason why YHWH denied the desert generation access to the Promised Land.[40] This view is supported by Coats's analysis of Israel's rebellion in the wilderness.[41] Coats argues that Israel's lack of food merely provided the setting for the murmurings and that, to this extent, Israel's food problem was merely the presenting issue. The real issue—that is, the substance of the rebellion—was a desire to go back to Egypt and the life they had before the Exodus. Their rebellion was, essentially, apostasy.[42] Exod. 16.3 provides a good example. The Israelites complain, 'Would that we had died by the hand of YHWH in the land of Egypt when we were sitting by the pots of flesh, when we were eating bread to the full'. The memory of food (supposedly) left behind in Egypt forms the immediate motivation for the murmuring. But the rosy picture of life in Egypt (slave labourers eating boiled flesh?) puts the emphasis, by dint of the exaggeration, on the fact that they left Egypt at all. Hence, the substance of the rebellion is not lack of food but the fact that they had been

---

38. Wright, *Deuteronomy*, p. 237.
39. Benjamin, *Deuteronomy and City Life*, p. 220.
40. Benjamin, *Deuteronomy and City Life*, p. 220. Cf. Ps. 95.7b-11, although the words סורר ומורה do not themselves appear in these verses.
41. G.W. Coats, *Rebellion in the Wilderness: The Murmuring Motif in the Wilderness Traditions of the Old Testament* (Nashville: Abingdon Press, 1968).
42. Cf. the argument of Heb. 3.7-19, citing Ps. 95.7-11.

taken out of Egypt. The complaint expresses not only a desire to return to the state of life they had before the Exodus, but also the wish that the Exodus itself had never happened.[43] This is the rebellion for which the wilderness generation were disqualified from entering the Promised Land, underlining the idea that סורר ומורה signifies apostasy. Just as corporate Israel refuses to heed instruction from YHWH, so the son in Deut. 21.18-21 who is סורר ומורה refuses to take instruction from his parents. His behaviour is tantamount to a renunciation of the parental bond. It is also tantamount to apostasy, insofar as the parental instruction that he rejects relates to the commands of YHWH (see 2.5.1.1 below).

2.3.2. 'He Will Not Obey our Voice' (Deuteronomy 21.20b)

What is at stake here? Is it simply a matter of an Israelite father telling his son to bring in the fatted calf and being told to get it himself? Hardly. We have seen that the charge of being 'stubborn and rebellious' signifies an obstinate refusal to listen to, or to obey, the voice of authority. This applies whether the voice of authority belongs to the parents or whether, as in the case of corporate Israel, it belongs to YHWH himself. Throughout the Hebrew Bible, hearing is associated with obedience. The one who hears is the one who obeys. Similarly, the one who refuses to hear is a synonym for one who disobeys. There is a binary opposition between active listening and obedience, on the one hand, and the refusal to hear and rebellion, on the other.

This opposition is apparent in the epilogue to the Covenant Code, where the people are commanded concerning the angel of YHWH (Exod. 23.20), 'Pay attention to him and listen to what he says (ושמע בקלו; JPS "obey him"). Do not rebel (תמר) against him' (Exod. 23.21).[44] In this verse, the word translated 'rebel' is derived from the root מרר (to be bitter) and not from the root מרה (to be rebellious), as used in Deut. 21.18 and 20. However, the verbs are quite similar phonetically. In any case, it is apparent that rebellion is the opposite of listening. For this reason, the parents' charge 'he will not obey our voice' recapitulates the charge of being 'stubborn and rebellious'. It clarifies the stereotype of the rebellious son.

Crucially, the charge presupposes the parents' teaching function in relation to the character and commands of YHWH. It is not simply a matter of

---

43. Coats, *Rebellion in the Wilderness*, p. 89. This is of course a theological interpretation that is not necessarily to be attributed to all the participants in the narrative.

44. There are many other examples, notably the command to heed the words of the 'prophet like Moses' (Deut. 18.15-19).

disobedience with respect to a few domestic chores. This presupposition is established early on in Deuteronomy itself,

> Only take heed, and keep your soul diligently, lest you forget the things which your eyes have seen, and lest they depart from your heart all the days of your life; make them known to your children and your children's children—[10] how on the day that you stood before the LORD your God at Horeb, the LORD said to me [Moses], 'Gather the people to me, that I may let them hear my words, so that they may learn to fear me all the days that they live upon the earth, and that they may teach their children so' (Deut. 4.9-10).

It is also clear from the early chapters of Deuteronomy that one of the typical settings for parental instruction is the home,

> you shall teach them [YHWH's words] diligently to your children, and shall talk of them when you sit in your house, and when you walk by the way, and when you lie down, and when you rise (Deut. 6.7, cf. 11.19).

To conclude, refusing to obey the parents' voice explicates the charge of being 'stubborn and rebellious'. Both have in mind the stereotypical person who does not heed the voice of authority. Moreover, to the extent that his 'refusal to listen' refers to parental instruction in regard to YHWH's commands, the phrase underlines the idea that סורר ומורה has overtones of apostasy.

2.3.3. *'He Is a Glutton and a Drunkard' (Deuteronomy 21.20c)*
Again we must ask, what sort of person are we talking about here? I shall argue that the typification here has overtones of apostasy and is at one with the behavioural pattern described in the first charge ('This our son is stubborn and rebellious') and in the second charge ('he will not obey our voice'). We may demonstrate this by examining the usage of the words זולל (a glutton), סבא (a drunkard) and the phrase זולל וסבא ('a glutton and a drunkard').

2.3.3.1. *זולל*. 'He who keeps the law (נוצר תורה) [or who "heeds instruction", JPS] is a wise son, but a companion of gluttons (זוללים) shames his father' (Prov. 28.7). Gluttony is associated with departing from *torah* and with failing to heed 'instruction'. Like the drunkard (see 2.3.3.2 below), the glutton is characterised as someone who has no interest in YHWH's commands.[45] Prov. 23.20 ('Be not among winebibbers, or among glutton-

---

45. Hirsch, *Deuteronomy*, p. 419 typifies the glutton (זולל) as the man who knows

ous [בזללי] eaters of meat') suggests a binary opposition between זלל ('to be worthless') and יקר ('to be valued, honoured').[46] If so, the glutton may be associated with the lowest in society.

For ancient moralists such as Philo, gluttony was unnatural not because gluttons have a desire to eat unnatural things but because the glutton was insatiable. For Philo gluttony is a common result of επιθυμια ('lust'),

> When it [επιθυμια] takes hold of the region of the belly, it produces gourmands, insatiable, debauched, eagerly pursuing a loose and dissolute life, delighting in winebibbing and gluttonous feeding, base slaves to strong drink and fish and dainty cakes, sneaking like greedy little dogs round banqueting halls and tables, all this finally resulting in an unhappy and accursed life which is more painful than any death.[47]

Instead of being satisfied with a decent meal, the glutton gorges himself until he is sick, even causing himself to vomit so that he can continue eating. The glutton goes beyond nature (and is therefore unnatural) because he overindulges a natural appetite. In this way, gluttons lose control of their appetites—and not only for food. Food abuse, it was thought, led to sexual perversion.

> [Gluttons] begin with making themselves experts in dainty feeding, winebibbing and the other pleasures of the belly and parts below it. Then sated with these they reach such a pitch of wantonness, the natural offspring of satiety, that losing their senses they conceive a frantic passion, no longer for human beings male or female, but even for brute beasts.[48]

Gluttony was analogous to bestiality, for if gluttony was too much food, bestiality was too much sex. In both cases, it was thought, a natural desire was taken to unnatural extremes.[49]

2.3.3.2. סבא. As with the glutton, the drunkard is also characterized as someone who has little concern for YHWH's commands. The prophet Hosea castigates the northern kingdom of Israel in the following terms, 'Ephraim is joined to idols, let him alone. A band of drunkards (סבאם),

---

'no higher bliss than a large juicy steak' and who has sunk into a 'brutish pandering to the senses' characterized by 'animal-like gorging'.

46. E.g. Jer. 15.19, 'If you utter what is precious (יקר) and not what is worthless (מזולל), you shall be as [the] mouth [of God]'.

47. Philo, *Special Laws*, 4.91.

48. Philo, *Special Laws*, 3.43.

49. D.B. Martin, 'Heterosexism and the Interpretation of Romans 1.18-32', *Bib. Int.* 3 (1995), pp. 332-45 (343).

2. *The Wrath of God on the Sons of the Disobedience* 53

they give themselves to harlotry; they love shame more than their glory' (Hos. 4.17-18). This link between drunkenness and whoredom echoes the juxtaposition of harlotry (זנות) and wine (ויין) in Hos. 4.11. The context (loss of understanding) typifies the drunkard as someone who cares little for anything beyond his sensual desires.

A similar typification occurs in Isa. 56.12, '"Come", they [Israel's watchmen] say, "let us get wine, let us fill ourselves (ונסבאה) with strong drink (שכר); and tomorrow will be like this day, great beyond measure"'. In this verse, the drunkenness of Israel's leaders typifies their complacency and their inability to grasp the true state of affairs described in Isa. 56.9 (the beasts on the way to the feast).[50] It is part and parcel of their blindness (Isa. 56.10), their lack of knowledge (Isa. 56.10) and their sensual self-absorption (Isa. 56.11). Drunkards are one of the social groups summoned by the prophet Joel to a national lament (Joel 1.5) and are singled out as those who ordinarily have little care for religion.[51] Again, the drunkard is a stock figure of the person who has no concern for YHWH.

Philo goes further, comparing the rebellious son to the degenerate Israelites who worshipped the golden calf (Exod. 32.17-19).[52] In his view, Deut. 21.20 referred to drunkenness of the most intense sort.[53] It was 'the poison which causes folly, indiscipline, smoulders within the man, then bursts into fire and flame impossible to quench, and consumes the soul through its whole being with the conflagration'.[54] For Philo 'strong liquor' symbolized several things, 'foolish talking and raving,…complete insensibility,…insatiable and ever-discontented greediness…[and] the nakedness which embraces the rest and manifests itself in all the qualities just mentioned'.[55] From this it follows that the rebellious son 'adds sins to sins, great to small, new to old [as well as] voluntary and involuntary'.[56]

---

50. J.A. Motyer, *The Prophecy of Isaiah* (Leicester: InterVarsity Press, 1993), pp. 468-69.
51. R. Dillard, 'Joel', in Thomas Edward McComiskey (ed.), *The Minor Prophets: An Exegetical and Expository Commentary Vol. I: Hosea, Joel and Amos* (Grand Rapids: Baker Book House, 1992), pp. 1-237 (258).
52. The Midrash hints at a similar link when it claims that, 'the making of the golden calf was on account of wine', *Num. R.* 9.24.
53. Philo, *On Drunkenness*, 8.27.
54. Philo, *On Drunkenness*, 8.27.
55. Philo, *On Drunkenness*, 1.4.
56. Philo, *On Drunkenness*, 1.4.

2.3.3.3. *זולל וסבא*. The words זולל וסבא do not appear together outside Deut. 21.20 with the same frequency as זולל וסבא. However, there is an interesting juxtaposition in Prov. 23.19-22,

> Hear, my son, and be wise, and direct your mind in the [proper] way. [20] Be not among winebibbers (בסבאי־יין) or among gluttonous eaters of meat (בזללי בשר); [21] for the drunkard (סבא) and the glutton (זולל) will come to poverty, and drowsiness will clothe a man with rags. [22] Hearken to your father who begot you, and do not despise your mother when she is old.

The warning about the fate of drunkards and gluttons in Prov. 23.21 is sandwiched between an emphatic imperative ('listen, you!', שמע־אתה, v. 19) and an injunction to obey one's father and to honour one's mother (v. 22). A clearer tip of the hat to Deut. 21.18-21 is hard to imagine.[57] Like Deut. 21.18-21, Prov. 23.19-22 warns against gluttony and drunkenness; echoes the motif of listening to the voice of the father; and appeals to the fifth commandment (see also 2.5.1 below). Prov. 23.19-22 also incorporates the motif of keeping bad company (viz. 'do not be of those'/'do not be among', cf. Prov. 28.7, see 2.3.3.1 above) and emphasizes habitual behaviour. Glutting meat implies more than an occasional feast and guzzling wine implies more than the occasional hangover. Reference is made elsewhere in the same chapter to the morning drinking bout, 'As often as I wake, I go after it again' (Prov. 23.35b).

From a semiotic point of view, the phrase 'a glutton and a drunkard' may be regarded as a visual manifestation of a particular lifestyle. Designating someone as a drug addict, for example, immediately evokes a way of life that goes far beyond taking drugs. We are supplied with part of the picture and our social knowledge of the stereotype enables us to fill in the rest. In the same way, the designation 'a glutton and a drunkard' may typify a lifestyle that includes excessive eating and drinking, but which also goes beyond it to include more destructive forms of behaviour.[58] It signifies other deviant forms of behaviour that contribute to our understanding of seriousness. There are various hints of the prurient lifestyle of habitual drunkards in the Hebrew Bible (e.g. Hab. 2.15, 'Woe to him who

---

57. For possible connections between Deuteronomic theology and Proverbial wisdom see, e.g. J. Blenkinsopp, *Wisdom and Law in the Old Testament: The Ordering of Life in Israel and Early Judaism* (Oxford: Oxford University Press, 1983).

58. Rotenberg, and Diamond. 'Biblical Conception of Psychopathy', p. 37 are probably right to argue that the 'stubborn and rebellious' son presents us with a recognizable 'stereotype', however, as we have seen, it may be anachronistic to present this typology as a 'psychological profile' (see 2.2.4).

makes his neighbours drink of the cup of his wrath, and makes them drunk, to gaze on their shame!'). In the New Testament, drunkenness is part of 'doing what the Gentiles like to do, living in licentiousness, passions, drunkenness, revels, carousing, and lawless idolatry' (1 Pet. 4.3). In both cases, drunkenness is seen as a typical example of an apostate or a pagan lifestyle.

The association between 'a glutton and a drunkard' and keeping the wrong sort of company in Prov. 23.19-22 reinforces this idea of a deviant lifestyle. In Deut. 21.18-21 it suggests a person who eats and drinks more with his like-minded companions than with his own family, creating greater potential (and support) for his own rejection of parental authority.

2.4 *The Rebellious Son as a 'Son of Belial'*

A possible example of a 'stubborn and rebellious son', after the manner of the social stereotype described in Deut. 21.18-21, is the behaviour of Hophni and Phinehas, the sons of Eli (1 Sam. 2.12-17). It must be recognized at the outset that 1 Sam. 2.12-17 does not use the language of Deut. 21.18-21. However, 1 Sam. 2.12-17 is relevant because we have argued that Deut. 21.18-21 presents us with a narrative typification. This means that the question of whether Deut. 21.18-21 applies in a given case does not depend on the answer to semantic questions such as: 'what if he was stubborn but a teetotaller?' (as *per* Brichto)[59] or 'suppose he drank (cheap) Italian wine instead of expensive wine?' (as *per Sanh.*).[60] The relevant question is: 'does his behaviour fit the stereotype?' There are a number of respects in which the sons of Eli in 1 Sam. 2.12-17 fit the stereotype of the 'rebellious son'.

Firstly, we know that they are gluttons. The normal practice at Shiloh was supposed to be that the attendant thrust his fork into the pot and whatever stuck to it was brought up for the priest (1 Sam. 2.13-14). The sons of Eli violated this system of pot luck by choosing the best portions for themselves (1 Sam. 2.15). They also included the fatty portions in their selection (which were supposed to be burnt for YHWH, see Lev. 17.6.), they demanded roasted (rather than boiled) meat (1 Sam. 2.15) and they insisted on getting their share before YHWH's portion was offered up (1 Sam. 2.15-16). For these reasons their offence is characterized as 'despising YHWH's offering' (1 Sam. 2.17). True, the word זוללים is not used but

---

59. Brichto, 'Kin, Cult, Land', p. 32.
60. *Sanh.* 8.2.

gluttonous behaviour can be present even when the word 'gluttony' is absent. The point is that as far as Eli's sons were concerned, filling their stomachs was more important than discharging their priestly duties. The word זוללים only occurs in Prov. 28.7 and to insist on its presence here is to expect biblical law to conform to a modern 'legislative' or 'semantic' approach (see 1.2.1 above). A second echo comes in the form of Eli's (weak) discipline (1 Sam. 1.22-25). His verbal reproof is not as forceful as the chastisement of Deut. 21.18, although some allowance should be made for the fact that he is 'very old' (1 Sam. 1.22). Thirdly, we are told that the sons are aggressive and violent, using the threat of force to get their own way (1 Sam. 2.16). In this respect too, they are like the rebellious son of Deut. 21.18-21. Deut. 21.19 alludes to his violence, describing how the father and mother 'seize' him (תפש, a forceful verb) and bring him before the elders. The son is overcome by the use of force. Fourthly, we are told that the sons would not listen to their father's voice (1 Sam. 2.25). As with Deut. 21.18-21 this refusal to heed is a continuing process, as implied by the phrasing, 'when [Eli] *would* hear what his sons were doing to the Israelites he *would* say to them' (1 Sam. 2.22, my italics). Finally, the sons meet an untimely end (1 Sam. 4.17, cf. 1 Sam. 2.25).

It might be objected that there is no explicit reference to the sons' drunkenness. However, their drunkenness is implicit in the description that they are described as 'sons of Belial' (בני בליעל, 1 Sam. 2.12, see further below). Earlier in the narrative, Hannah begs Eli not to think of her as a 'daughter of Belial' (בת־בליעל, 1 Sam. 1.16) when he mistakenly accuses her of behaving like a drunkard. The chances are high that Eli's sons were not only gluttons but also drunkards. We know from Judg. 21.19-21 that there were vineyards around Shiloh. If the sons were 'ripping off' the Israelites in respect of one sort of sacrifice, it is likely that they did the same with the others, including the libation offerings.

In addition, we noted at 2.3.3.1 and 2.3.3.2 that the 'glutton' and the 'drunkard' typified the person who had no regard for YHWH's commands. 1 Sam. 2.12 explicitly characterizes the sons of Eli as men who had 'no regard for the LORD'. We also considered at 2.3.3.3 that the phrase 'a glutton and a drunkard' typified a lifestyle that included food and alcohol abuse but that also went beyond it to include other dissolute forms of behaviour. This is also the case with the sons of Eli. According to the MT,[61] '[the sons] lay with women who served at the entrance of the Tent of

---

61. Though not according to LXX, R.W. Klein, *1 Samuel* (Waco, TX: Word Books, 1983), n. 22b.

Meeting' (1 Sam. 2.22). This is, after all, what we might expect. Gluttony, drunkenness and promiscuity are all part of the same behaviour pattern insofar as they are characterized by 'excessive indulgence'. This is consistent with Philo's description of the stubborn and rebellious son as one who has made 'a god of the body'.[62] To sum up, the sons of Eli, as described in 1 Sam. 2.12-17, fit the stereotype of the 'stubborn and rebellious son'. They are incorrigible sons who do not heed the rebuke of their father and are more interested in indulging their sensual appetites than in following YHWH's commands.

Interestingly, there is a label for this stereotype in the text, namely, 'sons of Belial' (1 Sam. 2.12). This suggests a possible relationship between the stereotype of the 'rebellious son' and being called a 'son of Belial'. Other biblical texts confirm the existence of a possible relationship between the stereotype of Deut. 21.18-21 and the designation 'son of Belial'. In 1 Sam. 10.27, 'sons of Belial' scoff at King Saul and show him disrespect by failing to bring gifts. This echoes the refusal of the 'rebellious son' to respect authority. In Judg. 19.22, the phrase 'sons of Belial' describes the men of Gibeah who demand relations with the visiting Levite and who fatally abuse his concubine (Judg. 19.25-28). This is consistent with the deviant lifestyle of the 'glutton and a drunkard'. In Ps. 18.5, 'rivers of Belial' are thought to refer to the forces of chaos and these dark undertones are made explicit in post-biblical literature, where Belial is identified as the spirit of darkness.[63] Finally, 2 Sam. 20.1 introduces us to a 'son of Belial' (איש בליעל) 'named Sheba, the son of Bichri (בן־בכרי), a Benjaminite' who revolted against David after Absalom's death. The narrative account of this unsuccessful revolt (2 Sam. 20.1-22) refers eight times to Sheba as 'the son of Bichri'. Clines suggests some wordplay with the popular etymology of the clan name Bichri.[64] בכרי sounds like בכרה ('young camel').[65] Camels are, of course, famously recalcitrant and aggressive creatures. A young camel 'never takes more than about three steps in any direction'[66] and to this day provides 'a dramatic illustration for anything

---

62. Philo, *On Drunkenness*, 1. 95.
63. E.g. *T. Levi* 19.1. Cf. V. Maag, 'Belija'al im Alten Testament', *TZ* 21 (1965), pp. 287-99 (294-95).
64. D.J.A. Clines, 'X, X *Ben* Y, *Ben* Y: Personal Names in Hebrew Narrative Style', *VT* 22 (1972), pp. 266-87 (277).
65. The feminine version appears in Jer. 2.23, Isa. 60.6.
66. K.E. Bailey and W.L. Holladay, 'The "Young Camel" and "Wild Ass" in Jer. 2.23-25', *VT* 18 (1968), pp. 256-60, cf. Jer. 2.23.

unreliable'.⁶⁷ The implication seems to be that Sheba, the son of בכרי, is a true son of a בכרה. He is 'stubborn, rebellious and self-willed'.⁶⁸ Clines concludes from this that 'sons of Belial' are those who break loose from accepted standards of morality or order.⁶⁹ Again, this is very close to the social stereotype envisaged in Deut. 21.18-21.

The question is, did every 'son of Belial' conform to the stereotype of the 'rebellious son'? This depends on how central the various characteristics of the 'son of Belial' are to the stereotype described in Deut. 21.20. Not every person who was called a 'son of Belial' may have been charged under Deut. 21.20. Following Wittgenstein's idea of family resemblances,⁷⁰ it is possible that the biblical characteristics of the 'son of Belial' may only have been part of the set of characteristics (or family resemblances) of the 'rebellious son'. On their own, these characteristics might not be sufficient. However, there is not enough evidence to answer this question with certainty.

To conclude, there is a possible relationship between the popular stereotype of the 'rebellious son' and being labelled a 'son of Belial'. This relationship exists at the level of social knowledge. Certain characteristics of the son of Belial (gluttony, refusal to heed, obstinacy, violence and sexual deviance) echo the narrative typification of the 'stubborn and rebellious son'. The rebellious son may even typify the socially destabilizing forms of behaviour associated with the son of Belial. The seeming overlap between the stereotype of the 'stubborn and rebellious son' and the label 'son of Belial' does not exclude the possibility that there are other antisocial characteristics associated with the 'stubborn and rebellious son' that are not associated with the 'son of Belial'. Nor does it necessarily imply that every 'son of Belial' was also a 'stubborn and rebellious son'. But the overall picture is consistent with Philo's description of the stubborn and rebellious son as 'a leader in godlessness'.⁷¹ 'Such was he who said: "Who is He that I should obey Him" and again "I know not the LORD"'.⁷² As we have argued above, the rebellious son is worse than a delinquent. He is essentially an apostate.

---

67. Bailey and Holladay, 'The "Young Camel"'.
68. Clines, 'Personal Names', p. 277.
69. Clines, 'Personal Names', p 277 n. 2.
70. For the notion of 'family resemblance' see L. Wittgenstein, *Philosophical Investigations* (trans. G.E.M. Anscombe; Oxford: Basil Blackwell, 1958), I, paras. 66-76.
71. Philo, *On Drunkenness*, l. 18.
72. Philo, *On Drunkenness*, l. 19.

2.5. Seriousness of Offence

We have argued that the behavioural pattern described in Deut. 21.20 constitutes a narrative typification that has much in common with the 'son of Belial'. 'Seriousness of offence' consists in two main factors: first, it is a violation of the fifth commandment (see 2.5.1 below) and second, it is a violation of the covenant community (see 2.5.2 below).

2.5.1. *Violation of the Fifth Commandment*

'Seriousness of offence' in Deut. 21.18-21 is closely tied to the fifth commandment ('Honour your father and your mother', Deut. 5.16, cf. Exod. 20.12).[73] It is not unusual to tie offences to this commandment. Jesus links the fifth commandment with Exod. 21.17 ('Whoever curses his father or his mother shall be put to death') and Lev. 20.9 ('If anyone insults his father or his mother, he shall be put to death; he has insulted his father and his mother—his bloodguilt is upon him') (Mt. 15.4; Mk 7.10). There are several literary reasons for regarding Deut. 21.18-21 as a violation of the fifth commandment.

Firstly, there is the immediate literary context. Wenham and McConville note a chiastic structure in Deut. 21.1-23, in which the mirror of Deut. 21.18-21 is Deut. 21.10-14 (the law of the captive maid).[74] A common theme in both Deut. 21.10-14 and Deut. 21.18-21 is the separation of children from their parents. This suggests that filial relationships based on proper behaviour and respect for parents are central to the meaning of Deut. 21.10-14 and Deut. 21.18-21.[75] Secondly, there is the wider literary context. A number of scholars (including Kaufman,[76] Miller,[77] Olson[78] and

---

73. P. Miller, 'The Place of the Decalogue in the Old Testament and its Law', *Int* 43 (1989), pp. 229-42 (236) sees Deut. 21.18-21 as one of a number of laws (along with Exod. 21.15, 17; Lev. 20.9 and Deut. 27.16) that spell out the implications of the commandment to 'honour' parents. Carmichael, *Laws of Deuteronomy*, p. 140 claims that Deut. 21.18-21 is a reworking of Exod. 21.15 and Exod. 21.17.

74. Gordon J. Wenham and J.G. McConville, 'Drafting Techniques in some Deuteronomic Laws', *VT* 30 (1980), pp. 248-52 (251).

75. Wenham and McConville, 'Drafting Techniques', p. 251.

76. S.A. Kaufman, 'The Structure of the Deuteronomic Law', *Maarav* 1 (1979), pp. 105-58 (109).

77. Miller, 'Place of the Decalogue', p. 239.

78. D.T. Olson, *Deuteronomy and the Death of Moses* (Philadelphia: Fortress Press, 1994), p. 64.

Wright[79]) point to the Decalogue-structure of Deuteronomic law. Deut. 21.18-21 is broadly related to the fifth commandment insofar as Deuteronomy 12–26 itself largely follows the sequence of the Ten Commandments. On this view, Deut. 21.18-21 is an extension, or a reinterpretation, of Deut. 5.12. Inevitably, this macro-structural approach has its weaknesses. Scholars disagree on the precise relationship between the commandments and the various 'statutes and ordinances' of Deuteronomy 12–26.[80] However, this criticism is not fatal because the 'Decalogue pattern' in Deuteronomy 12–26 is not an exact science.[81] I share Wright's conclusion that although the analysis is not clear-cut, it is likely that the Decalogue has influenced the ordering of the legal material in Deuteronomy.[82] The form and the content of the fifth commandment clarify the nature of the offence in Deut. 21.18-21 and amplify its seriousness.

2.5.1.1. *Form.* The legal form of the fifth commandment is unusual in several ways. Firstly, there is a dearth of prescriptive texts demanding honour in covenant contexts.[83] This is despite the fact that honour and shame were central to Israel's covenant relations.[84] For this reason the fifth commandment (Exod. 20.12; Deut. 5.16) is a quite exceptional imperative. Secondly, the commandment 'Honour' (כבד) is a gentler or weaker imperative than 'you shall' or 'you shall not'. It counsels, recommends, rather than imposes, compels.[85] Daube sees it as the only ordinance in the Pentateuch couched in this mood (with one possible exception).[86] The statutory imperative is thus

---

79. Wright, *Deuteronomy*, pp. 4-5.

80. E.g. Kaufman 'Deuteronomic Law' and Olson, *Deuteronomy*, p. 64 outline chs. 6-28 differently.

81. In spite of their differences, Kaufman, 'Deuteronomic Law', p. 113, Olson, *Deuteronomy*, p. 64 and Miller, 'Place of the Decalogue', p. 239 all relate Deut. 16.18–18.22 to the commandment to 'honour your parents'. This is based on the long tradition in Judaism and Christianity that sees the fifth commandment as instructing not only the proper attitude to parents but the right attitude to *all* other authorities.

82. Wright, *Deuteronomy*, p. 4.

83. Olyan, *Deuteronomy*, p. 218.

84. Olyan, *Deuteronomy*, p. 218.

85. D. Daube, *Ancient Jewish Law* (Leiden: E.J. Brill, 1981), p. 92.

86. This is the Sabbath commandment (Exod. 20.8-11). However, Daube, 'The Form is the Message' (in *idem, Ancient Jewish Law*), p. 94 argues that although the imperative in the fourth commandment ('Remember', וזכרת) is closer to the imperative form in the fifth commandment (כבד) than to the command 'you shall' or 'you shall not', it is not the same.

2. The Wrath of God on the Sons of the Disobedience 61

'unique—or, if you prefer,—near unique'.[87] Thirdly, the commandment follows an unusual pattern of demand and reward (cf. Eph. 6.2).[88] The reward for keeping the commandment is 'that you may long endure on the land that the LORD your God is assigning to you' (Exod. 20.12) or 'that you may long endure, and that you may fare well, in the land that the LORD your God is assigning you' (Deut. 5.16). Only Deut. 22.6-7 promises a similar combination of long days and well-being. The explanation appears to be simple. As with the fifth commandment, 'we owe piety to parents even in nature'[89](cf. Deut. 21.10-13). To sum up, the legal form of the fifth commandment highlights its singularity and importance and, accordingly, the seriousness of its breach.

2.5.1.2. *Content.* Part of the honour due to parents under the fifth commandment is tied to respect for the teaching they impart (see Deut. 4.9). Parents were the custodians of Israel's 'national assets'[90] viz. her faith, history and traditions. They preserved the stories that lay at the heart of Israel's self-identity including the Exodus, the giving of *torah* and the gift of the Land. Parents were to explain to their children the significance of key events, institutions and memorials (Exod. 12.26-27; 13.14-15; Deut. 6.20-24 and Josh. 4.6-7; 4.21-23). Fathers played a leading role (Prov. 3.1; 4.2; 7.1) though a mother was expected to take an equal share (Prov. 1.8). The attack on foreign wives in Deut. 7.3-4 and Ezra 9.2, 10.2 may indirectly attest to the role of mothers in transmitting religious values to their children (cf. Prov. 6.20; 31.1).[91] An attack on the authority of parents is most serious because 'it threatens the most precious heritage of Israel, its knowledge of God'.[92] This is consistent with the overtones of apostasy noted in the parents' charge in 2.3, above.

Phillips claims that the aim of the commandment was to ensure that sons would automatically maintain the faith of their parents.[93] In similar

---

87. Daube, 'Form is the Message', p. 94.
88. Daube, 'Form is the Message', p. 98.
89. Daube, 'Form is the Message', p. 99.
90. Christopher J.H. Wright, 'Family', in *ABD*, II, pp. 761-69 (764).
91. P.A. Bird, *Missing Persons and Mistaken Identities: Women and Gender in Ancient Israel* (Philadelphia: Fortress Press, 1997), p. 30.
92. V.S. Poythress, *The Shadow of Christ in the Law of Moses* (Phillipsburg, NJ: P. & R. Publishing, 1991), p. 88.
93. A. Phillips, *Ancient Israel's Criminal Law* (Oxford: Basil Blackwell, 1970), p. 81.

vein, Craigie argues that the issue in Deut. 5.16 is 'the continuity of the covenant'.[94] Noting a parallel between Deut. 5.16 and Deut. 4.40 ('that you may live long and it may go well for you on the land') he argues that if the children were receptive and learned the faith of their fathers from their parents, both children and parents would prosper in the Land (4.9-10, 40).[95]

Certainly, the fifth commandment is 'not merely a recipe for happy families'.[96] This is because the fifth commandment (as with the *torah* as a whole) was part of the structure of Israel's covenantal relation with YHWH. The fifth commandment may be seen as an attempt to protect the family internally from the disruption of its domestic authority structure.[97] Wright argues that this was important because the national relationship between Israel and YHWH depended on the survival and stability of family units living on their portions of land. This in turn depended on maintaining a healthy authority structure within the family itself.

We noted briefly in our discussion of סורר, in 2.3.1.1, above, that the relationship between YHWH and Israel was analogous to that between a father and his son. This is of some significance. Deuteronomy consistently uses the relationship between a father and his son to describe YHWH's relationship with his people.[98] Harrelson notes that the parent–child relationship as applied to YHWH and Israel occurs in a context of great intimacy (Exod. 4.22-23, cf. Deut. 8.5).[99] Israel was carried in the wilderness 'as a man carries his son' (Deut. 1.31) whilst elsewhere the Israelites are reminded, 'You are sons of the LORD your God' (Deut. 14.1).[100] At any

---

94. P.C. Craigie, *The Book of Deuteronomy* (Grand Rapids: Eerdmans, 1976), p. 158.
95. Craigie, *Deuteronomy*, p. 158.
96. Wright, *Deuteronomy*, p. 77.
97. C.J.H. Wright, 'The Israelite Household and the Decalogue: The Social Background and Significance of Some Commandments', *TynBul* 30 (1979), pp. 101-24 (105).
98. D.J. McCarthy, 'Notes on the Love of God in Deuteronomy and the Father–Son Relationship between Yahweh and Israel', *CBQ* 27 (1965), pp. 144-47.
99. W. Harrelson, *The Ten Commandments and Human Rights* (Philadelphia: Fortress Press, 1980), p. 99.
100. Such texts are consistent with the practice of naming peoples as masculine and countries as feminine, J.J. Schmitt, 'The Gender of Ancient Israel', *JSOT* 26 (1983), pp. 115-25 (116). Since the word 'Israel' primarily denotes the name of a people, this consistency results in a masculine image. 'Israel' is therefore characterized as a 'son', There are, however, two exceptions to this rule in the MT, namely 1 Sam. 17.21 and 2 Sam. 24.9. Schmitt, 'Gender of Ancient Israel', p. 116 regards the latter as an irregularity corrected by the Chronicler's rendering of the verse in 1 Chron. 21.5.

rate, parenting had a divine dimension in ancient Israel. Carmichael draws attention to the juxtaposition in Lev. 19.3, 'Every one of you shall revere his mother and his father, and you shall keep my sabbaths: I am the LORD your God'.[101] As in the Decalogue, the Sabbath rule is juxtaposed with the rule about parents because procreation links up with the original creation. This may have made the violation of the fifth commandment particularly serious.[102] Special respect is conferred on parents who have been co-creators of life with God. 'Remember that through your parents you were born: and what can you give back to them that equals their gift to you?' (Sir. 7.28).[103] The fifth commandment, accordingly, enjoins an attitude towards parents that parallels the proper attitude towards YHWH of honour, fear and reverence.[104] Jackson sees the fifth commandment (as expressed in the Covenant Code, Exod. 20.12) as a parallel to the first commandment (Exod. 20.2).[105] It too is designed to evoke *feelings* of loyalty and respect. Both commandments are a demand for an affective state. Reverence for parents is paralleled with reverence for YHWH.

Finally, it should also be noted that rebellion against one's progenitors was regarded as unnatural (cf. Isa. 1.2-3). Bockmuehl places this rebellion in the same category as Amos 6.12, viz. 'the corruption of what is perceived and acknowledged to be a healthy state of nature'.[106] This may also have been an aspect of seriousness.

2.5.1.3. *Filial Disobedience: The Whole Story?* Many commentators regard filial disobedience as a complete account of seriousness of offence in Deut. 21.18-21. However, without undercutting the force of 2.5.1.1 and 2.5.1.2, above, there may be further elements of seriousness. For whilst filial disobedience is a serious offence, many commentators tend towards hyperbole when seeking to justify the execution of the rebellious son on these grounds alone. Sometimes it seems as though the offence of filial

---

101. Carmichael, 'Laws of Leviticus 19', p. 246.
102. 'Earthly parents spend themselves for the children. And in many an instance the reward received is what YHWH also received...contemptuous disregard, violation of all bonds of loyalty. It must not be so' (Harrelson, *Ten Commandments*, p. 102).
103. For duties to parents see Exod. 20.12, 21.15, 21.17, Lev. 19.3a, 20.9, Deut. 5.16, 27.16.
104. Miller, 'Place of the Decalogue', p. 238.
105. Jackson, 'Literary Presentation', p. 191 (cf. *Qod.* 1).
106. M. Bockmuehl, 'Natural Law in Second Temple Judaism', *VT* 45 (1995), pp. 1-44 (23).

disobedience has to be rhetorically inflated to make it justify the death penalty (for example, Stulman's recent claim that 'filial disrespect is perceived as a serious threat to the cosmic and social order)'.[107]

These suspicions are confirmed by the fact that the charge of being 'a glutton and a drunkard' is really the capital one in evidentiary terms and not the charge of being a stubborn and rebellious son (see 2.6 below). Overall then, seriousness of offence in Deut. 21.18-21 appears to be more than a simple case of filial disobedience. Of equal, or perhaps greater importance, is what his stubborn and rebellious behaviour says about his attitude towards YHWH and the covenant community, an attitude that is symbolized most markedly by eating and drinking (see 2.5.2 below).

2.5.2. *Violation of the Covenant Community*

I have argued that the charge of being 'a glutton and a drunkard' explicates what it means to be 'stubborn, rebellious and not heed the parents' voice'. It is part and parcel of the same lifestyle and not a separate offence. Nonetheless, the charge of being 'a glutton and a drunkard' does take the modern reader by surprise. It is not the behavioural example we expect. Why is gluttony and drunkenness a serious offence? Gluttony and drunkenness is a more serious charge than it appears. This is because eating and drinking in ancient (as in modern Rabbinic) Judaism was a powerfully concentrated language of great semiotic significance. The wrong sort of eating and drinking could easily constitute a challenge to Israelite religious and social structures (cf. the diabolical behaviour of the sons of Eli in 2.4 above). It is a publicly observable rebellion that calls into question is continuing membership of the covenant community.

2.5.2.1. *The Semiotics of Food.*

Food, whether it be a matter of eating, not eating, starving or fasting is a powerfully concentrated language that symbolizes behaviour among members of a social group.[108] How one eats; how much; and with whom (all relevant factors when considering the typification of a glutton) can be seen as a direct expression of social, political and religious relationships.[109] Eating together is a social event that involves all who share the meal in a complex web of reciprocity and mutuality. It

---

107. L. Stulman, 'Sex and Familial Crimes in the D Code: A Witness to Mores in Transition', *JSOT* 53 (1992), pp. 47-63 (55).

108. D. Neufeld, 'Eating, Ecstasy and Exorcism (Mark 3.21)', *BTB* 26 (1996), pp. 152-62 (159).

109. Neufeld, 'Eating, Ecstasy', p. 159.

2. *The Wrath of God on the Sons of the Disobedience* 65

symbolizes a complex set of relationships and feelings, and it expresses the boundaries of group identity. For these reasons, food was a controversial issue in ancient Israel and it was one of the means by which condemnation and exaltation were conveyed.[110]

Food, therefore, was a medium through which attitudes towards both YHWH and the covenant community could be communicated. The act of eating fosters feelings of brotherhood, commonality, trust and intimacy. By the same token, gluttony could express breach of covenant with YHWH and the breakdown of relationships within the covenant community. A number of verses warn that material wealth and satiety can lead to pride and arrogance and to forgetting one's dependence upon YHWH (see e.g. Deut. 8.12-14; 11.14-16; 31.20; 32.15 and cf. Deut. 8.3). The same connection is made in Nehemiah's retrospective, '[Israel's descendants] ate, and were filled and became fat, and delighted themselves in thy great goodness. Nevertheless they were disobedient and rebelled (וימרו וימרדו בך) against thee and cast thy law behind their back and killed thy prophets' (Neh. 9.24-26).

2.5.2.2. *Food, Glorious Food?* We saw at 2.3.3 above that, for Philo, the seriousness of gluttony and drunkenness lay in the fact that it frequently led on to other vices. How far these attitudes, typical of some of the more ascetic Graeco-Roman traditions, underpinned Deut. 21.18-21 is hard to determine. However, it is consistent with the argument that the phrase 'a glutton and a drunkard' is not simply concerned with gluttony and drunkenness. Rather, it typifies a lifestyle that includes excessive eating and drinking but which may also go beyond it to include more destructive forms of behaviour (see 2.3.3 and 2.4, above).

2.5.2.3. *The Charge against Jesus.* This approach to Deut. 21.18-21 may shed some light on the charge against Jesus of being 'a glutton and a drunkard' (Mt. 11.19; Lk. 7.34). Jesus' use of the phrase 'a glutton and a drunkard' borrows from or is attributed to his critics. The immediate issue is Jesus' practice of welcoming the outcast into the new Israel. This could only have been regarded as rebellious by those who adhered to strict ritual, cultic and ethnic limits; boundaries which were, among other things, determined by food (cf. 2.5.2.1 above). Frequently in the synoptic gospels the

---

110. Neufeld, 'Eating, Ecstasy', p. 159.

issue of 'eating' and 'not eating' sparks off conflict between Jesus and (variously) his family, the crowds and the religious authorities. His disciples pick grain on the Sabbath and eat with unwashed hands, whilst Jesus and his followers do not fast and Jesus himself eats with tax collectors and sinners.[111] For those who continued to define the people of God in this way, rather than by their relationship to Jesus, Jesus could only have been perceived as a threat to their tradition. He was regarded as a menace and as a source of great dishonour to his family and to the community. As such, he deserved the same fate as the rebellious son in Deut. 21.18-21.[112]

This reading is in keeping with our analysis so far, that Deut. 21.20 is a serious charge levelled against someone who is thought to be a dangerous apostate. It is brought against someone whose behaviour challenges the boundaries of Israel's self-definition, boundaries that were defined not least by food. In Jesus' case, the boundaries were challenged by his habit of having private parties with the local 'low-life'.

Significantly, the immediate context (in both Matthew and Luke) alludes to Deut. 21.18-21. Jesus describes 'the people of this generation' (in so many words) as being stubborn and rebellious.[113] 'To what, then, can I compare the people of this generation ? What are they like ? They are like children sitting in the market-place and calling out to each other: "We played the flute for you, and you did not dance; We sang a dirge, and you did not cry"' (Lk. 7.31-32 and cf. Mt. 11.16-17). The picture is of people who are so unresponsive and impossible to please that it does not matter whether the 'game' being played is that of 'weddings' or 'funerals'. John and Jesus were radically different, but their hearers refused to hear the voice of YHWH in either the sombre or the joyful. Jesus may be accused of being a 'glutton and a drunkard' but his critics are the ones who are 'stubborn and rebellious'. Jesus goes on to say, 'For John the Baptist came neither eating bread nor drinking wine, and you say, "He has a demon". The Son of Man came eating and drinking, and you say, "Here is a glutton and a drunkard, a friend of tax collectors and sinners"' (Lk. 7.33-34; cf. Mt. 11.18-19). Again, the phrase a 'glutton and a drunkard' is associated with keeping the worst and lowest forms of company (cf. Prov. 13.19-22 and 2.3.3.3 above).

---

111. Neufeld, 'Eating, Ecstasy', p. 158.
112. Cf. Neufeld, 'Eating, Ecstasy', p. 159.
113. See R.T. France, *The Gospel according to Matthew* (Leicester: InterVarsity Press, 1985), pp. 196-97.

2. The Wrath of God on the Sons of the Disobedience 67

Implicit, too, in Jesus' use of the term 'a glutton and a drunkard' is that he is prepared for execution.[114] Jesus perceives that his practice of welcoming tax collectors and prostitutes into the new Israel provides the basis of a plot to destroy him. Indeed, in Matthew's account, such a plot emerges in the very next chapter (Mt. 12.14). This argument is consistent with Brown's thesis that the laws of Deuteronomy, especially Deuteronomy 13, played a vital role in stacking up the charges against Jesus.[115] To the official Judaism of Jesus' day, Jesus was a false prophet who sought to justify his teaching and practices by signs and wonders. The performance of miracles was regarded by some as proof of guilt and as providing clear-cut evidence to justify the purging of evil. If Brown is right and if Jesus was put to death in accordance with the laws of Deuteronomy, it is hardly surprising that the charge of Deut. 21.18-21 was invoked.[116] Jesus could have been presented as a rebellious son who deserved to be executed in accordance with Mosaic law. I argued at 2.4 above that the 'rebellious son' was the narrative typification of the son of 'Belial', which in turn has associations with the underworld. Notably, Jesus is accused of being in league with Beelzebub (Mt. 12.24-28; Mk 3.22-30; Lk. 11.14-20). We note especially the close link between food in Mk 3.20 (or the lack of it), the action of Jesus' family ('He is out of his mind', Mk 3.21) and the charge of devilry (Mk 3.22).

At any rate, the gospels' use of the phrase 'a glutton and a drunkard' underscores a number of key points. Firstly, they reiterate that eating was a powerfully concentrated language in ancient Judaism of great semiotic significance (cf. 2.5.2.1 above). The wrong sort of eating could easily constitute a challenge to Israelite religious and social structures. Secondly, the glutton and drunkard was seen as a destabilizing figure who kept the wrong sort of company and threatened the traditions of the community (cf. 2.3.3.3 above). Thirdly, the parallel between having a demon and being 'a glutton and a drunkard' recalls the association between the gluttony of the

---

114. H.C. Kee, 'Jesus: "A Glutton and a Drunkard"', *NTS* 42 (1996), pp. 374-93 (391).

115. C. Brown, *Miracles and the Critical Mind* (Grand Rapids: Eerdmans, 1984), p. 288.

116. Wright, *Deuteronomy*, p. 440 n. 273 suggests that this opens up another possible dimension of Lk. 15.11-32 (the parable of the prodigal son). Here the younger son is precisely a 'rebellious son', who squanders the inheritance of his father in riotous and wanton living. The parable is told to defend Jesus against the charge of 'receiving sinners and eating with them' (Lk. 15.2).

sons of Eli and the sons of Belial (1 Sam. 2.12). Finally, the charge of being 'a glutton and a drunkard' was thought to justify the death penalty; if not formally, at least in folk memory (cf. 2.1 above).

2.6. *Different Jurisdictions, Different Forms of Proof*

I have argued that the charge of being 'a glutton and a drunkard' is integral to the text of Deut. 21.18-21 where it explicates the stereotype of being 'stubborn and rebellious' and of not heeding the parents' voice. However, I have still to explain why the behavioural pattern of being 'a glutton and a drunkard' appears in v. 20 and not in v. 18 (see 2.1, above).

The reason is that Deut. 21.18-21 envisages two different jurisdictions (the family and the elders). These jurisdictions have different powers of punishment. The parents have the power to inflict corporal punishment on their son (Deut. 21.18) and to bring him before the elders (Deut. 21.19)[117] but unlike the Roman practice of *ius vitae necisque*[118] the parents in Deut. 21.18-21 do not have the power to put their son to death. Only the elders

---

117. For the scope of the parents' actions, cf. M. Frishtik, 'Physical Violence by Parents against their Children in Jewish History and Jewish Law', *JLA* 10 (1992), pp. 79-97 (93-94).

118. The *ius vitae necisque* refers to the right of the Roman *paterfamilias* to put to death those in his *potestas*. How far this was part of Roman social life is a matter of debate. Most writers take it for granted that the *ius vitae necisque* was a fact of Roman life, at least in the early period. W.W. Buckland, *A Textbook of Roman Law from Augustus to Justinian* (ed. P. Stein; Cambridge: Cambridge University Press, 1966), p. 123 states the traditional view: 'the father's power of life and death was very real in early law', whilst F. Schulz, *Principles of Roman Law* (Oxford: Clarendon Press, 1936), p. 167 avers that the disciplinary powers of the *paterfamilias* were unfettered: 'any chastisement was permitted, even capital punishment'. The *ius vitae necisque* is allowed by Papinian (*Coll.* 4.8), Ulpian (*Dig.* 48.8.2) and Paul (*Dig.* 28.2.11). Most scholars argue that the practice waxed during the early period of the Republic and waned during Imperial times, although exactly when is disputed. B. Nicholas, *An Introduction to Roman Law* (Oxford: Clarendon Press, 1962), p. 67 argues that there were no attempts at restriction until the beginning of the second century CE and then only by extraordinary imperial intervention in particular cases. The *ius vitae necisque* was abolished by Constantine (*Cod.* 9.17.1) but according to another view it was extinguished in 365 CE by a constitution of Valentinian I (*Cod.* 9.15.1).

However, this picture of the social reality of the *ius vitae necisque* has been challenged by a number of scholars. R.P. Saller, *Patriarchy, Property and Death in the Roman Family* (Cambridge: Cambridge University Press, 1994), p. 115 argues that the most famous cases of *ius vitae necisque* come from what he calls the 'legendary era' of early Rome. He contends that the cases contain unreliable details that change from one

are competent to pronounce sentence of execution. Because these two jurisdictions have different powers to punish, they also require different standards of proof. Verse 20 requires a different standard of proof from v. 18 because the sanction is capital, rather than corporal, punishment. The imperfect repetition in vv. 18 and 20 reflects these differences between the two jurisdictions.

According to Deut. 21.18, the parents have complete discretion to 'chastise' their son if they think that he is violating the fifth commandment. They also have discretion to bring him before the elders if he persists. Their discretion is implied by the word 'shall' in v. 19. This is because the use of the imperfect in Hebrew does not distinguish between the mandatory and the permissive. It could equally be read 'his father and mother *may* take hold of him and bring him out to the elders'. This implies that the parents are in the best position to judge whether their son is סורר ומורה and is refusing to obey their voice. If he has violated the fifth commandment, they should know. After all, it is their voice he does not heed.

Here, the allegation of being 'a stubborn and rebellious son' is akin to a married couple's claim that their marriage has 'irretrievably broken down'. It is an unassailable claim because nobody knows the state of their marriage better than they do. The very nature of the parents' charge in Deut. 21.20a-b makes it difficult for anyone else to challenge. If *they* think he is stubborn and rebellious then he must be. Against a parent's accusation, who can stand?

The charge of gluttony and drunkenness in Deut. 21.20c, however, is different. Whereas the typical case of being 'stubborn and rebellious' and of refusing to heed the parents' voice takes place in a *private*, domestic,

---

version to another. Saller notes that some of the sources on which the traditional view relies are ambiguous. For example, R.W. Lee, *The Elements of Roman Law* (London: Sweet & Maxwell, 1956), p. 61 and Nicholas, *Roman Law*, p. 67 refer to the Catilinarian conspiracy of 63–62 BCE as an example of the *ius vitae necisque*. In this episode, the conspirators are joined by Fulvius, a senator's son. His father had him brought back and put to death and other fathers followed suit. However, Saller, *Patriarchy*, p. 115 sees this story (and others like it) as showing the value of putting loyalty to the *patria* ahead of loyalty to the *familia*. Saller, *Patriarchy*, p. 117 concludes that there is no clear evidence for the successful invocation of the *ius vitae necisque* in the classical era against a grown son except in defence of the *patria*. Likewise, W.V. Harris, 'The Roman Father's Power of Life and Death', in R.S. Bagnall and W.V. Harris, *Studies in Roman Law in memory of A. Arthur Schiller* (Leiden: E.J. Brill, 1986), pp. 81-95 (86) draws attention to the 'real rarity' of historical instances in which *vitae necisque potestas* was relied on with regard to adult sons.

setting, the charge of being 'a glutton and a drunkard'—with all that that involves regarding a visibly deviant lifestyle—refers to *publicly* observable behaviour. Verses 18 and 20 both allege that his behaviour conforms to a particular stereotype. In that respect, there is no difference between the behavioural patterns mentioned. Both claim that he is a certain sort of person. The difference lies in the nature of the evidence that is put forward to support this claim. In Deut. 21.18 it is sufficient if the parents alone think that he is a 'stubborn and rebellious son'. But for the elders to concur in the parents' judgment, there must be a different form of evidence in the form of publicly observable behaviour ('he is a glutton and a drunkard'). This different standard is required because the sanction is capital, and not corporal, punishment.

Thus, although the parents are in the best position to establish whether their son is 'stubborn and rebellious', the elders cannot simply rely on the parents' word. This is contrary to the view that the public execution acted as a warning against 'parents who might make irresponsible accusations against their children'.[119] This view ignores the two forms of proof that are present in Deut. 21.18-21. Irresponsible parents could not simply 'hand over' their children for public execution. The rebellious son was only executed if he was found to be 'a glutton and a drunkard'. Proving this charge was a matter for the community as a whole, not just the parents.

There must be safeguards for the alleged 'rebellious son' in case his parents bring him before the elders out of frustration, anger or malice. This means that a substantive, publicly observable, demonstration of the parents' allegation is required. This is the charge that he is 'a glutton and a drunkard' (זולל וסבא)[120] which relates to matters that can be publicly attested. Everyone knows the town drunk. It is the most obvious external indicator of a deviant lifestyle made manifest to the community.

This argument is consistent with the protective features of Deut. 21.18-21 noted by several writers. Patrick sees Deut. 21.18-21 as a shift in legal tradition that 'safeguards against [the] unlimited authority of parents'.[121] Olson notes that parental authority in Deut. 21.18-21 is shared by the

---

119. E.g. V.H. Matthews, 'Entrance Ways and Threshing Floors: Legally Significant Sites in the Ancient Near East', *Fides et Historia* 19 (1987), pp. 25-40 (27).

120. This may partly account for the lawgivers' interest in 'gluttony and drunkenness' as opposed to, say, 'hitting his parents' (cf. Exod. 21.15). 'Food abuse' typically takes place in public whereas 'elder abuse' typically takes place in private.

121. D. Patrick, *Old Testament Law* (London: SCM Press, 1985), p. 129.

father and the mother and is not centred on one individual.[122] He argues that this reflects Deuteronomy's concern for the careful distribution and balance of human power (cf. the 'decentralizing' and limiting of authority among judges, kings, priests and prophets in Deut. 16–18). Wright is guided by the preceding law (Deut. 21.15-17) in arguing that the mother's presence in Deut. 21.18-21 acts as a safeguard for her son.[123] As in the law of inheritance (Deut. 21.15-17), a son is not to suffer at the hands of an unjust father. Deut. 22.13-19 is a further example of a law that protects innocent family members from false accusation and execution (see Chapter 4, below).

To sum up, the parents' charge that their son conforms to the stereotypical 'rebellious son' must be backed up by publicly observable proof. The charge in Deut. 21.20, 'This our son is stubborn and rebellious, he will not obey our voice; he is a glutton and a drunkard' combines two different forms of proof, personal or private knowledge (on the part of the parents) and public knowledge (on the part of the community). The latter takes the form of independent eyewitness evidence of a deviant lifestyle.

2.7. Disinheritance: A Further Dimension of Seriousness?

There is, however, a further possible dimension to seriousness of offence in Deut. 21.18-21. This arises from the legal (as opposed to the filial) relationship that existed between parents and children in the ANE. The parties are related not only biologically as parents and children but also legally as testators and heirs. This may add a further dimension to seriousness of offence. Deut. 21.18-21 may not simply be a case of being a bad son (filial disobedience) but also a bad heir.

The motive clauses of both versions of the fifth commandment explicitly tie respect for parents to long life in the Land (Exod. 20.12 and Deut. 5.16).[124] Although the whole Decalogue is a condition for long life in the Land, the relationship between parent and child as testator and heir seems to have been the cornerstone of enjoying the inheritance.[125] Indeed, Israel's

---

122. Olson, *Deuteronomy*, p. 79.
123. Wright, *Deuteronomy*, p. 236.
124. Exod. 20.12 states, 'Honour your father and your mother, that your days may be long in the land which the LORD your God gives you'. Deut. 5.16 states, 'Honour your father and your mother, as the LORD your God commanded you; that your days may be prolonged, and that it may go well with you, in the land which the LORD your God gives you'.
125. Benjamin, *Deuteronomy and City Life*, p. 221.

unique self-understanding of being a chosen people who had received a holy Land might lead us to expect that relations between parents and children *qua* testators and heirs would be strictly regulated. It may therefore be that Deut. 21.18-21 is not just about having a more sensitive attitude towards one's parents[126] but about pursuing a certain sort of lifestyle (akin to a 'son of Belial') that ultimately jeopardizes his inheritance.[127] Being unfit to inherit the Land is a serious offence in Deuteronomy which repeatedly casts the people's relation to the Land as a metaphor of their relation to YHWH.[128]

Inheritance may be an important aspect of the 'father son' imagery vis-à-vis YHWH and Israel. Melnyk suggests that this imagery refers to relations between a father and his adopted son.[129] The following aspects of YHWH's relationship with Israel are similar to the stipulations found in ANE adoption clauses, namely, claiming the child as one's own, raising the child, providing an inheritance and punishing the rebellious child.[130] Three of these stipulations are crystallized in Jer. 3.19, 'I thought I would set you among my sons (אֲשִׁיתֵךְ בְּבָנִים) and give you a desirable land, the fairest heritage of all the nations; and I thought you would call me, "My Father", and would not turn from following me'. Jer. 3.19 makes three points: Israel is (1) appointed as son, (2) promised an inheritance and

---

126. Benjamin, *Deuteronomy and City Life*, p. 219.

127. Cf. the list of behaviours that prevent one from 'inheriting' the kingdom of God in the New Testament, 'Now the works of the flesh are plain: fornication, impurity, licentiousness, idolatry, sorcery, enmity, strife, jealousy, anger, selfishness, dissension, party spirit, envy, drunkenness, carousing, and the like. I warn you, as I warned you before, that those who do such things shall not *inherit* the kingdom of God' (Gal. 5.19-21, my italics). Cf. also 1 Cor. 6.9-10, 'Do you not know that the unrighteous will not *inherit* the kingdom of God? Do not be deceived; neither the immoral, nor idolaters, nor adulterers, nor sexual perverts, nor thieves, nor the greedy, nor drunkards, nor revilers, nor robbers will *inherit* the kingdom of God' (my italics).

128. Benjamin, *Deuteronomy and City Life*, p. 217. In the ANE, designating an heir was a legal process. The heir might be the eldest son, another child or even someone else's child. This heir carried the legal title 'son' and enjoyed special privileges during the life of his 'father'. This process could be legally reversed. Either the father or the son could repudiate the covenant and repudiation consisted both of actions and declarations which are publicly witnessed, Benjamin, *Deuteronomy and City Life*, p. 215.

129. J.L.R. Melnyk, 'When Israel Was a Child: Ancient Near Eastern Adoption Formulas and the Relationship between God and Israel', in M. Patrick Graham *et al.*, *History and Interpretation* (JSOTSup, 173; Sheffield: Sheffield Academic Press, 1993), pp. 245-59.

130. Melnyk, 'When Israel Was a Child', pp. 245-59.

2. The Wrath of God on the Sons of the Disobedience

(3) the adopted children are expected not to rebel.[131] The Hebrew phrase אשׁיתך בבנים may be seen as the inter-dialectal semantic equivalent of an Akkadian phrase meaning 'to establish for the status of an heir'.[132] This background of adoption, filial obedience and disinheritance is relevant to our understanding of Deut. 21.18-21 because it suggests that the rebellious son is disinherited.

Melnyk notes that the condition that the children should not 'rebel' was a common clause in ANE adoption contracts, especially if the father had bequeathed a large or a valuable inheritance.[133] If the conditions laid down in the adoption agreement were broken, the inheritance was the first to go. Breaking an adoption agreement often meant more, however, than disinheritance. Adoptive but rebellious children were commonly disowned, exiled and subjected to slavery.[134] Significantly, Israel's rebellion is punished in the same way. If Melnyk is correct and Canaan is seen as the valuable inheritance that YHWH bequeaths to his adopted son, Israel, it follows that filial respect is necessary for 'survival' in the Land (Deut. 32.45-47).

There is no express indication in Deut. 21.18-21 that disinheritance is part of the background to Deut. 21.18-21. Nonetheless, the narrative context of Deut. 21.18-21, the immediate literary context (Deut. 21.15-23), evidence of thematic repetition and the plea of the daughters of Zelophehad all suggest that Deut. 21.18-21 may be concerned with disinheritance.

2.7.1. Narrative Context

Deut. 21.18-21 appears in the context of a wider body of legislation (4.44–28.68) that, in turn, is presented as part of Moses' valedictory speech to the Israelites. The context is a covenant-renewal ceremony on the plains of Moab before the Israelites have crossed the Jordan. It is a speech addressed to those who are about to inherit land. The discourse itself is peppered with exhortations and warnings that remind the people how they must behave if they are to keep the Land. They are repeatedly warned about the stubbornness and rebellion of the previous generation who failed to inherit. To boot, the address is delivered by someone whose own rebellion prevents him from entering the Land (Num. 20.12).[135] All this is highly significant

---

131. Melnyk, 'When Israel Was a Child', p. 251.
132. Melnyk, 'When Israel Was a Child', p. 251.
133. Melnyk, 'When Israel Was a Child', p. 255.
134. Melnyk, 'When Israel Was a child', p. 256.
135. The seriousness of Moses' sin can be seen by comparing the narrative of

from a semiotic perspective with its interest in the identities of speaker and audience. Indeed, if we were trying to reconstruct the context within which a message such as Deut. 21.18-21 would be meaningful, we could hardly do better than this: a farewell address given by Moses to the obedient generation on the border of the Promised Land. The narrative and geographical context of Deut. 21.18-21 raises the possibility that the stubborn and rebellious son may have been understood not only as a bad son but also as a bad heir.

It may be that what takes being stubborn and rebellious out of the sphere of (mere) domestic discipline and into the public sphere is the fact that domestic discipline is incorporated as a condition of the covenant. Domestic discipline is part of covenantal law (Exod. 20.12), the reward for observance of which is indeed inheritance. Here inheritance means not merely inheritance of a parental estate, but inheritance of divinely promised land. This requirement may explain the relationship between the behaviour of the rebellious son and the implication of disinheritance.

2.7.2. Immediate Literary Context (Deuteronomy 21.15-23)

Deut. 21.18-21 is preceded by Deut. 21.15-17 (the law of the first-born) and it is followed by Deut. 21.22-23 (which concerns the body of an executed criminal). These three laws share the same basic construction ('if a man has', כי־יהיה),[136] a formula that occurs only here in Deuteronomy.[137] Plainly, they are interlinked. Some scholars might explain this by referring

---

Num. 20 with the similar situation of Exod. 17. Instead of showing the people that it was YHWH's intention to produce water for them, Moses' performance has directly the opposite effect. This amounted to a serious desecration of YHWH's name and reputation. Moses behaved like a 'stubborn and rebellious son'. As such Moses (as well as Aaron) was barred from entering the Land ('you shall not lead this congregation into the land that I have given them'). There is similarity between the language of Num. 20.12 ('Because you did not trust me enough') and Num. 14.11 ('how long will [this people] have no faith in me?'). Moses and Aaron's punishment (that of not entering the Land) is announced by YHWH in almost identical terms to that of the people. As J. Milgrom, *Numbers* (Philadelphia: Jewish Publication Society, 1990), p. 265 notes, Moses is 'condemned for revealing the very failing which he tried to rectify in his charges'. See also J. Lim Teng Kok, *The Sin of Moses and the Staff of God* (Assen: Van Gorcum, 1997).

136. See Deut. 21.15-17, 21.18-21 and 21.22-23.

137. The construction does not appear in Exodus or Numbers and it occurs only once in Leviticus (Lev. 22.12). A variation of the construction appears in Deut. 21.13 and Deut. 22.19, Benjamin, *Deuteronomy and City Life*, p. 212.

2. *The Wrath of God on the Sons of the Disobedience* 75

to the associative mind that appears to govern the arrangement of the Deuteronomic laws.[138] The argument might go as follows: Deut. 21.15-17 governs the relationship between fathers and sons and this gives way to the law in question (Deut. 21.18-21) which governs relations between parents and their sons and finishes with the spectacle of an executed son. This in turn leads naturally on to Deut. 21.22-23 which regulates the exposure of the condemned man's body. This rationale is straightforward and quite possibly correct. However, the unusual formulation of the three laws may suggest something more than thought-association. It may actually suggest a common theme, which may be inheritance.

In Deut. 21.15-17, the father who has more than one wife must give a double-portion to his first-born son, even when he might prefer to endow the son of another marriage. The law governs the father–son relationship in respect of inheritance. This means that Deut. 21.15-17 is not only concerned with parents and sons (in filial relationship) but also with testators and heirs (in legal relationship). The father–son relationship is regulated, not abstractly, but in relation to property.

An express reference is made in Deut. 21.16 to 'the day when he [the father] assigns his possession as an inheritance (נחלה) to his sons'. An explicit reference is also made to inheritance in Deut. 21.22-23, 'you shall not defile your land which the LORD your God gives you for an inheritance (נחלה)' (21.23). No mention is made of נחלה in Deut. 21.18-21, but since it has the same formal structure as the laws on either side of it and because, like Deut. 21.15-17, it is concerned with the father–son relationship, the implication may be that the rebellious son is not fit to become an heir. When the son was designated an heir (perhaps on the day his father '[assigned] his possessions as an inheritance to his sons' [21.16]), he assumed certain social, economic and religious obligations towards his testators.[139] A stubborn and rebellious son may have been one who is not fulfilling those obligations. He has failed to honour his parents, who are also his testators. After all, Deut. 21.18-21 is not restricted to the period

---

138. H.M. Weiner, 'The Arrangement of Deuteronomy XII–XXVI' in H. Loewe (ed.) *Posthumous Essays* (London: Oxford University Press, 1932), pp. 26-36 has suggested that transitions in the text of Deuteronomy are not purely lexical but are the product of an 'associative mind'. Discovering the underlying association of ideas, in which one idea triggers the next, is the key to understanding the organization of the book.

139. Benjamin, *Deuteronomy and City Life*, p. 220.

when the son is a child. It continues to regulate the relationship between parents and son when all the parties are adult.

There is a further possible connection between Deut. 21.15-17 and Deut. 21.18-21, based on the theme of inheritance. Like Deut. 21.15-17, Deut. 21.18-21 could be abused by an unscrupulous father who wanted to disinherit the son of an unloved wife. To prevent this from happening, the mother is involved in the whole proceedings. Reference is made to the son disobeying her voice (21.18, 20) and ignoring her chastisement (21.18). Her consent is therefore required if he is going to be disinherited. She is also involved in bringing him before the elders (21.19). The law in Deut. 21.18-21, like that of Deut. 21.15-17, may be designed to protect the son from an unscrupulous father. The mother's presence may be a safeguard to prevent the father from bringing a false charge of misbehaviour.[140]

2.7.3. *Thematic Repetition*
Rebellion and disinheritance are fully integrated into the wider themes of Deuteronomy. Two recurring motifs are: the presentation of Israel as YHWH's rebellious son and the conditional nature of the inheritance.

2.7.3.1. *Rebel Without a Cause.* The motif of Israel as YHWH's rebellious son, which I mentioned briefly in 2.2.1 and 2.3.1.1 above, is found in Moses' opening discourse, the main body of the legislation and the closing address. The opening discourse (Deut. 1.6–4.40) prefaces the main body of law (4.44–28.68), beginning with a retrospective of events following Israel's departure from Mount Sinai (1.6–3.29). It reminds them how they must behave if they are to keep the land, warning the people against stubbornness and rebellion and exhorting them to obedience.[141] Specific incidents of rebellion are recalled, notably the refusal to take the Land after hearing the spies' report ('you would not go up [to take the Land], but rebelled (ותמרו) against the command of the LORD your God' (Deut. 1.26). This stubbornness and rebellion causes YHWH, in Deut. 1.34-41, to reverse his promise to give the Exodus generation the Land.

---

140. J.H. Tigay, *Deuteronomy* (Philadelphia: Jewish Publication Society of America, 1996), p. 197.

141. The binary opposition between 'rebellion' and 'obedience' is presented as an elementary choice in Deuteronomy (along with 'blessing and curse' [Deut. 28] and 'life' and 'death' [Deut. 30.15-20]) and their consequences are either 'keeping' or 'losing' the land.

Israel's failure to listen to YHWH's voice also leads to a rout at the hands of the Amorites. 'I [Moses] spoke to you, and you would not hearken; but you rebelled (ותמרו) against the command of the LORD, and were presumptuous and went up into the hill country' (Deut. 1.43). Deut. 21.18-21 makes exactly the same point: rebellion and a failure to listen causes the reversal of all that has been promised.

The main body of the legislation is also peppered with reminders of Israel's rebellion, 'from the day you came out of the land of Egypt, until you came to this place, you have been rebellious (ממרים) against the LORD' (Deut. 9.7). The rebellion of the wilderness generation is reinforced in Deut. 9.23-24, 'you rebelled (ותמרו) against the commandment of the LORD your God, and did not believe him or obey his voice. You have been rebellious (ממרים) against the LORD from the day that I knew you.' Finally, the closing section of the book records one last (and prophetic) complaint, 'For I know how rebellious (מריך) and stubborn you are; behold, while I am yet alive with you, today you have been rebellious (ממרים) against the LORD; how much more after my death!' (Deut. 31.27).

2.7.3.2. *The Conditional Nature of the Inheritance.* The conditional nature of Israel's inheritance is reiterated throughout Deuteronomy. Obedience is necessary to obtain the inheritance. This is stressed in three main ways. Firstly, by Moses' failure to enter the Land, secondly, by the death of the Exodus generation in the wilderness and thirdly, by the statement in Deut. 4.1 that entry is dependent on obedience. If being an obedient son is central to inheritance in Deuteronomy, it is possible that disobedience in the case of the rebellious son also causes him to forfeit the land. Just as Israel does not have an unconditional right to the Land, so the son in Deut. 21.18-21 does not have an unconditional right to his father's property, either.[142]

2.7.4. *Summary*
The legal relationship between biblical parents and their children, in the form of testators and heirs, may be an additional aspect of seriousness of offence in Deut. 21.18-21. The narrative and immediate literary context both suggest that inheritance may be an issue. Deut. 21.18-21 may allow parents to disinherit the stubborn and rebellious son because they fear that

---

142. Benjamin, *Deuteronomy and City Life*, p. 221.

he will be a bad heir. Being unfit to inherit the land would be a serious offence within the framework of Deuteronomy which stresses the people's relationship to the Land as a metaphor of their relation to YHWH. It is consistent with one of the dominant themes of Deuteronomy, namely, the insistence upon obedience in order to possess and to enjoy the land.[143] It also allows us to take seriously the motive clauses of the Decalogue that expressly tie respect for parents with long life in the Land.

2.8. Conclusion

Deut. 21.18-21 describes the social stereotype of the 'rebellious son'. Verses 18 and 20 signify the typical behavioural patterns of a narrative stereotype. They are not discrete offences. It is a serious offence to be a rebellious son because it violates the fifth commandment. However, seriousness of offence is not limited to filial disobedience. The real issue is his pursuit of a deviant lifestyle that challenges Israelite religious and social structures and which is publicly signified by gluttony and drunkenness. This is unsurprising in a culture where food consumption takes on a semiotic status and is a sign. His offence is not merely delinquency, but is essentially apostasy. There is a close affinity between the stereotypical rebellious son and the 'son of Belial'. His lifestyle ultimately calls into question his continuing membership of the covenant community. The legal relationship between parents and children as testators and heirs may be an additional aspect of Deut. 21.18-21. If so, the law may allow parents to disinherit an unsuitable heir. Deut. 21.18-21 is internally structured around two spheres of jurisdiction. The charge of זולל וסבא ('a glutton and a drunkard') safeguards the rebellious son from malicious prosecution by establishing a different form of proof. If the elders, like the parents, are satisfied that he conforms to this stereotype, he is to be executed. But the offence cannot be limited to filial disobedience. His execution has a purifying effect upon the community, purging the evil from their midst.

143. Israel must obey YHWH in order to occupy the Land successfully (Deut. 4.1), to enjoy its bounty (Deut. 7.12-16) and to retain possession of it (Deut. 11.21). Disobedience delayed possession (Deut. 1) and could later lead to expulsion (e.g. Deut. 4.25-27).

Chapter 3

LINEAGE, TITLE AND THE BAREFOOT MAN:
SERIOUSNESS OF OFFENCE AND DEUTERONOMY 25.5-10

'And some there are who have no memorial, who have perished as though they had not lived... Their bodies were buried in peace, and their name lives to all generations.'

Sir. 44.9, 14

Deut. 25.5-10 is included in this book because it is a unique text. It is the only example of a biblical law whose punishment consists exclusively in a public-status degradation ceremony (Deut. 25.9-10). Further, the sanction is distinctively diachronic. It continues through time and has consequences for future generations (see Deut. 25.10, below). Exploring this text thus helps us to extend the semiotic range of seriousness of offence. Moreover, Deut. 25.5-10, like Deut. 21.18-21, reflects an underlying concern for the Land and for the obligations imposed by family relationships (see Chapter 2).

There are a number of registers of seriousness of offence in Deut. 25.5-10. The first performative register is the widow's initiative in appearing before the elders. The role assigned to the deceased's wife is an unusual feature of the case. Here, biblical law uncharacteristically attributes a major legal act to a dependent woman. She is to 'go up to the gate to the elders, and say, "My husband's brother refuses to perpetuate his brothers name (שם) in Israel; he will not perform the duty of a husband's brother to me"' (Deut. 25.8). The seriousness of the offence is such that the widow is granted immediate access to justice. This is similar to the complaint of the daughters of Zelophehad, 'Why should the name (שם) of our father be taken away from his family, because he had no son?' (Num. 27.4) which prompts Moses to seek a special, oracular, ruling (Num. 27.5). It is also similar to the case of the woman of Tekoa (2 Sam. 14.1-20), whose deceased's husband's 'name' (שם) is in danger of being wiped out (2 Sam. 14.7). Again, her plea prompts a swift response, this time from the king (2 Sam. 14.8-11). Such cases suggest that these situations were regarded as serious. How widely this performative register was broadcast depends on whether the phrase 'shall go up to the gate' (הֹשַׁעְרָה) in Deut. 25.7 envisages the open area that would have existed just inside the city, against the back wall of the gates[1] or the complex of rooms built into the city gate.[2] The latter may have provided a place for the discussion and settlement of disputes. For various reasons, it is likely that the woman's complaint was brought to the elders as they sat in private in the city gates. In a shame-conscious society such as ancient Israel,[3] one would not want a 'shameful' allegation to be brought in public until (a) the elders had a chance to investigate the matter and (b) the accused had been given an opportunity to speak for himself (the purpose of the 'interim stage' described in Deut. 25.8).

The second performative register is the elders' act of summoning the unwilling brother, 'the elders of his city shall call him, and speak to him' (Deut. 25.8). As with Deut. 25.7, it is questionable how far this performative register was broadcast. Again, it is likely that this discussion also took place in private. There is little point in holding the interim stage out in the open because the very process of litigation is itself shaming (Prov. 25.7-10). If the levir is already shamed he has no reason to capitulate. Psychologically, a public hearing is less conducive to the goal of the discussion which is to change the levir's mind.[4]

    1. Cf. excavations at Dan; A. Biran, 'Dan', in E. Stern *et al.* (eds.), *The New Encyclopaedia of the Holy Land* (London: Simon & Schuster, 1993), pp. 323-32 (325).
    2. Cf. recesses found during excavations at Gezer; W.G. Dever, 'Gezer', in E. Stern *et al.* (eds.), *The New Encyclopaedia of the Holy Land* (London: Simon & Schuster, 1993), pp. 496-506 (503-505).
    3. See L.M. Bechtel, 'Shame as a Sanction of Social Control in Biblical Israel: judicial, political and social shaming', *JSOT* 49 (1991), pp. 47-76; 'The Perception of Shame within the Divine–Human Relationship in Biblical Israel', in L.M. Hopfe, *Uncovering Ancient Stones: Essays in Memory of H. Neil Richardson* (Winona Lake, IN: Eisenbrauns, 1994), pp. 79-92; Olyan, 'Honour, Shame and Covenant Relations in Ancient Israel and its Environment', pp. 201-18. Cf. D. Daube, 'To Be Found Doing Wrong', in *Studi in onore di Edoardo Volterra* 2 (1969), pp. 1-13, criticized by S. Dempster, 'The Deuteronomic Formula *Ki Yimmase* in the Light of Biblical and Ancient Near Eastern Law', *RB* 91 (1984), pp. 188-211.
    4. We note in passing the scope this 'talk' provides for explaining the purpose of the law and for moralizing about the offence. This interim stage, characterized by reasoning and discussion, contains valuable lessons for the modern criminal justice process. The discussion tries to make the offender see sense and its goal is obedience to the law that is based on consent. From an institutional point of view obedience that arises from voluntary restraint is more efficient than obedience that is dependent on the

3. *Lineage, Title and the Barefoot Man*

The third register of seriousness is the levir's continuing refusal to perform the duty, 'and if he persists, saying, I do not wish to take her' (Deut. 25.8). The offence is made more serious because it is a repeat, and not a one-off offence (see 3.2.4.1, below). The fourth register is the performance of the חליצה ceremony,[5] 'his brother's wife shall go up to him in the presence of the elders, and pull his sandal off his foot, and spit in his face; and she shall answer and say, "So shall it be done to the man who does not build up his brother's house"' (Deut. 25.9). This was a serious punishment in a shame-conscious society (see 3.4.1–3.4.3, below). Again, there is a question as to how widely this register was broadcast. Deut. 25.10 does not specify the exact location for the חליצה ceremony. However, the reference to 'the presence of [lit. "in the sight of"] the elders' in Deut. 25.9 implies that the ritual is located in the same place as the interim stage (Deut. 25.8), that is, in private. Indeed, the reference to 'the presence of the elders' may indicate that there are no other witnesses. If correct, does this weaken the shaming power of the ritual, given that 'shame' stems from the *public* revelation of a person's failure or inadequacy?[6] Much depends on how widely we define 'public'. If we bear in mind that the elders would most likely have been relatives of the accused and that the power of shame is related to our having people whose opinions we care about[7] there is no reason to think that the presence of a smaller group reduces the intensity of the shame (indeed, quite the reverse).[8]

A fifth register is the levir's change of status, 'the name of his house shall be called in Israel, "The house of him that had his sandal pulled off"' (Deut. 25.10). This sanction qualifies as a performative register because the community 'performs' it in the act of implementing it. Renaming is a significant sanction in a name-oriented society (see 3.2.2, below).

In addition to describing these performative registers, the text also contains the following descriptive registers of seriousness. These include, firstly, the motivation given for the performance of the duty, 'that his [the dead brother's] name may not be blotted out' (Deut. 25.6). The importance

---

threat of sanctions. Even if the attempt fails, at least the offender is left in no doubt as to why he is being punished. In his heart of hearts, he may even approve. Such recognition is essential to the legitimacy of any criminal justice system.

5. The word חליצה is derived from the Hebrew root חלץ (to take/draw off).
6. Bechtel, 'Shame as Sanction', p. 49; Olyan, 'Honour, Shame', p. 204.
7. E.g. J. Braithwaite, *Crime, Shame and Reintegration* (Cambridge: Cambridge University Press, 1989) and 'Shame and Modernity', *BJC* 33 (1993), pp. 1-18.
8. That said, public acts are evident in Ruth 4.1-12.

of preserving the name is explored in 3.1.1–3.1.4, below. A further descriptive register is the addition of the words 'of Israel' in Deut. 25.6 ('that his name may not be blotted out of Israel') and 'in Israel' in Deut. 25.7 ('"My husband's brother refuses to perpetuate his brother's name in Israel"'). The invocation of 'Israel' may suggest that a venerable Hebrew tradition (preserving the name) is under attack.[9]

Anthropologists note that there are certain behaviours that, whilst generally disapproved, do not outrage public opinion nor cause it to react directly.[10] In such cases, public opinion has to be mobilized by a public statement of the crime and by hurling insults at the culprit by an interested party.[11] In the light of anthropological findings, perhaps we ought not to be surprised that the levir needed to be challenged publicly. After all, ancient Israelite society seems to have been only too willing to tolerate the levir's refusal. The levirate was never a popular duty and it was frequently evaded. Also, widows were never held in high public esteem and their interests, to judge from the prophets, were always in danger of slipping off everyone else's agenda. The widow may have had to take matters into her own hands if she was going to get justice. She had to bring into the open a matter (however private and painful) that everyone else might have been happy to ignore. Mobilizing public opinion would also have been necessary in this case because the punishment consisted in public shaming and had to be administered by the community as a whole. Even today, victims' families play a vocal role in galvanizing public opinion against those whom they hold responsible for personal tragedy (e.g. the *Marchioness*, Hillsborough and Dunblane tragedies in the UK). Mustering public opinion is seen by victims' families as essential to securing justice for their deceased.

In part, the woman's intervention undoubtedly reflects her necessarily intimate knowledge of the facts of the case. Imagine a 'sham' levirate mar-

---

9. Benjamin, *Deuteronomy and City Life*, p. 247.
10. Cf. Malinowski's findings concerning crime and punishment among the Trobianders (the inhabitants of the Trobiand Archipelago north-east of New Guinea), B. Malinowski, *Crime and Custom in Savage Society* (London: Routledge, 1966). Malinowski reports the case in which a boy had broken the tribal rules of exogamy by having relations with his maternal cousin. But whilst his behaviour was generally disapproved of, public opinion was not outraged by the knowledge of the crime nor did it react directly (p. 79).
11. Malinowski, *Crime and Custom*, p. 79. Within Trobiand society, 'criminal' behaviour could be tolerated so long as it was not 'squarely faced, put into words, openly stated and thus challenged', Malinowski, *Crime and Custom*, p. 121.

riage in which the widow lives in her brother-in-law's house but he refuses to consummate. As far as the outside world is concerned, he has done his duty. The absence of children is not of itself remarkable since a woman who was sterile married to one man, might remain so married to another. His deceit merely compounds her childless disgrace. Only the widow knows differently. She is the only person other than the levir who knows whether the duty was performed. For this reason alone, she is the obvious person to start proceedings. That said, we should not underestimate the potential embarrassment and humiliation caused to the woman in 'going public' about such an intimate matter. Ultimately, though, it was in her interests to do so, either to extricate herself from the marriage (according to the Rabbis, her marriage to anyone other than the levir was invalid)[12] or to shake off the stigma of childlessness.

In this regard her role is close to that of the גאל הדם ('avenger of blood'). In cases of manslaughter, this person was typically the victim's nearest family representative who was able (within certain, judicially approved limits) to kill the manslayer (e.g. Num. 35.9-29; Deut. 19.11-12). In all likelihood it was as close as biblical law could get to 'poetic justice' for this sort of offence. The dead victim obviously cannot take the life of the manslayer, but the victim's 'blood-substitute' or גאל הדם can and this is the next best thing. There is a parallel between the role of the גאל הדם and the widow in Deut. 25.5-10. In both cases an injustice has been committed against deceased persons who cannot participate in the process of judicial retribution. Both require another person to step in on their behalf to ensure that justice is done. The levir has 'blotted out' his brother's name and whilst nothing would be more fitting than that the brother should, for his part, blot out the levir's name, this is impractical. But his wife can do it for him by means of a symbolic ceremony. As with the case of the גאל הדם, poetic justice is secured so far as the case allows. In this regard, the wife is performing the role of her husband's גאל. This only highlights the irony manifest in the process. The גאל who fails to perform his duties is brought to book by the גאל who does stand up for the deceased's interests. The victim's name was effaced by a גאל and so it is fitting that the offender's name should be effaced by a גאל too.

---

12. S. Belkin, 'Levirate and Agnate Marriage in Rabbinic and Cognate Literature', *JQR* 60 (1969), pp. 275-329 (319).

3.1. *Offence Description*

The offence is described in the woman's charge as brought before the elders, '"My husband's brother refuses to perpetuate his brother's name (שֵׁם) in Israel; he will not perform the duty of a husband's brother to me"' (Deut. 25.7). By not uniting with his brother's wife, the levir fails to uphold the purpose of the law in Deut. 25.5-6. He refuses to provide his dead brother with a son and so causes his brother's שֵׁם to be extinguished.[13] This stated purpose takes priority over other explanations for the levirate.

There are of course all sorts of reasons why the levirate was a valuable institution. It protected the bridewealth exchanged between clans, it ensured the retention of friendly social relations between the two families and it was a good assurance of the security of the children and the widow. But none of these was its primary purpose. This is stated to be maintaining the dead brother's name. The reference to שֵׁם distinguishes the biblical practice of leviracy from other possible examples of this institution in the ANE. Scholars query the extent of levirate practice in the ANE. Certain ANE laws discuss the marriage of a brother to his widowed sister-in-law but, as Westbrook points out, whether these amount to examples of 'levirate' marriage depends on one's definition of 'levirate'.[14] In view of this ambiguity, it is probably safest to say that the biblical practice of levirate marriage adapted a common ANE custom to its own purposes.

In any event, the biblical texts cannot be reduced to exactly the same level of interpretation as those of the ANE. This is because there is an irreducible difference in the explicit motive clause regarding the 'name' of the dead brother. This interest in 'raising up a name' to keep the estate within the immediate family is conspicuously absent in the Hittite and Assyrian laws governing (so-called) 'levirate' marriage. The reference to שֵׁם distinguishes the biblical practice of leviracy from other possible examples of this institution in the ANE. The description of the offence is thus tied to the meaning of שֵׁם. This word has multivalent connotations[15]

---

13. Contra E. Neufeld, *Ancient Hebrew Marriage Laws* (London: Longmans, Green & Co., 1944), p. 33 who claims that 'the principal object of the biblical levirate is not expressly declared'.

14. R. Westbrook, 'The Law of the Biblical Levirate', in R. Westbrook, *Property and the Family in Biblical Law* (JSOTSup, 113; JSOT Press: Sheffield, 1991), pp. 69-89 (87).

15. Allen P. Ross, שֵׁם, in *NIDOTE*, pp. 147-51.

and so it is important to determine its precise meaning in the context of Deut. 25.6-7.

3.1.1. *Family Line*

In certain contexts, the word שׁם means family line or line of descendants. A man with no descendants has no שׁם (Isa. 14.22). Elsewhere in Isaiah, YHWH promises to give to the eunuchs, 'a hand and a name (יד ושׁם) better than that of sons and daughters...an everlasting name (שׁם עולם) that shall not be cut off' (Isa. 56.5). The reference to 'eunuchs' in Isa. 56.4 implies an association, in certain contexts, between שׁם and 'seed'.

This correlation is also found in Gen. 38.7-9. In Gen. 38.8, Judah commands that Onan raise up 'seed' (זרע) to his dead brother. This is significant because Gen. 38.7-9, like Deut. 25.5-10, deals with a form of levirate marriage (see 3.2.4.1 and 3.2.4.3, below). Likewise, Ps. 109.13 parallels a man's 'posterity' (אחריתו) with the 'names' (שׁמם) of his children. These texts suggest that שׁם has a metonymic force meaning 'progeny', possibly comparable to that of בית ('house', cf. Ps. 113.9, 'He gives the barren woman a home [בית], making her the joyous mother of children [בנים]').[16]

Family line appears to be the primary meaning of שׁם in Deut. 25.6-7. To perpetuate the name in the context of Deut. 25.7 means to continue or to perpetuate the family line. This squares with the justification given for the חלצה ceremony in Deut. 25.9, viz. '"So shall it be done to the man who does not build up (לא־יבנה) his brother's house"'. Here, the expression 'to build a house' means 'to establish a family' (cf. 2 Sam. 7.27; 1 Kgs 11.38 and 1 Chron. 17.10). That said, the word שׁם is multivalent. Thus, whilst the primary meaning of שׁם in Deut. 25.5-10 is 'family line' we must consider other contextual connotations.

3.1.2. *Property*

Several texts suggest a link between property and שׁם. Firstly, it is implicit in the complaint of the daughters of Zelophehad, 'Why should the name (שׁם) of our father be taken away from his family, because he had no son? Give to us a possession (אחזה) among our father's brethren' (Num. 27.4). Secondly, in Ruth 4.9-10 the son born to Boaz and Ruth perpetuates 'the name of the dead' (שׁם־המת) by inheriting the land. Boaz states, 'You are witnesses today that I am acquiring Ruth the Moabite, the wife of Mahlon, as my wife, so as to perpetuate the name of the deceased upon his estate,

---

16. Brichto, 'Kin, Cult, Land', p. 22.

that the name of the deceased may not disappear from among his kinsmen and from the gate of his home town' (Ruth 4.9-10). If 'gate' here means 'court', Ruth 4.10 may imply a system of land registration. Thirdly, Ezekiel 48 commences with the phrase 'these are the names (שמות) of the tribes' (48.1), before going on to state the portions of land that are assigned to each (48.1-29).

Together, these texts suggest that the שם maintained the legal claim of Israelite families to their land.[17] This practice may, in part, be due to the fact that contracts for the sale of land specified the location of a field by registering the names of owners of adjacent plots.[18] This is not unusual. An association between name and property is apparent elsewhere in the ANE. An example is the phrase *sakan sumsu* which occurs in the Armana letters, 'Behold the king has set his name in the land of Jerusalem; so he cannot abandon the lands of Jerusalem'.[19]

Succeeding to the name may therefore be a question of legal attribution in respect of a particular property. This is apparent in Gen. 48.6 where Jacob, having adopted Joseph's two eldest sons, declares that the future sons of Joseph will 'be called in the name of their older brothers [Ephraim and Manasseh] in their inheritance (על שם אחיהם יקראו בנחלתם)' (Gen. 48.6). In other words, for the purpose of inheritance they will be considered sons of their brothers, Ephraim and Manasseh. As we have seen, Ruth's marriage is intended 'to perpetuate the name of the dead in his inheritance (להקים שם־המת על־נחלתו)' (Ruth 4.10), that is, to continue the dead man's nominal ownership of his estate. Both Ruth 4.10 and Gen. 48.6 link שם with נחלה.

Deut. 25.6 uses similar language to both Gen. 48.6 and Ruth 4.10, although it is closer to the latter.[20] The first-born son of the levirate marriage 'shall succeed to the name of his brother (יקום על־שם) who is dead, that his name may not be blotted out of Israel'. In other words, as in Ruth 4.10, the son in Deut. 25.6 asserts the rights to the property that his dead father had. He is, legally, the bearer of the name.[21] A comparison with Gen. 48.6

---

17. Benjamin, *Deuteronomy and City Life*, p. 255.
18. J.M. Sasson, *Ruth* (Sheffield: Sheffield Academic Press, 1995), p. 45.
19. Gordon J. Wenham, 'Deuteronomy and the Central Sanctuary', *TynBul* 22 (1971), pp. 103-18 (113).
20. Deut. 25.6 uses the verb קום ('to establish', cf. Ruth 4.10) instead of the verb (קרא, 'to call', cf. Gen. 48.6).
21. Hirsch, *Deuteronomy*, p. 508.

may suggest that, in essence, the son in Deut. 25.5-10 is posthumously adopted by the deceased brother.²²

The property dimension of שם in Deut. 25.6 means that performing the duty was usually a sacrifice on the levir's part. It meant raising up a child for the widow and looking after property that would ultimately belong to that child as the deceased's successor. Normally, if a man died without issue his inheritance would pass to member(s) of the collateral family line, the closest being his brother(s). But if the brother performed the levirate, the inheritance that would otherwise have passed to the brother(s) would return to the deceased's line.

The temptation to leave the deceased without issue and to take over the property for himself, and his own descendants, must have been immense.²³ The willing levir may enjoy some benefit. For example, he could exploit the land and its produce for a number of years whilst the child was growing up. However, there must have been many cases when the disadvantages outweighed the advantages, for example where the inheritance was small and a poor levir would have been reluctant to provide for another wife.²⁴ The Jerusalem Talmud cites the unusual story of a levir burdened with the duty of marrying the twelve childless widows of his dead brothers.²⁵

It would take a generous man to act as levir (such as Boaz, see 3.2.4.2 and 3.2.4.3 below). In this regard Deut. 25.5-10 fits into the theme of 'generosity' which, as Wenham notes, is one of the great themes of Deuteronomy.²⁶ Israel must respond to YHWH's generosity by giving herself to

---

22. Tigay, *Deuteronomy*, p. 232.

23. This is against the view of a number of scholars such as H.H. Rowley, 'The Marriage of Ruth', *HTR* 40 (1947), pp. 77-99 (90 n. 47); Viberg, *Symbols of Law*, p. 156 who think it is inconceivable that the levir should benefit from a refusal. M. Burrows, 'Levirate Marriage in Israel' *JBL* 59 (1940), pp. 23-33 (29) states, 'there is no indication that the brother-in-law…would be the heir if there were no levirate marriage'. This is contrary to the implication of Gen. 38.9. The only alternative is that the widow inherits the property herself. We shall argue at 3.4.1.4 below that this is unlikely. However, if she does inherit and remarries outside her husband's family, then the ancestral estate will pass completely out of the hands of the original owner; E.W. Davies, 'Inheritance Rights and the Hebrew Levirate Marriage: Part 1', *VT* 31 (1981), pp. 138-44 (263), cf. the concern to prevent possible alienation of property in Num. 27 and 36.

24. Davies, 'Inheritance Rights I', pp. 259-60.

25. *Yer. Yeb.* 4.12.

26. Gordon J. Wenham, 'The Gap between Law and Ethics in the Bible', *JJS* 48 (1997), pp. 17-29 (26).

YHWH in loyalty and service. Generosity must also characterize human relationships. Thus loans must be given even if there is little hope of repayment (Deut. 15.7-11) and manumitted slaves must be given a golden handshake (Deut. 15.12-15). The importance of this theme may explain why the law in Deut. 25.5-10 makes mandatory a matter of customary law that had hitherto been left up to the parties concerned. A clue may be found in the location of its pronouncement: the plains of Moab at the entrance to the Promised Land. McConville points out that a recurring theme in Deuteronomy is the gift of the Land.[27] Israel's response to this gift is repeatedly cast in terms of a higher standard of ethical obedience. It may be argued that as YHWH's bounty to his people increases, so do his expectations of their moral behaviour. The promulgation of the levirate law in Deut. 25.5-10 is consistent with this general idea. A sacrificial act that was hitherto left up to the discretion of the individual is now enjoined upon the community as a mandatory command. YHWH's generosity in giving the Israelites the Land may even have been the springboard to willing performance of the duty.

To sum up, performing the levir's duty meant raising up a son who would continue the lineage of the deceased and who would succeed to the family inheritance. The levir is supposed to prevent the deceased's title to his landed inheritance from being extinguished. He is expected to provide the deceased with a successor to his estate and to keep the ancestral estate within the immediate family.

However, property is not the only aspect of שם in Deut. 25.5-10. This is apparent from Num. 27.1-11 and Numbers 36, both of which precede Deut. 25.5-10 in narrative terms. The events of Num. 27.1-11 and Numbers 36 are located 'on the steppes of Moab, at the Jordan near Jericho' (Num. 26.63, Num. 36.13), whereas the law of Deut. 25.5-10 is given 'on the other side of the Jordan' (Deut. 1.1). According to Num. 27.1-11 and Numbers 36, daughters are allowed to inherit in the absence of sons, provided they do not marry outside the tribe. If inheritance is the *only* issue at stake in Deut. 25.5-10, what do we need the law in Deut. 25.5-10 for? It achieves nothing. If the dead brother had no sons, but left behind a daughter, she would inherit the estate. Nor do we need the proviso in Deut. 25.6 to raise up a 'first-born son'. A daughter would do just as well. Yet the perspective of Deut. 25.5-10 seems to be that it is not enough that the שם should descend via the dead man's daughter (see 3.2.2). This is

---

27. J.G. McConville, *Grace in the End* (Carlisle: Paternoster Press, 1993).

consistent with the claim that the meaning of םש in Deut. 25.5-10 is not simply a matter of property.

3.1.3 *As a Patronymic*

Sons bore their father's personal name as a patronymic ('so-and-so son of X'). It is possible that the son of the levirate marriage took the dead brother's personal name as his patronymic, instead of that of his father. If so this is another sense in which the dead brother's 'name' could be maintained, at least for a generation or two.[28] Neufeld denies that Deut. 25.5-10 uses the word םש in a personal sense, citing Ruth 4.17.[29] This explicitly identifies Obed as the son of Boaz (Ruth 4.21). However, Neufeld ignores the possibility that the levirate offspring took the patronymic in their own lifetimes.[30] An ethnographic study of levirate marriage among the African Luo found that the degree to which the genitor (the biological father) was accorded recognition varied from case to case. Much depended on the quality of the relationship between the levir and the offspring of the union.[31] A compromise solution may have existed in ancient Israel. Offspring could have been known as the sons of the deceased brother during their own lifetime, whereas the genealogies recorded the genitor's contribution.

3.1.4 *Summary*

The description of the offence is tied to the meaning of םש in Deut. 25.5-7. This has several dimensions. Perpetuating the םש in Deut. 25.7 means continuing the family line (cf. Deut. 25.9). Succeeding to the םש in Deut. 25.6 means succeeding to the family inheritance that formerly belonged to the dead brother. The word םש may also refer to the deceased's personal name. All three dimensions are interlinked. Raising up a son on behalf of the deceased, therefore, performs several functions. The son continues the family line of the deceased and keeps the ancestral estate intact. He may also perpetuate the dead brother's name for several generations. The levir

---

28. Brichto, 'Kin, Cult, Land', p. 24 and E. Levine, 'On Intra-Familial Institutions of the Bible', *Bib.* 57 (1976), pp. 554-59 (558) claim (without citing sources) that except for eponymous ancestors who gave their name to a tribe or a clan, a patronymic goes back normally only one, or a few, generations.

29. Neufeld, *Marriage Laws*, p. 47 n. 1.

30. As suggested by Tigay, *Deuteronomy*, p. 232.

31. B. Potash, 'Wives of the Grave: Widows in a Rural Luo Community', in B. Potash (ed.), *Widows in African Societies* (Stanford: Stanford University Press, 1986), pp. 44-65 (59).

refuses to perform this duty and to fulfil these purposes. This is the substance of the woman's charge in Deut. 25.7.

3.2. *The Paradigm Case*

3.2.1. *'When Brothers Dwell Together'*

Deut. 25.5 seems to refer to brothers who continue to dwell together on their father's death without dividing up the family estate.[32] Westbrook argues that this is the reason why there is no reference to the father-in-law in Deut. 25.5-10: he is already dead.[33] If Deut. 25.5-10 is rightly characterized by this sort of partnership, it follows that the two brothers jointly own all the property. In English terminology the brothers are joint tenants rather than tenants in common. Thus, when 'one of them dies' the surviving brother is not 'heir' to the dead one. He does not 'acquire' the property by succession. Rather, he simply carries on being owner. His legal status is unchanged (although in practical terms he now has greater freedom to act in respect of the property than hitherto).[34] Thus it seems as though the son born of the levirate union stands in the place of his deceased father as a joint owner of the individual estate, and not merely of his father's (divided) share.

This is the paradigm case. Some scholars might object that since the general practice was almost certainly for the heirs to divide up the estate among themselves and each to set up a household of his own, the case of 'brothers dwelling together' is far from being the 'typical case'.[35] The fact that 'dwelling together' is extolled in Ps. 133.1 ('How good and how pleasant it is that brothers dwell together', JPS) suggests that 'common ownership' was the exception rather than the rule. Does this mean that Deut. 25.5-10 cannot be regarded as a 'paradigm case'? No. To say that an illustration is a 'paradigm case' or a 'typical case' does not necessarily entail the claim that it 'happens all the time'. Even situations that do not occur very often can give rise to a 'paradigm', *provided* there is a stock of social knowledge of what does happen or ought to happen in such circumstances. Deut. 25.5-10 is not a 'paradigm case' in the sense that it 'happened all the

---

32. Daube, D. '*Consortium* in Roman and Hebrew Law' *Juridical Review* 62 (1950), pp. 71-91; Westbrook, 'Biblical Levirate', p. 78.

33. Westbrook, 'Biblical Levirate', p. 78 though cf. Sasson, *Ruth*, p. 125.

34. Cf. MAL B.2, 3 (Roth, *Law Collections*, p. 176) and LE16 (Roth, *Law Collections*, p. 61).

35. E.g. Davies, 'Inheritance Rights I', p. 265.

3. *Lineage, Title and the Barefoot Man*

time'. However, it may have happened frequently enough for there to be a stock of social knowledge about it. Certainly, there is nothing unusual about the levir's behaviour. It conforms to the stereotype of the 'greedy rotter' who puts himself before family duty. We have heard it all before in the Onan story (Gen. 38.8-10). For this reason, Deut. 25.5-10 is still a 'paradigm case'.

As we saw in Chapter 1, much depends on whether we take a semantic or a narrative approach to the text. An example of a semantic approach is Davies's claim that the phrase 'when brothers dwell together' functions as a 'severe restriction'[36] on the operation of the rule. Here, the semantic approach implies the presence of an additional logical operator 'if (*and only if*) brothers dwell together'. Davies argues that the possibility of levirate marriage was often not open to the childless widow because the brothers would probably have followed the prevailing custom of dividing up the ancestral land. A semantic approach suggests that the duty rarely, if ever, fell upon the deceased's brothers.

A narrative approach, on the other hand, proceeds from judgments of relative similarity between the case in hand and the narrative stereotype. This means that the further one departs from the collective image in Deut. 25.5-10, the less sure one can be that the case is intended to apply to the real-life situation, or that it would be regarded as applicable by the audience. But because a narrative approach is not based on a semantic analysis of the words in which the narrative rule is expressed, it is possible for the paradigm to exert some influence. The difference between a semantic and a narrative approach to Deut. 25.5-10 is this: a narrative approach does not allow us to assume that simply because the brothers are not 'dwelling together', they are thereby absolved of all responsibility.

There is another important aspect to regarding Deut. 25.5-10 as a paradigm case. It is this: as we move further away from the paradigm case in Deut. 25.5-10, two things happen. Firstly, the more distant the next of kin, the less dishonour he suffers for refusing the duty.[37] The obligation(s) of

---

36. Davies, 'Inheritance Rights I', p. 265. Cf. D.A. Leggett, *The Levirate and Go'el Institutions in the Old Testament: With Special Attention to the Book of Ruth* (New Jersey: Mack, 1974), p. 48; F.E. Greenspahn, *When Brothers Dwell Together: The Preeminence of Younger Siblings in the Hebrew Bible* (Oxford: Oxford University Press, 1994), p. 54 and Sasson, *Ruth*, pp. 133-34.

37. Rowley, 'Marriage of Ruth', p. 85. Elsewhere, however, Rowley takes the standard view that Deut. 25.5-10 'limits' the duty to 'brothers dwelling together' (p. 80) and that Deuteronomy fails to '*prescribe* [my italics] any alternative to a brother-in-

levirate marriage presses less heavily on more distant relations. The measure of stigma in Deut. 25.9-10 is in direct ratio to the nearness of the relationship. Secondly, and by corollary, the more distant the next of kin, the more honour there is for the willing levir. There are no plaudits for the brother who performs the levirate. He is only doing his duty *as a brother*. By contrast, we would expect the far-flung relative to receive praise precisely *because* his noble behaviour is atypical. I shall develop this theme further in 3.2.4.2, below, with respect to Ruth 4.1-12.

3.2.2. *'And One of Them Dies and Has No Son (בן)'*

The paradigm case probably concerns a husband who dies soon after the marriage. The question is whether בן means 'son' (as *per* most mainstream translations, e.g. RSV, NKJ, NRSV and BBE) or simply 'child' (meaning either a son or a daughter, as *per* KJV, LXX). In the context of Deut. 25.5, it refers to a 'son'. This is indicated by the word הבכור in Deut. 25.6, which consistently refers to a first-born male in the Hebrew Bible. This is what we would expect because gender is a determining factor in the patrilineal transmission of name. 'Within patronymic signification, "his" tory itself—a written record of genealogy through name—actually stops with a daughter.'[38] Unlike a son, a daughter is only a 'temporary sojourner within her family, destined to seek legitimation and name outside its boundaries'.[39] For this reason, only the birth of a son contributes to the 'patrilineal project'.[40] Sons and not daughters are the vessels through which the father reproduces himself.

The preference for sons rather than daughters to carry on the family 'name' is not a purely ancient prejudice.[41] In any case, it appears on the evidence that daughters were not considered fully capable of perpetuating

---

law who should decline the duty' (p. 86). Rowley could have strengthened his argument by adopting a 'narrative' approach (see 3.2.4.3 below).

38. L.E. Boose, 'The Father's House and the Daughter in It', in L.E. Boose and B.S. Flowers (eds.), *Daughters and Fathers* (London: The Johns Hopkins University Press, 1989), pp. 19-74 (21).

39. Boose, 'Father's House', p. 21.

40. Boose, 'Father's House', p. 24.

41. 'America's favourite father' Bill Cosby admitted he 'ask[ed] God to give me a son because I wanted someone to carry on the family name', cited in Boose, 'Father's House', p. 22. Similar issues are at stake in modern family law when one of two unmarried parents seeks to change the child's surname against the other's wishes (e.g. *Dawson v. Wearmouth* [1999] 1FLR, 1167-81 and *ReC (Change of Surname)* [1998] 2FLR, 656-67)

the dead man's שם as understood in Deut. 25.5-7. Num. 27.7-11 allows daughters to inherit their father's property in the absence of sons. But, as we saw in 3.1 above, Deut. 25.5-10 is concerned not only with property but also with the two other dimensions of שם, which are continuing the dead man's family line (3.1.1) and perhaps also his personal name (3.1.3). If we assume that the provisions of Num. 27.7-11 (said to be given in the wilderness) are already in place at the time of promulgating Deut. 25.5-10 (said to be given at the border of the Land), then the levirate law of Deut. 25.5-10 suggests that daughters do not ultimately preserve the שם in this broader sense, even though they are restricted to marrying within the tribe (Num. 36.6-13).

Moreover, whilst Num. 27.7-11 allows the daughters to inherit land, even this arrangement may not be all that it seems. The language of Num. 36.5-9 is revealing. Moses outlines the conditions under which the law of Num. 27.7-11 is to be applied, saying, 'every man, the sons of Israel, will *cleave* (ידבקו) to the inheritance of the tribe of their fathers. And every daughter to acquire an inheritance of the tribe of the sons of Israel shall be wife to one of the lineage of the tribe of her father...and an inheritance shall not circulate from one tribe to another tribe; on the contrary: every man of the tribes of the sons of Israel shall *cleave* (ידבקו) to his inheritance' (my italics).[42] In this passage the verb דבק ('to cleave', cf. Gen. 2.24) is twice used in connection with the inherited land. But on both occasions it is used in respect of sons. It is not used in respect of daughters. As Sterring notes, 'the social and physical unity that the Genesis text ascribes for man and wife turns in Numbers 36 into a command for the man only, and with respect to his land'.[43] Thus, even the text that grants daughters the right to inherit in the absence of sons recognizes that their relationship to the inherited land is not and cannot be the same as the relationship that a son would have.

It might be argued that daughters are capable of carrying on the dead man's personal name. They can do this by making their husbands take his name as a patronym. We know from Ezra 2.61-62 and Neh. 7.63-64 that this was possible. Both texts describe how a priest married a man's daughter and was then called by his name (presumably as a patronym). The drawback is that both texts then go on to tell us that this man's descendants—

---

42. Translation from A. Sterring, 'The Will of the Daughters', in A. Brenner (ed.), *A Feminist Companion to Exodus to Deuteronomy* (Sheffield: Sheffield Academic Press, 1994), pp. 88-99 (94).

43. Sterring, 'Will of the Daughters', p. 94.

uniquely among the priests—could not find their genealogical records and so were disqualified from the priesthood (Ezra 2.62; Neh. 7.64). Clearly, this method was disadvantaged.

It might be objected that, on this reading, the daughters' hard-won rights in Num. 27.7-11 are defeasible by the law of the levirate (Deut. 25.5-10). But there is no need to assume that the rights of the daughters will be 'trumped' by the levirate offspring in every case. The daughters' right is not so defeasible that it is pointless giving it to them. It is not hard to imagine cases where their rights will not be annulled, for example, cases where the brothers do not 'live together', where the real-life case is too far removed from the paradigm, where the levir refuses to perform the duty, or where the woman remains sterile. In fact, given the unpopularity of the levirate institution (as witnessed in Gen. 38.9, Ruth 4.6 and the provisions of Deut. 25.7-10), Num. 27.7-11 may be seen as providing an alternative way of preserving the שם in the absence of sons.

Of course, it is not ideal. The effect of the ruling in Num. 36.6-9 is that the family property may ultimately go outside the family, even though it remains in the tribe; whilst the effect of the levirate is that it remains, albeit by a fiction, in the personal line of the deceased, so long as there are male heirs. However, it is better than nothing, and it may have been regarded as a more reliable, if limited, way of preserving the שם in the absence of sons.

3.2.3. *'Her Husband's Brother Shall Unite with Her: He Shall Take Her as his Wife and Perform the Levir's Duty'*

The paradigm case opens with a reference to 'brothers' (plural) dwelling together (Deut. 25.5). This implies that typically the levir was one of a number of brothers who, in the absence of the deceased's brother's sons or children, would take an equal share in the property.[44] In the case of the daughters of Zelophehad, the daughters shared their father's estate with Zelophehad's *brothers* (plural). But only one brother in Deut. 25.5-10 is identified as failing to perform his duty. A key question is: on what criteria is he summoned before the elders in 25.8? Deut. 25.5-10 gives no indication of who should perform the duty if there is more than one surviving relative in the same degree.

It is commonly supposed that the duty devolved upon the eldest first, although this view has its critics.[45] Gen. 38.2-5, 8-11 suggests that it was a

---

44. Cf. Job 42.15.
45. E.g. Greenspahn, *When Brothers Dwell Together*, p. 54.

matter of customary law and that the levirate duty devolved according to age.[46] One advantage of this view, according to Deut. 21.17, is that the eldest son is given a double portion. This may compensate him for what he would otherwise have gained by not performing the duty (i.e. the deceased's brother's share). It may also compensate him for the expense incurred in looking after his dead brother's estate until the offspring comes of age. How well it compensates the brother will depend on the number of other brothers the levir has. In this respect there may well be an element of 'rough justice' (not unknown in biblical law).[47] If this is correct, it increases the seriousness of the offence. It means that the 'first-born' refuses to perform the levirate, despite the fact that Deut. 21.7 gives him a double portion.

However, we need not assume that the paradigm case always points automatically to a particular brother. Recent ethnographic studies, especially those focusing on African societies, indicate a range of practices for choosing the levir. The levir may be appointed by his family,[48] by the lineage head or by a council of lineage elders.[49] The levir may even be the widow's choice. In certain African tribes the widow is free to select any member of the lineage subject, on occasion, to the elders' formal approval.[50] This possibility is consistent with the autonomy the widow displays in Deut. 25.5-10 (going up to the elders [25.9] and performing the חליצה ceremony [25.9-10]). If so, the woman in Deut. 25.7 may be complaining that it is her choice that is refused. Tamar, in a sense, exercises 'choice' in terms of her 'levir', although Ruth does not. Ruth has no choice of levir and Boaz has to challenge the one who has prior claim.

The bottom line is that, according to the paradigm case, a choice is to be made (by whatever means) from among 'brothers' who dwell together. But as we have already seen, in 3.2.1 above, this does not necessarily mean that simply because there are no brothers who dwell together, the paradigm thereby exerts no influence.

A semantic approach to Deut. 25.5-7 would restrict the meaning of the noun יבם (Deut. 25.5, 7, 'her husband's brother') to a biological brother-in-law who dwells together with his other brothers (and to no one else).

---

46. Cf. *Yeb.* 24a and Neufeld, *Marriage Laws*, p. 34.
47. Cf. Jackson, *Semiotics of Biblical Law*.
48. R.S. Oboler, 'Nandi Widows', in Betty Potash (ed.), *Widows in African Societies* (Stanford: Stanford University Press, 1986), pp. 66-83 (79).
49. Potash, 'Wives of the Grave', p. 7.
50. Potash, 'Wives of the Grave', p. 7.

Similarly, a semantic approach would restrict the meaning of the verb יבם (Deut. 25.5, 7; '[to] perform the duty of a brother-in-law') to the duty performed by a יבם (and by no one else).

By contrast, a narrative approach does not restrict the meaning of יבם. Instead, both the noun יבם and the verb יבם are seen as referring to a wider range of agnatic kin in one's own (and possibly the senior) generation. As we argued in 3.2.1, above, the duty is not restricted to the biological brother-in-law alone. This is consistent with the idea that kin terms in the Bible are not always descriptive and are sometimes used with 'classificatory depth'. For example, the word 'brother' is used as a classificatory kinship term that also means 'kinsman'. Many kinship terms have a specific and a general use within family relationships.[51] In the Bible, relatives with a quite different blood relationship to the ego nonetheless share the same kin term. This is because the 'kin term' goes beyond genetics to typify those people who share the same network of rights and obligations. It is, in fact, a narrative reading that centres on similar attitudes and patterns of behaviour (cf. Jesus' redrawing of the 'family of God': 'Whoever does the will of God is my brother, and sister, and mother' [Mk 3.35]). The dominant idea here is not a semantic one ('what is the literal [i.e. biological] meaning of this word?') but a narrative one ('what sort of person would act like this?').

3.2.4. *Comparing a Narrative Approach to Deuteronomy 25.5-10 with Genesis 38 and Ruth*

A narrative approach to Deut. 25.5-10 assumes a certain amount of flexibility on the part of the levirate. Support for the flexibility of this institution is found in Genesis 38 and Ruth 4, texts that, it is often claimed, also depict cases of levirate marriage. It is beyond the scope of this book to consider in any detail the precise nature of any relationship that may exist between Deut. 25.5-10, Genesis 38 and Ruth 4. However, to demonstrate the flexibility of leviratic marriage I shall highlight some of the similarities and the differences that exist between Deut 25.5-10 and Gen. 38.8-11 (see 3.2.4.1, below) and between Deut 25.5-10 and Ruth 4.1-12 (see 3.2.4.2, below). I shall then suggest that a narrative reading of Deut. 25.5-10 may go some way towards resolving the alleged anomalies between Gen. 38.8-11, Deut. 25.5-10 and Ruth 4.1-12 (see 3.2.4.3, below).

---

51. F.I. Andersen, 'Israelite Kinship Terminology and Social Structure', *BT* 20 (1969), pp. 29-39 (38).

3. *Lineage, Title and the Barefoot Man*

3.2.4.1. *Comparison between Deuteronomy 25.5-10 and Genesis 38.8-11.* It is generally assumed that levirate marriage underlies the narrative of Gen. 38.8-11.[52] Indeed, there are certain similarities between Deut. 25.5-10 and Gen. 38.8-11. Firstly, the duty appears to be compulsory in both cases (Gen. 38.8; Deut. 25.5). Judah orders Onan, 'Go in to your brother's wife, and perform the duty of a brother-in-law to her, and raise up offspring for your brother' (Gen. 38.8). Some scholars might question whether Deut. 25.5-10 is compulsory. Some might regard the 'shall' of Deut. 25.5 as permissive rather than mandatory and the phrase 'if he does not want to' as indicating that the levir has a genuinely free choice in the matter. Craigie goes so far as to claim that the levir has 'a legal right' to refuse his obligation.[53] However, vv. 5-6 are quite categorical, there is a clear prohibition on the woman marrying outside the family and the levir's duty is quite explicitly stated in the form of a (casuistic) command. In any case, if Deut. 25.5-10 is permissive rather than mandatory, why should there be a sanction against the levir if he exercises that choice? Brin, in the course of examining the legal formula 'if he shall not [do]', sees Deut. 25.7 as a striking example of a refusal to perform an obligatory law.[54] *Sifre* states that 'the commandment of levirate marriage precedes the commandment of חליצה', implying that there are not two possible courses of action but one law and response-punishment for those who refuse to carry out the law.[55] A second similarity between Deut. 25.5-10 and Gen. 38.8-11 is the unpopularity of the duty, probably because, as we have seen, it requires of the levir action contrary to his own interests (see 3.1.2 above). Thirdly, both offences are continuing actions. Onan's *coitus interruptus* is not a one-off act but a regular occurrence.[56] The consecutive perfect in Gen. 38.9 is used in a frequentative sense which implies that Onan continually refused to perform the obligation. Likewise, the levir in Deut. 25.5-10 is punished for his persistent refusal (Deut. 25.8). The Bible's interest in the persistence of the

---

52. E.g. Benjamin, *Deuteronomy and City Life*, pp. 246-47; Neufeld, *Marriage Laws*, pp. 34-36; N.H. Snaith, 'The daughters of Zelophehad', *VT* 16 (1966), pp. 124-127 (125), Tigay, *Deuteronomy*, p. 481 and Westbrook, 'Biblical Levirate', p. 69.
53. Craigie, *Deuteronomy*, p. 314.
54. G. Brin, 'The Formula "If He Shall Not (Do)" and the Problem of Sanctions in Biblical Law', in David P. Wright *et al.* (eds.), *Pomegranates and Golden Bells: Studies in Biblical, Jewish and Near Eastern Ritual, Law and Literature in Honour of Jacob Milgrom* (Winona Lake, IN: Eisenbrauns, 1995), pp. 341-61 (347-49).
55. Brin, '"If He Shall Not (Do)"', p. 349 n. 2.
56. E.W. Davies, 'Inheritance Rights and the Hebrew Levirate Marriage: Part 2', *VT* 31 (1981), pp. 257-68 (257 n. 1).

behaviour in question is an important dimension of 'seriousness of offence' (cf. Chapter 2 where the behaviour of the 'stubborn and rebellious' son is characterized by repeated offending, rather than one-off acts of delinquency).

However, there are also important differences. The main divergence is that Deut. 25.5-10 refers to brothers 'dwelling together' whilst Gen. 38.13-26 refers to the father-in-law (see especially Gen. 38.26). Another is the fact that Gen. 38.8 refers not to שם but to זרע ('seed'). Finally, there is a difference between the levir's outright refusal of the duty in Deut. 25.5-10 and Onan's pretended (and hence hypocritical) assumption of the duty (Gen. 38.8-10).

3.2.4.2. *Comparison between Deuteronomy 25.5-10 and Ruth 4.1-12.* It is frequently assumed that Ruth 4 is an example of levirate marriage performed by the גאל.[57] The idea that the marriage of Ruth and Boaz is conceived as a form of levirate marriage does not require us to assume that these sources reflect the same form of, or opinions about, levirate marriage. The question is whether the discrepancies between Deut. 25.5-10 and Ruth reflect two different institutions, or different versions of the same institution. We shall argue, firstly, that Ruth reflects a version of the institution of levirate marriage and, secondly, that the flexibility of levirate marriage is an argument in favour of taking a narrative approach to Deut. 25.5-10.

Similarities between Deut. 25.5-10 and Ruth 4.1-12 include the following. Firstly, the child born of Ruth and Boaz's union is legally deemed the son of the deceased Mahlon (Ruth 4.10). Secondly, the bystanders appear to regard Ruth and Boaz's marriage as similar to Judah and Tamar's union (Ruth 4.12). Thirdly, Boaz's rationale in Ruth 4.10, 'to perpetuate the name of the dead in his inheritance, that the name of the dead may not be cut off from among his brethren and from the gate of his native place' evokes the woman's charge in Deut. 25.7.

However, there are important differences between Deut. 25.5-10 and the details of the Ruth narrative. These have caused several scholars to question whether Ruth is an example of the levirate. Firstly, Sasson argues that the limiting case of 'brothers [who] dwell together' does not apply in Ruth.[58] Neither Boaz nor the nearer kinsman are brothers, nor sons of Naomi, nor do they dwell together. Secondly, whereas in Deut. 25.5-10

---

57. E.g. Benjamin, *Deuteronomy and City Life*, p. 247; Neufeld, *Marriage Laws*, pp. 37-38; Tigay, *Deuteronomy*, p. 481.

58. Sasson, *Ruth*, pp. 133-34.

(and Gen. 38) the levirate is compulsory, in Ruth it is not. Ruth was never under an obligation to enter the next of kin's household.[59] Thirdly, Deut. 25.5-10 emphasizes the ideal of perpetuating the name of the dead man in Israel as the main purpose behind levirate practice. In Ruth 4, although the שם of Mahlon is mentioned (Ruth 4.10), the emphasis falls on the redemption of Elimelech's land.[60] Fourthly, if the levirate duty was tied to purchase of land, and if Boaz wanted to marry Ruth and be in a position to accomplish both, he should have asked the גאל to release Ruth rather than merely desist from purchasing her.[61] Fifthly, there are also important differences between the חלצה ceremony and the judicial proceedings that are described in Ruth 4. In Deut. 25.7, 9-10, the initiative to obtain release from levirate obligations rests on the aggrieved woman. But there is no indication that Ruth is even present during the proceedings at the gate. Nor is there any indication that the nearer kinsman submits to the חלצה ceremony (though see 3.2.4.3 below). The act of sandal-removal is different both in its nature and its consequences from that of Deut. 25.5-10. Finally, Bledstein argues that the allusion to Genesis 38 in Ruth 4.12 is quite general and does not necessarily imply levirate marriage.[62] Sasson concludes that 'Ruth tells us nothing about the workings of this institution'.[63]

3.2.4.3. *Accounting for the Anomalies.* Scholars have found it difficult to reconcile historically the law in Deut. 25.5-10 with the cases described in Genesis 38 and Ruth 4 and have put forward various theories to explain the anomalies.[64] However, I shall argue in this section that these anomalies

---

59. Sasson, *Ruth*, pp. 133-34.
60. Sasson, *Ruth*, pp. 133-34.
61. Sasson, *Ruth*, pp. 133-34.
62. A.J. Bledstein, 'Female Companionships: If the Book of Ruth Were Written by a Woman', in A. Brenner (ed.), *A Feminist Companion to Ruth* (Sheffield: Sheffield Academic Press, 1993), pp. 116-33 (128-29).
63. Sasson, *Ruth*, p. 229, *ditto* D.R.G. Beattie, 'The Book of Ruth as Evidence for Israelite Legal Practice', *VT* 24 (1974), pp. 251-67 (265).
64. E.g. source-critical methods (e.g. M. Burrows, 'The Ancient Oriental Background of Hebrew Levirate Marriage', *BASOR* 77 [1940], pp. 2-15; Burrows, 'Levirate Marriage' and Rowley, 'Marriage of Ruth', pp. 84-85) that see, for example, Ruth as 'pre-Deuteronomic' and T. Thompson and D. Thompson, 'Some Legal Problems in the Book of Ruth', *VT* 18 (1968), pp. 79-99 (79, 88) who claim that the differences between the texts arise purely from the fact that Deut. 25.5-10 is 'law' whereas Gen. 38 and Ruth are 'stories.' V.H. Matthews, 'Honor and Shame in Gender-Related Legal Situations in the Hebrew Bible', in V.H. Matthews *et al.* (eds.), *Gender and Law in the*

are more apparent than real, and that they are best explained by taking a narrative approach to Deut. 25.5-10.⁶⁵

I argued at 3.2.1 above that, in contrast to a semantic approach to Deut. 25.5-10, a narrative approach does not restrict the meaning of יבם to the biological brother-in-law. Rather, both the noun יבם and the verb יבם are seen as referring to a wider range of agnatic kin. We see this narrative, rather than semantic, approach in Genesis 38. In Gen. 38.11, Judah withholds his youngest son from performing the levirate duty with Tamar, whom he regards as lethal. This creates an unusual situation in which he, Judah, is next in line to perform the levirate. This duty is formally recognized by Judah himself (Gen. 38.26). What the story shows is that, in real-life cases, where the circumstances are removed from the standard case, the duty could (and, indeed, ought) to be performed by other, possibly senior, agnatic kin. The blood brother is still the paradigm levir but this does not prevent the duty from falling on male members of the family who are not as close an agnate of the deceased, if the case is an unusual one. Genesis 38 certainly presents problems for those wedded to a semantic interpretation of levirate marriage.⁶⁶ However, it is perfectly consistent with a narrative approach.

Similarly, Ruth's situation is several stages removed from the paradigm case of Deut. 25.5-10. For a start, she is not even an Israelite and her humble approach to Boaz (Ruth 3.9) is anything but that of a claimant to a legal right. Yet although she is a Moabitess, she prefers to marry within the family of her deceased husband, Mahlon, in order to preserve his name and property, than to seek a suitor from outside his family. Ruth supports a narrative reading according to which the levirate duty was by no means confined to brothers dwelling together, but extends to all male members according to the proximity of their relationship to the deceased. The exact nature of the relationship between Elimelech, the Nearest Redeemer, and

---

Hebrew Bible and the Ancient Near East (JSOTSup, 262; Sheffield: Sheffield Academic Press, 1998), pp. 97-112 (101 n. 17) suggests, rather vaguely, that variations between Deut. 25.5-10 and Ruth may be based on 'cultural-legal evolution or simply the difference between narrative form and legal pronouncement'.

65. Cf. the approach taken by the Karaites (Beattie, 'Book of Ruth', p. 259) and the Samaritans (Neufeld, *Marriage Laws*, p. 44). For a modern example of a 'narrative' approach see Thompson and Thompson, 'Legal Problems', pp. 89-90, 94.

66. E.g. Greenspahn, *When Brothers Dwell Together*, pp. 52-53 finds Gen. 38 'suspect, since its description differs from [Deut. 25.5-10]'.

3. *Lineage, Title and the Barefoot Man*

Boaz is not clear.[67] But it shows that if the Nearest Redeemer refuses, the duty devolves on those who are the next closest in terms of familial order.

Ruth 4.1-12 also demonstrates the proposition, at 3.2.1 above, that, on a narrative reading of Deut. 25.5-10, less dishonour is incurred by a more distant relation who refuses to perform the duty. The lesser seriousness of this offence is reflected in a less ignominious ritual. Thus in Ruth 4.1-12, the Nearest Redeemer is not subject to the full-scale חליצה ceremony, contrary to the view of Josephus.[68] Nonetheless, there may still be a muted form of disgrace. This surfaces in the fact that we are never told the Nearest Redeemer's name and in the odd way that Boaz calls him אלמני פלני (Ruth 4.1), which may be translated 'Mr So-and-So'.[69] If the word אלמני is related to the root אלמנה ('widow'), perhaps he is being called a 'widow-basher' or the like? In a book that pays close attention to genealogies (Ruth 1.2-4; 4.18-22) and to names ('call me Mara', Ruth 1.20), the fact that the levir's name is left unmentioned may not be an oversight. It suggests that, just as the Nearest Redeemer chose to ignore the duty of perpetuating an Israelite's name in the land, so his own name will not be recorded for posterity.[70]

Moreover, it follows that, just as less dishonour is incurred by the more distant relation who refuses to perform the duty, so more honour is won by the distant relation who does perform the duty. This too is demonstrated in Ruth 4.1-12. When Boaz agrees to take Ruth as his wife, he is regarded not as a man performing his legal duty (as would have been the case under the paradigm of Deut. 25.5-10), but as a generous benefactor. Boaz's benevolence is striking because it is far removed from the paradigm case. The record of King David's genealogy (Ruth 4.18-22) is, perhaps, a measure of the divine praise and reward that attaches to fulfilment of the duty in exceptional (and non-paradigmatic) circumstances.[71]

To sum up, the further we move away from the paradigm case of brothers living together, the less public censure there is of the unwilling levir and the more public praise there is for the willing levir. This is what we

---

67. Beattie, 'Book of Ruth', pp. 199-200 summarizes the possibilities canvassed in Rabbinic literature.

68. 'Boaz called the senate to witness, and bid the woman to loose his shoe, and spit in his face, according to the law', *Ant.* 5.9-4.

69. Sasson, *Ruth*, pp. 102-103.

70. See C.M. Carmichael, 'A Ceremonial Crux: Removing a Man's Sandal as a Female Gesture of Contempt', *JBL* 96 (1977), pp. 321-36 (335).

71. Cf. Belkin, 'Levirate and Agnate Marriage', p. 287.

find in the narratives of Genesis 38 and Ruth. It provides, in my view, a more satisfactory account of the supposed anomalies presented by these texts than traditional source-critical methods. So instead of regarding Ruth as pre-Deuteronomic (say) it could be argued that Ruth is an application of Deut. 25.5-10, in which the details of the Ruth and Boaz situation are several stages removed from the paradigm. To this extent, scholarly difficulties in reconciling the law in Deut. 25.5-10 with the events of Genesis 38 and Ruth 4 stem from a semantic reading of Deut. 25.5-10. We suggest that a better explanation of the differences between these texts may lie in a narrative approach to Deut. 25.5-10.

3.3. *Seriousness of Offence*

The consequence of the levir's refusal is that his brother's name will be 'blotted out in Israel' (Deut. 25.6). This is recapitulated in the charge that the brother's name will not be 'perpetuated' (Deut. 25.7). It is restated in the חלצה ceremony, which is a punishment for 'the man who does not build up his brother's house' (Deut. 25.9). These descriptions emphasize the harm that is done to the deceased brother, and to his potential family line. Deut. 25.5-10 presents the dead brother as the primary victim. The woman does not complain that she has been done down, but that her husband has been. She sues for justice on his behalf. In evaluating the seriousness of this offence, therefore, we shall concentrate on its impact upon the dead brother.

Several texts suggest that this is indeed a serious offence. The celebrated story of Tamar, who tricks her father-in-law into performing the levirate duty in Gen. 38.12-19, shows that the importance of providing 'a memorial for the childless man' places the levirate duty beyond other moralities.[72] Likewise, the woman of Tekoa is able to persuade David that the principle of leaving a son to carry on his father's name is more important than the principle that bloodguilt must be avenged (2 Sam. 14.4-11). Similarly, in Deut. 25.5-10 the levirate law takes precedence over the ban on incest (Lev. 18.16=20.21).[73] The seriousness of Deut. 25.5-10 is also suggested by the literary arrangement of the book of Deuteronomy.

---

72. S.B. Frost, 'The Memorial of the Childless Man', *Int* 26 (1972), pp. 437-50 (443).

73. I take the view that both Lev. 18.16 and Lev. 20.21 are capable of being interpreted as placing a ban even when the husband is dead. There is an interesting opposition between the penalty of Lev. 20.21 (childlessness) and the purpose of Deut. 25.5-10 (to produce a child).

According to Deut. 1.1, Deut. 25.5-10 is delivered at the entrance to the Promised Land as part of a body of legislation described as 'all the commandments and the statutes and the ordinances which you shall teach them, that they may do them *in the land which I give them to possess*' (Deut. 5.31; my italics). All the commands from 6.1 onwards are qualified by the geographical boundaries of the Land.[74] The underlying values of Deut. 25.5-10 (brothers should do their duty to one another and keep the ancestral land within the family) are consistent with the great Deuteronomic themes of 'land' and 'brotherhood'.[75]

Ancient Israel feared 'the obliteration of the name above all eventualities'.[76] Blotting out the name had a number of serious consequences for the deceased brother. It robs him of his right to descendants and it is tantamount to his personal extinction. This is seen in 3.3.1 and 3.3.2 below.

3.3.1. *Loss of Descendants*

Descendants are one of the principal forms of blessing in the worldly piety of the Hebrew Bible. An ancestor and his descendants are thought of as one, living on through solidarity with their offspring.[77] To deny a man his posterity is therefore a serious matter. According to Ps. 128.3, the wife of the man who fears the LORD 'will be like a fruitful vine within your house; your children will be like olive shoots around your table'. The continuation of his family line (e.g. Ps. 128.6) is important because it is central to being able to enjoy YHWH's blessings, not least the blessing of life in the Land. Ps. 25.13 promises that, '[the man who fears the LORD]... shall abide in prosperity, and his children shall possess the land' (cf. Ps. 69.36 [H. 69.37] 'the children of his [God's] servants shall inherit [Zion and the cities of Judah]'). Not only is it a blessing in itself to have children, it is also the means to enjoy future blessing.

The reverse is also true. We saw in 3.1.2 above that the loss of a lineage risks alienating the family estate. Barrenness was a disgrace (e.g. Gen. 30.1), whilst Ps. 21.10 [H. 21.11] exults in the hope that YHWH will punish Israel's enemies by cutting off their family line.

---

74. In fact, the phrase 'in the Land' frequently recurs after this point; e.g. 5.31 [H. 5.28], 5.33 [H. 5.30], 6.1, 6.3, 6.10, 6.18, 6.23, 7.1, 8.1.

75. See McConville, *Grace in the End*, pp. 46-47.

76. Sasson, *Ruth*, p. 133.

77. Cf. Preuss, זרע, in *TDOT*, IV, pp. 143-62 (161), 'whoever has descendants lives and his life has a future.'

Daube points out that whilst there is no duty of procreation in the Hebrew Bible (procreation being a blessing and not a commandment, Gen. 1.28), Deut. 25.5-10 is an example of a case where a man must, nevertheless, do his best to sire offspring.[78] Here the duty is commanded, not for oneself, but for the deceased brother's benefit. Daube writes, 'It is in the very nature of a boon that, while as far as your own person is concerned, you are free to take it or leave it, you must not withhold it from others'.[79] Since it is a blessing to have one's name carried on by subsequent generations, the surviving brother is to help the dead one to enjoy it.[80] This analysis may help us to understand why Deut. 25.4 precedes Deut. 25.5-10. Deut. 25.4 states, 'You shall not muzzle an ox while it is threshing'. It is unfair to deprive an ox of its share of the grain. Likewise, it is unfair to deprive the dead brother of his 'share' in the world.[81]

3.3.2. *Threat of Personal Extinction*

There is an intimate connection between the 'name' and existence (e.g. Eccl. 6.10, 'Whatever has come to be has already been named [שמו נקרא])'. In a similar vein, YHWH's promise that his people's name shall remain is a pledge of their continuing existence: 'For as the new heavens and the new earth which I will make shall remain before me, says the LORD; so shall your descendants and your name (זרעכם ושמכם) remain' (Isa. 66.22). Annihilation of the name spelt 'absolute death'.[82] For this reason, David laments: 'My enemies say of me in malice: "When will he die, and his name (שמו) perish?"' (Ps. 41.5 [H. 41.6]).

The idea that שם and existence are connected suggests that blotting out the name amounts to 'total personal extinction'.[83] For example, the command in Deut. 12.3 to wipe out the names of the pagan deities upon entering the land is seen as tantamount to destroying the religion that those images represented, 'you shall tear down their altars, and dash in pieces

---

78. D. Daube, *The Duty of Procreation* (Edinburgh: Edinburgh University Press, 1997), p. 6.

79. Daube, *Duty of Procreation*, p. 6.

80. Cf. Burrows, 'Levirate Marriage', p. 31, 'a man's right to have a son holds good even after he is dead'.

81. Carmichael, *Laws of Deuteronomy*, p. 239. J.T., Noonan Jr, 'The Muzzled Ox', *JQR* 70 (1979), pp. 172-75 and C.M. Carmichael, ' "Treading" in the Book of Ruth', *ZAW* 92 (1980), pp. 248-66 find a sexual innuendo linking Deut. 25.4 and Deut. 25.5-10.

82. J. Pedersen, *Israel: Its Life and Culture* (2 vols.; London: Oxford University Press, 1959), p. 256.

83. Pedersen, *Israel*, pp. 255-56.

3. *Lineage, Title and the Barefoot Man*

their pillars...you shall hew down the graven images of their gods, and destroy their name (את־שמם) out of that place' (Deut. 12.3). Zimmerman avers, 'Complete annihilation of a human being is not only accomplished through his physical death, but through the obliteration of his name'.[84] Personal and lineal extinction appears to lie behind second-millennium covenant-treaties where the deity threatens to 'blot out the [transgressor's] name and seed from the land'.[85] To this extent, the levir's duty was nothing less than to save his brother from being 'utterly quenched as a person'.[86]

3.4. *Seriousness of Punishment*

The levir's punishment is for him to be subjected to the חלצה ceremony (Deut. 25.9-10). Its purpose is to demote the levir within the community's status hierarchy. The formula found at the close of the ceremony ('Thus shall be done to the man who...') signifies the levir's change of status. In Est. 6.11, the same phrase (ככה יעשה לאיש אשר) signifies Mordecai's change of status (although in his case, the change is positive, rather than negative).

The חלצה ceremony can be characterized as a shaming ritual for the following reasons. Firstly, shame impacts on identity, changing the perception of who a person is.[87] The sting of shame is 'the fatal equation..."I did therefore I am"'.[88] This is epitomized in Deut. 25.10 by renaming the man, 'The house of him that had his sandal pulled off'. To borrow from Braithwaite's modern work on shaming, this name has the cast of a master-status trait that is intended to subsume all other identities. It becomes, henceforth, the most important thing that can be known about him. Secondly, shame often arises where there is a reversal of expectations.[89] This is seen in the reversal of gender roles in Deut. 25.9. The woman assumes the dominant/active/powerful role in the ceremony whilst the levir is put in the submissive/passive/powerless position. Thirdly, the essence of shame is to

---

84. F. Zimmermann, 'Folk Etymology of Biblical Names', in *Volume du congrès* (VTSup, 15; Leiden: E.J. Brill, 1966), pp. 311-26 (313).

85. D.J. Wiseman, 'Law and Order in Old Testament Times', *VE* 8 (1973), pp. 5-21 (16).

86. J.A. Motyer, 'Name', in *NBD*, pp. 799-802 (863).

87. Bechtel, 'Shame as a Sanction', p. 49.

88. L. Smedes, *Shame and Grace: Healing the Shame We Don't Deserve* (London: Triangle, 1993), p. 18.

89. Bechtel, 'Shame as a Sanction', p. 49.

89. Smedes, *Shame and Grace*, p. 54.

be looked on as an object. This is achieved in Deut. 25.10 when the levir is stripped of his name and is made to feel like a non-person. Fourthly, the woman's complaint relates to an intimate matter (Deut. 25.9). Daube notes that 'the tendency for shame to come to the fore [in sexual matters] is pretty universal'.[90] Not surprisingly, the levir is the subject of shame. 'The sexual domain is indeed shame's birthplace and forever and everywhere remains its *point d'appui*.'[91] Fifthly, shame depends on some form of shared moral consensus. This is achieved in Deut. 25.9 by performing the ritual in the presence of the elders who are representatives of the community. Indeed, the ritual itself plays an important part in Israel's socialization process, creating a kind of 'feedback loop'. By communicating and reinforcing shared moral values it helps to consolidate Israel's value-base. It also inculcates sensitivity to shame among those who either see the ceremony or hear about it. The woman enacts the moral values of the community. She is the Mummer in the legal process which then, as now, is theatre. Finally, the ceremony involves a form of divestiture (sandal-removal). This is a common ritual that is often used to humiliate those found guilty of dishonourable conduct. Clerics are 'defrocked' of their vestments and soldiers are 'stripped' of their uniforms.[92] Divestiture may exploit the hypothesized link between feelings of 'loss' (here, of clothes, or a sandal) and the sense of 'shame'.[93]

The חלצה ceremony is clearly a far less serious penalty than that of the death penalty described in Chapter 2. It is, however, a moderately severe penalty in a shame-conscious society.[94] In such a society there is great sensitivity to even the slightest degree of perceived diminishment (often resulting in efforts to restore honour and shame the violator). A surprising number of scholars deny that the חלצה ceremony is a penalty at all,[95] whilst

90. D. Daube, 'Shame Culture in Luke', in M.D. Hooker and S.G. Wilson (eds.), *Paul and Paulinism: Essays in Honour of C.K. Barrett* (London: SPCK, 1982), pp. 355-72 (363).

91. Daube, 'Shame Culture', p. 363.

92. Benjamin, *Deuteronomy and City Life*, p. 253.

93. Cf. Smedes, *Shame and Grace*, p. 12.

94. See Bechtel, 'Shame as a Sanction'; Bechtel, 'Perception of Shame'; Olyan, 'Honor, Shame and Covenant Relations', pp. 201-18. Cf. Daube, 'To Be Found Doing Wrong', criticized by Dempster, 'Deuteronomic Formula'.

95. I. Mendelsohn, 'The Family in the Ancient Near East', *BA* 11 (1948), pp. 24-40 (31) claims that 'the law nullifies itself by providing no penalty for its non-observance', whilst Davies, 'Inheritance Rights II', p. 260 avers that 'no penalty was imposed on the brother-in-law who refused his obligation.'

others downplay its significance.⁹⁶ Some go so far as to claim that it confers a benefit on the levir!⁹⁷ Such readings are ahistorical, insofar as they belittle the seriousness of shame in the Bible and the ANE.

Social shaming is a means of adapting individuals to the expectations of a given society.⁹⁸ According to Daube, Deuteronomy is considerably more shame-oriented than the other books of the Pentateuch.⁹⁹ Although his argument is trenchantly criticized by Dempster¹⁰⁰ there is undeniably a shame-cultural background to Deut. 25.5-10. Here, public degradation and disgrace is the lot of those who fail to conform.

The חליצה ceremony dramatizes the levir's change of status in the following ways. Firstly, by the act of sandal-removal, which leaves the levir barefoot; secondly, by the act of spitting in the levir's face and thirdly, by the act of renaming. Each of these acts is both descriptive and performative. By exploring their symbolic meaning, we can demonstrate how the חליצה ceremony functions as a register of seriousness.

3.4.1. *The Sandal-Removal*

In addition to their use as footwear, sandals were widely used in the ANE for symbolic purposes.¹⁰¹ They may symbolize different things in different

---

96. Viberg, *Symbols of Law*, p. 157 thinks the removal of the sandal is possibly a formal punishment, but regards this as 'uncertain'. Westbrook, 'Biblical Levirate', considers that the law of the levirate is not enforced, first, on the grounds that biblical law is 'notoriously shy of enforcing positive duties' and, second, that since the brothers' father is dead, there is no one to exercise authority over the surviving brother. He concludes that ultimately the levir is 'subject only to his own conscience and family pride' (Westbrook, 'Biblical Levirate', p. 82).

97. Davies, 'Interitance Rights II', p. 262 suggests that the ritual was performed for the levir's convenience. He commends the law for providing 'a ceremony by which he could formally renounce his obligation', a view recently followed by Matthews, 'Honor and Shame', p. 101. Hirsch, *Deuteronomy*, p. 514 describes the shaming ceremony as 'an act of publicly clearing any lack of fraternal love...[that] expresses the deepest feelings of love and readiness for brotherly actions in which the attachment of Jewish families has its roots'. Rabbinic opinion sees the 'renaming' as a symbol, not of shame, but of praise, *Yer. Yeb.* 13a although this interpretation reflects the fact that the Rabbis were basically opposed to the levirate and preferred the matter to be resolved by חלצה, seen now as mutual release.

98. F. English, 'Shame and Social Control', *TA* 5 (1975), pp. 24-28.

99. Daube, 'To Be Found Doing Wrong', p. 355.

100. Dempster, 'Deuteronomic Formula'.

101. Carmichael, 'Ceremonial Crux', pp. 321-24; E.A. Speiser, 'Of Shoes and Shekels', *BASOR* 77 (1940), pp. 15-20; Viberg, *Symbols of Law*, pp. 157-64.

contexts. Conflicting theories have been put forward to explain the meaning of the sandal and the act of sandal-removal in Deut. 25.9. We shall consider three of these in 3.4.1.1–3.4.1.3, before proposing a different explanation in 3.4.1.4.

3.4.1.1. *Freedom.* Several scholars argue that the sandal signifies oppression[102] and that the act of sandal-removal signifies freedom.[103] By removing the shoe, the widow gains her freedom. She is released from her legal obligation to marry the levir, and from his claim upon her. However, if this theory was correct we might expect the levir to remove the sandal. This is because, in the Bible, freedom is normally acquired as the result of the master's declaration or some act of his.[104] It would be highly unusual for a subject person to gain independence by a declaration or ceremonial act of his or her own.[105] Consequently, I reject this theory on the grounds that it does not adequately explain why the woman removes the sandal.

3.4.1.2. *A Rite of Passage.* A second approach sees the sandal as symbolizing the husband's authority and its removal as a symbolic rite of passage that marks her transition from an old identity to a new one.[106] This approach is based on the belief that the woman automatically becomes the levir's lawful wife upon her husband's death. A rite of passage is therefore necessary to dissolve the marriage so that the wife can become a free woman again.[107] However, this theory ignores the unusual sequence of the clauses in Deut. 25.5, '[he] shall go in to her, and take her as his wife'. This differs from the usual construction as expressed in Deut. 22.13, 'if any man takes a wife and goes in to her'.[108] This suggests that there is no automatic marriage on the brother's death. Deut. 25.5 emphasizes the duty of the levir to take the widow of the deceased as his wife. This is confirmed by Rabbinic interpretation of Deut. 25.5 which holds that intercourse is necessary if the levir is to take the place of the deceased brother.[109] The widow only becomes the levir's wife when he performs the duty.

102. Brichto, 'Kin, Cult, Land', p. 19.
103. Sasson, *Ruth*, p. 146; Tigay, *Deuteronomy*, p. 231.
104. E.g. Exod. 21.26-27; Deut. 21.14.
105. Westbrook, 'Biblical Levirate', p. 84.
106. Paul A. Kruger, 'The Removal of the Sandal in Deuteronomy XXV 9: "A Rite of Passage"?', *VT* 46 (1996), pp. 534-38.
107. Kruger, 'Removal of the Sandal', p. 538.
108. Benjamin, *Deuteronomy and City Life*, p. 246.
109. Belkin, 'Levirate and Agnate Marriage', pp. 282-83.

3. *Lineage, Title and the Barefoot Man*

3.4.1.3. *Fertility.* A third possibility is that the sandal is used as a symbol of fertility. It is likely that an agricultural society would have associated the earth with fertility. Certainly, ancient Israel's traditions present the ground as 'the womb from which man emerges',[110] (cf. Gen. 2.7, 'the LORD God formed man of dust from the ground'). To this extent, the sandal may be regarded as a symbol of fertility because it has contact with the ground.[111] The sandal, too, is covered with sand. This recalls YHWH's promise of 'descendants' to Abraham that would be as numerous as 'the sand which is on the seashore' (Gen. 22.17). Indeed, the word for 'descendants' in Gen. 22.17 is זרעך, suggesting a conceptual link between זרע and grains of sand.[112] The levir has refused to raise up seed for his brother (cf. Gen. 38.8-9). Therefore, the woman takes the sandal off his foot to signify that the privilege of intercourse is taken away from him. This need not conflict with the explanation given for the 'sandal-removal' ceremony in Ruth 4.7 because, I have argued, the meaning of the ceremony in Ruth is different anyway (see 3.2.4.2).

In addition, Carmichael observes that the nominal form of the verb used for 'sandal removal' in Deut. 25.9 (חלץ) refers to a man's loins (three times in the sense of his virility, Gen. 35.11, 1 Kgs 8.19 = 2 Chron. 6.9).[113] He suggests that the verb חלץ may well have had special significance in contexts such as Deut. 25.9 where the notion of generative strength is present. A similar association is found in Isa. 20.2 where the prophet removes sackcloth from his loins and, in a parallel action, is commanded to 'take off' (תחלץ) the sandals (singular in some manuscripts) from his feet (again, singular in some manuscripts).[114]

There are a number of reasons for favouring this procreative interpretation of the ritual (which differs substantially from Carmichael's sexual allegorizing).[115] Firstly, it is a simple explanation that includes all the

---

110. V.P. Hamilton, *The Book of Genesis Chapters 1–17* (Grand Rapids: Eerdmans, 1990), p. 158.

111. I am indebted to Dr Brian Lancaster for this observation.

112. Cf. Job 29.18 which associates 'sand' with 'multiplication' and 'increase': ' "I shall die in my nest, and I shall multiply (ארבה) my days as the sand"'.

113. Carmichael, 'Ceremonial Crux', p. 330.

114. Carmichael, 'Ceremonial Crux', p. 330 n. 33.

115. Carmichael claims that Deut. 25.4-12 cannot be understood except as a coded reference to the story of Tamar and Onan in Gen. 38, with the account of the sandal-removal signifying Onan's withdrawal from intercourse (cf. Gen. 38.9). Carmichael argues that the 'foot' is a symbolic penis and that the 'sandal' is a symbolic vagina and that the rite symbolically and publicly disengages the two. However, while feet are

relevant data, unlike 3.4.1.1 and 3.4.1.2 above. In particular, it explains why the woman takes off the levir's sandal. It is also fitting because procreation is integral to the meaning of the verb יבם (i.e. '[to] perform the duty of a brother-in-law'). An unpublished letter by Albright connects the Hebrew verb יבם with the Akkadian word *bamatu* ('loins') and this may suggest that the Hebrew root יבם denotes 'procreation'.[116] A second advantage is that if the sandal symbolizes fertility, the ceremony effectively

occasionally used as a euphemism in the Hebrew Bible, there are no examples of the sandal as a metaphor for the vagina. Carmichael's reasoning is somewhat convoluted, 'her [the woman's] doing the action...is by way of transferring Onan's action with Tamar to him because of the view that his non-action amounts to the same thing as Onan's quasi-one' (Carmichael, 'Ceremonial Crux', p. 329). But the woman is not Onan, nor is she trying to be. Carmichael forces the ritual of Deut. 25.9-10 into a narrative framework it does not fit.

A further objection to Carmichael's approach is that it divorces the shaming of the levir from any social reality. Carmichael, *Law and Narrative in the Bible: The Evidence of the Deuteronomic Laws and the Decalogue* (Ithaca: Cornell University Press, 1985), p. 296 n. 16 avers that 'no such sanction existed in the Deuteronomist's time or at any previous time', claiming that, insofar as the refusal of the levir 'belonged to the sphere of the family, the law as a public instrument would have looked away' (presumably, that it would have been a private and not a public matter). Deut. 25.5-10, on this view, is just a reflection of literary history and not of real history; a sort of neo-midrashic *haggadah*. Apart from its alleged narrative references, Deut. 25 has, for Carmichael, no meaning. Carmichael's claim that Deut. 25.5-10 is a historian's 'coded meditation' on the Onan story that has to be decoded by properly-versed *literati* is seen by Levinson, 'Carmichael's approach', p. 248 as Carmichael's 'most spectacular assertion'. Carmichael's approach to this text can be criticized on four main grounds: first, that he makes the final editing of Deuteronomy impossible to understand, because his account leaves no logical point in Israel's history in which it could have been written; second, that he posits a type of authorship that has no precedent in the ANE; third, that his approach provides few obvious methodological controls and fourth, that although Carmichael rightly emphasizes the importance of literary history, his actual exegesis persistently isolates the laws of Deuteronomy from both cuneiform and Israelite literary history (Levinson, 'Carmichael's Approach'). The result is to subvert the intelligibility and significance of Deut. 25.5-10 as a text (cf. Levinson, 'Carmichael's Approach', p. 257). It is an 'exegesis of despair' (Levinson, 'Carmichael's Approach', p. 242) within which the history of interpretation becomes simply the history of exegetical error. Finally, in spite of Carmichael's stress on the literary character of the laws he oddly disregards similar idioms in other biblical texts (e.g. his startling omission of Ruth 4.7-8). Suffice it to say that the existence of a form of the custom in Ruth (see 3.2.4.2 and 3.2.4.3) militates against Carmichael's assertion that Deut. 25.5-10 can *only* be interpreted allegorically.

116. Cited in Burrows, 'Hebrew Levirate Marriage', pp. 6-7.

symbolizes the nature of the offence (i.e. the levir's refusal to impregnate the woman). Thirdly, it is authentic to the text insofar as it views the sandal-removal from the actor's, that is, the widow's perspective. Moreover, if the sandal symbolizes fertility, it follows that she is in the best position to remove the sandal and, thereby, the privilege of fertility. After all, she is the only person (apart from the levir) who truly knows whether he has performed the duty or not. Fourthly, this interpretation incorporates an element of poetic justice. The ritual ends with the levir standing barefoot. This exposure may be an ironic comment on his refusal to uncover himself before the widow. Finally, this interpretation is supported by the literary presentation of Deut. 25.5-12. What is the link between Deut. 25.5-10 and the strange provision of Deut. 25.11-12 which prescribes a severe punishment for the woman who seizes a man's genitals in defence of her husband? The severity of the penalty in Deut. 25.12 suggests that Deut. 25.11 has in mind genital injury, possibly resulting in a haematoma or orchitis.[117] Her action risks making the man infertile and thus infertility seems to connect Deut. 25.5-10 and Deut. 25.11-12. Taking away the levir's right to inseminate the widow is an authoritative act that, like the spitting and renaming (see 3.4.3 and 3.4.4 below), subjugates the levir in relation to the widow. We have already seen that sandal-removal is a sign of deference to a higher authority (see 3.4.1.2 above). Clearly the act of forcibly removing the sandal places the levir in an abject position vis-à-vis the woman. There may be a hint of 'poetic justice' here: the levir who refuses to act as the 'dominant' partner by inseminating the widow is rendered 'submissive' before the woman. This interpretation is an attractive one. However, it suffers from the weakness that there is currently no evidence that attests to this use of the sandal elsewhere in the ANE. Accordingly, the explanatory power of this proposal seems limited.

3.4.1.4. *Property*. Finally, a number of scholars suggest that the 'sandal' symbolizes the ratification of a transaction.[118] It is thought that 'taking possession' of land meant 'walking' over it and that this, in time, was symbolized by the 'sandal' with which one 'treads the land'. In their view, the חלצה ceremony allows the widow to assume the right to her deceased husband's estate. Proponents appeal to the historical notice attached to Ruth 4.7 which also describes a sandal-removal ceremony, 'Now this was

117. Tigay, *Deuteronomy*, p. 483.
118. J.A. Loader, 'Of Barley, Bulls, Land and Levirate', in F. Garcia Martinez *et al.* (eds.), *Studies in Deuteronomy* (Leiden: E.J. Brill, 1994), pp. 123-38 (136).

the custom in former times in Israel concerning redeeming and exchanging: to confirm a transaction, the one drew off his sandal and gave it to the other, and this was the manner of attesting in Israel'. The reference to 'former times' implies that the practice has since been superseded. But if it went back to the original understanding of Deut. 25.9-10, it could be argued that sandal-removal in Deut. 25.9-10 is also bound up with the transfer of property.

Expressed in these terms, this view is not convincing for several reasons. Firstly, there are important differences between Deut. 25.9-10 and Ruth 4.7. There is a world of difference between taking off one's sandal and handing it to another and having one's sandal forcibly removed by someone else. In Ruth 4 it is not clear whose shoe is bandied about during the ceremony, nor do we know who receives it or removes it from the foot.[119] Also, in Ruth 4.7 all of the parties agree to the transaction, whereas Deut. 25.7 depicts the woman as bringing a complaint against the levir.[120] Moreover, '[the] ceremony in Ruth represents concession of a right, in Deuteronomy it represents failure to perform a duty'.[121] Secondly, in the light of the inheritance schema presented in Num. 27.8-11, it is hard to see how the levir can be thought of as releasing the property to the widow. His offence lies precisely in the fact that he is keeping it. If the property is released to anyone it is to him. Bechtel suggests that the 'sandal removal' symbolizes the surrender of the property to the levir.[122] But for this to make any sense, we would expect the *levir* to remove the *woman's* sandal. It does not explain why the woman releases the levir's sandal. Finally, several scholars suggest that by this act the woman gains her dead husband's estate.[123] But although women are sometimes depicted as owning money and property (e.g. Judg. 1.14; 17.2-3; 2 Kgs 8.1-6; Job 42.15; Ruth 4.3), there are no cases in the Hebrew Bible where a childless widow is depicted as possessing her deceased husband's land. If the woman could inherit a

119. Sasson, *Ruth*, p. 143.
120. C. Pressler, *The View of Women Found in the Deuteronomic Family Laws* (New York: W. de Gruyter, 1993), p. 70.
121. Westbrook, 'Biblical Levirate', p. 81.
122. Bechtel, 'Shame as a Sanction', pp. 60-61.
123. Thompson and Thompson, 'Legal Problems', p. 93; E. Otto, 'False Weights in the Scales of Biblical Justice? Different Views of Women from Patriarchal Hierarchy to Religious Equality in the Book of Deuteronomy', in V.H. Matthews *et al.* (eds.), *Gender and Law in the Hebrew Bible and the Ancient Near East* (JSOTSup, 262; Sheffield: Sheffield Academic Press, 1998), pp. 128-46 (139).

portion of the estate, it would reverse the roles of the parties. The levir would be the party most interested in enforcing the duty. Although Deut. 25.5-10 says nothing about the destination of the estate in the event of חליצה, the presumption must be that the estate goes to the brother(s), including the levir (as argued at 3.1.2 above). This means that there is no transfer of the estate in Deut. 25.9. Rather, it goes where it would have gone anyway, in the absence of a levirate marriage, that is, to the surviving brothers. This being so, no ceremony of transfer is required. There may be a partial parallel in the slavery laws (Exod. 21.4-6). No ceremony attends the release of the Hebrew debt-slave after six years because that is a reversion to his 'normal' status (Exod. 21.4). A ceremony is only required if there is to be a change of status to permanent slavery (Exod. 21.5-6). We may conclude, therefore, that the ceremony does not symbolize ceding the property to the widow, because that is manifestly what the levir does not do.

But whilst the ceremony may not describe what the levir has done, it may well describe what he *ought* to have done. By wresting the sandal off his foot, the widow demonstrates what ought to have occurred, namely, that the levir ought to have raised up an heir who would succeed to the dead brother's title. This interpretation allows us to take seriously the association between the sandal and property in Ruth 4.7 whilst avoiding the pitfalls presented by other advocates of property-release in Deut. 25.9-10.

3.4.2. *The Barefoot Man*
The act of removing the sandal leaves us with the image of a man standing barefoot. This image functions as a descriptive register (when the law is read) and as a performative register (when it is carried out). It is a potent image for several reasons. Firstly, it visually places the levir in a position of vulnerability and defencelessness. These are the very emotions associated with shame (cf. Ps. 89.39-40 [H. 89.40-41] where loss of dignity is associated with vulnerability and defencelessness). We note in passing that this is another example of how biblical law seeks to evoke certain feelings (see Chapter 6, below). Secondly, to go barefoot was itself a source of shame in ancient Israel and a mark of poverty, especially when 'a pair of sandals' was a proverbial expression for something of small value (cf. Amos 8.6). 'Walking naked and barefoot' is a source of shame in Isa. 20.2-4 where it typifies the exiled. Jer. 2.25 counsels, 'Keep your feet from going unshod' whilst David's ascension of the Mount of Olives barefoot, following Absalom's rebellion, is a sign of his humiliation (2 Sam. 15.30).

In a shame-conscious society such as ancient Israel, the barefoot man stood for the sort of person whom everyone else looked down upon. In the context of Deut. 25.9-10, the sight of the levir standing barefoot signifies that he now belongs to the lowest of the low. In the competitive world of inter-clan and inter-tribal rivalry, having one's sandal removed was the Israelite equivalent of being suddenly relegated to the bottom of the Third Division. As Daube notes, 'in a shame environment it is the ensuing ridicule that hurts most'.[124]

3.4.3. *Spitting in the Levir's Face*
Spitting in the face signifies the strongest rejection and contempt (e.g. Num. 12.14 where a daughter is expected to feel shame for seven days if her father spits in her face). Like the act of sandal-removal, it is designed to maximize the levir's humiliation. Carmichael suggests that the act of spitting is a coded reference to Onan's (misdirected) semen in Gen. 38.9. However, the argument would be stronger if the spitting was performed by the levir, rather than by the woman.[125] The spitting is 'a desperate assault'[126] that lowers him in public esteem. Job complains that his persecutors 'abhor me, they keep aloof from me; they do not hesitate to spit at the sight of me' (Job 30.10). Likewise, 'shame and spitting' (Isa. 50.6) form a natural pair in the indignities heaped upon the Suffering Servant.

3.4.4. *The Renaming*
'Sticks and stones may break my bones, but names will never hurt me.' Nothing could be further from the truth in ancient Israel. How shameful the reputation of being 'Unsandalled' was in Israelite society is explored in 3.4.2 above. But there can be no doubt that it was harmful in a culture where names signified status and identity. Bechtel argues that, because the sanction attacked the levir's status, it threatened 'the very survival of the family in the community'.[127] However, it is impossible to be sure as to the precise impact of this reputation. The renaming of the levir, 'The house of him that had his sandal pulled off' is presented as the culmination and consequence of the חליצה ceremony (Deut. 25.10). A key question is whether the phrase 'The house of him that had his sandal pulled off' refers

---

124. Daube, 'Shame Culture', p. 359.
125. Carmichael, 'Ceremonial Crux', p. 329.
126. Daube, 'To Be Found Doing Wrong', p. 359.
127. Bechtel, 'Shame as a Sanction', p. 61.

to a continuing state ('The house of him who is unsandalled') or to something that has been done to him ('The house of the one who has been unsandalled'). In other words, does it refer to 'the house of a person who is in the state of having his sandal taken off' or is it a description of 'the house who has had his sandal taken off'? Syntactically, the Hebrew (הנעל בית חלוץ) can express 'the house of he who is in the state of having had his sandal removed', but on pragmatic grounds it is more acceptable to adopt a process interpretation. Thus, I take the view that the name in Deut. 25.10 describes a process. He is called 'The house of him that had his sandal pulled off' on account of what has been done to him (i.e. the חלצה ceremony).[128]

It is not clear, however, whether the renaming is performed by the woman as part of the ceremony. It would be quite remarkable if the renaming was performed by the woman. This is because naming in the Bible is the prerogative of a superior (cf. Gen. 2.19-20). Likewise, 'renaming' typically expresses the authority of the name-giver over the subject who is named or renamed. This is commonly seen in regard to places that have changed ownership (e.g. as a result of conquest with 'Kenath' becoming 'Nobah' in honour of its eponymous conqueror, Num. 32.42). There is, of course, a difference between renaming places and renaming people but the extrapolation is a reasonable one (cf. Gen. 17.5; Jn 1.42). However, if the woman did rename the levir, it would not be altogether surprising. It is consistent with the high degree of authority that she exercises over him in the course of the ceremony (cf. the acts of sandal-removal and spitting, above). Being renamed by a woman could be an additional aspect of his humiliation.

On the other hand, it may be that the statement in Deut. 25.10 is an editorial comment. The stigma may have been assimilated into the levir's family name in two ways: one, in common parlance and two, in genealogical records. In common parlance, the name could have been assimilated into the two-unit patronymic 'X בן Y', in which case we might expect it to last for two generations. A key question is whether the new name would have been assimilated into Israelite three-unit names ('X בן Y בן Z', where Z is the paternal grandfather), four-unit names (e.g. 1 Kgs 11.26) or six-unit names (1 Sam. 9.1), in which case the stigma could have been extended for longer. Ultimately, it is impossible to say how long the disgrace typically lasted as we do not have any examples of this name-form outside

---

128. I am indebted to Prof. Dennis Kurzon for his advice on this matter.

Deut. 25.10. Probably, it was a matter for the local community to decide, since they were the ones who actually enforced it.

We might expect the 'name' to survive longer in written records although, again, how long is impossible to quantify. Evidence for extensive genealogies in the ANE includes the Assyrian, Babylonian and Sumerian king lists. Documentary evidence of land-ownership lawsuits, whose histories go back over three or four centuries, indicate that extended genealogical data were kept among land-owning people (e.g. the property dispute recorded on the walls of the Egyptian tomb of Mes [or Mose], a minor official under Rameses II).[129] Mes, of course, was not an 'ordinary' person, and we have no examples of similar documents in the case of 'ordinary' Egyptians. However, the strength of oral tradition in ancient Egypt and ancient Israel suggests that even where such information was not written down, it could still have been remembered.

To be the bearer of a bad name was a serious matter in a society that attached high value to a 'good name' (e.g. Prov. 22.1; Eccl. 7.1 where a 'good name' is to be preferred above 'great riches' and 'precious ointment', respectively).[130] There are several reasons for this. Firstly, in such a society, names summarize narratives. 'Through names language mediates between time and place and commemorates an occurrence in a particular locale.'[131] Hess's study of the use of personal names in Genesis 1–11 suggests that names function within the biblical text as a kind of 'onomastic commentary',[132] progressing the narrative and providing important clues to theme and direction.[133] Thus, for example, the name of 'Shem' prepares the reader for the chosen means of 'making a name' for humanity through Abram's call and blessing of Genesis 12 rather than through that proposed in the Tower of Babel incident.[134]

In such a culture, mentioning a name or reciting a list of names (as in a

---

129. G.A. Gaballa,*The Memphite Tomb-Chapel of Mose [Text and Translations]* (Warminster: Aris & Phillips, 1977).

130. Cf. also R. Simeon in *Ab.*, 'There are three crowns: the crown of *Torah*, the crown of priesthood and the crown of royalty, but the crown of a good name excels them all.'

131. D. Ben-Amos, 'Comments on Robert C. Culley's "Five Tales of Punishment in the Book of Numbers"', in S. Niditch (ed.), *Text and Tradition: The Hebrew Bible and Folklore* (Atlanta: Scholars Press, 1990), pp. 35-45 (38).

132. R.S. Hess, *Studies in the Personal Names of Genesis 1–11* (Neukirchen–Vluyn: Neukirchener Verlag, 1993), p. 158.

133. Hess, *Personal Names*, p. 161.

134. Hess, *Personal Names*, p. 157.

genealogy) can be a shorthand way of evoking an entire narrative (witness the book of Chronicles and the start of Matthew's Gospel). Likewise, the purpose of renaming is essentially narrative: it is the story of an event. Changes in place-names, for example, mostly reflect events that have happened there (or have yet to happen).[135] Renaming is a recurrent feature of the punishment narratives in the book of Numbers (e.g. Taberah [Num. 11.1-3], Kibroth-hattaavah [Num. 11.34] and the Waters of Meribah [Num. 20.13]). People as well as places are renamed and this too reflects the occurrence of an event. Ancient Israel had a tradition in which a 'birth-name' was replaced later with an 'event-name'.[136] Classic examples include Abraham (Gen. 17.5), Sarah (Gen. 17.15), Edom (Gen. 25.30), Israel (Gen. 32.28 [H. 32.29]) and Jerubbaal (Judg. 6.32). The levir's new name, on our process interpretation, perpetuates the story of the חלצה ceremony. Like Taberah, Kibroth-hattaavah and the Waters of Meribah, it retells the story of a punitive event. This standing reminder of his criminal record effectively destroys his reputation in the community. This is because there is a close association between name and reputation in ancient Israel. By the same token, those who act upon the name by raising it to high esteem can also lower it. Thus the man who brings a false accusation against his new bride 'brings up an evil name upon her' (Deut. 22.19) by giving her a bad reputation. Men of bad reputation are said to be 'name-less' (cf. Job 30.8, where the phrase 'a base and nameless brood' may also be rendered, 'Scoundrels, *nobodies*, stricken from the earth' [my italics]). In general terms, 'to have a name' means to have 'greatness' (2 Sam. 7.23). Only a 'man of name' could fill the position of 'a chief among the people' (Num. 16.2). Names and reputations were lost and won when the characters and deeds of people became widely known (e.g. 1 Sam. 18.30; 1 Kgs 5.11).

Secondly, and allied to this, renaming is a serious matter in ancient Israel because the name was thought to be closely related to the nature of its bearer.[137] By analysing a man's name one might find a clue to his personality or ancestry[138] and, in the light of this discovery, deal with him

---

135. O. Eissfeldt, 'Renaming in the Old Testament', in P.R. Ackroyd and B. Lindars (eds.), *Words and Meanings: Essays Presented to D.W. Thomas* (Cambridge: Cambridge University Press, 1968), pp. 69-79 (72).

136. Andersen, 'Kinship Terminology', p. 30.

137. O.S Rankin, 'Name', in A. Richardson (ed.), *A Theological Word Book of the Bible* (London: SCM Press, 1967), pp. 157-58 (157), Zimmerman, 'Biblical Names', p. 311.

138. E.g. in 2 Sam. 16 Shimei, who assaults David with curses and stones during his

accordingly. Names to beware included 'Jacob' (Gen. 27.36) and 'Nabal' (1 Sam. 25.25). For this reason, a man could be given a new name in the light of a revaluation of his character. Where the change is positive (e.g. 'Abram' to 'Abraham' [Gen. 17.5] and 'Jacob' to 'Israel' [Gen. 32.28 (H. 32.29), 35.10]) it is equivalent to 'regeneration'. The new name signifies that he is a new man. In Jacob's case, the name-change was also prophetic in force, describing the character of the man who was to be. By the same token, where the change is negative (e.g. Jeremiah's oracle against the unjust priest Pashhur, Jer. 20.3), the name-change symbolizes degeneracy.[139] Deut. 25.10 is an example of the latter. It rebrands the levir as the sort of man who will not stand by his brother. As such, his new name represents local intelligence in a concise form. It serves as a warning to others inside (and outside) the community as to the sort of person he is.[140]

Thirdly, the scope of the renaming. His whole 'house'[141] is blackened. The infamy of an entire 'house' is a classic example of 'communal punishment'. Daube argues that communal punishment is designed to stop subversive activities, not by targeting specific individuals, but by striking at the group in which they originate. 'Even modern parents who believe in individual responsibility are apt to ostracise a whole family just because

flight from Jerusalem, is introduced as 'the son of Gera *of the family of the house of Saul*' (2 Sam. 16.5, my italics). This is enough to explain his behaviour, as 2 Sam. 16.7-8 goes on to tell us ' "Begone, begone, you man of blood, you worthless fellow! *The LORD has avenged upon you all the blood of the house of Saul, in whose place you have reigned*; and the LORD has given the kingdom into the hand of your son Absalom"' (my italics). Shimei sees David's exile as cause to gloat because he is a relative of Saul.

139. It could be argued that Passhur's new name ('Terror-on-every-side') is not inherently shameful, unlike the levir's. However, in both cases the new names express YHWH's condemnation of their behaviour.

140. Social knowledge was often appended to English surnames as well. Daube, 'Form is the Message', p. 71 notes that a person's dwelling was once part of his 'name', for example, 'John Smith the Mill'.

141. The phrase 'House of the Unsandalled one' raises the question, whose 'house' is being referred to? S. Rattray, 'Marriage Rules, Kinship Terms and Family Structure in the Bible', in *Society of Biblical Literature 1987 Seminar Papers* (Society of Biblical Literature, 1987), pp. 537-44 (541) suggests that biblical Hebrew differentiates between the two kinds of family distinguished by anthropologists: the family of orientation (i.e. the family one is born into, the בת אב) and the family of procreation (i.e. the family one creates by marrying and having children of one's own, the בית). If so, the referent of 'House' may be the levir's own 'house', that is, the one that he has himself created.

one member of it has committed theft.'¹⁴² Again, there is an element of 'poetic justice'. The name attaches to the levir's posterity because he denied his brother's posterity. His 'house' bears the shame because the levir would not build his brother's 'house'. His name lives on—but only to preserve his notoriety. The punishment, like the offence, has generational consequences. Perfect calibration would, of course, require that the number of generations that the levir's 'name' endured should correspond exactly to the number of generations that the brother's family would have survived had the levir performed his duty. This is, humanly speaking, impossible to calculate because the brother's family could have died out naturally anyway. Only YHWH could know how many generations' stigma was appropriate. But to the extent that the Israelites understood their communal resolutions of local disputes to be the very means of securing divine justice, it is possible that the length of time the levir's name endured was simply left in YHWH's hands.

There is a parallel to this sort of talionic 'name-punishment' in the Tower of Babel episode (Gen. 11.1-9). In both cases the offence is tied to a 'name' and the punishment takes the form of a name that endures, but is derogatory. In Gen. 11.4 the express purpose of the people's building project is to 'make a name' for themselves. But their construction is named 'Babel' (Gen. 11.9, 'confusion') which also sounds like the word for 'folly' (בלל). For sure, the 'name endures, but only to commemorate 'their failure, not their success'.¹⁴³ Both the name 'Babel' and 'House of the Unsandalled' have an important didactic function. 'Babel' teaches 'the failure of godless folly'¹⁴⁴ by incorporating the sound of 'folly' into the title. Similarly, the failure of the levir is embodied in his name, 'the House of the Unsandalled', and it teaches the value of building up the family line. Like Babel, too, it is ironic that the levir who had no concern for his brother's 'name' finds the tables turned and himself the object of excessive concern about his 'name'. The brother 'gets his own back'.

3.5. Conclusion

The offender refuses to perform the levir's duty. His offence consists in his unwillingness to sire a male child who can continue the family line

---

142. D. Daube, *Studies in Biblical Law* (Cambridge: Cambridge University Press, 1947), p. 183.
143. G.J. Wenham, *Genesis 1–15* (Dallas: Word Books, 1987), p. 239.
144. Wenham, *Genesis 1–15*, p. 235.

and, in so doing, succeed to the property and establish the deceased's title to his inheritance. The offence menaces the deceased brother by blotting out his name. This was a serious offence because it posthumously denied the brother the blessing of descendants. This results in the alienation of the ancestral land and in the deceased's personal and lineal extinction. The seriousness of this offence is reflected in the חלצה ceremony. This was a potentially severe penalty in a status-sensitive society. The seriousness of the offence is perfectly captured in the symbolism of the חלצה ceremony, culminating in the talionic ('name for name') renaming of the levir and his house.

Chapter 4

PROSTITUTION AND THE JEALOUSY OF GOD AND MAN: SERIOUSNESS OF OFFENCE IN LEVITICUS 21.9 AND DEUTERONOMY 22.20-21

> 'I sense the presence of the phallic god and, in the current exaltation of the instinctual, a bowing down to the dark gods in the blood'.
> Leanne Payne, *The Broken Image*[1]

This chapter juxtaposes Lev. 21.9 and Deut. 22.20-21 and assists our understanding of seriousness of offence in biblical law, firstly, because of some important similarities. The same charge is brought in both cases, namely the accusation of לזנות which is usually translated 'playing the harlot'. I shall argue that the word לזנות refers to similar behaviour in both cases, namely, that both women are engaged in prostitution (see 4.2 and 4.3 below). Both women also bring dishonour upon themselves and their fathers (see 4.1 below). Moreover we shall see that in both cases, seriousness of offence is related to the women's status. The priest's daughter abuses her cultic status (see 4.2.5.2) whilst the commoner's daughter abuses her status as a betrothed woman (see 4.3.3.2).

So much for the similarities. The second reason for juxtaposing Lev. 21.9 and Deut. 22.20-21 is the striking difference in the form of the punishment. The priest's daughter is 'burned with fire' (Lev. 21.9) whereas the commoner's daughter is stoned to death (Deut. 22.21) (see 4.1). This contrast allows us to explore whether there is any correlation between seriousness and the offender's social status.

It might be objected that the comparison in this chapter between Lev. 21.9 and Deut. 22.20-21 is methodologically dubious because the two texts belong to separate bodies of law. Specifically, it might be doubted whether the punishment of burning in Lev. 21.9 can be contrasted with the stoning in Deut. 22.20-21, in view of the fact that the penalty of burning is

---

1. L. Payne, *The Broken Image* (Eastbourne: Kingsway, 1988).

nowhere prescribed in Deuteronomy so that it cannot be said that Deuteronomy does not subject the offender to its supreme penalty. Similarly, it might be objected that Lev. 21.9 shows how seriously the profanation of the priestly family was regarded, but since Deuteronomy does not contain any law governing the priesthood we cannot tell how the writers of Deuteronomy would have felt about that, compared with Lev. 21.9. Such criticism is misplaced, however. This chapter does not make any claim for interdependency at the level of the original sources. The claim is only made at the level of redaction. As argued in Chapter 1, this book takes a holistic and canonical approach to the question of seriousness because the world of seriousness is accessible only through the world of the text (see 1.6 above). The key issue is the semiotic significance of a given punishment and how it functions in the textual world presented by the texts. Since semiotic choices made in the final editing of the text are an important aspect of sense-construction, it is fitting that we should rely on the understanding of the final editors at the end of the redaction process.

4.1. *Performative Registers in Leviticus 21.9*

The main performative register in Lev. 21.9 is the execution of the priest's daughter. 'She shall be put to the fire.'

4.1.1. *Burnt Alive?*
It is not clear whether the fire is simply a way of disposing of the corpse (the offender having been executed by some other means) or whether it is the means of execution itself. Most commentators take the former view, invoking the execution of Achan in Joshua 7 as a parallel.[2] Josh. 7.15 describes Achan's offence (stealing the חרם) in the same terms as that of Lev. 21.9 (נבלה בישראל). The punishment in Josh. 7.15 is also stated in similar terms to Lev. 21.9. Josh. 7.25-26 describes a stoning and a burning and thus some take the view that the priest's daughter is stoned *before* she is burnt.[3] However, Josh. 7.25 is not conclusive. The double reference to stoning in Josh. 7.25 and the ambiguity over exactly who or what is stoned and burned means that the role of fire in Joshua 7 is not clear-cut. The LXX omits the account of the burning and so does the NEB. The reason for the multiple punishments of burning and stoning is probably because each part

---

2. E.g. P.P. Jenson, *Graduated Holiness* (JSOTSup, 106; Sheffield: JSOT Press, 1992), p. 123 n. 2.
3. Jenson, *Graduated Holiness*, p. 123 n. 2.

of Josh. 7.25 refers to a different object. It is likely that Josh. 7.25 follows a similar order to Josh. 7.24 (viz. 'all Israel stoned him [Achan] with stones; they burned them [the חרם] with fire, and stoned them [Achan's family and animals] with stones'). This would mean that only the חרם was actually burnt. Consequently, Joshua 7 provides only ambiguous support for the idea that the priest's daughter is stoned to death. I take the view that the girl is burned to death[4] because fire was a known form of execution in ancient Israel (e.g. Gen. 38.24 and Judg. 12.1) and elsewhere in the ANE. Even if she is not put to death by fire, the pyre still functions as a *post-mortem* register of seriousness.

4.1.2. *Ashes to Ashes*
Burning is structurally opposed to the rotting of dead flesh. Reducing a body to ashes was viewed extremely seriously in a culture that prized proper burial. Every Israelite expected to be interred, in one of three places, their capital city (e.g. Isa. 22.16), the family tomb or the common burial field (2 Kgs 23.6). Not to receive a proper burial was a recognized curse (1 Kgs 13.22; see also Deut. 28.26; 1 Kgs 14.11 and Jer. 16.4). The execution in Lev. 21.9 means that the young woman cannot be given a proper burial and marks her as an accursed object.

'Burning the body' also meant charring the bones. This excited particular horror in ancient Israel (e.g. 2 Kgs 23.16 and Amos 2.1). There is a thematic contrast in 1 Kgs 13.1-31 between the dishonourable 'burning of bones' (1 Kgs 13.2) and the honourable preservation of a dead body through burial (1 Kgs 13.31). In contrast to the former, the latter involves no violence to the body after death (cf. 1 Kgs 13.28 where the lion does not maul the dead body of the prophet). Burning the body maximized the humiliation and punishment of the deceased and added infamy to death. The seriousness of burning bones may lie in the idea that an individual's identity was never wholly lost as long as the bones or significant portions thereof were safely conserved, hence the practice of ossilegium (secondary burial of bones).[5] 1 Sam. 31.11-13, which describes the immolation of Saul and his sons, is the exception that proves the rule. Indeed, 1 Sam. 31.13 is careful to record that the bones were preserved and given a proper burial. There is some suggestion of a belief that a felicitous condition in the after-

---

4. H.H. Cohn, 'The Penology of the Talmud', *ILR* 5 (1970), pp. 53-74 (59).
5. Frost, 'Memorial', p. 438.

124   *The Signs of Sin*

life depended on the proper preservation of remains.[6] Interestingly, the Rabbis developed a method of burning the offender that left the body intact, hence the practice of strangling the convict and throwing a burning wick into his mouth to burn the intestines.[7] It was a form of 'death by fire' that did not involve mutilating the body.

The ideological structure of Leviticus made it especially serious to burn the body of a priest's daughter. Here, holiness is 'wholeness' and is symbolized by physical perfection. There is a polarity between the 'whole' and the 'defective'. Only priests free from bodily defects were allowed to serve YHWH at the altar (Lev. 21.17-21) because 'only the perfect witnessed to the holy'.[8] Neither the priests (Lev. 21.5-6) nor the ordinary Israelites (Lev. 19.27-28) are allowed to deface their bodies. Reducing the body of the priest's daughter to ashes relocates her at the opposite end of the holiness spectrum. It symbolizes the fact that she has deprived herself of 'holiness' by 'profaning herself' (Lev. 21.9).

4.1.3 *Fire in Ancient Israel*

Fire is a multivalent symbol in ancient Israel because it is both destructive and beneficial. Fire is widely used in the Bible to destroy[9] and thus it is a sign of total destruction.[10] Yet fire also purifies. The process of refining metals in a furnace is a symbol of cleansing judgment.[11] This duality is

---

6. E.g. Brichto, 'Kin, Cult, Land', pp. 4-5, 35-38; J.J. Niehaus, 'Amos', in T.E. McComiskey (ed.), *The Minor Prophets: An Exegetical and Expository Commentary*. I. *Hosea, Joel and Amos* (Grand Rapids: Baker Book House, 1992), pp. 315-494 (358).
7. *M. Sanh.* 7.2.
8. J.E. Hartley, *Leviticus* (Dallas: Word Books, 1992), p. lx.
9. E.g. Exod. 32.20, Deut. 7.5, 7.25 (idols), Deut. 12.3 (Asherim), Josh. 11.6, 11.9 (chariots) and Josh. 6.24, Judg. 18.27 (cities).
10. E.g. Isa. 66.15-16. Fire typifies 'YHWH in action' (e.g. Ps. 50.3; Isa. 31.9). The fire that comes from before YHWH to consume the sacrifices (Lev. 9.24) is possibly the reason why YHWH as a judge of sin is described as a 'consuming fire' (Deut. 4.24). Fire from YHWH devours Nadab and Abihu (Lev. 10.2), 250 men in the 'sons of Korah' incident (Num. 16.35), the 'murmurers' of Taberah (Num. 11.1) as well as the two captains and their armies who confront Elijah (2 Kgs 1.10, 12 and 14). Deut. 29.22 attributes the upheaval of Sodom and Gomorrah to YHWH's anger whilst Amos threatens a whole series of nations with divine destruction by fire (Amos 1.4, 7, 10, 12, 14; 2.2, 5). Cf. Rev. 18.7-9 for an association between 'playing the prostitute,' 'divine punishment' and 'burning'.
11. E.g. Isa. 1.25; Jer. 6.27-30, Ezek. 22.17-22, Mal. 3.2, Zech. 13.9, Ps. 66.10, Prov. 17.3. Cf. also the use of fire as a means of plague control in the aftermath of Baal Peor (Num. 31.21-23).

reflected in Lev. 21.9 where fire expresses both total destruction of the offender and the purification of the community. The priest's daughter is physically burned, unlike the commoner's daughter in Deut. 22.21. This is because of the greater degree of sanctity intrinsic in the priesthood.

Within the general symbolic structure of the priestly sacrificial system, burning the priest's daughter recalls the burnt offering. This 'over-cooking' is the most radical and total form of sacrifice because there is no food left at the end of it. It signifies that the offering has been given to YHWH in its entirety.[12] From a priestly perspective, burning is a radical punishment. We might expect the punishment to have this semiotic significance because the priesthood were, basically, cooks who on this occasion are roasting one of the family.

The 'burning' strengthens the association between Lev. 21.9 and Deut. 22.20-21. In Deut. 22.21 the purpose of stoning is to 'purge the evil from the midst of you' (Deut. 22.21) where the verb translated 'purge' is the *piel* of בער (to 'burn' or 'consume'). The use of real fire in Lev. 21.9 signifies that the offence of the priest's daughter is more serious than that of a commoner and that a real burning and a more intensive purgation is required.

4.1.4. *Tamar: The Lady Not for Burning*

The punishment in Lev. 21.9 is similar to Gen. 38.24 in which Judah commands of Tamar, likewise under the stain of prostitution, 'Bring her out, and let her be burned'. If, as I argue, there is a relationship between the status of the priest's daughter and being burned by fire, why is Tamar who is not a priest's daughter burnt? Three possible answers can be given. Firstly, one can imagine cases where the law in Lev. 21.9 could be applied to non-priests. An offence committed by the daughter of another person of elevated rank (e.g. the daughter of a king) might be regarded as more serious than that committed by the daughter of an ordinary citizen. Tamar was the daughter-in-law of Judah, Abraham's grandson and a prominent tribal leader, and may have been singled out on these grounds as a special case. Secondly, the setting of the Tamar story precedes the period of the priesthood. The idea of being related to a prominent tribal leader may have been roughly equivalent to the later law of Lev. 21.9 regarding the priest's daughter. A third possibility may be that the reference to burning in Gen. 38.24 reflects local customary law.

---

12. M. Bal, *Death and Dissymmetry: The Politics of Coherence in the Book of Judges* (Chicago: University of Chicago Press, 1988), p. 97.

4.2. *Descriptive Registers in Leviticus 21.9*

In addition to describing these performative registers, Lev. 21.9 also contains a number of descriptive registers of seriousness. These include the ritual consequences of the offence.

4.2.1. *She 'Profanes Herself'*

Firstly, the daughter 'profanes herself (תחל) by playing the harlot' (Lev. 21.9). The reflexive *niphal* of the verb חלל ('to profane') means 'to pollute or to defile oneself'. This can occur either ritually or sexually. A priest can 'profane himself' (להחלו) by contact with dead bodies (Lev. 21.4) whilst the priest's daughter 'profanes herself' (תחל) by 'acting the prostitute' (Lev. 21.9). We may hypothesize that the cultic consequences to the girl who 'profanes herself' through prostitution are similar to the consequences suffered by the priest who 'profane[s] himself' through contact with a dead body. Both examples of 'profaning oneself' in Leviticus 21 relate to the priestly family, and suggest that 'profaning oneself' has something to do with the loss of cultic status.

This is strengthened when we consider that the word חל ('profane') is one of four common Priestly words that reflect the priest's 'graded' conception of the world, the others being קדש ('holy'), טהור ('clean') and טמא ('unclean').[13] The relationship between these key terms is indicated by Lev. 10.10, 'you [the priests] must distinguish between the holy (קדש) and the profane (חל), and between the unclean (טמא) and the clean (טהור)'. From this and other texts, it is clear that 'holy' and 'profane', 'clean' and 'unclean' are opposed pairs.[14] A strict parallelism between these terms might suggest that the pairs are equivalent in some respect (viz. 'holy = clean' and 'profane = unclean'). However, Jenson argues that this is inconsistent with the strong contrast in the Priestly texts between 'holiness' and 'impurity'.[15] It is preferable therefore to assume a chiastic structure to the parallelism in Lev. 10.10, viz. the words 'holy and clean' and 'profane and unclean' are aligned but not synonymous terms. To put it another way, holiness is akin to cleanness but strongly opposed to profanity and uncleanness. The result is a 'parallelogram' in which the vertical relationships between the pairs ('holy → profane' and 'unclean → clean') are more

---

13. Jenson, *Graduated Holiness*, p. 40.
14. Jenson, *Graduated Holiness*, p. 43.
15. Jenson, *Graduated Holiness*, p. 44.

4. *Prostitution and the Jealousy of God and Man* 127

strictly defined than the horizontal relationships ('holy → clean' and 'profane → unclean').

The 'holy' may be defined as that which belongs to the divine sphere. 'Holiness' is a relational term which means 'belonging' to God or 'consecrated' to God.[16] It applies to places, people, objects and times. A special act of YHWH is required to make an earthly thing or a person 'holy'. Lev. 21.9 is preceded by the words, 'I the LORD, who sanctify you, am holy' (Lev. 21.8). Jenson suggests that the 'holy/profane' pair represents (positively and negatively) the divine sphere. Consequently, 'holiness' and 'profanity' are respectively characterized by the subject's presence in or absence from the divine sphere.[17] The word חל is the opposite of קדש.[18] Activity described by the root חלל deprives someone or something of holiness.[19] The priest's daughter shares the objective holiness of her father.[20] When the priest's daughter 'plays the harlot' she no longer shares in this holy status and so 'profanes herself'. This is appropriate because it means she loses the cultic status she abused.

4.2.2. *She 'Profanes' her Father*

A second descriptive register is that the priest's daughter profanes (מחללת) her father (Lev. 21.9). The *piel* form of חלל means 'to defile or pollute something or someone else'. Examples of things that are ceremonially profaned in the Hebrew Bible (all in the *piel*) include: the Sabbath (Exod. 31.14), a holy thing of the LORD (Lev. 19.8), the Sanctuary (Lev. 21.12) and the 'holy things' (Lev. 22.15). In all of these cases the referent has some degree of holiness. The Name of YHWH is profaned when other nations cease to respect it as a result of Israel's misconduct (Lev. 18.21; 22.32; Ezek. 36.20; 36.21).

Sometimes an individual can be profaned as a result of another person's sexual wrongdoing. The prohibitions of Lev. 19.29 and Lev. 21.15 indicate, respectively, that an Israelite father is capable of 'profaning' his daughter whilst the high priest is likewise capable of 'profaning' his offspring. Else-

---

16. J. Joosten, *People and Land in the Holiness Code* (Leiden: E.J. Brill, 1996), pp. 123-24.
17. Jenson, *People and Land*, p. 55.
18. W. Dommershausen, חלל, in *TDOT*, IV, pp. 409-17 (416).
19. O.E. Collins, 'The stem *znh* and prostitution in the Hebrew Bible' (Unpublished PhD dissertation, Brandeis University, 1977), p. 174.
20. Cf. Lev. 22.13 which states that a widowed daughter who has no offspring may partake of the cultic offerings.

where חלל is only used in Gen. 49.4 to describe how Reuben 'profaned' his father's 'bed', which is thought to refer to Reuben's sleeping with his father's concubine (Gen. 35.22).[21] This indicates that חלל can refer to sexual defilement independently of cultic associations.

Either way, the underlying idea is that when an individual is 'profaned' his or her reputation is dishonoured. This is confirmed by the fact that the secondary meaning of חלל in the *piel* form is to dishonour or to violate the subject's honour. Examples of subjects include the crown of the Davidic kingdom (Ps. 89.39), the kingdom of Judah (Lam. 2.2), and Tyre (Isa. 23.9). In like manner the priest's daughter who becomes involved in cultic prostitution dishonours her father. She attacks the moral integrity and honour of the priestly family by making a laughing-stock of its leader and head (cf. *Sanh.* 52a, 'If he [the father] was regarded as holy, he is now regarded as profane; if he was treated with respect, he is now treated with contempt; and men say "Cursed is he who begot her, cursed be he who brought her up, cursed be he from whose loins she sprung"'). Significantly Lev. 21.9 immediately concludes a section in which the priests are exhorted to be holy (Lev. 21.1-9). Priests must be holy to YHWH and must not 'profane the name of their God' (Lev. 21.6). Similarly the priest's daughter is not to profane herself lest she 'profanes her father' (Lev. 21.9). There is some suggestion that the priest's relationship to his daughter is comparable to the relationship between YHWH and the priest, at least in terms of the capacity to profane.

Finally, there is also a significant parallel between Lev. 19.29 and Lev. 21.9. Lev. 19.29 envisages the situation where the father 'profanes' (תחלל) his daughter through harlotry (see further 4.2.3) whilst Lev. 21.9 envisages the case where the (priest's) daughter profanes (תחל) her father. Priests are not to profane their daughters and the daughters of priests are not to profane their fathers. Notably, parents' responsibilities towards their children (in Lev. 19.29) are stated before childrens' obligations towards their parents (Lev. 21.9). This recalls the case of rebellious son in Chapter 2 where the responsibilities of the father in relation to his son (Deut. 21.15-17) precede the son's responsibilities towards his parents (Deut. 21.18-21).

4.3. *Offence Description (Leviticus 21.9)*

Lev. 21.9 states that the priest's daughter is burnt for 'playing the harlot' (לזנות).

---

21. Dommershausen, חלל, p. 416.

4.3.1 'Playing the Harlot'

The word לזנות is the infinitive construct of the verb זנה. The basic meaning of the root expressed in the verb זנה is 'to engage in sexual relations outside of or apart from marriage', hence the primary definition of 'to commit fornication'.[22] Cognate usage exhibits a similarly broad meaning. As a general term for extramarital sexual intercourse, זנה is limited in its primary usage to female subjects since it is only for women that marriage is the primary determinant of legal status and obligation.[23] While male sexual activity is judged by the status of the female partner and is prohibited or penalized only when it violates the marital rights of another man, female sexual activity is judged according to the woman's marital status. זנה is a more general or inclusive term than נאף (to commit adultery).[24] זנה includes adultery (the violation of a husband's sexual rights) and the activity of the professional prostitute who has no husband nor sexual obligation to any other male. זנה is the usual verb for the activity of a prostitute,[25] who is even called a זונה. In Hebrew thought the prostitute is essentially a professional or habitual fornicator whose role and profession are defined by her sexual activity with men to whom she is not married.[26] זנה is commonly used as a metaphor to condemn Israel's 'affairs' with other gods.[27] For Israel to turn away from her covenant relationship with YHWH to idols is as illegitimate in the context of that relationship as it is for the woman who forsakes her husband to have intercourse with other men.

4.3.2. *Leviticus 21.9 and Cultic Prostitution*

Does the use of the verb זנה in relation to a priest's daughter in Lev. 21.9 imply cultic prostitution? To answer this, we must consider the prevalence of cultic prostitution in the ANE (4.3.2.1 below), the possible association of the verb זנה with cultic prostitution (4.3.2.2 below) and the possible significance of Lev. 19.29 (4.3.2.3 below).

---

22. P. Bird, 'To Play the Harlot', in Peggy L. Day (ed.), *Gender and Difference in Ancient Israel* (Minneapolis: Fortress Press, 1989), pp. 75-94 (76); S. Erlandsson, 'Zanah', in, *TDOT*, IV, pp. 99-104 (99).
23. Bird, 'To Play the Harlot', p. 77.
24. Bird, 'To Play the Harlot', p. 77.
25. E.g. Gen. 38.24; Hos. 2.5 [H. 2.7].
26. Bird, 'To Play the Harlot', p. 78.
27. The verb זנה is used of apostasy in Lev. 17.7, 20.5-6; Num. 14.33, 15.39, 25.1; Deut. 31.16; Judg. 2.17, 8.27, 8.33; 1 Chron. 5.25; 2 Chron. 21.11, 21.13; Pss. 73.27, 106.39; Erlandsson, 'Zanah', p. 99.

4.3.2.1. *Cultic Prostitution in ANE*. The belief that cultic prostitution was common in the ANE has been widely criticized in recent years on the ground that this belief is typically based on non-contemporary sources or ambiguous texts.[28] Consequently, '[there is] mounting hesitancy to claim clear, unambiguous testimony for the existence of sacred prostitution among several Near Eastern religions'.[29] Even Yamauchi, who contends that the practice was widespread, notes that whilst 'it is generally assumed that the worship of the major Ugaritic goddesses...involved sacred prostitution...there are no explicit texts which can prove this'[30] and 'the most explicit references to sacred prostitution in Syria and Phoenicia are to be found in later texts'.[31] The perhaps arbitrary translation of certain Akkadian terms as 'harlot', 'whore' and 'prostitute'[32] results in a higher percentage of the population being identified as secular or cultic prostitutes than may be justified.[33] Modern scholarship is characterized by a cautious approach which accepts that whilst prostitutes may have functioned at times in the cultic sphere and hierodules may have had functions involving sexual activity, the actual scope of their activities must be carefully determined according to the circumstances of each case.[34] The meaning of key terms such as זונה and קדשה remains a matter for debate although it is generally argued that neither refers to cultic prostitution. Bird argues that the word זונה ('prostitute') is associated with public squares, inns and highways and not with sanctuaries or cultic activity[35] and that the word קדשה ('consecrated woman')[36] simply denotes a cultic functionary and does not in itself

---

28. R.A. Oden Jr, *The Bible Without Theology: The Theological Tradition and Alternatives to it* (San Francisco: Harper & Row, 1987), pp. 131-53; B.A. Brooks, 'Fertility Cult Functionaries in the Old Testament', *JBL* 60 (1941), pp. 227-53; D.R. Hillers, 'Analyzing the Abominable: Our Understanding of Canaanite Religion', *JQR* 75 (1985), pp. 253-69; E.J. Fisher, 'Cultic Prostitution in the Ancient Near East?: A Reassessment', *BTB* 6 (1976), pp. 225-36.

29. Oden, *Bible Without Theology*, p. 140.

30. E.M. Yamauchi, 'Cultic Prostitution', in H.A. Hoffner Jr (ed.), *Orient and Occident* (Neukirchen–Vluyn: Neukirchener Verlag, 1973), pp. 213-22 (219).

31. Yamauchi, 'Cultic Prostitution', p. 219.

32. Brooks, 'Fertility Cult Functionaries', p. 231.

33. Brooks, 'Fertility Cult Functionaries'.

34. Bird, 'To Play the Harlot', p. 76.

35. Bird, 'To Play the Harlot', p. 87. Cf. Fisher, 'Cultic Prostitution', p. 231.

36. Brenner, 'Female Prostitution', p. 78; J.G. Westenholz, 'Tamar, *qedesa*, *qadistu* and Sacred Prostitution in Mesopotamia', *HTR* 82 (1989), pp. 245-65 (248).

imply sexual activity.³⁷ Gruber concurs that the biblical קדשה is not a cultic prostitute,³⁸ although she does take the view that she is a prostitute. Nor does Gruber find any Ugaritic evidence to date that *qadistu* or *qedesah* are cultic prostitutes.³⁹ No settled meaning has yet been found for the Akkadian *qadistu*. Gruber identifies a number of possible meanings for this term, including those of wetnurse, midwife, cultic singer, archivist and, in later times, a sorceress but not that of a prostitute, cultic or otherwise.⁴⁰ We may conclude that discovering unambiguous evidence for cultic prostitution in the Bible and the ANE remains quite difficult.⁴¹ Some scholars such as Westenholz and Frymer-Kensky go too far in claiming that 'there was no such institution as sacred prostitution in Mesopotamia'⁴² and that 'the whole idea of a sex cult—in Israel or in Canaan—is a chimera, the product of ancient and modern sexual fantasies'.⁴³ More balanced is Oden's maxim that 'whatever conduct can be imagined will, if it is socially feasible, be put into practice by some people somewhere and for some time'.⁴⁴ Since cultic prostitution puts no strain on the imaginations of peoples either ancient or modern we are justified in presuming that the institution did exist. However, the present lack of clear, unambiguous evidence in the ANE means that the details of this institution are a matter of conjecture.

4.3.2.2. *Cultic Prostitution in Leviticus 21.9?* Bird notes that neither the verb זנה nor the noun זונה in their primary uses refers to cultic activity or have cultic connotations. Hence, the normal context which one would assume for זנה/לזנות is non-cultic, unless there is evidence to the contrary. Yet there are some cases where the verb זנה is used in cultic contexts. Hos. 4.10, referring either to the children of the priest, or to the priests

---

37. Bird, 'To Play the Harlot', p. 87; Westenholz, 'Sacred Prostitution', p. 248. See also T. Binger, *Goddesses in Ugarit, Israel and the Old Testament* (JSOTSup, 232; Sheffield: Sheffield Academic Press, 1997), pp. 118-20.
38. M.I. Gruber, *The Motherhood of God and Other Studies* (Atlanta: Scholars Press, 1992), pp. 17-47.
39. Gruber, *Motherhood of God*, pp. 18-23.
40. Gruber, *Motherhood of God*, p. 42.
41. Oden, *Bible Without Theology*, p. 132.
42. Westenholz, 'Sacred Prostitution', p. 260.
43. T. Frymer-Kensky, *In the Wake of the Goddesses* (New York: The Free Press, 1992), p. 199.
44. Oden, *Bible Without Theology*, p. 153.

generally,⁴⁵ states 'they shall play the harlot (הזנו) but not multiply, because they have forsaken the LORD to cherish harlotry (זנות)'. It is thought that the prophet is here correcting an erroneous belief on the part of a corrupt priesthood that fertility could be secured by ritual intercourse. Cultic prostitution also seems to be in view in Hos. 4.13 and 4.14.⁴⁶ Andersen and Freedman suggest that the attention given to the behaviour of daughters and daughters-in-law in Hos. 4.13b-14a can be seen as more serious if they are all relatives of the priest.⁴⁷ Andersen and Freedman contend that the language of 4.14b makes it clear that 'promiscuity and sacrifice were part of a full-scale cult'.⁴⁸

The word לזנות occurs only five times in the Hebrew Bible (Lev. 20.5, 20.6, 21.9, Num. 25.1 and Deut. 22.21). In three of these cases (Lev. 20.5, 20.6 and Num. 25.1) it is used in a figurative sense to refer to apostasy. In Num. 25.1-2, the reference to prostitution appears to be actual as well as symbolic insofar as the syncretism includes sexual rites of pagan worship (cf. Num. 25.6-8 where the 'harlotry' is clearly sexual). The same combination in Num. 25.1-2 of eating, drinking, bowing down to foreign gods and sexual activity is seen in Exod. 32.6 where the expression 'rose up to play' almost certainly refers to sexual cultic rites. It is possible that the references to לזנות in Lev. 20.5 and Lev. 20.6 may also refer to cultic prostitution. A parallel text to Lev. 20.5 (Lev. 18.21) which refers to the cult of Molech occurs in the context of illicit sexual intercourse (Lev. 18.1-30). The reference to 'wizards' in Lev. 20.6 suggests sexual rites in this text because of the association between sorcery and the זונה (Nah. 3.4).⁴⁹

It is possible, therefore, that the prostitution (לזנות) in Lev. 20.5, 20.6 and Num. 25.1 takes place in a cultic setting. The question is whether the prostitution in Lev. 21.9 (also described as לזנות) also takes place in a cultic setting.

The literary context of Lev. 21.9 certainly suggests that it is possible. Lev. 21.1-9 begins with the command that priests shall not defile themselves 'for the dead' (Lev. 21.1) whilst Lev. 21.5 forbids cultic practices

45. F.I. Andersen and D.N. Freedman *Hosea* (AB; New York: Doubleday, 1980), p. 362.
46. Andersen and Freedman, *Hosea*, p. 369.
47. Andersen and Freedman, *Hosea*, p. 370.
48. Andersen and Freedman, *Hosea*, p. 370.
49. For the possible relationship between sorcery and sexual rites see Isa. 57.3 which occurs in a larger context replete with cultic imagery, see Isa. 57.5-9.

4. Prostitution and the Jealousy of God and Man

associated with the cult of the dead, such as shaving a bald spot on the head, disfiguring the edge of the beard and lacerating the skin. This is significant for our understanding of Lev. 21.9 because there is a link between the cult of the dead and certain fertility rites. This is supported by the biblical memory of Baal Peor as preserved in Ps. 106.28: 'Then they [the wilderness generation] attached themselves to the Baal of Peor, and ate sacrifices offered to the dead'. We know from elsewhere that the Baal Peor incident involved wrongful sexual intercourse on the part of the Israelites (cf. Num. 25.6-8). Clearly, if Lev. 21.9 does take place in a cultic setting, it is an additional aspect of seriousness (see 4.4.3 below).

4.3.2.3. *The Typical Case Envisaged by Leviticus 19.29.*
Lev. 19.29 is a prohibition on forcing daughters into prostitution,

> Do not profane your daughter by making her a harlot (להזנותה) lest the land fall into harlotry and the land become full of wickedness.

The *hiphil* of זנה means 'to force into prostitution'. The addressees are the כל־עדת בני־ישראל (Lev. 19.2) from which we may conclude that the ban is directed at Israelite fathers.[50] The practice is discouraged on the ground that prostitution will spread throughout the country. Unlike other ANE texts (see below), no sanctions are stated in Lev. 19.2 for the father who disobeys.

The practice of parents (usually fathers) putting their daughters 'out to work' as prostitutes was known in the ANE and is recorded in a small number of legal documents.[51] The earliest example is thought to be a Sumerian text from the reign of Rim-Sin of Larsa (c. 1822–1763 BCE) which indicates that natural parents had the right to agree that their daughter would work as a prostitute for an adoptive mother.[52] Another text (AASOR 16 51) takes the form of a royal proclamation addressed to palace staff at Nuzi. This forbids fathers from making prostitutes of their daughters without permission from the king.[53] If the father violated this order, another daughter would be taken from him and added to the palace staff and the father would pay a fine. The proclamation implies that a Nuzi

---

50. For a discussion of the identity of the כל־עדת בני־ישראל, see 5.2.2 below.
51. J. Fleishman, 'Father's Authority to Prostitute his Daughter in Mesopotamian and Biblical Law' (Paper delivered at 1998 Conference of the Jewish Law Association in Ramat Rahel, Israel).
52. Fleishman, 'Father's Authority', pp. 2-3.
53. Fleishman, 'Father's Authority', pp. 4-5.

father who was not a 'servant of the palace' or one of the 'people of the house' was allowed to prostitute his daughter.

Lev. 19.29 has some bearing on our understanding of seriousness of offence in Lev. 21.9 and Deut. 22.13-21 because it may help us to explain why the daughter's sexual behaviour reflects badly upon her father. In Lev. 21.9 her behaviour 'profanes' her father whilst in Deut. 22.21 the execution is held at the father's front door. Why in both cases does her sexual behaviour affect her father? The conventional reason is that the father has a duty to guard his daughter from sexual access by other males. This may well be true for the priest in Lev. 21.9 but we shall see that this reasoning is unsatisfactory for the father in Deut. 22.13-21. Lev. 19.29 suggests an alternative explanation for both Lev. 21.9 and Deut. 22.13-21: the father is blamed for his daughter's prostitution because he put her out to work in the first place.

One final question is whether the typical case of fathers putting their daughters out to prostitution refers to cultic prostitution or to secular prostitution. Lev. 19.29 does not explicitly refer to either. However, the literary context suggests that cultic prostitution may again be in view. Lev. 19.26-31 refers to augury and witchcraft (v. 26), the cult of the dead (vv. 27-28), the need for proper cultic worship (v. 30) and to mediums and wizards (v. 31). We cannot be certain that the paradigm case of Lev. 19.29 is cultic but if so it is, again, an additional element of seriousness (see 4.4.3 below).

4.3.3 *Summary*
To sum up, the verb זנה in Lev. 21.9 typifies prostitution. The literary context of Lev. 21.9 and the paradigm case of Lev. 19.29 suggest that the additional element of cultic prostitution may be in view, although we cannot be certain.

4.4. *Seriousness of Offence*

4.4.1. *Status*
A key element of seriousness is the daughter's abuse of her cultic status. As we noted in 4.2.1 and 4.2.2 above, the consequences of her abuse are that she 'profanes' both herself and her father (Lev. 21.9). In contrast to the commoner's offence in Deut. 22.20-21, which relies on the fact that the offence was committed whilst she was betrothed, no reference is made in Lev. 21.9 to the marital status of the priest's daughter. She is guilty

whether she is betrothed or not. This confirms that in Lev. 21.9 her status as a member of the priestly family is the key factor in determining seriousness of offence.

4.4.2. *Location*
The location of the priestly families during the wilderness wanderings may also be relevant to seriousness of offence in Lev. 21.9. Num. 3.38 states that during this period the priestly family protected the Tabernacle on its eastern side whilst the Levites threw a protective cordon around the other three sides (Num. 3.23, 3.29 and 3.33). The priestly family was located at the eastern side because this was holiest flank of the Tabernacle.[54] The daughter's offence could have been committed somewhere within the priestly encampment and thus not far from the entrance to the Tabernacle itself. Even if her offence is committed in some other location, her return to the priestly encampment inevitably brings the profane into close proximity to the holy. This is a serious matter because moral impurity, as well as ritual impurity, defiles the Sanctuary (Lev. 20.3, Ezek. 5.11).[55]

4.4.3. *Imitating Pagan Practices*
We noted the likelihood that the priest's daughter was engaged in cultic prostitution at 4.2.4 above. If this is correct, it adds a further dimension to seriousness of offence. Cultic prostitution was a serious offence for any Israelite. Deut. 23.17 excluded not only fertility rites from the worship of YHWH but also the involvement of Israelites as cult prostitutes at Canaanite shrines.[56] Since priestly families bore primary responsibility for maintaining Israel's cultic identity (e.g. Lev. 10.10-11), it was a particularly serious matter for a priest's daughter to be involved.

4.5. *Performative Registers in Deuteronomy 22.20-21*

Turning to Deut. 22.20-21, the performative registers are as follows. Firstly, the young woman is brought out to the door of her father's house to be executed (Deut. 22.21). This location is unique for an execution in the Hebrew Bible. Secondly, the young woman is stoned to death by the men of her city (Deut. 22.21). Stoning is a more common and less serious

---

54. See Chapter 6, below.
55. J. Klawans, 'The Impurity of Immorality in Ancient Judaism', *JJS* 48 (1997), pp. 1-16 (3).
56. Collins, 'Prostitution in the Hebrew Bible', p. 89.

4.6. Descriptive Registers in Deuteronomy 22.20-21

In Deut. 22.20-21 descriptive registers include the statement that the daughter has 'wrought folly in Israel' (נבלה בישראל) by playing the harlot (Deut. 22.21). The legal idiom 'X did נבלה בישראל' appears in six texts.[59] For Driver, נבלה signifies moral and religious insensibility[60] whilst for Phillips נבלה signifies the 'extreme gravity' of an offence.[61] It is an act of crass disorder or unruliness that breaks up relationships at every level, including relationships with YHWH, between tribes, within the family, in marriage and in business.[62] The stem נבל is associated with ruin and deterioration[63] and thus נבלה can mean an act that is destructive or degrading. In Deut. 22.21, נבלה emphasizes the degrading, destructive aspect of the woman's prostitution. It also has overtones of disgrace, dishonour and contempt and signifies moral insensitivity (cf. 2 Sam 13.12-13, Prov. 17.21). The stem נבל occurs with the stem זנה in several other texts (Hos. 2.5-12 [H. 2.7-14] and Nah. 3.4-7). Several contextual elements in these passages emphasize the degrading nature of prostitution (Hos. 2.5 [H. 2.7]; 2.10 [H. 2.12]; Nah. 3.4, 6) and are consistent with the use of נבלה in Deut. 22.21. The reference to the woman 'degrading herself' through

---

57. There is only one other case where נבלה is visited with capital punishment, Josh. 7.15 (4.1.1.2 above). However, there are several examples in which נבלה results in death. These include the forcible intercourse of Shechem (Gen. 34.7), resulting in the events of Gen. 34.25-26, and that of Amnon (2 Sam. 13.12), resulting in the events of 2 Sam. 13.28-29, the behaviour of the men of Gibeah (Judg. 19.23-24, 20.6) which culminated in the near-massacre of the tribe of Benjamin (Judg. 20.46) and the punishment meted out to the false prophets Ahab and Zedekiah (Jer. 29.21-23).

58. Pedersen, *Israel*, p. 428 and Ludwig Köhler, *Hebrew Man* (London: SCM Press, 1956), p. 112.

59. Gen. 34.7; Deut. 22.21; Josh. 7.15; Judg. 20.6, 10; 2 Sam. 13.12 and Jer. 29.23.

60. S.R. Driver, *A Critical and Exegetical Commentary on Deuteronomy* (Edinburgh: T. & T. Clark, 1895), p. 256.

61. A. Phillips, 'Nebalah—a term for serious disorderly and unruly conduct', *VT* 25 (1975), pp. 237-42 (242).

62. Phillips, 'Nebalah', p. 239.

63. Collins, 'Prostitution in the Hebrew Bible', pp. 162, 166.

---

form of capital punishment than 'burning'.[57] The body is marred though not to the same degree as that of the priest's daughter in Lev. 21.9. Subsequent burial is also possible, although some scholars claim that stoning prevents the victim from being interred in the family tomb.[58]

harlotry in Deut. 22.21 is comparable to the statement in Lev. 21.9 that the priest's daughter 'profanes herself'. A final descriptive register in Deut. 22.20-21 is the purpose of the execution, 'so shall you purge the evil from the midst of you' (Deut. 22.21). Elements of this formula occur a number of times in *Deuteronomy*[64] and the formula also appears in two cases of נבלה (Deut. 22.21 and Judg. 20.13). The 'evil' in Deut. 22.21 refers specifically back to Deut. 22.14, where the husband brings an 'evil name' upon his wife. If the charge is true (Deut. 22.20) it follows that evil is in their midst and it is this evil that must be 'purged'.

4.7. *Offence Description (Deuteronomy 22.20-21)*

The offence described in Deut. 22.20-21 is subsidiary to the main case described in Deut. 22.13-19. The death penalty in Deut. 22.21 cannot be taken independently from the context of Deut. 22.13-19 because the opening of Deut. 22.20 ('But if the thing is true') refers back to the accusation brought in Deut. 22.14. Therefore to understand 'seriousness of offence' in Deut. 22.20-21 we must first reconstruct the paradigm case of Deut. 22.13-21.

The traditional view of the girl's offence in Deut. 22.20-21 is that she lost her virginity before her wedding-night. This is the view held by the overwhelming majority of scholars.[65] However, I shall argue in this section that the traditional view is mistaken. I shall begin by noting a number of problems with the traditional approach (4.7.1) before outlining an alternative approach to Deut. 22.13-21 (4.7.2) and a reconstruction of the paradigm case of Deut. 22.13-21 (4.7.3).

---

64. Deut. 17.12, 21.21, 22.22, 22.24 and 24.7.

65. Most recently expressed by P.O.C. Mullins, 'The Status of Women in Family Life: A Comparative Study of Old Testament Times', *Milltown Studies* 41 (1998), pp. 51-81 (59). Other proponents include C. Pressler, 'Sexual Violence and Deuteronomic Law', in A. Brenner (ed.), *A Feminist Companion to Exodus to Deuteronomy* (Sheffield: Sheffield Academic Press, 1994), pp. 102-112 (30) (Deut. 22.20-21 makes 'entering into a first marriage as a non-virgin' a capital offence); J. Plaskow, *Standing again at Sinai: Judaism from a Feminist Perspective* (Harper: San Francisco, 1991), p. 4; A. Rofé, 'Methodological Aspects of the Study of Biblical Law', in B.S. Jackson (ed.), *Jewish Law Association Studies II: The Jerusalem Conference Volume* (Atlanta: Scholars Press, 1986), pp. 1-16 (3-4) and T. Frymer-Kensky, 'Virginity in the Bible', in V.H. Matthews *et al.* (eds.), *Gender and Law in the Hebrew Bible and the Ancient Near East* (JSOTSup, 262; Sheffield: Sheffield Academic Press, 1998), pp. 79-96.

4.7.1. *Problems with the Traditional Approach*

The first problem is that the traditional interpretation conflicts with the wider literary structure of Deut. 22.13-29. Deut. 22.20-21 is the second of a series of six highly structured cases spanning Deut. 22.13-29 (see Figure 1).[66]

Figure 1. *Summary of cases presented in Deuteronomy 22.13-29*

Case no.	Verse(s)	Status of woman	Punishment (if any)	Execution site
Case 1	22.13-19	Married (presumably following betrothal)	Damages (100 shekels) No divorce	N/A
Case 2 [subsidiary to 1]	22.20-21	Married (presumably following betrothal)	Woman executed	At door of father's house
Case 3	22.22	Married	Man and woman executed	No location specified
Case 4 [Relations in town]	22.23-24	Betrothed בתולה (consents to intercourse)	Man and woman executed. Man said to have 'violated his neighbour's wife'	At city gate
Case 5 [Relations in open country]	22.25-27	Betrothed בתולה (raped)	Man executed Woman exempted	No location specified
Case 6	22.28-29	Unbetrothed בתולה (raped)	Damages (50 shekels) No divorce	N/A

All the laws in Deut. 22.13-29 contain the variable of marital status.[67] Deut. 22.13-21 concerns the behaviour of a בתולה whilst betrothed.[68] The

66. Pressler, 'Sexual Violence', p. 106; Wenham and McConville, 'Drafting Techniques', p. 250.

67. Pressler, 'Sexual Violence', pp. 106-107; Wenham and McConville, 'Drafting Techniques', p. 249.

68. Deut. 22.13 refers to a marriage and we are entitled to presume that this followed a period of betrothal, or inchoate marriage. Betrothal establishes the groom's exclusive claim over the bride, and it is normally enacted by the payment of bride-wealth. Upon betrothal, the woman is called the groom's אשה ('wife', cf. Deut. 22.24 where the third party who has relations with a betrothed בתולה is said to have 'violated his neighbour's wife'). Although the couple are not allowed to cohabit until the marriage proper, sexual intercourse with third parties is a capital offence (Deut. 22.23-27). The standard length of the engagement in ancient Israel cannot be ascertained (1 Sam. 18.17-19, 26-27) although later Jewish tradition held that there was customarily a twelve-month gap between betrothal and marriage.

4. *Prostitution and the Jealousy of God and Man*

traditional approach assumes that the law is concerned with the betrothed woman's premarital virginity. But the literary structure of Deut. 22.13-29 suggests that the primary concern of Deut. 22.13-21 is not whether the girl was a virgin at the time of the offence but whether she was betrothed. The traditional view implies that *any* intercourse by an unmarried woman is capital. But there is no penalty in biblical law for the unbetrothed girl who engages in consensual relations (Exod. 22.16-17; [H. 22.15-16]). The reason why consensual relations are capital in Deut. 22.13-21 but not in Exod. 22.16-17 is because the בתולה is ארשׂה ('betrothed') in Deut. 22.20-21 whereas in Exod. 22.16-17 the בתולה is not ארשׂה. This signals that the girl's offence in Deut. 22.20-21 is to have had intercourse *during the period of betrothal*.[69] This makes her offence one of quasi-adultery. It is marital status, not virginity, which defines 'seriousness' in Deut. 22.20-21. This is not surprising. Biblical law and biblical narrative repeatedly cast the seriousness of female sexual offending in terms of how it affects male sexual privileges.[70] The same is true of other laws in the ANE. Marital status is central to the cuneiform adultery laws (e.g. MAL A.14 where a key issue is whether the male adulterer knew of the woman's marital status).[71]

A second and related problem for the traditional view is the argument that בתולה refers to 'virgin'[72] and that the בתולים or 'tokens of virginity' are the evidence of a perforated hymen on the wedding-night.[73] Wenham notes that none of the cognate terms used in other Semitic languages have the meaning of 'virgin'[74] and that only when the word בתולה is qualified

---

69. Contra Rofé, 'Methodological Aspects', p. 3 who claims that Deut. 22.20-21 contradicts other family laws in Deuteronomy by not distinguishing between the status of betrothed and unbetrothed girls. But Deut. 22.20-21 *does* distinguish between being 'betrothed' and 'unbetrothed'.

70. K. Stone, *Sex, Honor, and Power in the Deuteronomistic History* (JSOTSup, 234; Sheffield: Sheffield Academic Press, 1996), *passim*.

71. Roth, *Law Collections*, p. 158.

72. T. Wadsworth, 'Is There a Hebrew Word for Virgin? *Bethulah* in the Old Testament', *ResQ* 23 (1980), pp. 161-71; C. Locher, *Die Ehre einer Frau in Israel* (Göttingen: Vandenhock & Ruprecht, 1986); Stone, *Sex, Honor*, p. 108; Carolyn S. Leeb, *Away from the Father's House: The Social Location of na'ar and na'arah in Ancient Israel* (JSOTSup, 301; Sheffield: Sheffield Academic Press, 2000), p. 43; Frymer-Kensky, 'Virginity', pp. 93-95; Matthews, 'Honor and Shame', pp. 108-11; Boose, 'Father's House, p. 66.

73. E.g. Tigay, *Deuteronomy*, p. 203.

74. Gordon J. Wenham, '*Betulah*: A Girl of Marriageable Age', *VT* 22 (1972), pp. 326-48 (326-29).

by the phrase 'whom no man has known' (e.g. Gen. 24.16, Num. 31.18, Judg. 11.37-39) can we be sure that the primary reference is to a *virgo intacta*. Even here, notes Hugenberger, '[such expressions] may have less to do with a claim to technical virginity than with the more public and observable fact that such a woman had not yet experienced the consummation of a marriage'.[75] A case in point is Num. 31.17, where Israelite soldiers are commanded to kill 'every woman who has known a man'. For Laffey this implies the superiority of the 'unused female sexual partner'[76] but as Hugenberger rhetorically points out, 'How were the Israelite soldiers to check for the requisite virginity? By impromptu medical examinations?'[77] Rather, the phrase stands by synecdoche for marital status and not for technical virginity. The meaning of בתולה must be determined by context and we shall see in 4.7.2 below that the alternative meaning of 'menstruant' is preferred. Pressler contends that בתולה means 'virgin' in Deut. 22.13-21 because 'words often acquire technical meanings when used in a legal context'. Indeed they do in *modern* legal contexts (cf. the legal meaning of the word 'assault') but to assume that they did so in ancient Israel is to assume the very point at issue. Pressler assumes a 'semantic' and 'legislative' approach to the meaning of בתולה but I shall argue that Deut. 22.13-21 is better served by a narrative approach (see 4.3.2 below).

In similar vein, doubt may be cast on the traditional view that the word בתולים refers to the evidence of a broken hymen and that the שמלה ('garment', Deut. 22.17) refers to the bed linen used on the wedding-night. These readings are problematic and raise the question of how the parents obtain the evidence (do they do service washes?). Matthews has recently proposed that there existed a 'ritual of examination' on the wedding-night that required the bridegroom, or perhaps an objective witness such as a midwife, to present the physical evidence to the in-laws.[78] But this is implausible because as Wenham points out, the garment in Deut. 22.21 is such that 'the husband is prepared to gamble very heavily that the girl's parents cannot produce it'.[79] If the שמלה are the bed sheets, no one knows better than the husband whether or not they are stained with the בתולים. If they are stained there is no point in the husband bringing an accusation.

---

75. G.P. Hugenberger, *Marriage as a Covenant* (Leiden: E.J. Brill, 1994), p. 263.
76. A.L. Laffey, *Wives, Harlots and Concubines: The Old Testament in Feminist Perspective* (Phiadelphia: Fortress Press, 1988), p. 18.
77. Hugenberger, *Marriage as a Covenant*, p. 263.
78. Matthews, 'Honor and Shame', p. 109.
79. Wenham, '*Betulah*', p. 334.

4. *Prostitution and the Jealousy of God and Man* 141

He knows in advance that his parents-in-law can produce the evidence (Deut. 22.17), that he will be proved wrong and that he will be punished (Deut. 22.18-19). Wadsworth argues that the law legislates for the stupid husband who knows that his parents-in-law can produce the evidence but gives his wife an 'evil name' anyway. 'The law must still grant the possibility that he might do it and be wrong and then punish him for it.'[80] However, it still remains unlikely that a husband who had inside knowledge would willingly choose the punishment of Deut. 22.18-19. It is simply not a convincing reading of Deut. 22.13-19. For this reason, I seek an alternative approach to Deut. 22.13-19 that makes better sense of the husband's actions.

The traditional reading also suffers from the additional problem that not all virgins have intact hymens or bleed the first time they have sexual relations.[81] On the traditional view, a girl who is genuinely a virgin but is, for whatever reason, *sans* בתולים could be executed. It could be argued that the 'virgin who fails to bleed' is an exceptional case and that the law is only concerned with 'typical' cases. But that is not a convincing argument here because, unlike other texts which stress the role of witnesses in capital cases (Deut. 17.6-7), the determining factor in Deut. 22.13-21 is the physical evidence of the שמלה. Whatever the שמלה is, it must be able to distinguish between virgins who bleed on their wedding night and those who do not. Otto recently admitted that 'the evidence of the garment does not really prove adultery during an inchoate marriage',[82] but goes on to claim that the redactor simply 'put up with these inconsistencies'.[83] But rather than brush the argument aside, a more satisfactory approach would be to reconsider the nature of the evidence. I shall advance a reading of the בתולים and the שמלה at 4.7.2 below that does not risk executing the virgin who is *sans* בתולים.

A final problem for the traditional view concerns the location of the offence. Figure 1 shows that in the literary unit of Deut. 22.13-29 there are two cases of a בתולה who has consensual relations whilst betrothed (Deut. 22.20-21 and Deut. 22.23-24). Both are stoned to death but the execution site differs. The literary structure of Deut. 22.13-29 signifies that this contrast is highly significant because these are the only offences for which a

---

80. Wadsworth, 'Virgin', p. 165.
81. Tigay, Jeffrey H., 'Examination of the Accused Bride in 4Q159: Forensic Medicine at Qumran', *JANESCU* 22 (1993), pp. 129-134 (129-30).
82. Otto, 'False Weights', p. 137.
83. Otto, 'False Weights', p. 137.

location is specified (see Figure 1). The first betrothed בתולה is stoned at the entrance to her father's house[84] (Deut. 22.20-21) whilst the second betrothed בתולה is stoned at the entrance to her city (Deut. 22.23-24). The city gate is the normal place of execution in Deuteronomy (e.g. Deut. 17.5, Deut. 22.24 and implied in Deut. 21.18-21) whereas the location in Deut. 22.20-21 is unparalleled in biblical law. Both girls are betrothed and commit similar offences (consensual intercourse) so why are they executed in different places? This significant difference is overlooked by commentators.[85] The traditional approach states that the execution at the door of the father's house signifies the father's responsibility to ensure his daughter's virginity prior to marriage.[86] However, this cannot be correct. If it is true that fathers have a *general* duty to guard their daughters until they are married then the same reasoning must apply to the father of the betrothed girl in Deut. 22.23-24. Yet she is executed at the city gate and there is no suggestion that her father has failed in his duty. Leeb, an exponent of the traditional view,[87] claims that no mention is made of the father in Deut. 22.23-24 because 'she was not under his supervision when the event occurred'.[88] But this is precisely the argument that is used to blame the father in Deut. 22.20-21 (i.e. 'he didn't supervise her properly')! On this view there is no difference between the father's 'failure' in Deut. 22.13-21 and Deut. 22.23-24. One is as irresponsible as the other. I shall argue at 4.7.2 below that the location does indeed blame the father but for a reason *other* than failing to protect his daughter's virginity.

---

84. Deut. 22.21 presumably envisages the 'doorway' of the standard house (L.E. Stager, 'The Archaeology of the Family in Ancient Israel', *BASOR* 260 [1985], pp. 1-36 [11]), or the main entrance to a multiple family compound (Stager, 'Archaeology of the Family', p. 18).

85. E.g. Craigie, *Deuteronomy*; Pressler, 'Sexual Violence'; and Wright, *Deuteronomy*. Phillips, *Ancient Israel's Criminal Law*, p. 116 suggests that this location 'dramatised the offence as against family institutional law' but there are any number of offences against 'family institutional law' that are not punished at the door of the father's house. Frymer-Kensky, 'Virginity', p. 95 mistakenly highlights the significance of stoning ('an offence against hierarchy', cf. the critique of Finkelstein at 1.4.2) but overlooks the significance of the location.

86. Cf. Collins, 'Prostitution in the Hebrew Bible', p. 116; W.W. Hallo, 'The Slandered Bride', in *Studies Presented to A. Leo Oppenheim* (Chicago: University of Chicago Press, 1964), pp. 95-105 (102).

87. Leeb, *Father's House*, p. 144.

88. Leeb, *Father's House*, p. 144.

4.7.2. *An Alternative Approach to Deuteronomy 22.13-21*

We begin with an alternative approach to the meaning of בתולים and בתולה. Wenham has argued that בתולים is a regular Hebrew form for abstract nouns designating age groups[89] and that it therefore refers to 'tokens of adolescence' (i.e. menstruation) rather than 'tokens of virginity'.[90] Cognate evidence confirms that the term refers to an age-group approximately equivalent to the English term 'adolescent' but applied specifically to females. It does not mean virginity per se, it simply acknowledges the onset of puberty and therefore the potential to bear children. From this Wenham infers that בתולה means a girl of marriageable age who may or may not be a virgin.[91] She is a girl who has come of age, that is, a menstruant. Wenham's approach is followed by Day who proposes that a woman could be described as a בתולה until the birth of her first child. Hence there could be a married בתולה.[92] This is persuasive because if entry to the age group is marked by menarche and the potential to bear children, it is logical to suppose that the exit is reached when that potential has been reached. בתולה thus describes the transitional phase between childhood and being fully and demonstrably a woman by virtue of giving birth.[93] This means that the next 'normal' change in a female's social status in ancient Israel is from menstruant to motherhood and not marriage or first intercourse. If בתולים refers to menstruation, then the husband's complaint ('I did not find בתולים in her', Deut. 22.13) is that his wife showed no signs of menstruation in the month following marriage.[94] This failure could be due to her conceiving on the wedding-night but it may also be due to her 'playing the harlot' prior to the marriage. Deut. 22.13-21 is

---

89. Wenham, *'Betulah'*, p. 331.
90. Wenham, *'Betulah'*, p. 331.
91. Wenham, *'Betulah'*, p. 326; J.J. Schmitt, 'Virgin', in *ABD*, pp. 853-54 (853).
92. Day, P. L. 'Why is Anat a Warrior and Hunter?', in D. Jobling *et al.* (eds.), *The Bible and the Politics of Exegesis: Essays in Honour of Norman K. Gottwald on his Sixty-Fifth Birthday* (Cleveland, OH: The Pilgrim Press, 1991), pp. 141-46 (144-45).
93. It is important to recognize that menstruation in ancient Israel would have been a very different social experience to that of modern Western women. Menstruation today is largely a product of contraception and of an increase in the childbearing years with the result that the average healthy woman now spends a total of nearly seven years menstruating. Menstruation would have been less frequent in ancient Israel, owing to a combination of factors, including the fact the woman spent her years between the onset of menses and the menopause either pregnant or breast-feeding (which delays the return of the menses), Gruber, *Motherhood of God*, p. 67.
94. Wenham, *'Betulah'*, p. 334.

concerned with the paternity of an unexpected pregnancy that occurs immediately after marriage. Behind Deuteronomy 22 is the husband's concern regarding the child's paternity. Paternity, unlike maternity, is not self-evident. The בתולים are not so much tokens of virginity as a pregnancy test.[95] There is perhaps a parallel here with Gen. 38.24 where Tamar's pregnancy is also the evidence of her having 'played the harlot' (זנתה). The issue is not whether the girl is a virgin but whether she is already pregnant.

There is an example of menstruation being used as a 'pregnancy' test elsewhere in Deuteronomy, although this is not cited by Wenham. This is the case of the war captive maid in Deut. 21.10-14. The text asserts that the waiting period before the man assumes sexual access to the woman is 'a full month' (ירח ימים, Deut. 21.13). One might have expected a shorter mourning period of perhaps seven days (e.g. Gen. 50.10, 1 Sam. 31.13, 1 Chron. 10.12). In addition, why is the period 'a full month' as opposed to, say, a thirty-day mourning period (שלשים יום, Num. 20.29, Deut. 34.8)? Washington suggests that an obvious solution is that waiting 'a full month' is long enough for the woman's menstrual cycle to be completed[96] and means the man can be assured of the paternity of any children resulting from intercourse. This is important since the woman is a non-Israelite, probably not a virgin and possibly the wife of another man among the defeated enemy. The purpose of the law is not therefore to give adequate time for mourning but rather to prevent the man from engaging in intercourse until it is clear that the woman is not pregnant. As with Deut. 22.13-21, the purpose of the law is to ensure his claim to paternity. Significantly, there is a parallel between Deut. 21.10-14 ('taking' the woman [21.11], 'going into her' [21.13] and 'taking no delight in her' [21.14]) and Deut. 22.13 ('taking a wife', 'going into her', and 'spurning her').

Wenham's approach can thus be recast as a 'narrative' approach to Deut. 22.13-21 in contrast to the 'semantic' approach offered by Pressler (in 4.7.1), which tries to give בתולה a special 'legal' or technical meaning. A narrative approach sees בתולה as a well-known social stereotype: a marriageable girl who has come of age, but whose womb has not been opened

---

95. Wenham, '*Betulah*', p. 336.
96. H.C. Washington, ' "Lest He Die in the Battle and Another Man Take Her": Violence and the Construction of Gender in the Laws of Deuteronomy 20–22', in V.H. Matthews *et al.* (eds.), *Gender and Law in the Hebrew Bible and the Ancient Near East* (JSOTSup, 262; Sheffield: Sheffield Academic Press, 1998), pp. 185-213.

by birth or miscarriage.⁹⁷ Such a girl is likely to be a virgin but this is not essential to the stereotype. It may be that conflicting scholarly views on the question whether בתולה means 'virgin' are simply the result of 'a confusion of reference with meaning',⁹⁸ since in the ANE a marriageable young woman would almost certainly be a virgin. The stereotype of the בתולה as a 'marriageable young girl' carries a social presumption of virginity but the main emphasis is on her age and nubility and the fact she has not conceived. The question is which sense is primary at the linguistic level. Although the overall sense of בתולה is related to age the word acquires different connotations in different contexts, as we saw in 4.7.1 above. Where the bride-price is at issue (as in Exod. 22.16-17 [H. 22.15-16]) the primary connotation of age is virginity but where paternity is at issue (as in Deut. 22.13-21) the connotation of age is an unopened womb. In both cases the בתולה is a menstruant who has not conceived. The בתולים are the typical proof of whether a girl has reached adolescence and once she has reached adolescence the absence of בתולים is the typical proof of whether she has conceived.

This typification of בתולה is preferable to the traditional view which places a higher value on virginity in ancient Israel than seems to be warranted by the biblical texts. Stone refers to the emphasis upon 'female sexual purity as a prerequisite for marriage'.⁹⁹ The standard explanation for valuing premarital chastity has been that men want their wives to be virgins so they can be sure that any babies are theirs.¹⁰⁰ But if paternity is really the concern then proof of menstruation at the time of marriage is just as good as proof of virginity.¹⁰¹ Virginity is not essential to settle the question of paternity.

Wenham's approach has been criticized by a number of scholars but these criticisms are largely misplaced. Pressler argues that Wenham's proposal makes Deut. 22.20-21 an instance of adultery, thereby making

97. As argued by Sasson, *Ruth*, p. 133.
98. Hugenberger, *Marriage as a Covenant*, p. 253 n. 159.
99. Stone, *Sex, Honour*, p. 115.
100. Frymer-Kensky, 'Virginity', p. 81.
101. Contra Collins, 'Prostitution in the Hebrew Bible', p. 118 who claims that virginity is the central issue in Deut. 22.21 'to ensure the paternity of the first offspring of the marriage' and Matthews, 'Honor and Shame', p. 108 who states that virginity assures the husband that 'his semen will not be mixed with that of any other man'. The same effect can be achieved if she is guarded from sexual access for several months and is not pregnant at the time of the marriage.

146   *The Signs of Sin*

Deut. 22.23-24 (which is concerned with adultery) repetitious. But as we noted in 4.7.1 above, Deut. 22.20-21 and Deut. 22.23-24 are not identical cases because the location of the execution is different. In any case, if Pressler is right, we should also have to describe Deut. 22.25-27 as 'repetitious'. The fact is that there are three cases of 'betrothed girls' in Deut. 22.13-29 and what Pressler calls 'repetition' is simply an aspect of the literary structure of the pericope (see Figure 1 in 4.7.1 above). Repetition is in any case characteristic of biblical law.[102] Frymer-Kensky claims that equating בתולים with menstruation is unparalleled 'in a world where bloody-sheet inspection is a well-known institution for enforcing the virginity of daughters'.[103] However, anthropology merely generates hypotheses. It does not determine the meaning of a biblical text. In this case, whilst anthropological evidence might suggest that Deut. 22.13-21 is concerned with virginity this does not appear to be supported by the biblical text. Among other reasons, as we saw in 4.7.1 above, the traditional approach makes it hard to account for the husband's actions. More importantly, whilst the use of menstruation as a pregnancy test may not be paralleled in the modern Mediterranean it does seem to be paralleled elsewhere in Deuteronomy (Deut. 21.10-14). This is of far greater significance than contemporary practice. Even Frymer-Kensky notes that there is a 'radical and revealing difference between the biblical practice and that found elsewhere',[104] namely that whereas in other cultures the groom or his parents take possession of the sheets on the wedding nights, in Deuteronomy the parents of the wife take the sheets. Frymer-Kensky describes this as 'a strange twist'[105] but does not appreciate that this is a serious flaw in the traditional approach of which she is an exponent.[106] Stone objects

---

102. Cf. J.W. Watts, 'Public Readings and Pentateuchal Law', *VT* 45 (1995), pp. 540-57 and 'Rhetorical Strategy in the Composition of the Pentateuch', *JSOT* 68 (1995), pp. 3-22.

103. Frymer-Kensky, 'Virginity', pp. 79-80 n. 2. Tigay, *Deuteronomy*, p. 203 claims this practice was well known among various Jewish and Arab communities in the Middle East until recent times. M.J. Giovannini, 'Female Chastity Codes in the Circum-Mediterranean: Comparative Perspectives', in D.D. Gilmore (ed.), *Honour and Shame and the Unity of the Mediterranean* (Washington DC: American Anthropological Association, 1987), pp. 61-74 (61) notes that ritual displays of virginity (bloody sheets, night-gowns) following the consummation of a marriage are 'very pervasive' in Mediterranean culture.

104. Frymer-Kensky, 'Virginity', p. 95.
105. Frymer-Kensky, 'Virginity', p. 95.
106. Frymer-Kensky, 'Virginity', pp. 79-80.

that 'a failure to menstruate scarcely seems like the sort of problem for which a young woman might be executed',[107] overlooking the possibility that pregnancy and therefore paternity are at stake. Finally, Wadsworth objects that menstrual stains 'only' prove that the girl was not pregnant before marriage.[108] But this is precisely the point at issue. If the girl was already pregnant on her wedding-night, the paternity of the child is called into question and this was a serious matter (see 4.7.4.1 below).

4.7.3. *Reconstructing Deuteronomy 22.13-21*

I noted at 4.7.1 that there is a crucial difference between Deut. 22.20-21 and Deut. 22.23-24 in the location of the executions. I argued that the execution at the entrance to the 'father's house' in Deut. 22.20-21 signifies some blame on the part of the father that does *not* apply to the father in Deut. 22.23-24. It follows that the nature of the offence in Deut. 22.20-21 must be something more than merely a failure to protect the daughter from male advances, since that would equally apply to the father in Deut. 22.23-24. The father in Deut. 22.13-21 is responsible for his daughter's offence in a way that the father in Deut. 22.23-24 is not.

The daughter's offence is described in Deut. 22.21 as לזנות בית אביה ('playing the harlot in her father's house'). We saw at 4.2.2 above that זנה is the usual verb for the activity of a prostitute and that Lev. 19.29 prohibits fathers from giving up their daughters to prostitution. It is thus plausible to suggest that the reason why the father is held responsible for the daughter's offence in Deut. 22.20-21 but not for the daughter's offence in Deut. 22.23-24 is because the father in Deut. 22.20-21 put his daughter out to prostitution during the period of betrothal.

If this is correct, the paradigm case of Deut. 22.13-21 may be reconstructed as follows. The case concerns a father who puts his daughter out to work as a (cultic or secular) prostitute.[109] This is contrary to Lev. 19.29 which does not specify a penalty for the offender. The active role of the father and the passive role of the daughter in Lev. 19.29 is consistent with their respective roles in Deut. 22.13-21. It is also consistent with the fact that none of the women in the whole pericope of Deut. 22.13-29 appears to initiate any sexual activity. Throughout Deut. 22.13-29 sexual activity is initiated by men (Deut. 22.13, 22.22, 22.23, 22.25 and 22.28). It is also

---

107. Stone, *Sex, Honour*, p. 109.
108. Wadsworth, 'Virgin', pp. 165-66.
109. See 4.3.2.2 above for a discussion of whether the typical case of prostitution in Lev. 19.29 is cultic or secular.

consistent with the proactive role of the father in Deut. 22.13-21. The slander is brought against the girl (Deut. 22.13) but it is the father in Deut. 22.13-21 who is the active subject. The father of the נערה submits the בתולים to the elders (Deut. 21.15), presents his case (Deut. 21.16-17) and receives the fine from the man who has brought the false accusation (Deut. 22.19).

It may be that the daughter in question had been working as a prostitute for some time before the period of betrothal. There does not seem to be a bar on an ordinary Israelite man marrying a former prostitute. The prohibition in Lev. 21.7 against a priest or the high priest marrying a prostitute implies that it is acceptable for a common Israelite to marry a prostitute. Hosea is explicitly commanded by YHWH to marry a prostitute (Hos. 1.2). Elsewhere in the ANE, paras. 27[110] and 30[111] of the Laws of Lipit-Ishtar (c. 1930 BCE) show not only that sexual contact with a prostitute was legal but also the willingness of some men to forsake their wives in favour of marrying a prostitute. Since one of the main purposes of marriage is the production of children, ancient Israelite society may even have thought there was some benefit in marrying a woman, such as a prostitute, who had once been pregnant or given birth to a living child.[112] Such a woman may be thought to have an advantage over the virgin in that she has proven her fertility and her ability to bear children. She may well be seen as a 'safer' bet. In an age where many women died in childbirth and when polygamy was permitted, the belief that all brides should be 'new' may not have prevailed in ancient Israel.[113] This is consistent with the overall theme that I have been developing, namely that Deut. 22.13-21 is concerned with paternity and not with virginity (see 4.7.2 above).

The drawback of course to marrying a prostitute who has had multiple sexual partners is that the paternity of her children cannot be guaranteed. In her critique of Wenham's hypothesis, Pressler argues that 'it is difficult to understand why it would be assumed that the husband was not the father, or why the husband would express an accusation that his wife was pregnant at the time of the marriage'.[114] It is easy to understand why if the woman was a former prostitute. As a result, some method is needed of ensuring that the offspring of the marriage (especially the first-born)

110. Roth, *Law Collections*, p. 31.
111. Roth, *Law Collections*, p. 32.
112. Frymer-Kensky, 'Virginity', p. 81.
113. Frymer-Kensky, 'Virginity', p. 80.
114. Pressler, 'Sexual Violence', p. 27.

belongs to the husband. This is easily satisfied if the father agrees not to make his daughter a prostitute during the period of betrothal. It amounts to a pledge that his daughter will not be pregnant with another man's seed when the time comes for her to begin cohabitation. Provided the father keeps his word, the husband can have confidence that the first-born child of the marriage will be his. This might explain why the father has a special responsibility towards the betrothed husband in Deut. 22.13-21 that he does not have in Deut. 22.23-24. When the husband gives his wife 'an evil name' in Deut. 22.14 he challenges the father-in-law and accuses him (rightly or wrongly) of giving him a daughter who was already pregnant at the time of the marriage.

Seen in this light Deut. 22.13-21 is a dispute *between men*, that is, between father and son-in-law. It is not simply a dispute between husband and wife. This is consistent with Stone's thesis that in the Bible, men establish and negotiate their relations with one another through their relations with women.[115] In the Bible, women often serve as 'a conduit of a relationship' between men. Because of this, men often manipulate their relations with women to achieve particular goals in the realm of their relations with other men.[116] Thus all sorts of male–female relations, such as those presented in Deut. 22.13-21, can be interrogated for what they tell us about male–male relations. Deut. 22.13-21 can be read as another example of sexual activity that has consequences for relationships between men. If so, the woman in Deut. 22.13-21 may simply be a signifier of the power relations between the husband and his father-in-law.

If the husband thinks that his wife is already pregnant and that his father-in-law has made a fool of him, it is vital that he challenges the father-in-law as soon as possible. There are a number of reasons why the husband brings the charge so soon after the marriage. Firstly, if the period of betrothal was quite short other people might assume that the conception was a 'honeymoon pregnancy' and that the child was his. Secondly, it was normal practice for a husband who has become the victim of another man's sexual assertiveness to 'go public' (cf. YHWH's reaction to Israel's prostitution in Hos. 2.12 [H. 2.10]).[117] The husband has been symbolically feminized by a sexual competitor and masculine honour demands an immediate

---

115. Stone, *Sex, Honor*, p. 47.
116. Stone, *Sex, Honor*, p. 48.
117. T.E. McComiskey, 'Hosea', in Thomas Edward McComiskey (ed.), *The Minor Prophets: An Exegetical and Expository Commentary*. I. *Hosea, Joel and Amos* (Grand Rapids: Baker Book House, 1992), pp. 1-237 (39).

challenge. We may support this by noting themes of male honour (Deut. 22.30 [H. 23.1]) and (literal) emasculation (Deut. 23.1 [H. 23.2]) in proximity to Deut. 22.13-29. In Deut. 22.13-21 the husband cannot challenge the man who had relations with her because he does not know who he is. However, he can avenge his honour by challenging the father who put her out to work. Thirdly, adult male mortality rates may have meant that nine months was simply too long to expect a man to wait when he had the option of divorce and of siring children by another woman (cf. Deut. 24.5 which exempts a newly married man from military service for one year, allowing him sufficient time to sire an heir in case he is killed in battle).[118] Fourthly, nine months may also have been too long to expect the woman to be under the stain of suspicion, if she is innocent.

The daughter's guilt or innocence is settled by producing the שׂמלה ('garment', Deut. 22.17). The traditional view sees the שׂמלה as the blood-stained cloths on which the marriage is consummated, although I argued at 4.7.1 above that this makes it hard to account for the husband's actions. Following Wenham's argument that בתולים means 'tokens of adolescence'[119] it is preferable to see the שׂמלה as a piece of the daughter's clothing that is stained with menstrual blood. In Deut. 22.17 the שׂמלה probably refers to the robe of a betrothed woman which is worn throughout the period of betrothal. This is consistent with the use of clothes to convey status visually in ancient Israel (see 5.3.1.2). Married or betrothed women were distinguished from other classes of women by their dress (saying in effect: 'hands off!').[120] Tamar's status as an (un)betrothed בתולה is indicated by her clothing, 'She was wearing an ornamented tunic [cf. Gen. 37.3] for maiden (בתולה) princesses were customarily dressed in such garments' (2 Sam. 13.18, JPS). In both Israel and Mesopotamia, the bride was veiled or otherwise clothed by her husband to demonstrate publicly her entry into his family.[121] Van der Toorn notes that the act of 'veiling' and 'clothing' (covering the head and clothing the body) occur together in an

---

118. C.L. Meyers, 'The Roots of Restriction: Women in Early Israel', in Norman K. Gottwald (ed.), *The Bible and Liberation* (Maryknoll, NY: Orbis Books, 1983), pp. 289-306 (295).

119. Wenham, '*Betulah*', pp. 334-35.

120. P.A. Bird, 'The Harlot as Heroine', *Semeia* 46 (1989), pp. 119-39 (135 n. 15).

121. K. Van der Toorn, 'The Significance of the Veil in the Ancient Near East', in David P. Wright *et al.* (eds.), *Pomegranates and Golden Bells: Studies in Biblical, Jewish and Near Eastern Ritual, Law and Literature in Honour of Jacob Milgrom* (Winona Lake, IN: Eisenbrauns, 1995), pp. 327-39 (338).

Old Babylonian deed of marriage.[122] The fact that a woman is clothed by a man indicates that she belongs to him (cf. the description of the Babylonian בתולות in Isa. 47.1-3). MAL A. 40-41 stipulate that a cult prostitute who is married must veil herself on the street.[123] It is likely that the betrothed woman as well as the married woman wore special clothes, especially given that the violation of a betrothed woman (Deut. 22.23-27) was treated as seriously as that of a married woman (Deut. 22.22). Because clothes normally convey status in ancient Israel, a change in status is frequently signified by a change of clothes. Thus the act of removing the 'garment (שמלה) of captivity' (Deut. 21.13) may be understood as removing the status of captivity.[124] Deut. 21.10-14 is a pertinent example because I argued at 4.7.2 above that this case is also concerned with menstruation and paternity. It is possible that the new clothes worn by the captive woman in Deut. 21.10-14 are also checked for proof of menstruation and constitute dateable evidence as to whether the woman is already pregnant. If so, the change of clothes has a similar function to Deut. 22.13-21.

If the בתולה ('menstruant') does not become pregnant whilst she is betrothed the שמלה will bear the stain of menstruation. This is how her parents are able to produce dateable evidence. It is identifiably the same שמלה that the young woman wore during betrothal. When betrothal is over and the daughter begins cohabiting with her husband the שמלה is handed over to her parents. If it contains the stains of menstruation, the parents can subsequently adduce it as dateable proof that their daughter was not pregnant prior to the marriage (Deut. 22.17). This explains why the husband has to take a gamble and risk punishment if he is proved wrong (Deut. 22.18-19). He has no access to the evidence and does not know for certain whether his suspicions can be rebutted. The use of clothing to prove or disprove sexual contact and the gamble on whether or not the other party is able to produce it is not unknown today. Not long ago President Clinton gambled on whether Monica Lewinsky could produce the infamous 'little black cocktail dress' to prove they had an intimate relationship.

How does the fact that the בתולה had not menstruated at some time in the past few months constitute proof that she was not pregnant at the time of the marriage? After all, it is well known that irregular periods are the

---

122. Van der Toorn, 'Significance of the Veil', p. 335.
123. Roth, *Law Collections*, pp. 167-69.
124. Pressler, 'Sexual Violence', p. 13.

norm for the first years of menstruation and it is also true that stress (including stress induced by a forthcoming marriage) can result in skipped periods. However, if the girl had begun to menstruate regularly and if the probationary period was, say, several months it would be very unusual if the girl did not have a period during that time. Moreover, if the daughter did have a tendency to skip periods then one would expect her parents to negotiate a longer probationary period. Certainly, as a question of proof, the failure to menstruate during the period of betrothal is a fairer evidentiary test than the broken hymen demanded by the traditional approach. If the בתולים are 'tokens of virginity' the daughter can be executed if her hymen had been broken for reasons other than sexual conduct. But if the בתולים are 'tokens of adolescence' (i.e. menstruation) there is far less chance of executing an innocent daughter. On the subject of proof it goes without saying that biblical standards of proof are, not unexpectedly, different from ours. The evidence of menstrual stains on the robe of the betrothed daughter may be another example of what Jackson calls an 'arbitrary evidence rule' in which a particular concrete test (בתולים on the שמלה) is conclusive of a wider issue ('playing the prostitute' whilst betrothed). An example of an 'arbitrary evidence rule' is the test of 'getting up and walking abroad on a staff' (Exod. 21.19) which signifies that the injured man has made a sufficient degree of recovery that any subsequent death cannot be his assailant's fault.[125] Clothes are used as criminal evidence (falsely, as it turns out) in the Joseph narrative (Gen. 37.31-33). There may originally have been a preference for this kind of material evidence as being (apparently) more objective than witnesses (e.g. 'hot possession' in Exod. 22.4 [H. 22.3], where the stolen animal found in the hands of the thief is conclusive of guilt). The use of 'real' evidence in this case probably reflects the difficulty of finding witnesses for this sort of offence.

If the girl is innocent, payment is made to the father 'for publicly defaming a בתולה of Israel'. This reconstruction implies that the payment is made 'for publicly defaming the father of a בתולה'.[126] The issue is whether the father has successfully discharged his duty as guarantor. Marriages were contracted through the payment of a bridewealth by the groom to the bride's father (cf. Gen. 34.12, Exod. 22.16-17 [H. 22.15-16], 1 Sam.

---

125. Jackson, *Semiotics of Biblical Law*, pp. 84-85.
126. Boose, 'Father's House', p. 66, although Tigay, *Deuteronomy*, p. 203 notes that there is no point in giving the fine to the bride. She is under her husband's authority, and he can take it from her.

18.25). The 50 shekels paid by the violator of an unmarried virgin (Deut. 22.28-29) is likely to be the fixed sum for the bridewealth. The cuneiform laws allow a groom to reclaim double the amount which he had paid, if his father-in-law failed to follow through on the contract by delivering his daughter (CE 25,[127] CH 160,[128] HL 29[129]). Presumably a groom could claim breach of contract where the father had failed in his duty as a guarantor. The husband may have slandered his bride in order to get out of the marriage and to recover double the bridewealth. The slanderous husband is fined the amount that the bride's father would have to pay if the charges were upheld and the contract proved to have been broken. Notably, the price is double what the rapist owes the father in Deut. 22.28-29. This suggests that defaming the father is significantly more serious than the rape of an unbetrothed בתולה (which takes away the father's choice as to whether to give his daughter in marriage). If the father has pledged not to make her work during betrothal, it may help to explain why the onus is on the father to prove his innocence, rather than on the husband to establish guilt. It is after all her father who responds to the charge (Deut. 22.16-17), referring repeatedly to 'my daughter' (Deut. 22.16, 17).

If the girl is guilty she is stoned at the entrance to the father's house. She is stoned because she had consensual relations during betrothal but her father is also held responsible because he put her out to work as a prostitute. Normally the man who had relations with a betrothed בתולה is also stoned but since his identity is not known in this case only the woman is executed. The father is not stoned because there is no suggestion that he slept with her. However, he is punished in two ways, first by losing his daughter and second by the location. The daughter's execution in Deut. 22.21 is more severe than the 'loss' suffered by the Nuzi father who prostitutes his daughter and loses her to the royal household (see 4.3.2.3 above). In addition, the location is clearly punitive because it lays the blame quite literally at the father's door. Some stigma remains attached to his 'house' either materially in the form of a pile of stones[130] or metaphorically. The family have an execution site for a doormat and they are scarred and

---

127. Roth, *Law Collections*, pp. 62-63.
128. Roth, *Law Collections*, p. 111.
129. Roth, *Law Collections*, p. 221.
130. Cf. 2 Sam. 18.17, Josh. 7.26, 8.29, 10.27, although this custom may have been reserved for notorious or royal criminals. For ordinary criminals, burial was thought sufficient, 1 Kgs 2.31-34, cf. Deut. 21.22-23, E.F. De Ward, 'Mourning Customs in 1, 2 Samuel (Part II)', *JJS* 23 (1972), pp. 145-66 (146).

shamed every time they go in or out of that house. The location is a signifier of the father's shame because he did not fulfil his pledge to withdraw her from prostitution. The location may also signify the setting of the offence. Gen. 38.14 describes how Tamar 'sat down בפתח ("in the entrance") to Enaim'. It may be that when the father put his daughter out to prostitution she advertised her trade by sitting at the פתח to her father's house. This is consistent with other ANE laws and legal documents where an extraordinary site of execution reflects the nature of the offence.[131]

Some may argue that this reconstruction assumes too much. If these are the circumstances, why does the law not spell them out? The answer may be, as noted in 1.5.2, above, that ancient Israel was a high-context society. Biblical law, in common with other biblical texts, often assumes rather than explains the cultural presuppositions of its authors and audiences. It is hardly surprising that a text that deals with betrothal, menstruation and paternity in ancient Israel, not to mention fathers who put their daughters out to prostitution, might need some unpacking for a modern audience.

Others may find this reconstruction of Deut. 22.13-21 speculative. However, it is inevitable that with a difficult text of this kind there is going to be some degree of speculation. The same criticism applies to the traditional view. The truth is that no one has yet been able to determine the meaning of this text conclusively. But whilst my reconstruction may be speculative, it satisfies the fourfold test demanded of all good theories. First it gathers in *all* the relevant data, including the difficult question of why the husband takes a gamble on the evidence and risks punishment. It explains why the husband does not know whether the parents can produce the בתולים. Second, it is consistent with what we know about biblical law and biblical society. The case makes sense in the light of the well-documented concern for paternity in biblical law and biblical society. This is preferable to an account that relies upon a poorly attested concern for virginity. Finally, this reconstruction sheds light upon other areas including the literary arrangement of Deut. 22.13-29. In particular it helps to explain why the father in Deut 22.20-21 is held responsible for the behaviour of his betrothed בתולה in a way that the father of the betrothed בתולה in Deut 22.23-24 is not.

To conclude, I suggest that Deut. 22.13-21 deals with the situation where the woman has played the harlot, that is, been a professional prostitute during the period of betrothal. I submit that this is the most reasonable

---

131. LH 21, 25 (Roth, *Law Collections*, p. 85), LH 256 (Roth, *Law Collections*, p. 129), HL 166 (Roth, *Law Collections*, p. 233).

solution to the understanding of seriousness in Deut. 22.20-21 because it fits both the framework of Deut. 22.13-21 and the wider setting of Deut. 22.13-29.

4.8. *Seriousness of Offence*

4.8.1. *Paternity*

I have argued in 4.3.1 and 4.3.2 that paternity is a key issue in Deut. 22.13-21. Uncertainty as to paternity is a serious matter in ancient Israel (cf. Num. 5.11-31) where lineage is defined in terms of the father. The husband must be certain that his children are his own. As Plaskow writes, the subject of biblical law might be women, the interest behind the laws is 'the purity of the male line... [Women are placed] firmly under the control of first fathers, then husbands, so that men can have male heirs they know are theirs'.[132] The biological integrity of the husband's family is at stake. This is especially important when, as in Deut. 22.13-21, the doubts concern the paternity of the first-born son (cf. Deut. 21.17).[133]

4.8.2. *Status*

Her status as a betrothed woman at the time of the offence is a key element in understanding seriousness. The husband's allegation in Deut. 22.14 relates to the period of betrothal before the בתולה was married. This is consistent with the observation that no formal sanctions attach in biblical law to the sexual activity of an unbetrothed commoner's daughter (see 4.3.1 above). The seriousness of the offence in Deut. 22.20-21 consists not in the fact that she has lost her virginity or even that she had once played the prostitute. It consists in the fact that she played the prostitute during the period of betrothal.

4.9. *Conclusion*

The offence in both Lev. 21.9 and Deut. 22.20-21 is that of לזנות ('prostitution'). Seriousness of offence depends on the status of the offenders. The woman in Lev. 21.9 abuses her status as the daughter of a priest whilst the בתולה in Deut. 22.20-21 abuses her status as a betrothed woman. Status is

---

132. Cf. Plaskow, *Standing again at Sinai*, p. 4.
133. I. Mendelsohn, 'On the preferential status of the eldest son', *BASOR* 156 (1959), pp. 38-40; J. Milgrom, 'First-born', in Keith Crim *et al.* (eds.), *Illustrated Bible Dictionary: Supplementary Volume* (Nashville: Abingdon Press, 1976), pp. 337-38.

also a key element in explaining the different forms of capital punishment in Lev. 21.9 and Deut. 22.20-21. The higher cultic status of both the priest and his daughter (Lev. 21.9) is the main reason why the latter's offence is more serious than that of a commoner (Deut. 22.20-21).

Chapter 5

SIN, STATUS AND SACRIFICE:
SERIOUSNESS OF OFFENCE AND LEVITICUS 4.1-35

> 'What we have written is not a story of detection, of crime and punishment, but of sin and expiation. It is possible that you have not known what sin you shall expiate, or whose, or why. It is certain that the knowledge of it must precede the expiation.'
> T.S. Eliot, *The Family Reunion* (Part II, sc. ii)

Leviticus 4 is a case-study in seriousness. The nature of the offence (inadvertent sin) remains stable throughout (see Lev. 4.2, 13, 22 and 27), but important variations occur in the type of sacrifice and the type of sacrificial ritual. These variations appear to be correlated with the identity of the offender, allowing us to explore status as a possible element of seriousness of offence. To the extent that seriousness manifests a concern for grading and classifying, it is not surprising to find a presentation of seriousness in a priestly text. This is because the Priestly worldview is dominated by the belief that order emerges through the correct separation of categories.[1]

5.1. *Leviticus 4.1-35 as a Text for Seriousness*

Lev. 4.1-35 can be treated as a discrete unit for the purpose of this chapter. Questions may be raised about the relationship between Lev. 4.1-35 and Lev. 5.1-13 but these do not affect the argument of the present chapter. Although Lev. 4.1-35 has much in common with Lev. 5.1-13, the latter is much less helpful for understanding 'seriousness'. This is because the main registers of 'seriousness' are expressed in sacrificial rituals which are

---

1. F.H. Gorman Jr, *The Ideology of Ritual* (JSOTSup, 91; Sheffield: JSOT Press, 1990), p. 59; D.P. Wright, 'The Spectrum of Priestly Impurity', in G.A. Anderson and S.M. Olyan (eds.), *Priesthood and Cult in Ancient Israel* (JSOTSup, 125; Sheffield: Sheffield Academic Press, 1991), pp. 150-81 (153).

described at length in Lev. 4.1-35 (see 5.3 below). By contrast, Lev. 5.1-13 does not describe the sacrificial rituals, bar a very brief discussion in Lev. 5.9 and 5.12, and so it is not included in my analysis.

Questions may also be raised about the relationship between Leviticus 4 and Num. 15.22-29. The similarities between these two sets of provisions may suggest some literary dependence, although in what direction is not clear. The word בשגגה is used repeatedly in both passages (Lev. 4.2, 4.22, 4.27, cf. Num. 15.24-29). In addition, Num. 15.24a bears a striking resemblance to Lev. 4.13, whilst Num. 15.25a has a clear parallel in Lev. 4.20b, 4.26b, 4.31b, 4.35b. Finally, the Hebrew text of Num. 15.27a is identical to Lev. 4.27a. Fishbane argues that Num. 15.22-29 is an exegetical expansion of Leviticus 4 and that this establishes the priority of the latter.[2] Rendtorff, by contrast, argues that Leviticus 4 is dependent upon Num. 15.22-29.[3] It is also possible that neither Leviticus 4 nor the Num. 15.22-31 pericope is a homogeneous unit and that each passage contains material that dates from different periods. If so, any literary 'borrowing' may not all be in the same direction, with Num. 15.22-26 showing some literary dependence on Lev. 4.13-21 and Lev. 4.27-31 showing some dependence on Num. 15.27-29.[4]

On the other hand, the differences between the two texts are sufficiently striking to raise the possibility that neither text is completely dependent upon the other and that each may represent an independent tradition. Firstly, Leviticus 4 refers to an accidental transgression committed 'from among all the commandments (מכל מצות)' which the LORD has commanded not to be done (cf. vv. 2, 13, 22, 27), whilst Num. 15.22-31 commences with the further-reaching statement 'and if you unintentionally transgress and do not do any of it [lit. all] these commandments (כל־האלה המצות) which YHWH spoke to Moses'. Secondly, Leviticus 4 deals with four types of offender whereas Num. 15.22-31 only considers two. Thirdly, there are differences in terms of the type of sacrifice required. Fourthly, reference is made to the 'stranger' in Num. 15.26, 15.29 and 15.30, but not in Leviticus 4. Finally, the statement in Num. 15.30-31 that no sacrifice can atone for deliberate or 'high-handed' sins has no counter-

---

2. M. Fishbane, *Biblical Interpretation in Ancient Israel* (Oxford: Clarendon Press, 1985), p. 191.

3. R. Rendtorff, *Die Gesetze in der Priesterschrift* (Göttingen: Vandenhoeck & Ruprecht, 1954).

4. E.W. Davies, *Numbers* (Grand Rapids: Eerdmans, 1995), p. 157.

part in Leviticus 4, or anywhere else for that matter.[5] Scholars have tried to rationalize the differences between the texts in different ways.[6] Suffice it to say that the precise nature of the relationship between Leviticus 4 and Num. 15.22-31 is beyond the scope of this chapter. The safest provisional conclusion is probably that of Davies who avers, 'the nature of the literary relationship between the two passages is probably far more complex than has generally been supposed'.[7]

    5.   Davies, *Numbers*, pp. 156-57.

    6.   A. Toeg, 'A Halakhic Midrash in Num. XV.22-31', *Tarbiz* 43 (1973) I-II (Summary), pp. 1-20 has tried to 'square the circle' by seeing Num. 15.22-31 as a halakhic *midrash* of Lev. 4. Toeg treats the apparent discrepancy in the sacrifices demanded by the two texts as an example of the 'exegetic interpolation technique'. In Num. 15.24-29 expiation of the unwitting sin is by a bull as a burnt offering and by a male goat as a חטאת ('purification-offering'). Lev. 4, on the other hand, only demands the bull as a חטאת and does not require any burnt offering. Toeg argues that the author of Num. 15.22-29 understood the language of Lev. 4.14 ('the קהל shall offer a bull of the herd as a חטאת') as a conflated version of the following, 'a bull of the herd—*for a burnt offering, and a goat*—as a חטאת' (interpolation in italics). On Toeg's view Lev. 4.14 can be 'cut' and 'explained' to harmonize with Num. 15.22-29. I. Knohl, 'The Sin Offering in the "Holiness School" (Num. 15.22-31)', in G.A. Anderson and S.M. Olyan (eds.), *Priesthood and Cult in Ancient Israel* (JSOTSup, 125; Sheffield: Sheffield Academic Press, 1991), pp. 192-203 heavily criticizes this view. For Toeg to be correct we would expect the writer of Num. 15.22-29 to make every effort to preserve a similar textual framework to that of Lev. 4. In this way the reader can clearly understand that it is the author's intention to correct and explain a difficult text (Knohl, 'Sin Offering', p. 194). But in fact, as Knohl shows, Num. 15.22-29 is full of changes and additions that are quite unnecessary according to Toeg's explanation. Knohl, 'Sin Offering', p. 195 concludes that Num. 15.22-29 is not an 'exegetic interpolation' but rather a revised and renewed version of Lev. 4 that has only a weak affinity with the original text. Knohl's own explanation for why Num. 15.22-29 gives priority to the burnt offering over the חטאת appeals to source criticism, claiming that the חטאת laws in Lev. 4 derive from the Priestly *torah* (P) whilst the חטאת laws in Num. 15.22-29 originate in the Holiness School (H), Knohl, 'Sin Offering', 197. To this extent Knohl and Toeg are agreed. Both hypothesize that the Num. 15.22-29 חטאת text is familiar with the corresponding text in Lev. 4 and simply revises it. But traditional methods of source criticism founder on the fact that each passage appears to be more complex than the other. It is possibly for this reason that scholarship has failed to reach a consensus in spite of a detailed analysis of the two texts, Davies, *Numbers*, p. 156. J. Milgrom, *Leviticus 1–16* (New York: Doubleday, 1991), p. 267 considers that the two texts represent independent traditions about the חטאת, whilst P.J. Budd, *Leviticus* (Grand Rapids: Eerdmans, 1996), p. 85 suggests that Num. 15.22-31 is a reworking of earlier priestly material in Exodus and Leviticus.

    7.   Davies, *Numbers*, p. 157.

5.2. Registers of Seriousness

I divide Lev. 4.1-35 into four cases. These are Case A (Lev. 4.3-12), Case B (Lev. 4.13-21), Case C (Lev. 4.22-26) and Case D (Lev. 4.27-35). Broadly speaking, there are four main registers of seriousness. These are, firstly, the type of sacrifice (see 5.3.1 below), secondly, the nature of the blood rite (see 5.3.2 below), thirdly, the identity of the ritual object cleansed by the blood (see 5.3.3 below) and fourthly, the method used to eliminate the animal carcass (see 5.3.4 below). Performative registers include, firstly, the act of bringing different types of animal for sacrifice (Lev. 4.4, 4.14, 4.23, 4.28 and 4.32). The sacrifices vary according to the identity of the offender. They are a young bull for הכהן המשיח (Lev. 4.4) and כל־עדת בני־ישראל (Lev. 4.14), a male goat for a נשיא (Lev. 4.23) and, finally, a female goat (Lev. 4.28) or a female lamb (Lev. 4.32) for the member of the עם הארץ. The declining economic value of the sacrifice reflects the seriousness of the offence (see 5.3.1.1 below). It is also possible that the visual appearance of each animal symbolizes the offenders' visual prestige. If so, this may be another respect in which the act of bringing different types of animal for sacrifice functions as a register of seriousness (see 5.3.1.2 below). A second performative register is the performance of the blood rites (Lev. 4.5-7, 16-18, 24-25, 30 and 34). Leviticus 4 describes two different blood rites, one in which the blood is brought into the Holy Place (in the case of הכהן המשיח [Lev. 4.6] and the כל־עדת ישראל [Lev. 4.17]) and another in which the blood is not brought into the Holy Place (in the case of the נשיא and the member of the עם הארץ). This registers the seriousness of the offence because the blood rite signifies the extent to which the Sanctuary has been polluted because of the offenders' sin (see 5.3.2 below). A third performative register (related to the second performative register) is the question which of the horned altars is daubed with blood. In the case of הכהן המשיח (Lev. 4.7) and the כל־עדת ישראל (Lev. 4.18) it is the incense altar located in the Holy Place. However, in the case of the נשיא (Lev. 4.25) and the errant member of the עם הארץ (Lev. 4.30 and 34) it is the altar of burnt offering located in the courtyard. This aspect of the blood rite is also a register of seriousness because it, too, signifies the extent to which the Sanctuary has been polluted because of the offenders' sin (see 5.3.3 below). A fourth performative register is the means by which the priest disposes of the animal carcass. In the case of הכהן המשיח (Lev. 4.11-12) and the כל־עדת ישראל (Lev. 4.21) the carcass is carried outside the camp to a clean place and burnt. This is not, however, required in the case of the נשיא and the member of the עם הארץ. It is a register of seriousness because it shows how much impurity was caused to the Sanctuary by the offence (see 5.3.4 below). It advertises the greater seriousness of the offence in Cases A and B as opposed to Cases C and D. It is worth noting that, in contrast to the other performative registers (viz. bringing the animals for sacrifice and performing the blood rites) which are witnessed only by the priests and the offeror(s), this performative register (burning the carcass outside the camp) is broadcast to a wider audience.

5.3. *Offence Description*

5.3.1. *Inadvertent Sin*

The offence is an inadvertent act committed בשגגה ('in error'). The word שגגה occurs in other legal contexts (e.g. Lev. 5.15, 22.14 and the parallel text of Num. 15.26, 15.27-29) and refers to sin of which it is easy to remain unaware. In Leviticus 4, שגה means sinning without realizing it[8] as a result of mistake, ignorance or inadvertence. Examples of שגגה include the 'slip of the tongue' (Eccl. 5.6 [H. 5.5]) and the error (misjudgement?) of a ruler (Eccl. 10.5). The word שגגה may derive either from the verbal root שגג meaning 'to commit error'[9] or 'to sin inadvertently' or שגה meaning 'to go astray'.[10] These roots suggest several factors that might reduce culpability including lack of intention[11] and drunkenness. The word שגה is used of those who cannot walk in a straight line because they are under the influence of alcohol (e.g. Prov. 20.1). This may suggest that the 'inadvertence' of Leviticus 4 refers to ignorance of some relevant fact or quality as a result of intoxication. But in whatever manner the sin occurred, a sacrifice was required as soon as the sin became known. The knowledge that the offender has committed an inadvertent sin may be prompted by the

---

8. For a discussion of whether ignorance of having committed a sin necessarily involves the unconsciousness of the act, see N. Kiuchi, *The Purification Offering in the Priestly Literature* (JSOTSup, 36; Sheffield: JSOT Press, 1987), pp. 25-31.

9. Or 'to move in error', Kiuchi, *Purification Offering*, p. 31.

10. Seidl, שגג/שגה, in, pp. 1058-1065 (1058); J. Milgrom, 'The Cultic שגגה and its Influence in Psalms and Job', *JQR* 58 (1967), pp. 115-25 (116) argues that the two roots coalesce (e.g. in Job 12.16).

11. בשגגה may also reduce culpability because it signifies a lack of intention (e.g. Gen. 43.12. Cf. also Num. 35.11 and Josh. 20.3).

offender's guilty conscience[12] or it may be brought to light by some other means.

5.3.2. *Knowledge of an Inadvertent Sin*
Lev. 4.14 states, 'when the sin which they have committed becomes known (ונודעה)'. This corresponds to the fact that when the כל־עדת ישראל commit the offence they do so 'unwittingly and the thing is hidden from the eyes of the assembly and they do any one of the things which the LORD has commanded not to be done and are guilty (ואשמו)' (Lev. 4.13). In Lev. 4.13, when the כל־עדת ישראל commit the offence they do not know that they are doing it. When the כל־עדת ישראל realize their wrong they are to bring a sacrifice. However, the word ונודעה in Lev. 4.14 is ambiguous because the letter ו in ונודעה can be translated either 'and' or 'or'. This means that the 'knowledge' spoken of in v. 14 may be *consequent* upon the awareness of guilt described in Lev. 4.13 (ואשמו) or it may refer to an *alternative* means by which knowledge of an inadvertent sin is brought to light.

We can settle the matter by noting that two different types of conjunctions are used in Leviticus 4. The first is the (ambiguous) ו conjunction that appears in Lev. 4.13-14 and the second is the או conjunction that appears in Lev. 4.22-23 and Lev. 4.27-28,

> When a ruler sins, doing unwittingly any one of all the things which the LORD his God has commanded not to be done, and is guilty (ואשם) if the sin which he has committed is made known to him (או־הודע) he shall bring as his offering a goat, a male without blemish (Lev. 4.22-23).

> If any one of the common people sins unwittingly in doing any one of the things which the LORD has commanded not to be done, and is guilty (ואשם) when the sin which he has committed is made known to him… (או־הודע) (Lev. 4.27-28).

The conjunction או in both Lev. 4.22-23 and in Lev. 4.27-28 means 'or'. The phrase או־הודע is therefore an alternative to ואשם. The word ואשם in Lev. 4.22 does not therefore mean 'thereby' incurring guilt. It refers to one of the two ways in which the offender discovers that he has done wrong. Either he discovers it himself (ואשם) *or* it is made known to him (או־הודע). Accordingly, we ought to translate Lev. 4.22-23 and Lev. 4.27-28 as follows,

---

12. Milgrom, *Leviticus*, p. 243; Gordon J. Wenham, *Leviticus* (Grand Rapids: Eerdmans, 1979), p. 99.

> When a ruler sins, doing unwittingly any one of all the things which the LORD his God has commanded not to be done, and is guilty [i.e. 'realizes his guilt'] *or* the sin which he has committed is made known to him, he shall bring as his offering a goat, a male without blemish (Lev. 4.22-23).

> If any one of the common people sins unwittingly in doing any one of the things which the LORD has commanded not to be done, and is guilty [i.e. 'realizes his guilt'] *or* the sin which he has committed is made known to him he shall bring for his offering a goat, a female without blemish, for his sin which he has committed (Lev. 4.27-28).

This interpretation of Lev. 4.22-23 and Lev. 4.27-28 influences our understanding of the ambiguous ו conjunction in Lev. 4.13-14. We should understand the ambiguity of Lev. 4.13-14 in the light of the conjunctions used in Lev. 4.23-24 and 4.27-28 and interpret Lev. 4.13-14 as follows,

> If the whole congregation of Israel commits a sin unwittingly and the thing is hidden from the eyes of the assembly, and they do any one of the things which the LORD has commanded not to be done and are guilty [i.e. 'realize their guilt'] (ואשמו), *or* when the sin which they have committed becomes known (ונודעה), the assembly shall offer a young bull for a sin offering (my italics).

This means that אשם can have both objective and subjective aspects.[13] The sinner brings the חטאת to the sanctuary when he realizes his guilt, or is informed by others.[14] Since no institution is mentioned as giving the warning, perhaps nothing more than informal notification need be assumed.

5.3.3. *Against a Prohibitive Command of the LORD*

The heading in Lev. 4.2 refers to the situation where a person sins inadvertently, 'in any of the things which the LORD has commanded not to be done (מכל מצות יהוה אשר לא תעשינה) [lit. "any of the LORD's commandments which are not to be done"] and does any one of them'. Cases A–D concern a sin of commission, committed by someone who, at the time, did not realize that what they were doing was wrong.[15]

---

13. Kiuchi, *Purification Offering*, p. 34.
14. Kiuchi, *Purification Offering*, p. 34.
15. This creates an overlap with Num. 15.22-29. Num. 15.22 refers to 'all' (כל, Num. 15.22) the LORD's commandments, positive and negative, performative and prohibitive (Milgrom, *Numbers*, p. 265; Fishbane, *Biblical Interpretation*, pp. 190-91, contra B. Levine, *Leviticus* [Philadelphia: Jewish Publication Society of America, 1989], p. 395). This seemingly contradicts Leviticus 4 insofar as these passages appear

5.3.4. Inadvertence and Pollution

Inadvertent sin was a serious offence in ancient Israel.[16] This is signified by the need to bring a חטאת ('purification offering').[17] The primary purpose of the חטאת ritual appears to be to purge the Sanctuary of uncleanness[18] and sin.[19] The blood of the חטאת is never applied to a person. Apart from Leviticus 4, the blood of the חטאת is only brought by an individual in cases of severe physical impurity, as with the parturient, leper or gonorrheic (Leviticus 12–15). None of these individuals is daubed with the purgative blood. Rather, atonement is made 'on' the holy objects in the

---

to require different sacrifices for the inadvertent violation of prohibitive commandments. This takes us back to the question of the relationship between these two passages, see 5.1.1 above.

16. Contra M. Douglas, *Leviticus as Literature* (Oxford: Oxford University Press, 2000), p. 148, 'Surely the unintended or inadvertent sin is not very serious'.

17. Milgrom persuasively argues in favour of this translation in a series of publications: J. Milgrom, 'A Prolegomenon to *Leviticus* 17.11', *JBL* 90 (1971), pp. 149-56; 'Israel's Sanctuary: The Priestly *Picture of Dorian Gray*', *RB* 83 (1976), pp. 390-99; 'Review of *Sühne als Heilsgeschehen*'. *JBL* 104 (1985), pp. 302-304 and *Leviticus*. He is followed by Hartley, *Leviticus*, Kiuchi, *Purification Offering*; B.J. Schwartz, 'The Bearing of Sin in the Priestly Literature', in David P. Wright *et al.* (eds.), *Pomegranates and Golden Bells: Studies in Biblical, Jewish and Near Eastern Ritual, Law and Literature in Honour of Jacob Milgrom* (Winona Lake, IN: Eisenbrauns, 1995), pp. 3-21 and Wenham, *Leviticus*, although some commentators such as Budd, *Leviticus*; R.K. Harrison, *Leviticus: An Introduction and Commentary* (Leicester: InterVarsity Press, 1980); Knohl, 'Sin Offering' and N. Zohar,'Repentance and Purification: The Significance and Semantics of חטאת in the Pentateuch', *JBL* 107 (1988), pp. 609-18 prefer the traditional translation 'sin offering'. Kiuchi, *Purification Offering*, p. 161 is right to stress that whilst the use of the phrase 'purification offering' conveys more comprehensively to the modern mind the basic function of the חטאת than the term 'sin offering' we should not allow this to obscure the fact that the חטאת is still concerned with sin.

18. Milgrom, 'Israel's Sanctuary'; 'Review'; *Leviticus*. Milgrom's thesis has found widespread support and is followed, though not necessarily in all of its details, by Hartley, *Leviticus*, pp. 55-56; Schwartz, 'Bearing of Sin' and Wenham, *Leviticus*, p. 96. For important modifications of Milgrom's approach see Levine, 'Intra-Familial Institutions' (differentiating between the 'riddance rite' and the 'expiation rite'); Kiuchi, *Purification Offering* (arguing that purification of the sancta is not wholly unrelated to the expiation of sin) and Zohar, 'Repentance and Purification' (stressing the personal purification of the sinner as the purpose of the חטאת ritual).

19. Sin can itself be an intense form of uncleanness, Kiuchi, *Purification Offering*, p. 161.

Sanctuary (Lev. 4.7, 4.18, 4.25, 4.30 and 4.34).[20] This is because the purpose of the חטאת sacrifice is to purge the Sanctuary.[21] Certain sins cause impurities that pollute the Sanctuary (Lev. 15.31, 20.3 and Num. 19.20).[22] We know from elsewhere in Leviticus that the Sanctuary is not only polluted by direct contact but also by indirect contact (e.g. Lev. 16.16 where purgation rites are described for areas to which the Israelites have no access).[23] Drawing an analogy with Oscar Wilde's *Picture of Dorian Gray*, Milgrom argues that impurity has a 'dynamic, aerial quality' that marks the Sanctuary from afar.[24] 'Sin may not leave its mark on the face of the sinner, but it is certain to mark the face of the sanctuary, and unless it is quickly expunged, God's presence will depart.'[25] The blood of the חטאת cleanses the Sanctuary and its sancta of the impurities that they have attracted as a result of the offeror's sin[26] and functions as a kind of 'ritual detergent'. Inadvertent sin was thus a serious offence because it pollutes the Sanctuary where YHWH dwells and since YHWH would not dwell in a polluted Sanctuary it risks his departure (see further Chapter 6). Impurity threatened the status of the Sanctuary as a consecrated area that is bounded and set apart. Defiling the Sanctuary by inadvertent sin risked the collapse of the sacred order and the eruption of chaos.[27] The חטאת ritual was

20. Milgrom, 'Review', p. 303.
21. Milgrom, *Leviticus*, p. 254.
22. For the spectrum of priestly impurity see Wright, 'Priestly Impurity'.
23. Milgrom, 'Israel's Sanctuary', p. 394.
24. Milgrom, 'Israel's Sanctuary', p. 393.
25. Milgrom, 'Israel's Sanctuary', p. 398.
26. Milgrom 'Israel's Sanctuary', 'Review', *Leviticus*, pp. 254-58, followed by Hartley, *Leviticus*, pp. 57-58. Contra B.A. Levine, *In the Presence of the LORD: A Study of Cult and Some Cultic Terms in Ancient Israel* (Leiden: E.J. Brill, 1974), pp. 67-77, who argues that impurity is 'demonic' and that the blood is apotropaic, and M. Douglas, 'Atonement in Leviticus', *JSQ* 1 (1993), pp. 109-30 (116, 118, 123 and 127-29), who argues that the basic meaning of atonement is to repair a torn protective covering. It is not necessary to choose between these theories. The complex nature of rites of atonement allows for secondary meanings. Milgrom's thesis does not exclude the possibility, raised by Levine and Douglas, that atonement has a protective as well as a purificatory character. Indeed 'protection' is a logical consequence of 'purification'. The Sanctuary is purified and because of this the sinner and the community are protected from YHWH's wrath. Blood protects as well as purifies.
27. For the relationship between pollution and chaos see T. Frymer-Kensky, 'Pollution, Purification and Purgation in Biblical Israel', in C.L. Meyers and M. O'Connor (eds.), *The Word of the Lord Shall Go Forth* (Winona Lake, IN: Eisenbrauns, 1983), pp. 399-414 (408-409) discussing, among other texts, Jer. 4.23-27.

necessary to cleanse the Sanctuary and to re-establish its sacred boundaries.[28] Inadvertent sin was a serious offence for the priests because it threatened the holiness of the Sanctuary. In this respect, seriousness of offence in Leviticus 4 is united to one of the overall themes of Leviticus, namely 'how to protect the holiness of the house of God'.[29]

5.4. *Offender Status*

The status and identity of the offenders is an important aspect of seriousness of offence in Leviticus 4.

5.4.1. *Identity of* הכהן המשיח *(Case A [Leviticus 4.3-12])*

Lev. 4.3 refers to הכהן המשיח ('the anointed priest'). The question is whether this refers to the ordinary priesthood or only to the high priest. Ordinary priests could be referred to as 'the anointed priests' (הכהנים המשחים, e.g. Num. 3.3) because they had been sprinkled with the sacred anointing oil (Lev. 8.30). Nevertheless, there remains a sense in which the high priest alone could be referred to as 'the anointed priest' because he was the only priest who had the sacred anointing oil (Exod. 30.22-33) poured upon his head (Lev. 8.12, cf. Lev. 21.10).[30] The definite form of v. 4 ('*the* anointed priest') confirms that the subject of Lev. 4.3-12 is the high priest alone and not the priestly class as a whole. The use of the definite article in Lev. 4.3 contrasts with Lev. 4.22 where the reference to '*a* ruler' (נשיא) shows that the subject is a whole class of rulers and not one particular person (see 5.2.3). The conclusion that Lev. 4.3 refers to the high priest does not necessarily mean that the ordinary priests are ranked with the עם הארץ of Lev. 4.27. This is because we do not have to assume that Leviticus 4 is exhaustive. Indeed, the use of the phrase עם הארץ often *excludes* (rather than includes) the priesthood (see 5.2.4 below). Consequently, the ordinary priests may *not* be formally included in Leviticus 4. If so, Leviticus 4 presents the case of the high priest (Lev. 4.3-12) but not the case of the ordinary priest.

28. Gorman, *Ideology of Ritual*, p. 234.
29. M. Douglas, 'Poetic Structure in Leviticus', in David P. Wright *et al.* (eds.), *Pomegranates and Golden Bells: Studies in Biblical, Jewish and Near Eastern Ritual, Law and Literature in Honour of Jacob Milgrom* (Winona Lake, IN: Eisenbrauns, 1995), pp. 239-56 (247).
30. Milgrom, *Leviticus*, p. 231. Contra Budd, *Leviticus*, p. 81 who contends that הכהן המשיח refers to an ordinary priest.

Uniquely among Cases A–D, the high priest's wrong '[brings] guilt upon the people (לאשמת העם)' (Lev. 4.3).³¹ BDB translates Lev. 4.3 as 'sin to the *becoming guilty* of the people' (my italics), that is, so that the people incur guilt.³² The phrase explicitly attributes guilt to the people, although it is not clear how exactly this guilt arises.

The key question is whether the people were actively involved in 'becoming guilty' or not. There are two possible scenarios. One is that the high priest does something inadvertently and the people are guilty without doing anything. The first scenario may reflect the high priest's solidarity with the people.³³ Milgrom sees לאשמת as a 'consequential אשם' that signifies that the high priest's action has somehow affected the whole nation.³⁴ Bonar suggests that the high priest was guilty of some mistake in his cultic service, or accidentally polluted some of the holy vessels.³⁵ This may have caused injury to the people as a whole because it misrepresented the sacrificial system. The second possible scenario is that the high priest does something and the people follow suit (e.g. the high priest commands the people to observe a cultic feast on the wrong day and the people obey). Here the people are actively involved in 'becoming guilty' because the high priest's erroneous decision causes the whole community to err.³⁶

Regardless of how one interprets Lev. 4.3, the sin of the anointed priest is greater than either that of the נשיא (4.22-26, see 5.4.3, below) or one of the עם הארץ (Lev. 4.27-31, see 5.4.4, below). This is consistent with the unique appointment of the high priest 'for YHWH' (Exod. 28.1, 28.3, 29.1). Compared to the נשיא and the errant member of the עם הארץ the

---

31. This has been variously translated 'according to the sin of the people', 'to the sinning of the people' (A.A. Bonar, *A Commentary on Leviticus* [London: Banner of Truth, 1972 (1846)], p. 66), 'to the detriment of the people' (Milgrom, *Leviticus*, p. 231), or 'so that blame falls upon the people' (JPS). For the meaning of אשם see D. Kellerman, אשם, in *TDOT*, I, pp. 429-37.

32. BDB 1979, p. 80.

33. D.J. Pursiful, *The Cultic Motif in the Spirituality of the Book of Hebrews* (Lewiston, NY: Edwin Mellen Press, 1993), p. 49.

34. Milgrom, *Leviticus*, p. 231.

35. Bonar, *Leviticus*, p. 67.

36. C.F. Keil and F. Delitzsch, *Leviticus* (Grand Rapids: Eerdmans, 1976 [1876]), p. 303 wrongly claim that the high priest sins in his official capacity as representative of the nation before YHWH. In fact, the high priest only acts in a truly 'representative' capacity once a year on the Day of Atonement (as signified by his change of clothing, Lev. 16.4, 16.23-24). There is no reason to suppose that he is acting in a 'representative' capacity in Lev. 4.3-12 where his clothes class him as one 'set apart'.

high priest's inadvertence is more serious because he has a higher obligation to know and to practise *torah*. It is the duty of the high priest, as a member of the priestly class, to know the Law and to teach it to the people (Lev. 10.10-11, cf. Mal. 2.7). That the Law is particularly associated with the priesthood is implicit in several texts (Jer. 18.18 and Ezek. 7.26). It is restated in the context of Jehoshaphat's reforms (2 Chron. 19.11) and reaffirmed following the Exile (Neh. 8.2). Ezra himself is described as 'Ezra the priest, the scribe, learned in matters of the commandments of the LORD and his statutes for Israel' (Ezra. 7.11). A number of texts hold the priests directly responsible for not knowing the Law and for not teaching it to the people. 'My people are destroyed for lack of knowledge...since you [the priest] have forgotten the law of your God' (Hos. 4.6). The result was that 'For a long time Israel was without the true God, and without a teaching priest, and without law' (2 Chron. 15.3). This responsibility places a higher obligation on the priest to know and follow *torah*.[37] This makes his sin of ignorance more serious.

5.4.2. *Identity of* כל־עדת ישראל: *(Case B [Leviticus 4.13-21])*

Lev. 4.13 refers to two institutions, the כל־עדת ישראל and the קהל. Reference is also made in Lev. 4.15 to זקני העדה ('elders of the congregation'). However, the זקני העדה is not synonymous with either the כל־עדת ישראל or the קהל and is limited to a small group of representatives who lay their hands on the sacrifice. By contrast, כל־עדת ישראל and קהל appear to refer to a large multitude of people. These groups are equivalent to either the entire nation (the apparent upper limit, see below) or to all Israelite men over 20 (the apparent lower limit, see below).

The evidence suggests that כל־עדת ישראל refers to the whole body of Israel and not to any specific body of representatives.[38] This is confirmed by the use of the similar phrase כל־עדת בני־ישראל which occurs more

---

37. Cf. Jer. 5.5 where 'the great' includes the priesthood as well as the secular leaders of Judah. Jesus' parable of the Good Samaritan assumes that the priest has the greatest responsibility to obey the law, followed by the Levite and then by the Samaritan (Lk. 10.30-37).

38. The כל־עדת ישראל is a far broader group than the עדה referred to in Num. 35.24. In Exod. 12.3 and 12.47 כל־עדת ישראל refers to those ('every man') who are commanded to take part in the Passover. In Josh. 22.18, Joshua warns the Transjordan tribes who have set up their own altar, 'if you rebel against the LORD today, he will be angry with כל־עדת ישראל tomorrow'. He invokes the sin of Achan as a precedent, 'Did not Achan the son of Zerah break faith in the matter of the devoted things, and wrath fell upon כל־עדת ישראל?'

frequently than כל־עדת ישראל in the Hebrew Bible. In Num. 1.2-3, YHWH commands Moses to 'take a census of כל־עדת בני־ישראל by the clans of its ancestral houses [i.e. of its tribes] listing the names, every male, head by head. You and Aaron shall record them by their groups, from the age of twenty years up, all those in Israel who are able to bear arms.' This indicates that the כל־עדת בני־ישראל consists of all Israelite men over 20. Against this, it might be argued that כל־עדת בני־ישראל refers to the whole nation of Israel (Exod. 16.1, 16.2, 16.9, 16.10, 17.1, 35.1, 35.4, 35.20; Lev. 19.2; Num. 1.2, 8.9, 13.26, 14.7, 15.25). However, as Wenham points out, if the כל־עדת בני־ישראל consists of 'all Israelite men over twenty', it would contain representatives of every Israelite family.[39] It could therefore be used, on occasion, to designate the whole nation.[40] Interestingly, כל־עדת בני־ישראל is used in Num. 15.25 which has some parallels to Lev. 4.13, 'And the priest shall make atonement for כל־עדת בני־ישראל, and they shall be forgiven; because it was an error'.

The parallelism between כל־עדת ישראל and קהל in Lev. 4.13 ('If the כל־עדת ישראל commits a sin unwittingly and the thing is hidden from the eyes of the קהל') suggests that the two groups are synonymous. This synonymity appears to be confirmed in other texts. Although the term קהל can, on occasion, mean a select group (e.g. Ps. 26.5, 'I hate the company of evildoers [קהל מרעים]') phrases such as כל־קהל and כל־קהל ישראל are presented as being close to the meaning of כל־עדת ישראל. The phrase כל־קהל is used in Exod. 16.1-3 as a parallel to כל־עדת ישראל. Turning to כל־קהל ישראל, Josh. 8.35 states, 'there was not a word of all that Moses commanded which Joshua did not read before כל־קהל ישראל, and the women, and the little ones, and the sojourners who lived among them'. This implies that the כל־קהל ישראל did *not* include women, children and sojourners. This picture of the כל־קהל ישראל is consistent with the picture of the כל־עדת בני־ישראל in Num. 1.2-3 which refers to Israelite men over 20. The phrase כל־קהל ישראל is also used in 1 Kgs 8.14, 8.22, 8.55 which is important because at 1 Kgs 8.65 the writer uses the phrase, 'all Israel, a great assembly (קהל גדול)'. This connects the phrase כל־קהל ישראל to the shorter term קהל גדול which is used in a number of texts to refer to the whole nation (Jer. 44.15). In fact, there is no apparent difference between קהל גדול and קהל because קהל is used to mean 'a host' (Ezek. 16.40, 23.46-47). In Joel 2.15-16, the whole nation is implied in the

---

39. Wenham, *Leviticus*, p. 98.
40. Wenham, *Leviticus*, p. 98.

command, 'call a solemn assembly (עצרה), gather the people (עם). Sanctify the congregation (קהל); assemble the elders, gather the children, even nursing infants.' There are other permutations, of which the most important are כל־קהל עדת בני ישראל (Exod. 12.6) and כל קהל עדת ישראל (Num. 14.5). We may conclude that כל־עדת ישראל and קהל should be treated as parallel terms in Lev. 4.13.

If this is correct, the sin in Lev. 4.13-21 is not committed by a small, representative, group but by a multitude that includes, at the minimum, all Israelite men over 20. The wilderness narratives present the כל־עדת בני־ישראל as a corporate body capable of both obedience and deliberate sin. In Num. 27.20, YHWH commands Moses to invest Joshua with some of his (Moses') authority, 'that כל־עדת בני־ישראל may obey'. Clearly, if the whole people can be regarded as a corporate body capable of obedience they can also be regarded as a single body capable of offending. An example of this 'corporate responsibility' is found in Num. 13.26–14.10 in which the spies return from Canaan to report their findings to 'Moses and Aaron and to כל־עדת בני־ישראל' (Num. 13.26). The latter hear their report (Num. 14.7) but their response is to stone them with stones (Num. 14.10, where the referent is simply to the עדה). If the 'whole congregation' can 'obey' and 'rebel', it can also sin 'inadvertently'. This does not require every single member of the nation to sin 'inadvertently'. It merely requires that the *majority* of 'males over 20' sin inadvertently. (Even the deliberate sin of the whole congregation, described in Num. 14, does not include Joshua and Caleb!) Num. 14.7 strengthens the idea that the כל־עדת בני־ישראל consists of all Israelite men over 20. Everyone over 20 who rebelled against the spies was part of the generation who died in the wilderness (cf. Num. 14.29).[41] Finally, reference is made in the wilderness narratives to כל־עדת בני־ישראל appearing before Moses (Exod. 35.1, 35.4, 35.20) and Aaron (Exod. 16.10) for instruction. Exod. 16.10 describes how 'Aaron spoke unto כל־עדת בני־ישראל', suggesting that the 'error' in Case A might have arisen when the high priest mistakenly taught the כל־עדת בני־ישראל (all males over 20) and all, or the vast majority, followed his direction.

5.4.3. *Identity of* נשיא *(Case C [Leviticus 4.22-26])*
The definitive meaning of נשיא is contained in the Hexateuch. This is because the term נשיא in the Hebrew Bible always refers to a pre-monarchical figure, apart from a few scattered references and Ezekiel's

---

41. Wenham, *Leviticus*, p. 98.

'idiosyncratic' usage.⁴² The נשיא appears to be a leader, potentially at either tribal (cf. Num. 3.32, Josh. 22.14) or sub-tribal (Num. 3.30, 3.35) level. The נשיאים are frequently equated with the title ראשי בית אבתם (Num. 7.2; 36.1), suggesting that the נשיא had to be a duly recognized head of a בית אב and each could also designate the tribal chief.⁴³ Each tribal subdivision or clan was designated as בת־אבה and each could have its own נשיא⁴⁴ (cf. Num. 3.32 where the three Levite clans had individual נשיאים with a chief נשיא over them). Speiser argues that *any* patriarchal grouping, large or small, was headed by its own נשיא who was probably elected in the case of larger groups (cf. Num. 1.16 and Num. 16.2).⁴⁵ Speiser's view that, among such groups, נשיא stands for a 'duly elected chieftain' has since been supported by the discovery of a semantic equivalent in Ugaritic.⁴⁶ This means that there were plenty of נשיאים in ancient Israel. Indeed, Num. 1.5-16, 13.1-15 and 34.16-28 provide three discrete lists of the chieftains of the twelve tribes, none of which duplicates another.⁴⁷

The נשיאים represented the chief political authority of their day⁴⁸ with the right to declare war (Josh. 22.14), make treaties (Josh. 9.15) and decide property issues (Num. 36.1). The leaders of other tribal groups with whom Israel came into contact were also called נשיאים (Josh. 13.21). An executive council of the נשיאים, acting as representatives of their tribes, probably made important decisions. Speiser contends that just as clans and tribes each had their respective נשיא the same title was also applied to the head of a combination or confederation of a number of tribes. In this way a נשיא could hold national as well as clan or tribal office.⁴⁹ In contrast to the singular נשיא of Ezekiel (e.g. Ezek. 34.24) there is no definite article in Lev. 4.22 and so I conclude that Lev. 4.22-26 refers to any single member of the class of נשיאים.

---

42. I.M. Duguid, *Ezekiel and the Leaders of Israel* (VTSup, 56; Leiden: E.J. Brill, 1994), p. 14. For the development of chiefly authority in Israel see J.W. Flanagan, 'Chiefs in Israel', *JSOT* 20 (1981), pp. 47-73.
43. Milgrom, *Leviticus*, p. 247.
44. Milgrom, *Leviticus*, p. 247.
45. E.A. Speiser, 'Background and Function of the Biblical Nasi', *CBQ* 25 (1963), pp. 111-17 (113).
46. Duguid, *Leaders of Israel*, p. 12.
47. Milgrom, *Leviticus*, p. 246.
48. Duguid, *Leaders of Israel*, p. 14.
49. Speiser, 'Biblical Nasi', p. 114.

5.4.4. *Identity of* עם הארץ *(Cases D1 [Leviticus 4.27-31] and D2 [Leviticus 4.32-35])*

Some scholars argue that the phrase עם הארץ (lit. 'people of the land') in Lev. 4.27 includes priests and Levites as well as commoners.[50] Milgrom notes that עם הארץ can have this meaning in certain contexts such as Ezek. 45.22, cf. Ezek. 7.27, 45.16.[51] However, it is inadvisable to rely on Ezekiel because Ezekiel's use of נשיא is unusual[52] and the same may also be true of his use of עם הארץ. Milgrom also cites Hag. 2.4 in support of the view that עם הארץ includes priests and Levites, 'But be strong, O Zerubbabel—says the LORD—be strong, O high priest Joshua son of Jehozadak; be strong all you people of the land—says the LORD'. But it is far more likely that Zerubbabel and Joshua here represent the *office* of leadership both secular and sacred. If so, the phrase 'the people of the land' simply refers to those who are neither secular leaders nor sacred leaders. If so, Hag. 2.4 posits exactly the same oppositions we find in Leviticus 4 (see 5.2.5). These oppositions are those that occur between 'sacred leader' and 'secular leader' (Cases A and C) and between 'leaders' (Cases A and C) and 'followers' (Cases B and D). The phrase עם הארץ in Haggai 2 and Lev. 4.27 does not include the priests and the Levites but rather *excludes* them.[53] On occasion, it has an even more exclusive sense (e.g. 2 Kgs 21.24, 23.30 where it refers to a political group). The phrase עם הארץ explicitly excludes the priesthood in certain contexts, for example in Jer. 1.18 which defines עם הארץ as the *absence* of leaders and priests. Jer. 1.18 is consistent with the idea that there is a basic opposition between 'leaders' (defined as 'princes' and 'priests') and 'followers' (defined as the עם הארץ). My position is that the same opposition is apparent in Leviticus 4. The phrase עם הארץ in Lev. 4.27 should therefore be taken at face value to refer to the general class of common people. Consequently, the typical offender in Lev. 4.27-35 is any individual member of the class of commoners.

---

50. Milgrom, *Leviticus*, p. 251; G. Bush, *Notes on Leviticus* (Minneapolis: James & Klock, 1976 [1852]), p. 47.

51. Milgrom, *Leviticus*, p. 251.

52. Duguid, *Leaders of Israel*, p. 14.

53. It might be argued that because I have excluded the priesthood from my reading of the 'anointed priest' in Lev. 4.3 (see 5.2.1 above), we ought therefore to *include* the priesthood in my reading of Lev. 4.27. Such an argument is based on the premise that Lev. 4 must be exhaustive in its scope. However, as we saw in 5.2 above, there is no reason to assume that Lev. 4 is intended to be comprehensive.

5.4.5. *Summary*

We can sum up as follows. Case A (Lev. 4.3-12) deals with the high priest who leads the people into sin whilst Case B (Lev. 4.13-21) concerns the multitude, apparently acting independently and without being prompted by the high priest. Leviticus 4 does not state the consequences of the high priest acting on his own and without bringing guilt upon the people.[54] Case C (Lev. 4.22-26) deals with the inadvertent sin of the נשׂיא whilst Case D (Lev. 4.27-35) deals with the inadvertent sin of the member of the עם הארץ. From this brief sketch, it appears that there is a binary opposition between Cases A and C. Case A presents the case of the *sacred* leader (הכהן המשׁיח) whilst Case C presents that of a *secular* leader (the נשׂיא). Both B (כל־עדת ישׂראל) and D (עם הארץ) envisage the people (*en masse*) who follow their leaders. To this extent there is also a structural opposition between leaders (in Cases A and C) and followers (in Cases B and D).

Finally, the three cases dealing with individuals are presented in descending order of status. They are the sacred leader (Case A), followed by the secular leader (Case C) and the commoner (Case D). In addition, Case D (Lev. 4.27-35) can be subdivided into two cases, D1 (Lev. 4.27-31) and D2 (Lev. 4.32-35), depending on whether the חטאת is a female goat (Lev. 4.28) or a female lamb (Lev. 4.32). Descending order of status appears elsewhere in biblical law and in the ANE. Exodus 21 is arranged in descending order of the victim's status, starting with injuries to a free man (Exod. 21.12-19) followed by injuries to a male slave (Exod. 21.20-21) and injuries to a female slave (Exod. 21.26-27). A similar descending order is found in Exod. 21.28-35 which moves from a 'man or woman' (Exod. 21.28, 29) to a 'son or daughter' (Exod. 21.31) and then to a male or female slave (Exod. 21.32) and finally to animals (Exod. 21.33-35). Declining status is also found in LH 196 and 198.[55]

---

54. It might be argued that Cases A and B simply deal with two different ways in which the people make a mistake: in Case A it is thanks to the high priest and in Case B the people make the mistake on their own. However, this differentiation overlooks the focus of each case. In Case A, the focus is on the responsibility of the high priest whilst in Case B the focus is on the responsibility of the כל־עדת ישׂראל.

55. Roth, *Law Collections*, p. 121. Notably the class distinction between 'nobleman' and 'commoner' in LH makes the commoner's injury less serious. There is no distinction between 'nobleman' and 'commoner' in Exod. 21 although there is a difference in the treatment of slaves (Exod. 21.26-27, 21.32).

5.5. Registers of Seriousness in Leviticus 4

Figure 2, below, presents the main registers of seriousness of offence in Leviticus 4. They are presented separately to simplify matters although the registers are of course interconnected.

Figure 2. *Registers of seriousness according to status of offender in Leviticus 4*[56]

Status of Offender	Registers			
	1. *Type of animal*	2. *Blood rite*	3. *Object cleansed*	4. *Disposal of carcass*
הכהן המשיח	Bull	Brought into Holy Place; 7 times toward the veil	Incense altar horns	Destroyed
כל־עדת ישראל	Bull	Brought into Holy Place; 7 times toward the veil	Incense altar horns	Destroyed
נשיא	Male goat	Not brought into Holy Place	עלה altar horns	Eaten
Member of עם הארץ	Female goat or Female lamb or Female sheep	Not brought into Holy Place	עלה altar horns	Eaten

Figure 2 shows that registers of seriousness of offence in Leviticus 4 (measured by type of animal, blood rite, object cleansed and carcass disposal) are related to the status of the offender. We shall examine each of these registers as follows.

5.5.1. *Register 1. Type of Animal*
The type of animal functions as a register of seriousness in two respects.

5.5.1.1. *Declining Economic Value.*
Firstly, the sacrifices are presented in terms of declining economic value. Sacrifices could be, and indeed were, regarded in financial terms (e.g. Deut. 14.24-26). This is not surprising because sacrifice was the central means of revenue collection in the biblical world,[57] with similar linguistic terms used for sacrifice and tax records.[58] The Tabernacle was a national 'storehouse' and, to this extent,

---

56. Adapted from Jenson, *Graduated Holiness*, p. 172.
57. G.A. Anderson, *Sacrifices and Offerings in Ancient Israel: Studies in their Social and Political Importance* (Atlanta: Scholars Press, 1987).
58. Levine, *Leviticus*, p. xxiii.

5. *Sin, Status and Sacrifice*

the role of Israel's priests was somewhat akin to that of modern financiers (cf. 2 Kgs 18.13-16).[59] The more serious cases are dealt with by more expensive sacrifices and the less serious cases are dealt with by less expensive sacrifices. The young bull brought by the high priest (Lev. 4.4) and כל־עדת ישראל (Lev. 4.14) is more valuable than the male goat brought by the נשׂיא (Lev. 4.23). This in turn is more valuable than the female goat (Lev. 4.28) or female lamb (Lev. 4.32) brought by the member of the עם הארץ. The superior economic value of males in general over females is confirmed in Lev. 27.1-8. This may be psychological[60] and may reflect Israelite patriarchal custom. Within the sacrificial system, male animals are generally preferred to females although there are exceptions (e.g. Gen. 15.9 and 1 Sam. 6.14). A single male animal may also be worth more than a single female on the ground that one stud can service many females.[61] Declining economic value is paralleled elsewhere in the priestly system (e.g. Lev. 5.6-13 and comparing Lev. 14.10 with Lev. 14.21-22) where it is based on the principle of affordability (Lev. 5.7c, 5.11 and 14.21). A semantic approach sees Leviticus 4 as a set of rules which specify the exact economic value of the sacrifice. Thus Anderson claims regarding Leviticus 4, 'The priest (*sic*), community, ruler, and individual had their own requirements *that could not be varied*' (my italics).[62] A narrative approach, however, would see Leviticus 4 as a series of paradigm cases in which the correlation between status, seriousness and expense signifies the need to bring a sacrifice that is broadly in line with the offeror's status. Davies takes a narrative approach to Leviticus 4 when he notes that the severity of penalties may well have fluctuated in practice according to economic or other conditions.[63] This kind of leeway in sacrificial matters is seen elsewhere in the ANE. Line 85A of the text of the 'Nin Dinger' ritual states

---

59. Matthews and Benjamin, *Social World of Ancient Israel*, p. 191. Matthews and Benjamin claim, without citing sources, that the priests assessed the net worth of a household on the basis of the goods brought by its representatives. Households were not to send diseased animals or agricultural produce in an attempt to reduce the value of their appraisal (the ancient equivalent of 'tax-evasion').

60. P.A. Bird, 'Images of Women in the Old Testament', in N.K. Gottwald (ed.), *The Bible and Liberation* (Maryknoll, NY: Orbis Books, 1983), pp. 252-88 (263).

61. Wenham, *Leviticus*, p. 100.

62. E.g. G.A. Anderson, 'Sacrifice and Sacrificial Offerings', in *ABD*, V, pp. 870-86 (875).

63. E. Davies, 'Ethics of the Hebrew Bible: The Problem of Methodology'. *Semeia* 66 (1994), pp. 43-53 (47).

that in a good year the 'Nin Dinger' priestess will receive 'thirty *parisu* of barley', but only 'fifteen *parisu* of barley' in a bad year.[64] A narrative approach would also take account of regional variations concerning the relative wealth of a particular type of offender (e.g. it is likely that a נשיא in the Negev would be poorer than a נשיא in Upper Galilee). A final advantage of a narrative approach is that it does not matter that the priests are not formally mentioned in Leviticus 4 (see 5.2.1 above). The priests' sacrifice does not have to be specified because it can be calculated on the basis of what the other parties ought to bring.

5.5.1.2. Declining Visual Prestige. Secondly, and related to 5.3.1.1 above, the sacrifices are presented in declining order of visual prestige. The young bull (Lev. 4.4, 14) is the animal of finest prestige.[65] It is visually more impressive than the male goat (Lev. 4.23), the female goat (Lev. 4.28) and the female lamb (Lev. 4.32). The visual appearance of the sacrificial animals is relevant because it correlates with the status of the offenders, who are themselves doubtless the carriers of visual markers of distinction. Clothes functioned as social markers in ancient Israel, signifying gender (e.g. Deut. 22.5), employment (Exod. 28.31-42, 2 Sam. 20.8) and power relationships (e.g. 2 Sam. 13.18, 2 Kgs. 25.29).[66] For these reasons, it is likely that the clothes of the נשיא signified his higher standing in relation to a member of the עם הארץ whilst the high priest, in his ephod (Exod. 28.6-12, 39.2-7), breastplate (Exod. 28.15-30) and robe (Exod. 28.31-35, 39.22-26), was the most splendidly attired of all individuals in ancient Israel. Particularly impressive animals symbolized those who held power and prestige in Israelite society. The correlation between the visual prestige of the animal and the visual prestige of the offender is a good example of 'biotic rapport', viz., the idea that the sacrificial animal has somehow to 'represent' the person bringing the sacrifice.[67] It is a further way in which

---

64. Cf. also l. 85 C, D.E. Fleming, *The Installation of Baal's High Priestess at Emar* (Harvard Semitic Studies, 42; Atlanta: Scholars Press, 1992), pp. 58-59.

65. Douglas, *Leviticus as Literature*, p. 142.

66. Cf. their use in the Joseph narrative (V.H. Matthews, 'The Anthropology of Clothing in the Joseph Narrative', *JSOT* 65 [1995], pp. 25-36) and the David narrative, where David's accumulation and Saul's simultaneous loss of clothing provides a valuable measure of their relative power (O.H. Prouser, 'Clothes Maketh the Man', *BR* 14 [1998], pp. 22-27).

67. R.J. Thompson, 'Sacrifice and Offering: I. In the Old Testament', in *IBD*, III, pp. 1358-366 (1360).

type of animal functions as a register of seriousness in Leviticus 4 although unlike 5.3.1.1, above, this register is communicated in visual rather than purely financial terms.

5.5.2. *Register 2: Blood Rite.*

A second register is the nature of the blood rite. I noted at 5.1.3, above, that the main purpose of the חטאת ritual is to cleanse the Sanctuary of impurity and to re-establish the boundaries of the holy. Figure 3, below, presents an aerial map of the Tabernacle. This shows the position of the various cultic objects and the relative holiness of different parts of the Sanctuary.[68] This will help us to understand how the blood rites of Leviticus 4 function as an element of seriousness in Leviticus 4.

The boundaries of the holy are as follows. The most sacred part of the Tabernacle is the innermost shrine, the Holy of Holies (קדש הקדשים, Exod. 26.33) accessible only to the high priest on the Day of Atonement (Lev. 16.32-34). Of lesser sanctity is the Holy Place (הקדש, Exod. 26.33) which is restricted to the priests. The courtyard (חצר, Exod. 27.9-19) around the Holy of Holies and the Holy Place belongs to a lower category of the sacred and is open to the laity.[69] The entrance to the Tent of Meeting, marked on Figure 3 (פתח אהל מועד, Exod. 29.4, 29.32, 29.42, Lev. 1.3, 3.2, 12.6, 16.7) refers to the area between the bronze altar and the entrance to the court.

Leviticus 4 describes two distinct blood rites. In the first rite, the blood is brought into the Holy Place and sprinkled seven times in front of the veil that separates the Holy Place from the Holy of Holies (Cases A and B, Lev. 4.5-6, 4.16-17). The sevenfold sprinkling of the blood is peculiar to Cases A and B. Bush suggests that the number seven signifies the 'full and perfect cleansing of sin'[70] and thus the aggravated heinousness of the offence in Cases A and B. If so, it may act as a further register of seriousness. In the second rite, the ritual is restricted to the courtyard and the blood is not brought into the Holy Place (Cases C and D, Lev. 4.22-26, 4.27-35). In all four cases the spatial extent of the blood rites is in direct proportion to the extent of the pollution caused by the offenders'

---

68. Cf. Jenson, *Graduated Holiness*, pp. 89-114.
69. See J. Milgrom, 'The Shared Custody of the Tabernacle and a Hittite Analogy', *JAOS* 90 (1970), pp. 204-209 (207-208 n. 25).
70. Bush, *Leviticus*, p. 43.

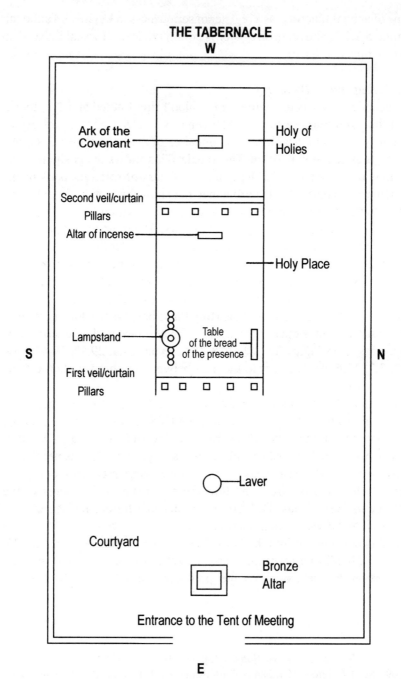

Figure 3. *Aerial view of Sanctuary showing grades of holiness*

inadvertence.⁷¹ In this way, the blood rites function as a register of seriousness. This correlation is consistent with the observation, above, that ritual preserves and protects the boundaries of the holy.⁷²

Figure 4, below, shows the extent of the blood rite in Cases A and B. The impurity caused by their inadvertent sin contaminates the Holy Place, and the courtyard. The blood applied on the curtain marks the outer boundary of the pollution caused by the high priest and כל־עדת ישראל.

A slightly different approach to seriousness is taken by Kiuchi who argues that it is the Holy of Holies, rather than the Holy Place that is defiled by the sin of הכהן המשיח or the כל־עדת ישראל.⁷³ Kiuchi argues that the veil cannot be separated functionally from the כפרת ('atonement slate') and approves Haron's observation that the veil is 'a kind of projection and "shadow" of the כפרת behind it'.⁷⁴ On this view, sprinkling the veil seven times does not refer to the curtain itself, which was not an instrument of expiation. Rather, sprinkling the veil is an indirect way of sprinkling the כפרת behind it. If Kiuchi is correct then it follows that the *whole* of Figure 2 should be shaded in as it would mean that the Holy of Holies would also be polluted by the sin of הכהן המשיח and the כל־עדת ישראל.

Figure 5 shows the extent of the blood rite in Cases C and D. In contrast to Figure 4, only the courtyard has been polluted. Consequently, the blood of the חטאת does not have to be brought into the Holy Place.

Figures 4 and 5 show that the impurity caused by the offenders in Cases A and B penetrates deeper into the Sanctuary than the impurity caused by the offenders in Cases C and D. We conclude from this that the inadvertent offending of the high priest and כל־עדת ישראל is more serious than that of the נשיא and the עם הארץ.

---

71. Milgrom, *Leviticus*, p. 257. Contra Budd, *Leviticus*, p. 81 who argues that the priest brings the blood into the Holy Place because the priest is implicated in the sin of Cases A and B, and the Holy Place is the area where the priest operates. This interpretation limits the range of Case B, which may be seen as a case where the people sin *without* being prompted by the high priest (see 5.2.2 above). Kiuchi, *Purification Offering*, p. 124 contends that the sprinkling of the blood towards the veil is necessitated by the fact that the sinner is הכהן המשיח or the כל־עדת ישראל, rather than by the fact that uncleanness reaches there.
72. Budd, *Leviticus*, p. 98.
73. Kiuchi, *Purification Offering*.
74. Kiuchi, *Purification Offering*, p. 125.

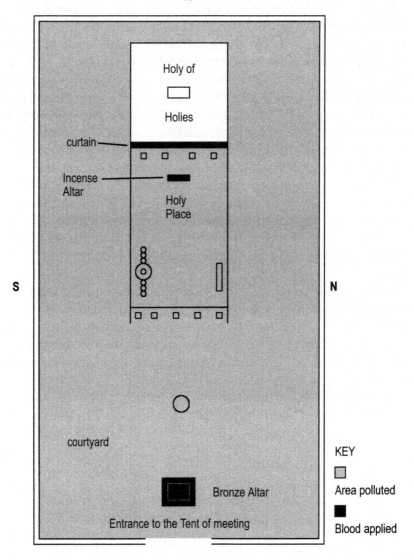

Figure 4. *Degree of pollution caused by the sin of the* כל־עדת ישראל *and the* הכהן המשיח

5. Sin, Status and Sacrifice   181

THE TABERNACLE

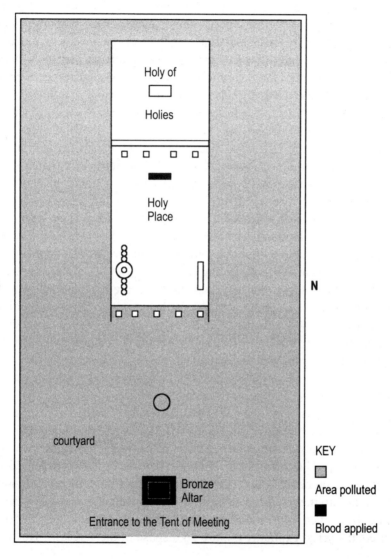

Figure 5. *Degree of pollution caused by the sin of the*
נשיא and the member of the עם הארץ

5.5.3. *Register 3: Object Cleansed*

A further register, related to 5.3.2 above, is the identity of the objects that are cleansed in the course of the ceremony. The blood of the חטאת is not daubed at random. It purges the very points that attract impurity. Pollution is drawn, not just to the Sanctuary—the implacable foe of impurity[75]—but, in particular, to its most sacred objects.[76] The bronze altar (which is the holiest object in the courtyard) and the incense altar (which is the holiest object in the Holy Place) are the holiest points of their respective areas (Exod. 29.37, Exod. 30.10). Like 'lightning-conductors' for impurity, they are the objects that attract contamination and have to be cleansed with the blood of the חטאת. In this way, as in register 5.3.2 above, the identity of the objects that are cleansed also indicates the extent of the pollution caused by the offenders' inadvertent sin. It functions as a register of seriousness because it shows how far impurity has penetrated the Sanctuary.

Figures 4 and 5, above, identify the objects that are applied with blood in Cases A–D. Figure 4, above, shows that in Cases A (Lev. 4.7) and B (Lev. 4.18) the blood of the חטאת is applied to the horns of the incense altar. Figure 5, above, shows that the blood of the חטאת is applied to the horns of the altar of burnt offering in Cases C (Lev. 4.25), D1 (Lev. 4.30) and D2 (Lev. 4.34). We may conclude that the inadvertent sin of the anointed priest and כל־עדת ישראל is thus more serious than the inadvertence of the נשיא and the עם הארץ. This is because it is a more serious matter to pollute the Holy Place and its sancta than it is to pollute the surrounding courtyard and its sancta.

5.5.4. *Register 4: Disposal of Carcass*

A fourth register is the manner in which the חטאת sacrifice is disposed of. In Cases A (Lev. 4.11-12) and B (Lev. 4.21) the priest is ordered to carry the carcass 'outside the camp to a clean place, where the ashes are poured out, and...[to] burn it on a fire of wood' (Lev. 4.12). This is in accordance with strict procedure, 'no חטאת shall be eaten from which any blood is brought into the tent of meeting to make atonement in the holy place; it shall be burned with fire' (Lev. 6.30 [H. 6.23]). Cases C and D do not direct the priest explicitly on how to dispose of the carcass.[77] However,

---

75. Milgrom, 'Israel's Sanctuary', p. 395.
76. Milgrom, 'Israel's Sanctuary', p. 393.
77. Levine, *Presence of the Lord*, p. 104 sees the difference between disposal of the carcass in Cases A and B and that of Cases C and D as evidence that there were originally two different חטאת rituals (one a 'rite of riddance' and the other a 'gift of expi-

unlike in Cases A and B, the implication is that the carcass is eaten by the priests (cf. Lev. 10.17). Notably Lev. 5.1-13, which follows on directly from Lev. 4.22-35, also appears to be concerned with חטאת that should be eaten. Milgrom suggests that the חטאת may not be eaten in Cases A and B because of the principle that no priest should profit from his own sin.[78]

This difference in the disposal of the carcass appears to lie in the fact that the blood of the חטאת in Cases A and B purges the inner Sanctuary, whereas the blood of the חטאת in Cases C and D only purges the outer altar.[79] The method of disposal functions as a register of seriousness because, as with 5.3.2 and 5.3.3 above, it signifies the degree of pollution caused by the offenders' act of inadvertence.

We have already seen that it is a more serious matter to contaminate the Holy Place than it is to contaminate the courtyard. Accordingly, the sacrifice in Cases A and B absorbs more impurity than the blood of the חטאת in Cases C and D.[80] This means that the blood of the חטאת has the potential to contaminate those who come across it. So too does the carcass, on the principle of *pars pro toto*. The whole animal partakes of the impurity of the blood.[81] Consequently, the remains of this sacrifice must be removed

---

ation'). Milgrom, 'Israel's Sanctuary', disagrees, claiming that the difference between the two חטאת rituals is a difference of degree, rather than of quality. They do not vary in function, but in the degree of impurity that they purge.

78. Milgrom, *Leviticus*, p. 264, cf. Budd, *Leviticus*, p. 80.

79. Milgrom, 'Israel's Sanctuary', pp. 261-64 finds support for his thesis in Lev. 10.16-20. Here, Moses makes it clear that the חטאת should have been eaten because the blood had not been brought into the inner Sanctuary (Lev. 10.18). From this it appears that the manner of disposal depends on the use to which the blood has been put. The crucial question is whether the blood has been brought into the holy place. If it has then the flesh must not be eaten. Kiuchi, *Purification Offering*, disagrees, claiming that the mode of disposal of the חטאת is determined by whether Aaron bears his own guilt, including the guilt arising out of his capacity as high priest.

80. Budd, *Leviticus*, p. 81 argues that the unique power of sacrificial blood lies in its ability to take away impurity without thereby becoming contaminated itself. For this reason, there is no need to suppose that the חטאת becomes contaminated or carries contamination away. Budd argues that if the carcass did become contaminated, it seems unlikely that the priests would ever be allowed to eat it, or that in other circumstances it could be carried away to a clean place (Lev. 4.12, 21). The view that the blood of the חטאת absorbs sin and uncleanness is criticized by Kiuchi, *Purification Offering*, on the grounds that this view fails to distinguish between uncleanness in the camp and uncleanness envisaged in the sancta.

81. Kiuchi, *Purification Offering*, p. 142 contends that both the eaten and the burnt חטאת are contagious, but that they show disparity in the contagiousness. Kiuchi argues

from the camp.⁸² The lesser impurity of the חטאת sacrifice in Cases C and D, by contrast, means that this carcass does not have to be removed.⁸³ We may conclude that, on this register, the inadvertent offences of Cases A and B are more serious than those of C and D.

5.5.5. *Summary*

Registers of seriousness in Leviticus 4 include type of animal, blood rite, object cleansed and the method of destroying the carcass. Underlying these registers are the interlocking constructs of status and space. Status is relevant when considering the symbolic link between the type of animal and the status of the offeror (see 5.3.1.2 above), the status of the zone used to perform the ritual (see 5.3.2 above), and the status of the object on which the blood is applied (see 5.3.3 above). Space is relevant when considering which area the blood is brought into (see 5.3.2 above), the location of the ritual object to be cleansed (see 5.3.3 above) and where the carcass is destroyed (see 5.3.4 above). Status and space are central to the priestly worldview and to the ritual order of the Tabernacle.⁸⁴ These are exactly the categories that we might expect the Priestly writers to use to communicate their beliefs concerning the seriousness of inadvertent sins. They indicate that Cases A and B are the two joint 'top-of-the-league' cases of seriousness. These cases are more serious than Cases C and D, as measured by type of animal, blood rite, object cleansed and method of

---

that the eaten חטאת conveys holiness within the Sanctuary whereas the burnt חטאת probably conveys holiness within the Sanctuary, but defiles its handler outside the camp.

82. 'Outside the camp' is typically where the unclean dwell, but the carcass itself is deposited in a 'clean place' (Lev. 4.12, 21). By contrast, Kiuchi, *Purification Offering*, pp. 141-42 argues that the rationale of burning חטאת is that when expiation involves the sin of Aaron (not only as an individual but also in his capacity as high priest) the חטאת must be burned outside the camp to remove his guilt. Kiuchi, *Purification Offering*, p. 135 argues that the burning of the חטאת probably symbolizes 'removal of guilt'.

83. Rather, it is necessary and appropriate for this sacrifice to be eaten by the priests. As in Cases A and B, the flesh of the חטאת is destroyed, but by different means, Milgrom, 'Israel's Sanctuary', pp. 261-64. Contra J. Dunnill, *Covenant and Sacrifice in the letter to the Hebrews* (Cambridge: Cambridge University Press, 1992), p. 96 who suggests, without citing sources, that the consumption of the flesh by the priests rather than by fire identifies them as vehicles of divine power and as mediators between human sin and God's holiness.

84. Gorman, *Ideology of Ritual*, p. 234.

carcass disposal. Finally, the register of type of animal introduces a distinction between Cases C and D, showing that Case C is more serious than Case D, as measured by type of animal.

5.6. Conclusion

Leviticus 4 holds a particular offence (sins of inadvertence) constant throughout but it prescribes different outcomes depending on the identity of the offender. This allows us to draw the following conclusions. Firstly, the inadvertent sin of the high priest who leads the people into sin is a more serious offence than the inadvertent sin of a נשיא. The sin of a sacred leader is more serious than the sin of a secular leader. Secondly, the sin of a נשיא is more serious than the sin of a member of the עם הארץ. The sin of a leader is more serious than the sin of a follower. Sin is great when great men sin. Thirdly, the sin of a high priest who leads the people into sin is equal in gravity to the collective sin of the people, acting on their own account. Finally, the inadvertent sin of the whole people, acting collectively, is more serious than the inadvertence of a single individual, whether a נשיא or a member of the עם הארץ. The question of whether the inadvertent sin of כל־עדת ישראל is more serious than an inadvertent sin of the high priest that does not bring guilt upon the people, is undetermined.

Chapter 6

THE SHEKHINAH DEPARTS:
SERIOUSNESS OF OFFENCE AND EZEKIEL 8.1-18

> The central neurosis of our time is emptiness.
> Carl Jung

Ezekiel 8 is relevant to our understanding of seriousness for several reasons. Firstly, there is the scale of the offence and its repercussions. Idolatry in the Temple causes the glory of God to depart (Ezek. 8.6, 9.3, 10.4, 10.18 and 11.23) and the result is Israel's collapse and exile. The stakes could not be higher. Secondly, it is relevant because the four abominations are not of equal gravity. Ezekiel 8 makes a judgment of *relative* seriousness. Thirdly, the case-study in Ezekiel 8 is presented to a distinct semiotic group: 'the elders' of Judah'. We might therefore assume a sophisticated message on the ground that, in ancient Israel, different levels of ethics were thought appropriate to different social classes owing to different levels of understanding of *torah* (cf. Jer. 5.4-5).[1]

6.1. *Performative Registers of Seriousness*

Ezekiel 8 contains a number of registers of seriousness. The main performative register is the departure of the *Shekhinah*[2]—the glory of YHWH—from the Temple. The loss of the divine presence is foreshadowed in the conventional translation[3] of Ezek. 8.6, 'Son of man, do you see what they

---

1. J. Barton, 'Ethics in Isaiah of Jerusalem', *JTS* 32 (1981), pp. 1-18.
2. The word *Shekhinah* is not found in the Hebrew Bible. It is a Talmudic term derived from the biblical verb שׁכן ('to dwell') and it literally means 'the act of dwelling'. It denotes the visible and audible manifestation of God's presence on earth (cf. Ezek. 10.4-5). See R. Patai, *The Hebrew Goddess* (Detroit: Wayne State University Press, 1990), pp. 96-111.
3. Contra M. Greenberg, *Ezekiel: 1–20* (New York: Doubleday, 1983) who argues that the subject of the verb is not YHWH but the House of Israel. This results in 'the

6. The Shekhinah Departs

are doing, the great abominations that the House of Israel are committing here, *to drive Me far from My Sanctuary?*' (my italics). The dread event finally occurs in Ezek. 9-11[4] where the fourfold departure of the glory of YHWH parallels the fourfold movement of the prophet in Ezek. 8.5-18.[5] 'Divine temple abandonment' was a well-established form of covenantal judgment in first- and second-millennium Mesopotamia[6] and was imposed by a god upon his people for breach of covenant. A typical example is the Middle-Assyrian 'Tukulti-Ninurta Epic' in which a wrathful pantheon abandon their temples and holy cities and leave the Kassite king (Kashtili-ash IV) to certain defeat.[7] Divine temple abandonment was an extremely serious sanction. When a god deserted his people and removed his protection, the result was military defeat, foreign dominion and exile.[8] It was a nightmare 'end-of-the-world' scenario rather like nuclear war for modern popular culture. A more total disaster is hard to imagine.

In the context of ancient Israel, divine temple abandonment was especially serious because the Presence of YHWH was the greatest blessing of the Mosaic covenant and his absence was the greatest curse. The filling of the Tabernacle by 'the presence of YHWH' is the destiny of Israel and the climax of the book of Exodus. Likewise, the jewel in Solomon's crown

---

great abominations that the House of Israel are committing here *removing themselves from My Sanctuary?*' (my italics). He claims that when the idiom רחק מעל is used in conjunction with humankind and God, the subject of the verb is always the people. For it to refer to God, one would expect a personal pronoun, indicating a change of subject, or, say, a *hifil* verb, showing that it was somebody else who was 'driven out'. Yet who else can be driven from the Sanctuary but YHWH?

4. See Ezek. 9.3, 10.4, 10.18 and 11.23.

5. D.I. Block, *The Book of Ezekiel* (Grand Rapids: Eerdmans, 1997), p. 273.

6. Block, *Ezekiel*, pp. 275-76, 298; J.J. Niehaus *God at Sinai: Covenant and Theophany in the Bible and Ancient Near East* (Carlisle: Paternoster Press, 1995), pp. 136-41.

7. Cf. also an inscription of Esarhaddon, describing the deity's flight from the temple of Esagila because of divine wrath at the sinfulness of the people, Niehaus, *God at Sinai*, pp. 137-39.

8. Protection was one of the most important obligations of a suzerain towards his vassal (cf. Ps. 27.5). The loss of YHWH's presence meant the loss of protection for his people. 'The security of Zion is grounded in its creation by Yahweh as the site of his royal residence', B.C. Ollenburger, *Zion, the City of the Great King* (JSOTSup, 41; Sheffield: JSOT Press, 1987), p. 147. It follows that when the great King leaves, Zion must fall. We note that 'abandonment' and 'loss of protection' were also a serious punishment insofar as the whole nation was exposed to shame (cf. Ps. 89.39-45), Bechtel, 'Perception of Shame', pp. 83-84.

was the arrival of the *Shekhinah* glory to the completed Temple, showing YHWH's intention to 'live' in his house with his people as his 'household' (1 Kgs 8.10-13). Only after the Presence of the LORD had filled the Temple could Solomon turn and bless 'the whole congregation of Israel' (1 Kgs 8.14). Ezekiel 8 dramatically reverses the order of events in 1 Kings 8. YHWH appears in theophany to demonstrate not his dwelling, but his departure. Whereas the arrival of the *Shekhinah* in 1 Kings 8 marked the completion of its journey from Mount Sinai and signified that the people's wandering is over, the departure of the *Shekhinah* in Ezekiel 8 signifies that the people's wandering must begin again.[9] For when YHWH abandons his 'house', his conquered and uprooted people must leave their homes as well. There is a parallel between what happens to YHWH's 'house' and what happens to his people's 'houses': the foreigners who loot YHWH's 'house' (7.21) will sack his people's homes as well (7.23-24). When the *Shekhinah* departs, exile begins.

The 'glory of the God of Israel' (Ezek. 8.4) which departs from the Temple is described in Ezekiel's first vision (Ezek. 1.1–3.15) as 'an immense cloud with flashing lightning and surrounded by a brilliant light' (Ezek. 1.4).[10] The language evokes a theophany and especially the theophany at Sinai. The fourfold reference to 'fire' in Ezek. 1.13 recalls the 'fire' which consumed Mount Sinai (Exod. 19.18) whilst Ezekiel's description of 'the semblance of a throne, in appearance like sapphire' (Ezek. 1.26) recalls 'the likeness of a pavement of sapphire' seen by Moses and the elders on the mountain (Exod. 24.9-10). This is significant in view of the argument advanced at 6.3.6 below that the four abominations are based on a narrative typification of idolatry in the Decalogue (Exod. 20.3-6). Ezekiel reminds his hearers of the Sinaitic covenant before describing the breach (Ezek. 8.3-18) that makes divine temple abandonment the only possible response. It is perhaps also significant that the prophet receives the first manifestation of YHWH in the form of a theophanic 'thunderous voice' (Ezek. 1.24). The combination of 'roar' and 'many waters' evokes the theophanic description of YHWH enthroned above the judgment waters of the Flood.[11] The presence of God and his departure evokes a scene of theo-

---

9. Niehaus, *God at Sinai*, p. 276.
10. The translation is from Niehaus, *God at Sinai*, p. 255.
11. Niehaus, *God at Sinai*, p. 259. See Ps. 29.3, 10, 'The voice of the LORD is over the waters, the God of glory thunders, the LORD, over the mighty waters… The LORD sat enthroned at the Flood, the LORD sits enthroned, King, forever.'

phanic judgment that is strengthened in view of the allusion to the Deluge in Ezek. 8.17 (see 6.6.1 below).

6.2. *Descriptive Registers of Seriousness*

The main descriptive register is naming the idols as 'abominations' (תועבות, Ezek. 8.6, 13, 15 and 17). The word תועבה is a highly emotive term that stigmatizes what God hates, 'Yet I persistently sent to you all my servants the prophets, to say, "I beg you not to do this abominable thing which I *hate*"' (Jer. 44.4, my italics). תועבה signifies that which is morally repugnant, both in and of itself and to God.[12] In particular, Leviticus and Deuteronomy associate תועבה with the deeds of the Canaanites that resulted in their being vomited out of the land.[13] תועבה thus refers to behaviour which risks expulsion from the Land.[14] This is probably why Ezekiel uses the word תועבה more than any other Hebrew author.[15] Part of Ezekiel's message is that Israel has been sent into exile because of her abominations (e.g. 'Thus said the LORD YHWH... I will execute judgments in your midst in the sight of the nations. *On account of all your abominations*, I will do among you what I have never done, and the like of which I will never do again' (Ezek. 5.5, 8-9; my italics). Hallo's review of ANE terms sharing the semantic field of 'divine abominations' shows that they embrace two widely divergent realms.[16] The first involves the infraction of ethical norms or standards of good conduct (e.g. having dishonest weights, ignoring the poor and so on). The second meaning of 'abominations' is concerned with the sacred nature of deity and, in the context of Israel, it refers to the practices of alien cults that were anathema to YHWH. This is the sense in which תועבה is used in Ezekiel 8. The effect of the four abominations is to 'goad' YHWH to 'fury' (8.17).

A second descriptive register which also has a strongly affective aspect is the description of the first abomination as 'the statue of jealousy that

---

12. W.H. Pickett, 'The Meaning and Function of *T'b/To'evah* in the Hebrew Bible' (PhD thesis submitted to Hebrew Union College, Cincinnati, 1985), p. 281.

13. Cf. Pickett, 'Meaning and Function of *T'b*', p. 285.

14. Pickett, 'Meaning and Function of *T'b*', p. 285.

15. 43 times, compared to 21 times for Proverbs and 16 times for Deuteronomy, P. Humbert, 'Le substantif *tô'ebah* et la verbe *t'b* dans l'Ancien Testament', *ZAW* 72 (1960), pp. 217-37 (219).

16. W.W. Hallo, 'Biblical Abominations and Sumerian Taboos', *JQR* 76 (1985), pp. 21-40.

provokes to jealousy' (סמל הקנאה, Ezek. 8.5). The word קנאה ('jealous') describes the 'passionate resentment'[17] that YHWH feels at seeing what belongs to him being given to another. It underscores the relational character of idolatry because only an exclusive and valued relationship arouses jealousy when threatened. This is consistent with Exod. 20.5 and 34.14 which present YHWH's jealousy as the reason for the prohibition of idolatry. According to Exod. 20.5, idolatry causes YHWH to requite the active hatred shown by idolatry with hatred, even as he requites love with love.[18] The use of forceful and emotive registers to elicit strong feelings of aversion is typical of the prophet's shock tactics (cf. Ezekiel 6, 16 and 23) which are designed to break down the resistance of a hardened audience (Ezek. 2.3-8, 3.7). Interestingly, this emotional reaction to idolatry is the very basis of judgment in Ezekiel 9. Only those 'who *moan and groan* because of all the abominations that are committed [in Jerusalem]' (Ezek. 9.4, my italics) are spared the carnage of Ezek. 9.5-7. Once again the affective connotations of תועבות are central: what seals the Jerusalemites' doom is that they simply do not care.

6.3. *Offence Description*

Ezekiel 8 presents four cases of idolatry in the Temple. The total is significant because four is the number of completeness in Ezekiel. It signifies that the Temple is totally corrupt and riddled with idolatry.

6.3.1. *Abominations Unmasked*

The offence is witnessed through the eyes of a priest who was among those deported a thousand miles from Jerusalem to Babylon when the city was first invaded by the Babylonians in 597 BCE (Ezek. 1.2-3).[19] The text takes the form of a visionary experience and is dated to the fifth day of the sixth month of the sixth year of King Jehoiachin's exile (Ezek. 8.1) which computes to 18 September 592 BCE in our calendar.[20] Although the veracity

17. Greenberg, *Ezekiel*, p. 168.
18. Jackson, 'Literary Presentation', p. 190.
19. The deportation subsequent to the initial invasion in 597 BCE meant that between 597 BCE and 587 BCE there were two 'Houses of Israel', the 'House of Israel-in-exile' and the 'House of Israel' left behind in Judah and Jerusalem. This explains why the 'elders' of Judah/ the House of Israel are both the subjects of the vision (8.11) as well as its audience (8.1). There are two groups of elders: those in exile and those (including Jaazaniah in 8.11) who are left behind in Jerusalem.
20. The dates in Ezekiel constitute a homogeneous system, the antecedents of

6. *The Shekhinah Departs*

of the vision is heavily debated there is ample justification for the traditional view that Ezekiel went into exile in 597 BCE and prophesied from Babylon.[21] There are several indications that the events to which he is an eyewitness occur on the day of the vision itself. Firstly, the divine agent who shows the prophet around the Temple always uses the word 'here' (פה) whereas the prophet always uses the word 'there' (שם). This suggests that the divine agent is present in Jerusalem whereas the prophet is not there 'in the flesh'. For the divine agent, Jerusalem is 'here' (i.e., immediately present) whereas to the prophet Jerusalem is 'there' (i.e., away from Babylon). These deictic expression are sufficient justification for treating the vision naturalistically. The vision refers to events that were happening in Jerusalem, at that moment, whilst the prophet was in Babylon. Secondly, Ezekiel's oracle of judgment upon Jerusalem (9.1–11.25) has added bite if we assume that Ezekiel 8 refers to current events. If this presumption is correct, Ezekiel 8 is not 'a prediction of a future event, but an extension of a present one'.[22] It is a vision of a distant land rather than a distant future. But it is not as though the elders had the benefit of a live satellite link-up with Jerusalem. Ezekiel presents, not a live report, but a prophetic interpretation of events. The purpose of Ezekiel's prophecy is to rebut the widespread questioning of YHWH's power (e.g. Ezek. 8.12b, 9.9) and to tell the deportees why they are in exile. They are not in exile because an impotent deity abandoned the Land but because a powerful Judge left his Temple in revulsion at its abominations. These abominations can be unmasked as follows.

---

which are grounded in the captivity of 597 BCE, K.S. Freedy and D.B. Redford, 'The Dates in Ezekiel in Relation to Biblical, Babylonian and Egyptian Sources', *JAOS* 90 (1970), pp. 462-85. The date for Ezek. 8.1 is derived from the internal chronology of Ezekiel which claims that the events of Ezekiel 8 take place a year and two months after those of Ezek. 1.1-2, e.g. G.A. Cooke, *The Book of Ezekiel* (Edinburgh: T. & T. Clark, 1936), p. 89.

21. D.N. Freedman, 'The Book of Ezekiel', *Int* 8 (1954), pp. 446-71 (455) states that 'whatever outside evidence we have tends to confirm the traditional position of the Book of Ezekiel.' At p. 455 he cites Rowley's conclusion: 'The ministry of Ezekiel I would place wholly in Babylonia in the period immediately before and after the fall of Jerusalem'. M. Smith, 'The Veracity of Ezekiel, the Sins of Manasseh, and Jeremiah 44.18', *ZAW* 87 (1975), pp. 11-16 (11) speaks of 'the return of scholarship to the opinion that Ezekiel worked in Babylonia during the twenty or thirty years after 593 BCE'. W.D. Stacey, *Prophetic Drama in the Old Testament* (London: Epworth Press, 1990), p. 183 claims that this is now the 'majority' position.

22. Stacey, *Prophetic Drama*, p. 183.

6.3.2. *The First Abomination (Ezekiel 8.3-6)*

This is 'the image of jealousy, which provokes to jealousy' (סמל הקנאה המקנה, Ezek. 8.3). The meaning of סמל is unclear, although Phoenician usage denotes a statue of either a divine or a human being.[23] King Manasseh places a פסל הסמל (2 Chron. 33.7) in the Temple, only to remove it later (2 Chron. 33.15). 2 Chron. 33.7 is seemingly a paraphrase of 2 Kgs 21.7 which openly speaks of a פסל האשרה ('graven representation of the אשרה [Asherah]', a Canaanite fertility goddess). Clearly there was a tradition that designated Manasseh's סמל as an Asherah. It is thus possible that the first abomination is an Asherah.[24] The position (מושב, Ezek. 8.3) of the סמל seems to be well known,[25] suggesting that an Asherah occupied the spot, off and on, since Manasseh's reign. There is something slightly sinister about the use of בבאה at the end of Ezek. 8.5 which JPS neatly translates: '[the] image *on the approach*' (emphasis added). The connection between the crime and its punishment is so close that it is almost as though the encroachment of the image on to the northern gate signifies the foreign armies themselves advancing from the north (cf. Jer. 1.13-14).[26] In another age, the statue might almost be seen as a symbolic Trojan horse.

6.3.3. *The Second Abomination (Ezekiel 8.3-6)*

The second abomination is set in a hidden room which is possibly part of a casemate wall. This type of construction consists of an outer and an inner wall joined together by cross-walls.[27] Not all the 'rooms' need have been filled (cf. Josh. 2.15, 2 Kgs 4.10) with the result that the prophet could

---

23. H. Torczyner, 'Semel Ha-qin'ah Ha-Maqneh', *JBL* 65 (1946), pp. 293-302 (298); D.J. Halperin, *Seeking Ezekiel* (Pennsylvania: Pennsylvania State University Press, 1993), p. 119.

24. Contra W. Zimmerli, *Ezekiel I: A Commentary on the Book of the Prophet Ezekiel Chapters 1–24* (trans. R.E. Clements; Philadelphia: Fortress Press, 1979), p. 238 who assumes that the first abomination is located at the outer gate of the city and therefore cannot be the same as the Asherah set up by Manasseh 'in the Temple [area?]' (2 Kgs 23.6 cf. 21.5). However, I argue at 6.6.3 below that the Temple is the location of all four abominations. If so, there is no reason why the idol in Ezek. 8.3-6 could not have been the reinstatement of Manasseh's Asherah in the Temple area.

25. Zimmerli, *Ezekiel I*, p. 238.

26. The direction from which the Assyrians attacked Jerusalem in 701 BCE and the Babylonians in 597 BCE and 587 BCE. Ezekiel knew very well that judgment comes from the north in the form of foreign invaders, having been among those deported from Jerusalem to Babylon after the first Babylonian invasion of 597 BCE.

27. G.E. Wright, 'Israelite Daily Life', *BA* 18 (1955), pp. 50-79 (57-58).

have emerged either into a room in the casemate wall itself or into a room that was part of the house attached to the casemate wall on its interior side.[28] Ezekiel's unusual mode of entrance (clearly the prophet could not gain access by conventional means) and the exclusivity of the gathering suggests that Ezek. 8.10-12 is an example of clandestine idolatry (cf. Deut. 27.15). However, this is unlikely because clandestine idolatry presupposes a society that is hostile to idolatry. This does not seem to be the case in Ezekiel 8. It is more likely that the secrecy is part of the internal dynamic of the cult and a means of preserving the rite for an élite. The 'vile abominations' (התועבות הרעות, Ezek. 8.9) are the secret engravings of 'all detestable (שקץ) forms of creeping things (רמש) and beasts (ובהמה) and all the fetishes (גלול י) of the House of Israel' (Ezek. 8.10). The word שקץ appears in Lev. 11.10-11 and, given the close relationship between Ezekiel and the Priestly writings,[29] it is possible that the second abomination refers to engravings of the forbidden creatures described in Lev. 11.10-11. If so, a priest such as Ezekiel would think it horrific that these illicit creatures have become the objects of worship. Notably, the only other use of the word מקטרת ('incense-burner', 8.11) appears in connection with King Uzziah who intrudes upon the priestly prerogative by offering incense before the altar (2 Chron. 26.19).[30] This implies an intrusion by the elders into a prohibited cultic sphere (cf. the role of the elders in Ezek. 8.16, see 6.3.5 below).

6.3.4. *The Third Abomination (Ezekiel 8.14-15)*
The third abomination is the spectacle of 'the women wailing for the Tammuz' (8.15). The Hebrew derives from the Sumerian 'Dumuzi' meaning 'the good (or "the right") son'.[31] It is thought that Tammuz worship was a mourning rite in which women lament for the disappearance of a young male figure who led a lonely and dangerous life as a shepherd[32] in the

---

28. S. Ackerman, 'A *Marzeah* in Ezekiel 8:7-13?', *HTR* 82 (1989), pp. 267-81 (270).

29. E.g. A. Hurvitz, *A Linguistic Study of the Relationship between the Priestly Source and the Book of Ezekiel* (Paris: Gabalda, 1982), p. 9.

30. Zimmerli, *Ezekiel I*, p. 241.

31. Notably T. Jacobsen, 'Toward the Image of Tammuz', in William L. Moran (ed.), *Toward the Image of Tammuz and other Essays on Mesopotamian History and Culture* (Cambridge, MA: Harvard University Press, 1970), pp. 73-103.

32. B. Alster, 'Tammuz', in K. van der Toorn *et al.* (eds.), *Dictionary of Deities and Demons in the Bible* (Leiden: E.J. Brill, 1995), pp. 1567-79 (1570) and see the literature review by O.R. Gurney, 'Tammuz Reconsidered: Some Recent Developments', *JSS* 7

desert.³³ Dumuzi's 'disappearance' is often associated with the autumn (when the leaves fell) and his subsequent 'revival' with the spring (when the leaves began to sprout). The date of the vision is consistent with the onset of autumn and with Dumuzi's 'disappearance'. Most of the surviving lamentation texts are written in a dialect spoken mainly by women,³⁴ consistent with the picture given in Ezekiel 8 of a woman's cult.³⁵ The laments are only known in Sumerian and not in any West Semitic texts.

6.3.5. *The Fourth Abomination (Ezekiel 8.16)*

The fourth abomination describes men 'worshipping שמש in the east' (8.16). This might refer to Shamash, the Mesopotamian deity who upheld covenants, however the word שמש, as used in the Hebrew Bible, is never an actual divine name.³⁶ If it does refer to Shamash, the elders' behaviour before Shamash, the supposed 'god of covenant', is highly ironic. This is because Israel's elders (the same group who ratified the covenant on Mount Sinai according to Exod. 24.9-11) are themselves turning their back on that very covenant. At the same time, these covenant-breakers imagine they are worshipping 'the god of covenant', an act which causes the *real* 'God of the covenant' to initiate the covenant curses.

However, it is probably more likely that the fourth abomination is a form of sun-worship contrary to Deut. 17.3 (cf. Deut. 4.19). According to 2 Kgs 21.3, 23.5 worship of the 'host of heavens' (comprising the sun, the moon and the planets) took place during the reigns of Manasseh and Amon. This text refers to a period when Judah was an Assyrian vassal and it is thought by some that the sun-cult may have been foisted on Judah as a token of her subjection.³⁷ Others claim that the sun-cult was not popular in

---

(1962), pp. 147-60. In Sumerian mythology, Dumuzi's true nature was that of the shepherd although Jacobsen, 'Image of Tammuz', seeks to add other aspects to 'Dumuzi's' identity.

33. Alster, 'Tammuz', pp. 1568–77.

34. The laments are expressed through such figures as the mother, the sister and the widow. Male representatives such as a sorrowing father or brother find no place. In addition, the great events that are celebrated in the cult are the events of a woman's life, Jacobsen, 'Image of Tammuz', pp. 90-91.

35. Jacobsen, 'Image of Tammuz', p. 90.

36. E. Lipiński, 'Shemesh', in Karel van der Toorn *et al.* (eds.), *Dictionary of Deities and Demons in the Bible* (Leiden: E.J. Brill, 1995), pp. 1445-52 (1445).

37. Though contrast M. Cogan, *Imperialism and Religion: Assyria, Judah and Israel in the Eighth and Seventh Centuries BCE* (SBLMS, 19; Missoula, MT: 1974).

Iron Age Syria-Palestine, in contrast to Egypt and Mesopotamia.[38] A third possibility is that the rite was not a straightforward case of sun-worship but a corrupt, solar interpretation of pure YHWH worship. The ancients believed that the face of a god (like the sun) radiated light and life to those who beheld it. A prayer of Nebuchadnezzar (604–562 BCE)—the very commander laying siege to Jerusalem—entreats, '[O Shamash] look with your radiant countenance, your happy face joyfully upon the precious works of my hands'.[39] There is tragic irony in the elders' turning their backs on YHWH's שלום to turn their faces towards a different sort of 'light'. It is because the elders bow down to this sort of 'radiance' that the 'radiance' of YHWH himself leaves the Temple (Ezek. 10.4). It is easy to see how metaphorical texts[40] which describe YHWH as his people's light[41] and the sun as a vivid symbol of his glory[42] could have been misused to corrupt pure YHWH worship, especially given that sun worship and YHWH worship overlapped in the biblical period. This may explain the statement, for example in Deut. 17.3, that YHWH 'never commanded' the worship of heavenly bodies. This would not have been necessary unless there was a tendency to treat solar symbolism as a licence for 'solar-YHWH' worship.

With this in mind we should note the possibility that the fourth abomination may therefore be a fusion of a YHWH festival with a solar rite, perhaps even a corrupt version of the Feast of Booths.[43] Interestingly, the

38. Lipiński, 'Shemesh', p. 1445.
39. Niehaus, *God at Sinai*, p. 124.
40. As S.A. Wiggins, 'Yahweh: The God of Sun', *JSOT* 71 (1996), pp. 89-106 is keen to stress in response to J.G. Taylor, *Yahweh and the Sun* (JSOTSup, 111; Sheffield: Sheffield Academic Press, 1993).
41. See also Ps. 78.14 and cf. Moses' luminosity (Exod. 34.29) and the famous Aaronic blessing (Num. 6.24-26).
42. Lipiński, 'Shemesh', p. 1448.
43. Some scholars argue that סכות (the 'Feast of Booths') originally took place around the time of the autumn equinox (e.g. J. Morgernstern, 'The Gates of Righteousness', *HUCA* 6 [1929], pp. 1-37 [32]; H.G. May, 'The Departure of the Glory of Yahweh', *JBL* 56 [1937], pp. 309-21 and T.H. Gaster, 'Ezekiel and the Mysteries', *JBL* 60 [1941], pp. 289-310). If correct, this might explain the interest in the 'sun' and the lament over the 'departure' of YHWH. The worshippers confuse 'YHWH' with the 'sun' and the onset of shorter days with YHWH's 'departure'. Exod. 23.16 and 34.22 state that סכות was celebrated during the last seven days of the year and immediately preceding the New Year's Day (the date of the autumn equinox) upon the tenth of the seventh month. Taylor, *Yahweh and the Sun*, p. 153 thinks that the precise timing of the Feast relative to the equinox is difficult, partly because of the uncertainty surrounding the nature of the ancient Hebrew calendar. Nonetheless, the date given for the

Mishnah contains a tradition of a solar rite in connection with the Feast of Booths. *Suk.* 5.4 describes a ceremony during סכות in which two priests accompanied by a multitude assembled at dawn at the eastern gate of the Temple area,

> Arrived there, they [the priests] turned their faces to the west and said, 'Our fathers who were in this place had their backs towards the Temple and their faces eastward, and they would prostrate themselves eastward towards the sun; but as for us, our eyes are towards Him [or "towards Yah"]'.

It is hard to see what significance this reference would have had in the context of the later celebration of סכות unless the rite (which has remarkable similarities to Ezek. 8.16) played some role within the same Feast at an earlier period.[44] Tractate *Sukkah* also refers to the practice during סכות in which pilgrims collected different sorts of branches, some of which were to be made into a festal plume. Every day during the water libation ceremony, a procession of priests walked around the altar waving the plumes whilst the watching pilgrims joined in addressing YHWH with the chorus of Ps. 118.25, 'Save us, we beseech thee O LORD!' This fits several details of Ezek. 8.16-18 including the altar, extending a branch to YHWH's nose; and the remark 'though they shout in my ears with a loud voice, I will not hear them' (Ezek. 8.18). Tractate *Sukkah* suggests that the shouting may have been an appeal for deliverance. Against this it could be argued that the Mishnaic tradition of 'branch-waving' is attested rather late. However, Taylor contends that in Lev. 23.40 branches of different kinds are referred to in the context of rejoicing before the LORD during סכות rather than for constructing the booths themselves. This suggests a relatively early date for the celebrative waving of branches at the Feast.[45] One final point: if Ezekiel 8 is set at the time of סכות, it parallels the dedication of Solomon's Temple at the time of a 'Feast' (1 Kgs 8.2) which, although not explicitly named, is generally thought to have been סכות.[46] The tragic irony is that whilst 1 Kings 8 describes the arrival of the *Shekhinah* into the Temple via the east gate, Ezekiel 8 describes its departure via the same route. Whilst we cannot be certain about what exactly the fourth abomination represents, the worshippers' behaviour is denounced as idolatrous, regardless of their

---

vision (calculated at 18 September) is sufficiently close to the autumn equinox (22 September) to raise the possibility that Ezek. 8 may have taken place at some time during סכות.

44. Taylor, *Yahweh and the Sun*, p. 152.
45. Taylor, *Yahweh and the Sun*, p. 157.
46. Taylor, *Yahweh and the Sun*, p. 153.

subjective beliefs. They have turned their backs on the Temple, rejecting YHWH in favour of the sun god. Their idolatry, indeed, may be all the worse for being disguised as proper worship.

6.3.6. *A Narrative Approach to Ezekiel 8*

The four abominations not only signify completeness but also suggest that Ezekiel 8 is set out according to a definite plan.[47] It is not a random jumble of alien cults. Indeed, it may be structured according to the prohibition of idolatry in Exod. 20.4-5. This text presents us with a collective image of what it means to 'act like an idolater'. Firstly, 'acting like an idolater' is particularly identified with 'making' images (Exod. 20.4, 'You shall not *make* for yourself a graven image', my italics) and, secondly, with the 'body language' of the worshippers (Exod. 20.5, 'You shall not *bow down* to them or *serve* them', my italics). Ezekiel 8 follows roughly the same pattern. The first two abominations (the סמל and the 'creeping things') emphasize *representation* (and hence the 'making' of idols) whilst the latter two abominations (the Tammuz and the שמש) stress the *activity* (worshipping Tammuz and the sun) and emphasize the worshippers' body language. Ezek. 8.14 refers to the 'wailing' women whose mourning rites would have been accompanied by gesticulations, whilst Ezek. 8.16 refers to the worshippers 'bowing low' to the sun and 'turning their backs' on the Temple (cf. Jer. 2.27 and 32.33). There is of course some merging of the two 'panels' of abominations. Ezek. 8.11 refers to the men 'standing' in cultic service where עמדים לפניהם means 'to stand as a servant' before another, whilst the references to 'censers' and 'incense' in Ezek. 8.11 also allude to service. Nonetheless, the primary emphasis of Ezek. 8.5-13 is on 'representations' (cf. Exod. 20.4) whilst the primary emphasis of Ezek. 8.14-16 is on 'service' (cf. Exod. 20.5). This structure is consistent with the

---

47. For this reason it is intrinsically unlikely that there is a fifth abomination in 8.17. The charge of 'lawlessness' (חמס) in 8.17 is an overall evaluation of what Ezekiel has already seen. The cultic offences described in Ezek. 8.3-16 are closely related to the moral offences of Ezek. 8.17 because idolatry and injustice go together. Because the moral imperative lay at the heart of Temple worship, the failure to worship YHWH in the proper way at his Temple meant that social wrongdoing could not be far behind. The rejection of YHWH opened the door to rampant injustice since it was faith in YHWH that underpinned the Israelite system of social and economic justice (see Wright, 'Family', pp. 224-25). The gunpowder trail of idolatry led into the Temple court and destroyed not only the physical Temple in 587 BCE but also the social order it represented.

narrative typification of idolatry in Exod. 20.4-5 and with the prophetic practice of taking Israel 'back' to Mount Sinai.

There is also an association between the order of the four abominations in Ezekiel 8 and the warning against idolatry in Deut. 4.16-19. Deut. 4.16 warns against making a סמל ('idol', cf. its use in Ezek. 8.3 and 5), Deut. 4.17 and Deut. 4.18 go on to forbid making the likeness of כל־בהמה ('any beast') or כל־רמש ('creeping things', cf. Ezek. 8.10) whilst Deut. 4.19 concludes with a warning against astral worship (cf. Ezek. 8.16). Notably, Deut. 4.16-19 contains five references to תבנית ('likeness', cf. Ezek. 8.10 and the ironic use of תבנית in Ezek. 8.3 to describe the 'likeness' of the *real* divine hand). Finally, Deut. 4.24 emphasizes that 'the LORD your God is a devouring fire, a jealous God' and this imagery also recurs in Ezekiel 8 (e.g. the use of 'jealousy' in Ezek. 8.3, 8.5, the reference to kindling 'anger' in Ezek. 8.17 and the fiery destruction of Jerusalem in Ezek. 10.2, 10.6).

6.4. *The Seriousness of Idolatry*

There has only ever been one alternative to the worship of the creator and that is the worship of the created. The dark exchange of idolatry, which replaces 'the truth of God for a lie' (Rom. 1.25), has always been censured as a cardinal sin[48] and the root of sorrow.[49] Withdrawing proper allegiance to the true God and offering allegiance to a false god is 'the most radical possible disruption of the very root of our responsibility to God'.[50] In Rabbinic tradition 'the prohibition of idolatry is equal in weight to all the other commandments of the Torah [put together]'[51] and, conversely, whoever rejects idolatry is 'as though he acknowledges the whole Torah'.[52] The prohibition of idolatry is the only command which the 'prophet-like-Moses' is not allowed to suspend.[53] According to *Sanh.* 74a, a Jew was allowed to violate the ordinances of *torah* under the threat of death, with the exception

---

48. M. Dahood, *Psalms I (1–50)* (New York: Doubleday, 1966), p. 125 sees it as 'the great crime (פשע רב)' of Ps. 19.13 (H. 19.14).

49. 'The worship of idols…is the beginning, cause and end of every evil' (Wis. 14.27).

50. Poythress, *Shadow of Christ*, p. 297.

51. *Hor.* 8a.

52. *Ḥul.* 5a.

53. *Sanh.* 90a.

of those forbidding idolatry, immorality and bloodshed, idolatry being ranked first in importance. What makes idolatry an especially serious offence?

6.4.1. *Ban on Idols*
The reason for the ban on idols is given in the Covenant Code where YHWH declares, 'You yourselves saw that I spoke to you from the very heavens: With me, therefore, you shall not make any gods of silver, nor shall you make for yourselves any gods of gold' (Exod. 20.22-23 [H. 20.19-20]). YHWH could not be represented because what the Israelites 'saw' was a voice. The same reasoning is found in Deuteronomy where a warning about falling into idolatry is preceded by the reminder, 'you saw no shape when the LORD your God spoke to you at Horeb out of the fire' (Deut. 4.15). This ban is logical given the use to which idols were put in the ancient world. An idol was a representation of a particular deity whose being was somehow thought to be present in the object. The ancients believed that idols were necessary in order to communicate with the deity and to receive blessing. This meant that, for Israel, idols were useless and illogical because YHWH spoke to Israel *directly* at Mount Sinai (Exod. 20.1-17 [H. 20.1-14]) and indirectly thereafter through Moses (Exod. 20.18-21 [H. 20.15-18]). There was no need for the mediation of idols.

6.4.2. *Breach of Covenant*
A structural analysis of the Ten Commandments confirms that idolatry was the most serious breach of the covenant between YHWH and Israel. This can be set out in terms of a semiotic square[54] (see Figure 6, below). Worshipping other gods (idolatry) violates the most fundamental rule of the covenant: 'You shall have no other gods before me' (Exod. 20.3).

---

54. The semiotic square distinguishes between two different types of opposites that are called in logic 'contradictories' and 'contraries'. When two terms are contradictory, not only does the assertion of the one entail the negation of the other, but the negation of the one entails the assertion of the other. For example, a person who is 'wet' cannot at the same time be 'dry'. However, when two terms are a contrariety, the assertion of one term entails the negation of the other, but the negation of one term does not entail the assertion of the other. For example, something that is 'black' cannot be 'white', but something that is not 'black' need not be 'white', Jackson, *Making Sense in Law*, p. 149.

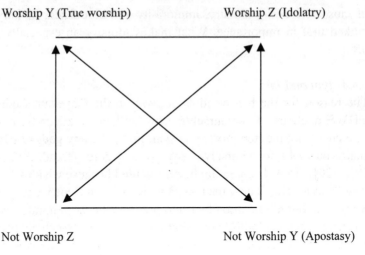

Figure 6. *A semiotic square showing the seriousness of idolatry*

In a semiotic square the diagonal lines represent contradictions while the top of the square represents a contrariety (or conventional opposition).[55] Sense-making processes tend to operate with binary oppositions (i.e., with a pair of terms usually regarded as opposites). It follows that the opposite of worshipping Y (YHWH) is worshipping Z (that is, an idol). It even includes worshipping YHWH *plus* something else, since the true worship of YHWH is exclusive (cf. Deut. 6.13, 1 Sam. 7.3 and Mt. 4.10). In this way, the semiotic square opposes true worship and idolatry as opposites. Going up the sides of the square, 'worship Y' is the privileged manifestation of 'not worship Z' and 'worship Z' is the privileged manifestation of 'not worship Y'. From this it is clear that the opposite to 'worshipping Y' (or YHWH) alone is idolatry and not, for example, apostasy. This is consistent with the order of the Decalogue Commandments. Jewish tradition has always regarded Exod. 20.2 ('I am the LORD your God who brought you out of the land of Egypt, the house of bondage') as the first Commandment or Utterance.[56] It is an implicit command to worship YHWH alone.[57]

55. Jackson, *Making Sense in Law*, p. 150.
56. How one classifies the Decalogue depends on whether one understands דברים to mean simply 'words' or 'commandments'. Jewish tradition understands Exod. 20.2 as the first 'Commandment' or 'Utterance' and Exod. 20.3-6 as the second 'Commandment' or 'Utterance'. This interpretation contrasts with that of Reformed and Orthodox Christians who understand Exod. 20.2-3 as the first 'Commandment' and Exod. 20.4-6 as the second 'Commandment'. This division implies that there is a difference between

The logical internal negation of this is the second דבר, 'You shall have no other gods beside me' (Exod. 20.3). Since the exclusive worship of YHWH is the first commandment, it follows that idolatry is the most serious breach of the covenant. It is no coincidence that Israel's first act of covenant disobedience was recalled as 'making' and 'worshipping' the golden calf (Exod. 32).[58]

The seriousness of idolatry within the overall structure of the Decalogue is confirmed by rhetorical criticism; the ban on idolatry (Exod. 20.3-6) is nearly twice as long as the last five commandments (Exod. 20.13-17 [H. 20.13-14]). This is a good indicator of its importance, especially if one accepts that the tradition of public readings shaped the composition and redaction of biblical law.[59] In similar vein it is notable that the commandment 'you shall have no other god besides me' (20.3) is repeated several times to maximize its didactic force.[60]

6.4.3. *Personal Context*

The seriousness of the offence is further underscored by the unique presentation of the charge. The prophet is transported to the crime-scene in a vision and is personally led around by a divine figure. By taking one man and showing him what is wrong, YHWH demonstrates the personal nature of the offence. The rhetorical question 'do you see?' (Ezek. 8.6) and variants thereof (Ezek. 8.9, 12, 13 and 15) highlight the fact that idolatry is a violation of YHWH's absolute claim upon Israel's devotion. It is 'a sin

---

the prohibition on worshipping 'other gods' in the first 'Commandment' ('You shall have no other gods before me', Exod. 20.3) and the ban on graven images in the second 'Commandment' ('You shall not make for yourself a graven image, or any likeness of anything that is in heaven above, or that is in the earth beneath, or that is in the water under the earth', Exod. 20.4). The phrase 'You shall not make for yourself a graven image' could just be interpreted as a ban on making images *of YHWH*. However, the continuation 'of anything that is in heaven above or of anything that is in the earth beneath or that is in the water under the earth' goes better with the notion that the referent of Exod. 20.4 is to graven images of 'other gods' rather than YHWH. This strengthens the Jewish position which regards the prohibition of the graven images as a continuation of Exod. 20.3, that is, the prohibition of worship of other gods.

57. Jackson, 'Literary Presentation', pp. 189-90.
58. Miller, 'Place of the Decalogue', p. 234.
59. See Watts, 'Public Readings' (1995).
60. 'You shall not make for yourself a sculptured image' (20.4) and 'you shall not bow down to them or serve them' (20.5).

within a system of interpersonal relationships'[61] comparable to adultery, disloyalty and betrayal.[62] It is, after all, the specific history of relations between YHWH and Israel that makes idolatry possible. The ban on idolatry in Exod. 20.3-6 is prefaced by the declaration, 'I am the LORD your God who brought you out of Egypt, out of the house of bondage' (Exod. 20.2). It is this pre-existing relationship that makes idolatry '[walking after] other gods which *you have not known*' (e.g. Deut. 11.28, my italics). What is lacking between Israel and another deity is knowledge (דעת), that is, a personal and intimate relationship. Israel leaves a God whom she has known for a nonentity that she does not know. For this reason, the Rabbis describe idolatry as 'strange worship'. It is misplaced and alien devotion which, from YHWH's perspective, is humiliating.[63] YHWH's solution to the problem is also cast in terms of human relationships, namely, a reunion accompanied by such feelings of shame and deep gratitude as to ensure that the idolatry will never recur (Ezek. 16.62-63).[64]

6.4.4. *The False Loves*

Any treatment of the seriousness of idolatry must put these relationships and the emotions they engender centre-stage. Ezekiel 8 highlights the emotions that are aroused by the offence, both on the part of the idolaters and on the part of YHWH. In all three cases where idolaters appear, their behaviour is described in terms that emphasize their emotional commitment. In the second abomination we are told that the reliefs are depicted over 'the entire wall' (8.10). The phrase סביב סביב (Ezek. 8.10) can be loosely translated 'everywhere you look'. This together with the repetition of כל in Ezek. 8.10 ('*all* detestable forms...' and '*all* the fetishes of the House of Israel', italics added) signifies that the worshippers have completely sold out. This is underscored by the 'thick cloud of incense' (8.11) which also signifies intense worship. The third abomination, with the

---

61. M. Halbertal and A. Margalit, *Idolatry* (trans. N. Goldblum; Cambridge, MA: Harvard University Press, 1992), p. 1.

62. E.g. Exod. 34.15-16 (idolatry as adultery and disloyalty) and Hos. 1.2, 2.5-10 [H. 2.7-12] (idolatry as betrayal). The comparison of idolatry with 'whoredom' in these texts recalls our discussion of 'harlotry' in Chapter 4. But, although the sin of idolatry can be characterized as harlotry, 'idolatry is worse than ordinary prostitution because... the fee is always being paid with the husband's money, [i.e. God's] as he is the sustainer of the world' Halbertal and Margalit, *Idolatry*, p. 13).

63. Halbertal and Margalit, *Idolatry*, p. 27-28. For the perception of shame within the divine–human relationship see Bechtel, 'Perception of Shame'.

64. Halbertal and Margalit, *Idolatry*, p. 19.

uninhibited wailing of the women, is also striking for its emotional intensity. Jacobsen notes that the most significant aspect of the cult is its 'altogether extraordinary potential of emotional intensity, depth and power'.[65] The *piel* form of בכה is particularly expressive of uninhibitedness.[66] The cult may be emotional because it is a projection of the worshippers' emotional needs upon the deity. Surviving dirges reveal a single, all-pervasive maternal instinct to find Tammuz, to be with him and to mother him. The death of the god thwarts this 'possessive drive', creating anger among his worshippers for having died and withdrawn himself. Jacobsen notes that although the Tammuz is a male god he is conspicuously lacking in 'manly' virtues such as courage and resourcefulness.[67] Instead, in a surprising reversal of the normal roles of 'god' and 'worshipper', he is presented as a passive, helpless figure who clings to his mother and sister. This, Jacobsen concludes, is not accidental. The Tammuz was loved for his immaturity and weakness, characteristics that invited maternal feelings of pity and compassion. The Tammuz was therefore a projection of desire, the desire to mother, comfort and generally to be necessary to another. Its emotional nexus is ultimately 'a straight one-sided drive to possess'.[68] According to Jacobsen the laments went 'on and on without ending, accompanied by shrill wailing flutes and the deep vibrant tones of the harp' abandoning the worshippers to 'transports of grief and religious exaltation'.[69] Finally, the devotion of the sun-worshippers is demonstrated by their posture ('[bowing] low', Ezek. 8.16).

This emphasis upon emotions is again consistent with the Ten Commandments. The ban on idolatry is preceded by the words, 'I am the LORD your God, who brought you out of the land of Egypt, out of the house of bondage' (Exod. 20.2). This evokes the feeling of loyalty.[70] Exod. 20.3-6 goes on to portray idolatry in sensual and affective terms. Stress is placed on physical acts of devotion ('you shall not *bow down* to them', my italics). This concern for the appearance of body language is reflected in tractate *'Abodah Zarah* which warns that, 'If a splinter has got into his [the worshipper's] [foot] whilst in front of an idol, he should not bend down to get

---

65. Jacobsen, 'Image of Tammuz', p. 99.
66. E.F. De Ward, 'Mourning Customs in 1, 2 Samuel (Part II)' *JJS* 23 (1972), pp. 1-27, 154.
67. Jacobsen, 'Image of Tammuz', pp. 94-96.
68. Jacobsen, 'Image of Tammuz', p. 94.
69. Jacobsen, 'Image of Tammuz', p. 99.
70. Jackson, 'Literary Presentation', p. 190.

it out, because he may appear as bowing to the idol; but if not apparent [i.e. if he will not appear by bending to be bowing to the idol] it is permitted'.[71] Stress is also placed on the smell and taste of sacrifice ('or *serve* them', my italics).[72] Idolatry, then, is not an abstract offence. A person is either for YHWH with all his being, or against him with equal fervour. False worship involves active devotion to other gods and engages a person's whole being. There was no room within Yahwistic religion for neutrality or half-heartedness.

6.4.5. *Aesthetic Revulsion*

By definition, תועבת arouse strong feelings. As we have seen, תועבת are things that are described as disgusting, detestable or loathsome. They are things for which the reader is expected to feel a kind of automatic revulsion. Note that they are not merely the objects of moral disapproval, nor are they even the most extreme expression of it. They are things that are actually sickening. Social commentators frequently describe horrific events of which they have no direct experience as sickening. Had they been physically present at the gruesome crime-scene (say), the chances are they really *would* have found it sickening. It is the sensory perception of the thing itself that creates the disturbance which we feel. Even the metaphorical use of 'sickening' depends on our immediate sense perceptions of things that make us sick. If this is true in our highly conceptual society, which hypothesizes ethics in abstract terms, how much more is it likely to be true of a culture that expresses its beliefs more concretely? Consequently, there are good reasons for supposing that what makes תועבת 'abominable' has something to do with their presentation to the senses.

In the Hebrew Bible תועבת are like disgusting food, suggesting some link with the sense of taste. Unwholesome sexual practices are likened to unwholesome food in chs. 18 and 20 of Leviticus. The visual defect described as תועבת in Deut. 17.1 hints at an aesthetic rejection. *Ditto* the confusion between male and female 'things' in Deut. 22.5. The sense construction of abominations thus appears to be not primarily rationalist, but semiotic, viz. in determining what makes a thing abominable, the appropriate question is not a rationalist one ('what general concept do these things have in common?') but a semiotic one ('how do these present themselves to the senses?'). Sight and smell appear to be important. The pas-

---

71. *'Abod. Zar.* 12a.
72. Jackson, 'Literary Presentation', p. 190.

sage repeatedly refers to 'eyes' (Ezek. 8.5, 8.18) and to 'seeing' (Ezek. 8.6, 8.9, 8.12, 8.13 and 8.15). Of course, such references are formal elements of a vision description.[73] But it may also have something to do with the presentation of abominations to the senses.[74] Ezek. 8.11 and 8.17 mention smell with references to the 'thick cloud of incense' and the worshippers putting 'the branch to their nose'. The latter is one of the *tiqqune sopherim*, a list of 18 passages in the MT that are thought to have undergone emendation for theological reasons. In Rabbinic tradition YHWH's exclamation, 'Lo, they put the branch to their nose', is an emendation of the far more shocking idea that the worshippers had thrust the branches to 'my (i.e. YHWH's) nose'.[75] Either way, smell is part of what makes this rite offensive.

This makes seriousness in Ezekiel 8 a question of sensibility. Idolatry is compared to the aesthetic rejection of anything that arouses disgust.[76] This is because idolatry occupies the nexus between intellectual conceptions on the one hand and perceptual and emotional experiences on the other.[77] It fuses ideas and feelings, representations and impressions. Perhaps this is why the sense-construction of idolatry is markedly semiotic.

A semiotic approach to the seriousness of idolatry is consistent with the Ten Commandments. Exod. 20.3 instructs, 'You shall have no other gods before me' (עַל־פָּנַי, literally, '*before my face*', my italics). The idiom may reflect the ANE belief that the divine temple was the deity's actual dwelling-place. An example is the early-morning rituals performed by the Egyptian priests at Edfu where the whole temple and its gods were awakened, washed, dressed, fed and made ready for a new day.[78] Israel's beliefs were in some respects similar: the Tabernacle was YHWH's 'house' and its accessories were his furniture. Anything that takes place in or around the

---

73. Zimmerli, 'Ezekiel', p. 236.

74. A similar feeling is expressed by J. Calvin, *Commentary on the Old Testament: Ezekiel, Daniel* (Grand Rapids: Baker Book House, 1979 [1565]), p. 282. 'If an immodest woman runs after an adulterer, her husband is justly enraged; but if she brings him before her husband, and wantons with him *before his eyes*... certainly such wanton lust cannot be endured' (my italics).

75. C. McCarthy, *The Tiqqune Sopherim* (Göttingen: Vandenhoeck & Ruprecht, 1981), pp. 91-92.

76. Provided 'aesthetics' is understood in its original meaning of 'feeling', Halbertal and Margalit, *Idolatry*, p. 5.

77. Halbertal and Margalit, *Idolatry*, p. 5.

78. H.W. Fairman, 'Worship and Festivals in an Egyptian Temple', *BJRL* 37 (1954), pp. 165-203 (180).

Temple is therefore done to YHWH's face. It is the immediacy of the experience that makes these abominations so repellent. Proximity thus appears to be an element in the seriousness of this offence (see 6.6 below). Moreover, the face is of course the location of the senses. Ezekiel 8 may thus be related to the biblical polemic against a belief in 'living idols', e.g. Ps. 115.5-6, 'They have mouths, but do not speak; eyes, but do not see... noses, but do not smell' (cf. Ps. 135.16). Faur argues that the purpose of these statements was to shatter the common notion that idols were capable of sensory perception.[79] Against this background, Ezekiel 8 may be claiming that YHWH, unlike the idols, is capable of sensory perception because he is the only true and living God.

6.5. *Social Status as an Element of Seriousness of Offence*

Seriousness of offence in Ezekiel 8 is also related to the social status of the worshippers. No worshippers are specified as being present at the first abomination (Ezek. 8.3, 8.5-6). However, the worshippers at the scene of the second and fourth abominations (the elders of the House of Judah, Ezek. 8.11, 8.12 and 8.16 [cf. 9.6]) are of a higher social status than the worshippers who are present at the third abomination (the 'women' of Ezek. 8.14). Chapters 4 and 5 of this book raise the hypothesis that social status is correlated with seriousness of offence in Ezekiel 8. This is likely, given that Chapter 4 (in the case of Lev. 21.9) and Chapter 5 draw upon priestly legal texts, and that the narrator of Ezekiel identifies himself as a priest (Ezek. 1.3).

6.5.1. *Noblesse oblige*

There are several indications that social status is an element of seriousness in Ezekiel 8. Firstly, we are told that the second abomination is worshipped by 'seventy men, elders of the House of Israel' (Ezek. 8.11). The willingness to name specific individuals, such as 'Jaazaniah' in Ezek. 8.11, suggests that this is an actual rather than a symbolic group. This does not, of course, rule out the possibility of symbolic overtones (such as an allusion to the representatives of Israel as they had once stood before YHWH at the making of the covenant, Exod. 24.9-11).[80]

---

79. J. Faur, 'The Biblical Idea of Idolatry', *JQR* 69 (1978), pp. 1-15 (13).
80. Zimmerli, *Ezekiel I*, p. 240.

The 'seventy' were leaders (probably an élite band of aristocrats) who functioned as the people's ruling council. One—'Jaazaniah son of Shaphan'—is singled out as 'standing in their midst' (Ezek. 8.11). This Shaphan may be the same Shaphan ben Azaliah who was 'scribe' to King Josiah.[81] Idol-worship by a man of distinguished family underlines social status as an element of seriousness. There may be an even more shocking reason for singling him out. 2 Kgs 22.10 relates that it was this Shaphan who conveyed the rediscovered *torah* (commonly thought to be a scroll of Deuteronomy) to King Josiah (2 Kgs 22.3-20). Shaphan's act of reading the scroll to the king spurred the monarch to reforming action (2 Kgs 22.11, 23.1-25). If this is the case, it is ironic that the son of a man closely associated with turning Israel towards the Law is 'up to his neck' in the idolatry condemned by Deut. 4.17-18.

Secondly, the 25 men in front of the portico at 8.16 are later identified as elders (9.6). One might have expected these men to have been identified as priests but in fact they are elders. A number of priests had been taken into exile (Ezekiel was himself a priest and one of the first wave of captives taken into exile, Ezek. 1.1-3) but the presence of Seraiah and Zephaniah (2 Kgs 25.18) and the prophet Jeremiah (Jer. 1.1) shows that Nebuchadnezzar left enough of the ruling class for the Judaean vassal state to function. The fact that the remaining priests allowed the elders to perform the role of priests is a further violation. Perhaps the hypothesized priestly symbolism of the number '25' (24 priestly classes [1 Chron. 24.7-19] and the high priest) is an ironic comment on the cultic pretensions of the elders who acted as if they *were* priests (see 6.3.3, 6.3.5 above and 6.6.6 below). The presence of a smaller number than the 'seventy' of Ezek. 8.11 might suggest an even more select group but this is uncertain. Either way, judgment begins with this group (9.5). It begins with those who are (or who should be) senior in their knowledge of YHWH. Exactly the same theme is present in the New Testament. Jesus declares, 'Every one to whom much is given, of him will much be required; and of him to whom men commit

---

81. Josiah reigned from approximately 640 to 609 BCE, hence this suggestion is consistent with the framework of Ezekiel's own chronology, which dates the vision to 592 BCE. Three 'sons of Shaphan' are named in the historical sources, two of whom were allies of Jeremiah. 'Shaphan' is also said to have had two grandchildren, one of whom became Governor of Judah after the Babylonian invasions of 589–587 BCE (Jer. 39.14). His brothers included: the distinguished scribe Gemariah (Jer. 36.10-12), the ambassador, Elasah (Jer. 29.3), and Jeremiah's powerful patron, Ahikam (Jer. 26.24, cf. 2 Kgs 22.12), Halperin, *Seeking Ezekiel*, p. 72.

much, they will demand the more' (Lk. 12.48). Likewise Peter proclaims, 'For the time has come for judgment to begin with the household of God; and if it begins with us, what will be the end of those who do not obey the gospel of God ?' (1 Pet. 4.17).

The importance of social status as an element of seriousness in Ezekiel 8 is confirmed by two separate sources. These are, firstly, the vision of the restored Israel in Ezekiel 40–48 and, secondly, the account of Jesus' departure from the Second Temple in Mt. 24.1-3.

6.5.2. *Ezekiel's Judgment on the First Temple*

Let us first deal with the vision of the restored Israel in Ezekiel 40–48. One of the purposes of the book of Ezekiel is to identify the specific sins and sinners that caused the Exile.[82] No one emerges entirely free of guilt, but nonetheless some are more responsible than others. This is shown in Ezekiel 40–48 where some groups in the restored Israel are downgraded or even excluded from the Promised Land in order to prevent any future exile. There is a clear correlation between those who are seen as chiefly responsible for the Exile and their corresponding lack of status in the restored Land. The prophet maintains a remarkably consistent attitude towards each of the different leadership groups within Judaean society.[83] This makes it possible to draw comparisons between the behaviour of the lay leadership in Ezekiel 8 and their corresponding treatment in Ezekiel 40–48. The lay leadership is singled out for particular blame, despite the fact that the whole house of Judah shares responsibility for the Exile (8.17). Within this grouping, the זקנים and the שרים are the two primary groups of lay leaders who are held responsible. The former group are especially associated with the sin of idolatry (see Ezek. 8, 14.1-8 and Ezek. 20). The latter group are particularly associated with the violent misuse of power for their own ends.[84] Of course this does not mean to say that the sin of idolatry is unique to this class of people. Their sins, especially of idolatry, are also those of the whole people. After all, the same charge of idolatry is laid against groups such as 'Jerusalem', 'the people of Israel' and 'the

---

82. Duguid, *Leaders of Israel*, p. 2.
83. Duguid, *Leaders of Israel*, p. 1.
84. There is no need to assume any 'hard and fast' distinction between the two groups since many of the שרים would also have been זקנים. Nonetheless, it is striking that where this specific terminology (זקנים or שרים) is used it is associated with specific sins, Duguid, *Leaders of Israel*, p. 123.

house of Israel/Judah'. Even so, when a specific group is identified out of this mass for blame in cultic matters it is invariably the זקנים.

The זקנים, whilst hardly alone in their sin, are leaders in the idolatry that causes the *Shekhinah* to depart. Accordingly, they are entirely swept away in Ezekiel's vision of the restored Temple. They are absent from chs. 40–48. Moreover, one of their chief functions in earlier times, that of acting as judges, is now given to the priests (Ezek. 44.24). This may be 'poetic justice' for their role in usurping the power of the priests (see 6.3.5 above and 6.6.6 below). Likewise, the people who followed their example are downgraded to the most circumscribed position in the new order. Having once defiled the Temple with idolatry they now have neither easy access to the restored Temple, nor a clearly defined role in worship. They are kept at a safe distance from the Temple and their view of the ceremonies taking place in the inner court would have been very limited.[85] Their participation in worship was limited to the following: contributing to the offering of the נשיא, proceeding through the *outer* court on major festivals and a brief act of prostration at the outer entrance of the gateway to the inner courtyard on Sabbaths and new moons. They were to have no opportunity to repeat their past abuse. However, they are the fortunate ones. Unlike the lay leadership they at least have a place in the Promised Land. Thus, social status is a factor in assessing seriousness of the offence.

6.5.3. *Jesus' Judgement on the Second Temple*

Secondly, central motifs in Ezekiel 8, namely, idolatry, lay leadership and the departure of the *Shekhinah* recur in a key passage of the New Testament. Mt. 23.35–24.2 narrates Jesus' departure from the Temple in a manner that alludes to the departure of the *Shekhinah* in Ezekiel 10. Jesus is presented as the *Shekhinah* whose departure from the Second Temple is a sign of judgment. Before Jesus leaves the Temple, echoes of Ezekiel 8 are heard in his lament over Jerusalem, 'O Jerusalem, Jerusalem… Behold your house is forsaken and desolate' (Mt. 23.37-38). The wording alludes to the divine temple-abandonment of Ezekiel 8. Notably, in the same context, Matthew draws attention to the precise location of Zechariah's murder 'between the sanctuary and the altar' (Mt. 23.35). The inclusion of this detail has puzzled commentators.[86] However, it may be another allusion to

---

85. Duguid, *Leaders of Israel*, p. 137.
86. E.g. S.B. Blank, 'The Death of Zechariah in Rabbinic Literature', *HUCA* 12-13 (1938), pp. 327-46 (345) claims that it is 'totally irrelevant in its context.'

Ezekiel 8, where the location between the Sanctuary and the altar is significant (Ezek. 8.16, see 6.6.4.4 below). Having left the Temple for the last time, Jesus prophesies to his disciples that the Second Temple, like the First, will be destroyed. 'You see all these [Temple buildings] do you not? Truly, I say to you, there will not be left here one stone upon another, that will not be thrown down' (Mt. 24.2). This is immediately followed by the statement that 'Jesus sat on the Mount of Olives' (Mt. 24.3), mirroring the tradition that the *Shekhinah* hovered over the Mount of Olives following its departure from the city. The biblical account of the flight of the *Shekhinah* describes how the *Shekhinah* 'stood at the door of the east gate of the house of the LORD' (Ezek. 10.19) before ascending from the midst of the city and standing on the Mount of Olives (Ezek. 11.23). R. Jonathan said, 'Three and a half years the *Shekhinah* abode upon the Mount of Olives hoping that Israel would repent, but they did not'.[87] Finally, there is an allusion to the role of the lay leadership whose idolatry was instrumental in driving the *Shekhinah* from the Temple in Ezekiel 8. It is seen in Jesus' extraordinary denunciation of the 'scribes and Pharisees' in Mt. 23.13-36 (the seven woes). For who are the scribes and the Pharisees but the lay leaders of Israel?

6.6. *Location as an Element of Seriousness*

Location is an element of seriousness in Ezekiel 8. Frequent use is made of deictic expressions such as פה ('here', Ezek. 8.6, 8.9 and 8.17) and שם ('there'; Ezek. 8.1, 8.3, 8.4 and 8.14) (see 6.3.1 above). We are told the exact spot where the abominations are located (Ezek. 8.5, 8.10, 8.14 and 8.16, see 6.6.4 below) and also the vantage-point from which they are seen (Ezek. 8.3, 8.7-10, 8.14 and 8.16, see 6.6.4 below). This concern for geography is not surprising. Ezek. 4.1–5.4 describes how the prophet is engaged immediately before he receives the vision in Ezekiel 8. He has been enacting an omen against Jerusalem by lying before a model siege-works for a prolonged period (390 days on his left side and 40 days on his right side). Ezekiel himself is the besieger (Ezek. 4.3), which requires that he face in a particular direction. In this position he has a very long time in which to 'mull over' the city's geography.[88] There are four ways in which location is an element of seriousness in Ezekiel 8. Firstly, the idolatry takes place at

---

87. *Lam. R.*, 25.
88. D.E. Fass, 'The Symbolic Uses of North', *Judaism* 148 (1988), pp. 465-73 (467-68) notes Ezekiel's particular preoccupation with the North.

the Temple of YHWH in Jerusalem (see 6.6.1 below) and secondly, it is performed at entrances (see 6.6.2 below). Thirdly, if we locate the four abominations carefully (see 6.6.4 below) we find a binary opposition between the inside and the outside of the Temple (see 6.7 below) and fourthly, we also discover a binary opposition between the northern and the eastern sides of the Temple (see 6.8 below).

6.6.1. *Jerusalem*

The defining issue is repeatedly the presence of idols *in Jerusalem*. It is Jerusalem that is prophesied against in chs. 4–5, it is *her* abominations that provide the primary justification for punishment and *she* is the epicentre of the holocaust that consumes the whole of Judah. There are several reasons for this. Firstly, Jerusalem is a powerful symbol of the kingship of YHWH (e.g. Jer. 8.19) because of the presence of the Ark and the Temple. Jerusalem symbolized YHWH's sovereignty, not only over Israel but over the whole world.[89] YHWH was enthroned on the Ark of the Covenant (e.g. Pss. 80.1 [H. 80.2], 99.1).[90] The Temple, likewise, expressed YHWH's rule in visible form. Mount Zion was the new Mount Sinai. To set up idols in Jerusalem where the great King dwelt was high treason. Even today, the most insulting place for republicans to burn an effigy of the Queen is at the gates of Buckingham Palace. This made the offence of vassal-rebellion even more serious. Israel's apostasy was all the worse for being committed in the very place of covenant remembrance.

Secondly, Jerusalem was the holy city, the one place on earth where YHWH had set his Name. She occupied the extreme end of the holiness spectrum[91] that is polarized in Ezekiel as 'Jerusalem versus the *Goyim* [Gentiles]' (Ezek. 5.5). Idolatry was a violation of holiness and a frequent source of חטאת ('sin').[92] Since the scale of pollution increased with the holiness of the violated object, it was accordingly a serious matter to defile

---

89. Ollenburger, *Zion*; F.R. McCurley, *Ancient Myths and Biblical Faith* (Philadelphia: Fortress Press, 1983), pp. 158-60.

90. McCurley, *Ancient Myths*, p. 155. The Ark of the Covenant is closely associated with kingship. It is said to represent the footstool of a king in its appearance, whilst the כרבים are thought to represent the guardians of YHWH's throne-room, or the throne itself. Naturally, the Ark is the focus of the covenant because it contains copies of the treaty (Exod. 25.16, 25.21, 40.20, Deut. 10.1-5).

91. Jenson, *Graduated Holiness, passim*.

92. Ezekiel often associates idols and idolatry with uncleanness, André 1980, pp. 338-40. Hosea, for example, equates 'the high places of Aven' with 'the sin of Israel', Hos. 10.8.

Jerusalem. The worst is the corruption of the best.[93] Idolatry *anywhere* in Israel defiled the Sanctuary, profaned the Name and induced YHWH to withdraw his Presence. How much worse, then, was the actual installation of pagan cultic objects at the Sanctuary itself?

Thirdly, what happened in Jerusalem was of global significance. She was the *axis mundi* and 'the centre of the earth' (Ezek. 38.12, JPS).[94] Ezekiel often calls Jerusalem 'the high mountain of Israel', a telling phrase that may allude to the mythological cosmic mountain.[95] This was a prevalent ANE motif.[96] Among the Canaanites, the earthly temple of the deity was considered a copy of the heavenly temple where the high god dwelt on the 'holy mountain'. This belief in a correspondence between the earthly copy and the heavenly prototype was evidently shared by the Israelites, as seen in the instructions for building the Tabernacle (esp. Exod. 25.40). Temples were thus thought to be 'cosmic' because they reflected the heavenly temple. The Temple on the cosmic mountain was itself cosmic in the sense that it represented 'the true Temple which is the source of order in the world'.[97] The idea of Mount Zion and its Temple as the 'cosmic mountain' is a common motif, so much so that the foundation of the Temple is portrayed as an event reaching back to the beginnings of time. Ultimately the Temple is not seen as being established by David or Solomon, but by God himself, 'He built his Sanctuary like the heavens, like the earth that he established forever' (Ps. 78.69). The seven years of Solomon's temple-building activity are sometimes seen as parallel to the seven days of creation. The exuberant interior design, with its motifs of 'cherubim and palm trees and open flowers' (1 Kgs 6.29, 6.32 and 6.35) echoes the creation of the world and symbolizes the cosmic order that has its locus in the Temple. The Temple is also seen as the moral centre of the universe. At the centre of the Holy of Holies stood the Ark of the Covenant, inside of which lay

---

93. *Neg.* 12.4 attests to the (later) belief that two classes of houses were considered beyond pollution, those outside Israel and those in Jerusalem.

94. McCurley, *Ancient Myths*, pp. 139-63.

95. R.J. Clifford, *The Cosmic Mountain in Canaan and the Old Testament* (Cambridge, MA: Harvard University Press, 1972); V. Hurowitz, *I Have Built You an Exalted House* (JSOTSup 115; Sheffield: Sheffield Academic Press, 1992), pp. 335-37.

96. In the ANE the temple is the architectural embodiment of the cosmic mountain, J.M. Lundquist, 'What is a Temple? A Preliminary Typology', in H.B. Hoffman *et al.* (eds.), *The Quest for the Kingdom of God* (Winona Lake, IN: Eisenbrauns, 1983), pp. 205-19 (207-208).

97. Clifford, *Cosmic Mountain*, p. 177.

6. *The Shekhinah Departs*   213

'nothing...but the two tablets of stone which Moses placed there at Horeb' (1 Kgs 8.9). Moral imperative was at the heart of Temple worship.

The priestly understanding of the Temple as the cosmic centre of the universe, the place where heaven and earth converge, means that abominations at Jerusalem threaten the whole earth and make a cataclysm inevitable. 'Things fall apart; the centre cannot hold/Mere anarchy is loosed upon the world.'[98] Nor are these global repercussions far-fetched. YHWH's words to Ezekiel at 8.17 ('the earth is filled with lawlessness') repeat exactly the words used upon the announcement of the Flood. 'I have decided to put an end to all flesh, for the earth is filled with lawlessness' (Gen. 6.13). The similarities do not end there. In both stories the words are the prelude to divine judgment from which only a protected few escape (Ezek. 9.1-11, cf. Gen. 7.1-23).

6.6.2. *Entrances*

A further dimension is that each abomination takes place before an entrance. Ezek. 8.3 refers to a 'gate entrance' and 8.7 to a 'courtyard entrance'. The pattern is repeated in 8.14 ('gate entrance to the Temple') and in 8.16 ('Temple courtyard...entrance to the Temple'). This is an element of seriousness because entrances were legally significant sites in the ANE. Firstly, they were seats of power. When priests, prophets and kings wanted to invest their statements with the authority of YHWH and the Law, they often stood at the entrances of temples, palaces and cities. Even in our culture entrances often symbolize the 'power' and 'authority' associated with the building. The Prime Minister speaks from the steps of No. 10 Downing Street, royal notices are fixed to the gates of Buckingham Palace, and a newly-wedded husband carries his wife over the threshold.

Secondly, one particular form of entrance is a gate and the gates were places of judgment. Entrances (especially city gates) were associated not only with the judicial process[99] but also with the execution of justice.[100]

---

98. W.B. Yeats, 'The Second Coming', in W.B. Yeats, *Selected Poetry* (ed. A. Norman Jaffares; London: Macmillan, 1962), p. 99.

99. Archaeologists have discovered a group of Assyrian legal tablets in a room associated with the 'gate of Shamash' (the Mesopotamian god of justice). The gate's association with the judicial process was so strong that it functioned as a sort of 'law library' (Matthews, 'Entrance Ways', p. 26).

100. When judgment is to be carried out on Jeroboam's wife, Abijah prophesies that her sick child will die (1 Kgs 14.12). The prophecy is fulfilled when she steps over the threshold of her house, judgment falls and the child dies (1 Kgs 14.17). In similar

Temple gates were places of judgment throughout the ANE.[101] Thirdly, gates formed the legal boundary between the inside and the outside world. Only free citizens could pass through the city gate without question or challenge. For this reason, the gate may have been the link that connected the average citizen to his or her temple and local community and which became, over time, the chief symbol of social stability and legal continuity. There is also evidence that entrances operated, in certain contexts, as a channel between two worlds, the world of humans and the enclosed world of the god and the king.[102]

The narrative of 1 Sam. 5.2-5 illustrates the seriousness of setting idols at temple entrances. The story relates how an image of the Philistine god Dagon is found lying on the floor of his own temple, prostrate before the captured Ark of the Covenant. 'The head of Dagon and both his hands', the narrator tells us with glee, 'were lying cut off *upon the threshold*' (1 Sam. 5.4, my italics). The location is significant because the entrance or threshold of a temple symbolized the power (or in this case, powerlessness) of the resident deity. The helplessness of Dagon before YHWH is conveyed by the broken palms on the threshold. The Philistines initiate the practice of 'jumping over the threshold of the temple' (1 Sam. 5.5) in response to their fallen idol. Again, this suggests the potency of the temple threshold. The fact that it occurs in Dagon's own temple only adds to the irony.

Setting up idols at the entrances to the Temple (Ezek. 8.3, 8.5, 8.7, 8.14 and 8.16) and especially before the House of YHWH itself (Ezek. 8.16) therefore aggravates the seriousness of the offence. It is an affront to YHWH's sovereignty. Notably, whilst ANE conquerors commonly installed the gods of defeated peoples in their own temples as 'captives' of their god, David burned the idols of the defeated Philistines (1 Chron. 14.12).[103] It is remarkable that, in contrast to the prevailing custom, David is unwilling to bring *any* sort of idol (even a captive one) into YHWH's

---

vein, 2 Kgs 10.8-9 describes how the basketed heads of Ahab's 70 sons were stacked in two piles 'at the entrance of the gate'. Cf. the dying concubine's struggle to reach the threshold in Judg. 19.26-27 which may symbolize a futile, last-ditch attempt to get justice, Matthews, 'Entrance Ways', p. 34.

101. Hurowitz, *Exalted House*, p. 290 n. 2; G.P.F. Van den Boom, '*Wd-ryt* and Justice at the Gate', *JNES* 44 (1985), pp. 1-25 (role of the temple gate as a place of justice in ancient Egypt).

102. Matthews, 'Entrance Ways', p. 26; van den Boom, 'Justice at the Gate'.

103. Niehaus, *God at Sinai*, p. 140.

6. *The Shekhinah Departs*

temple. Yet we find in Ezekiel 8 that the first abomination takes place before a 'gate entrance' (פתח שער, Ezek. 8.3) (see 1 in Figure 7 below). The second abomination is situated before a 'courtyard entrance' (פתח החצר, Ezek. 8.7) (see 2 in Figure 7 below). This pattern, of 'gate entrance' followed by 'courtyard entrance', is repeated in Ezek. 8.14 and Ezek. 8.16. Thus, the third abomination takes place before the 'gate entrance to the Temple' (פתח שער בית־יהוה, Ezek. 8.14) (see 3 in Figure 7 below). Finally, the fourth abomination is located in the 'Temple courtyard [at the]… entrance to the Temple' (פתח היכל יהוה…חצר בית־יהוה, Ezek. 8.16) (see 4 in Figure 7 below).

6.6.3. *Location and Relative Seriousness*

Most translations of the Bible and many commentators[104] assume an ascending order of seriousness. On this assumption, the transitory verses between one abomination and another (i.e. Ezek. 8.6, 8.13 and 8.14) are translated, 'You will see still *greater* abominations' (my italics). In support of this, commentators argue that the emphatic word עוד qualifies the noun תועבת in Ezek. 8.6 and 8.13. However, one could equally claim that in Ezek. 8.6 and 8.13, the emphatic עוד qualifies the verb (תשוב, 'turn *again!*') rather than the noun (although even here it might still be argued that there is a rhetorical transference). Commentators also appeal to the text's 'discourse structure', arguing that the abominations are presented in a sequential, cumulative fashion. But although the fourth abomination is climactic, this does not in itself prove that the narrator is making similar value judgments about the preceding three abominations. In contrast to the majority view, which ranks the four cases in ascending order of seriousness, I shall argue that there is only one gradation and that is between the first three cases and the last abomination. This is signalled by the comparative מ in Ezek. 8.15. Some might argue that the presence of a מ in 8.15 supports a comparative implication in 8.6 and 8.13 as well. But this is only an inference, the text does not say so explicitly. The only formal indication in the text of a comparative judgment is between the fourth abomination and the preceding three. The fourth abomination is not just worse than the third abomination, it is worse than all of them. Accordingly, the phrase ועוד תשוב תראה תועבות גדלות in Ezek. 8.6 and 8.13 should be translated 'other great abominations' and the phrase תועבות גדלות מאלה in Ezek. 8.15 should be translated 'greater abominations than these'. Ezekiel 8

---

104. E.g. Block, *Ezekiel*, p. 284 n. 7; Cooke, *Ezekiel*, p. 93, Duguid, *Leaders of Israel*, pp. 122-23; Halperin, *Seeking Ezekiel*, p. 38 and Zimmerli, *Ezekiel*, p. 237.

makes a judgment of relative seriousness by presenting the fourth abomination as worse than the preceding three. Some are more serious than others.[105] Zimmerli notes that the affirmative question of YHWH to the prophet ('have you seen?'), which each time prepares the prophet to see something worse, is absent from Ezek. 8.17b-18, confirming that the fourth abomination is indeed the climax.[106] I shall argue in this section that the location of the fourth abomination (Ezek. 8.16) is the main reason why this abomination is regarded more seriously than the preceding three.

6.6.4. *Locating the Abominations in the Temple*
All four abominations are located immediately in and around Solomon's Temple. The whole vision (Ezek. 8.1–11.24) is marked by unity of place. The massacre of Ezek. 9.11 takes place 'out of vision'. So too does the burning of the city. The command to burn the city (10.2) and the description of the 'fire' being given to the 'man...clothed in linen' (10.6-7) is broken off by the statement 'and [he] went out' (10.7). This suggests that the prophet's movements are restricted to a small area. We are thus justified in assuming that the Temple and its environs are the setting of Ezek. 8.3-13, although the Temple itself is not explicitly identified until v. 14.

The layout of Solomon's Temple, insofar as it can be reconstructed from the biblical evidence, is as follows. The Temple had only one court but this was enclosed by a larger court, creating a large Temple-Palace complex in which God and king lived side by side (1 Kgs 7.1-12, cf. excavations at Beth Shan),[107] an arrangement that flowed naturally from the fact that the king was the protector of the cult.[108] This meant that the south wall of the Temple enclosure was also the north wall of the royal enclosure. Several gates led from the inner courtyard (the 'court of the priests') to the outer court (the 'great court') (e.g. 2 Chron. 4.9). The Gate of the Courtiers lying to the south-guarded direct access between the

---

105. Contra the NEB translation of Ezek. 8.6, 8.13 and 8.15 and Calvin, *Ezekiel, Daniel*, p. 285 who denies that *any* of the abominations are worse than another. This overlooks the force of the comparative מ in 8.15 (מאלה) which can only be interpreted: 'great*er* abominations than these' (my italics). The existence of another מ in Ezek. 8.17 does not mean that there is a *fifth* abomination, even more serious than the fourth. This is because the מ in 8.17 appears with an infinitive (מעשות), whereas in 8.15 it appears with a demonstrative adjective (מאלה).

106. Zimmerli, *Ezekiel I*, p. 237.

107. M. Ottosson, *Temples and Cult Places in Palestine* (Uppsala: Acta Universitatis Upsaliensis, 1980), p. 113.

108. Ottosson, *Temples and Cult Places*, p. 112.

6. *The Shekhinah Departs*

palace and the Temple (2 Kgs 11.19). The absence of any buffer zone led to YHWH's complaint that the kings of Israel '[set] their threshold by my threshold and their doorposts beside my doorposts, with only a wall between me and them' (Ezek. 43.8). It meant that the kings '[defiled YHWH's] holy name by the abominations that they committed' (Ezek. 43.8). This complaint is made during Ezekiel's vision of the restored Temple (Ezekiel 40–46) which, unlike Solomon's Temple, had *two* courts of its own and no secular buildings in the enclosed area, reinforcing the idea that Solomon's Temple had no outer wall of its own.

The typical access to the Temple was via the king's palace that lay to the south. The worshipper passed through the outer court that enclosed the palace and the Temple and then entered the middle court that enclosed the palace. From thence they were able to reach the inner court that enclosed the Temple. The command to the prophet in Ezek. 8.5 to 'lift up' his eyes 'to the north' implies that the prophet has approached the Temple from the south. This is consistent with the picture of how the worshippers typically approached the Temple. The prophet is set down in the inner court, south of the entrance to the northern gateway (Ezek. 8.3). This interprets הפנימית in Ezek. 8.3 as an abbreviation for החצר הפנימית as used in Ezek. 10.3 (cf. the החצר החיצנה, Ezek. 10.5).

This presentation is contrary to the view of a number of scholars who propose that the action is not limited to the Temple and its immediate environs. Instead, they contend that the prophet is led in stages from the outer gate of Jerusalem to the inner part of the sanctuary.[109] However, there are several problems with this interpretation. Firstly, as argued in 6.6.3 above, seriousness of offence in Ezekiel 8 is not expressed as a steadily increasing incline but as a contrast between the first three abominations

---

109. Ackerman, '*Marzeah* in Ezekiel?'; Zimmerli, *Ezekiel*, p. 237, and Duguid, *Leaders of Israel*, pp. 112-13. Ackerman, '*Marzeah* in Ezekiel?', p. 269 claims that the picture of Ezekiel beginning his vision in the inner court (8.3), leaving (8.7) and working his way back, pausing outside the north gate of the inner courtyard (8.14) before re-entering the inner court is 'hardly a logical path to have followed'. She favours the Greek text which omits הפנימית in Ezek. 8.3. On the strength of this Ackerman, '*Marzeah* in Ezekiel?', p. 270 argues that Ezekiel finds himself first at the northern gate of Jerusalem's city walls and from there he goes to the gate which leads into the great court surrounding both Temple and palace (8.7). From thence he goes to the northern entrance of the inner court of the Temple (8.14) and finally into the inner court (8.16). Moving from the perimeter of the city to its heart, the prophet moves from 'secular' space to locations that are progressively more sacred (cf. Zimmerli, *Ezekiel*, p. 237).

and the fourth abomination. It is not about the prophet 'getting warm' the closer he gets to the Temple: it is a binary opposition between the fourth abomination which is in the Temple court and the other three which are outside it (see Figure 7, below). Secondly, whilst there is evidence that the priestly worldview envisioned 'spheres of holiness' in the Temple and the surrounding courtyard[110] there is no evidence that these 'gradations' extended to the host city. (Are we to suppose that offences become progressively less serious with distance within Shiloh, for example?) In any case, First Temple Jerusalem, unlike its modern successor, was not a sprawling metropolis with a 'Temple Mount'. In those days, Jerusalem was less of a city with a Temple in it than a Temple with a city round it. There is little sense, historically, in basing an argument on a distinction between the 'secular' city and the 'holy' Sanctuary.

In view of the divergent Greek and Hebrew traditions of Ezekiel 8, the safest course is to assume that the more difficult text is the more authentic one. Therefore, I prefer to follow the *lectio difficilior* of the MT which contains the word הפנימית in Ezek. 8.3. On this reading, Ezek. 8.3 refers to 'the entrance of the gate to the inner [court]' around the Temple, supplying 'court' as necessary for the sense. This 'inner court' corresponds to 'the outer court' of Ezek. 10.5. This reading interprets the word הפנימית as an abbreviation for החצר הפנימית (cf. Ezek. 10.3), corresponding to החצר החיצנה ('the outer court', Ezek. 10.5).[111]

We now turn to consider the movements of the prophet within the Temple compound. These are set out in Figure 7.

6.6.4.1. *Locating the First Abomination.* The prophet is standing inside the court facing the northern gateway (Ezek. 8.3). Looking through the gate to the outer court beyond he sees the first abomination 'north of the altar gate, in the entrance' (8.5, marked '1' in Figure 7). This equation of the northern gate with the 'altar' gate is consistent with what is known of how Solomon's altar was repositioned by later kings. Originally, the 'molten sea' occupied the south-east corner of the Temple (2 Chron. 4.10). The position of the large bronze altar (2 Chron. 4.1) is not stated, but the general concern for symmetry suggests that it was sited at the north-east corner. This is supported by the observation that when the altar proved to be too small to handle all the sacrifices at the dedication of the Temple,

---

110. Jenson, *Graduated Holiness*.
111. Cf. Block, *Ezekiel*, p. 277 n. 21.

6. *The Shekhinah Departs*

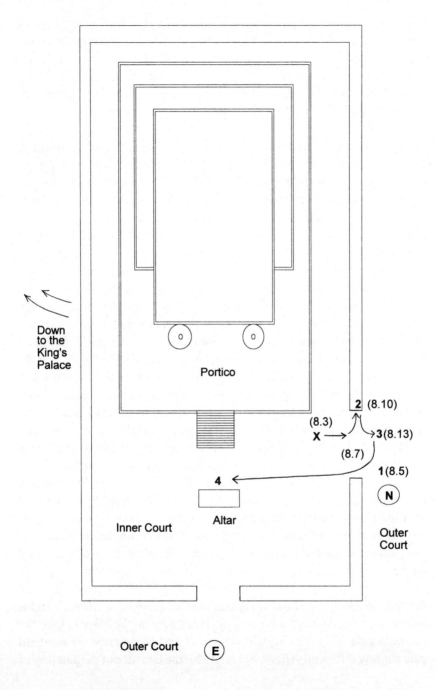

Figure 7. *Map of the prophet's movements according to Ezekiel 8*

Solomon 'consecrated the centre of the court that was in front of the House of the LORD' (1 Kgs 8.64). This would have been the space left between the two bronze objects. According to 2 Kgs 16.14, this altar was moved further to the north by King Ahaz, in order to make room for his new 'Damascus-style' altar. If so, it is not surprising that the northern gate would have been called the 'altar' gate.

6.6.4.2. *Locating the Second Abomination.* Secondly, the prophet is brought to 'the door of the court' (8.7, perhaps better translated 'the entrance to the enclosure'). This refers to the south opening of the northern gate, that gives onto the inner court.[112] Thereupon, he enters the gateway's interior. We can distinguish between the 'gate' (שער, a covered building of some size, like a college lodge) and the entrance (פתח) or 'door' within it. This had a large chamber, or chambers attached to it. Certain people had rooms in the 'upper' (i.e. the 'inner' court), allowing them to overlook the enclosure (e.g. Jer. 36.10). Such chambers may have been rooms inside a casemate wall. Josh. 2.15 describes how '[Rahab's] house was built into the city wall, so that she dwelt in the wall'. A hole in the wall reveals a secret entrance, giving access to a hidden chamber (marked '2' in Figure 7). Of course, the secret chamber could have lain either to the right or the left of the chamber, but for simplicity's sake I have marked '2' as being on the right of the northern gate, as seen from the inner court. The proximity of these chambers to the palace suggests that they were 'grace and favour' residences for servants of the king. Occupants from the time of Jeremiah—and therefore of Ezekiel—include Gemariah, one of the king's aides (Jer. 36.25, conceivably, 'Jaazaniah son of Shaphan', named in Ezek. 8.11, may have been Gemariah's brother; Jer. 36.12) and Nathan-Melech, the eunuch (2 Kgs 23.11). If these chambers were occupied by members of the ruling class, it would explain why the worshippers at this location were the elders of Judah (Ezek. 8.11). It would also explain the exclusivity of the gathering and the difficulty of gaining access to the rite (see 6.3.3 above).

6.6.4.3. *Locating the Third Abomination.* The prophet re-emerges and is led out through the northern gateway. He is now on the *other* side of the northern gate. This may explain why vv. 3 and 14 describe the northern gate slightly differently (Ezek. 8.3 refers to 'the entrance of the gateway of

---

112. Greenberg, *Ezekiel*, p. 169.

the inner [court] that faces north' whilst Ezek. 8.14 refers to 'the entrance of the north gate of the House of the LORD'). There is a difference in perspective because in Ezek. 8.3 the prophet sees the northern gateway from within the inner court, whereas in Ezek. 8.14 he sees it from the outer court. Here, in the *outer* court, is the location of the third abomination (marked as '3' on Figure 7). It is clear from Figure 7 that the first and the third abominations are in roughly the same location. It may be objected that, if so, why does the prophet not notice the Tammuz-worship in 8.3-5? We should remember that unlike the first abomination (the סמל in Ezek. 8.3-6), the third abomination (Tammuz-worship in Ezek. 8.15) does not require an image (see 6.3.4. above). It merely requires mourners. Consequently, the women could easily have made their appearance whilst the prophet was in the secret chamber. Alternatively, we may assume that the prophet observed the women in Ezek. 8.15, but withholds the information from his hearers for dramatic purposes. Ushedo notes the use of 'time manipulation' in the Bible to delay the reporting of certain incidents.[113]

6.6.4.4. *Locating the Fourth Abomination.* Finally, the prophet is led from the outer court back 'into the inner court of the House of the LORD' (8.16). He is led from the northern gate of the inner court to the eastern gate of the inner court. Ezekiel's journey through the enclosure from the northern to the eastern gate can be corroborated by noting the parallel journey taken by the six 'executioners' in Ezek. 9.1, 9.2 and 9.6. This correspondence emphasizes the justice of the punishment. The 'guided tour' in Ezekiel 8 is of the idolatry that is to be punished by the divine warriors.

Here he witnesses the fourth abomination that is practised 'at the door of the house of the LORD, between the porch and the altar' (8.16, marked as '4' in Figure 7). This was a particularly sacred part of the Sanctuary. According to Joel 2.17, this was where the priests were to weep and plead to YHWH on a fast day. It was an appropriately mediatorial position because it was situated between the altar (where sacrifice was made) and the Temple (the dwelling-place of YHWH). This text underlines the possibility that the elders in Ezek. 8.16 are usurping the role of the priests. *M. Kel.* 1.9 gives this area 'eight out of ten' for degrees of sanctity; second only to the Sanctuary itself.

---

113. B. Ushedo, 'Forensic Narration in the Book of Ruth', *Scripture Bulletin* 28 (1998), pp. 28-40.

6.6.5. *Outside versus Inside*

It is clear from Figure 7 above, that there is a binary opposition between the location of abominations '1'–'3' and that of '4'. The first three abominations all take place outside the enclosure[114] whereas the fourth, and last, takes place inside the enclosure. There is an opposition between 'outside' and 'inside' the enclosure. This would have been of great semiotic significance to a priest such as Ezekiel who would have been sensitive to spatial gradations in the holiness of the Temple. Solomon's Temple, like its precursor, the Tabernacle, is arranged according to the principle of graded sanctity. 'Graduated holiness' is conveyed spatially, among other means.[115] Since the Temple is the place where God dwells (in a limited sense), those places that are close to the divine presence are more holy than those places that are further away. Thus the adytum (the 'Holy of Holies') has a higher degree of sanctity than the main hall (the 'Holy Place') which in turn is holier than the precinct outside. The courtyard itself is a transitional area and so its status is rather ambiguous. However, there appears to be some gradation between the enclosure and the area beyond it. The presence of the divine 'furniture' (the 'sea', the 'altar' and so on) implies that the inner court is more sacred than the outer court. In addition, the phrase 'the Temple of the LORD' was often used to include the courtyard as well. This explains the sudden jump in relative seriousness between the first three abominations and the fourth, as registered by the comparative כ in Ezek. 8.15 (see 6.6.3 above).

6.6.6. *North versus East*

A further binary opposition in the presentation of Ezekiel 8 is that between north and east. The question is whether the abomination is committed on the northern or on the eastern side of the Temple. North and east are binary opposites in this context, because the north is the least favoured area of the Temple, and the east is the most important area.

The only entrance to the Tabernacle was from the east. Its supremacy is signified by its superior furnishings, being curtained with similar material to that used in the curtains of the Tabernacle itself (Exod. 27.16, cf. Exod. 26.31). The superiority of the east is reflected in the arrangement of the camp around the Tabernacle in the wilderness. The leaders of the people (the Aaronides and Moses) encamped at the eastern entrance (Num. 3.38)

---

114. '1' and '3' take place in the outer court, whilst '2' occurs in the wall of the enclosure and not in the enclosure itself.

115. Jenson, *Graduated Holiness*, pp. 89-114.

because it was the choicest part of the camp. Rotating clockwise, still facing the east, the southern side (on the right) was next in importance, followed by the west and then by the north. This results in a structural opposition between the 'east' (as the most desirable location) and the 'north' (as the least desirable location). The tribal groupings bear out this hierarchy. Notably, the Leah tribes make up the first two divisions located in the east and the south, but not in order of birth (cf. Gen. 29.31–30.24, Exod. 1.1-4). This is to enable Judah, Leah's fourth son, to be given the choicest role as the leader of the eastern unit (cf. Gen. 49.10) whereas the first-born, Reuben, is assigned the leadership of the southern unit.[116] The rotation continues with the Rachel tribes in the west (headed by Ephraim) and the Danite division in the north. We may draw upon the Tabernacle as a precedent on the assumption that the Tabernacle preceded the Temple. However, our argument does not necessarily depend on this. Regardless of the direction in which the influence runs (whether 'Temple → Tabernacle' or, say, 'Ezekiel → Temple → Tabernacle'), the same evaluation is made throughout, namely that the most favoured side of YHWH's dwelling was the east. It is almost certain that the author of Ezekiel 8, who identifies himself as a priest (Ezek. 1.3), drew upon this opposition in structuring the charge of idolatry. Notably, in Ezekiel's vision of the restored Temple, the *Shekhinah* enters from the east (Ezek. 43.1, 43.2 and 43.4). This contrasts with the view of Ackerman who argues that the prophet's movements in Ezekiel 8 are 'hardly a logical path to have followed'.[117] It is perfectly logical if we posit a structural opposition between 'north' and 'east'.

Figure 7 shows that abominations '1'–'3' take place in and around the northern gate, whereas '4' takes place at the eastern gate. This is another reason why the fourth abomination is the worst of all.

6.7. Conclusion

Ezekiel 8 is the anatomy of a catastrophe. The cause is idolatry, the most fundamental breach of the covenant, and the penalty is divine temple abandonment. When this happens and the *Shekhinah* departs, Jerusalem falls and the exile proper begins. Seriousness of offence is vital to the narrative because it establishes the justice and the power of YHWH. However, all idolatry is not the same. Seriousness of offence varies according to who does it, where it takes place and with what implications. This suggests that

---

116. Milgrom, *Numbers*, pp. 340-41.
117. Ackerman, '*Marzeah* in Ezekiel?', p. 269.

the biblical approach to seriousness is highly contextual, at least in the case of idolatry. The fourth abomination is worse than the preceding three abominations because it occurs in a sacred part of the enclosure and on the eastern side of the Temple, in contrast to the other three abominations that do not take place within the enclosure and which are oriented towards the north.

Chapter 7

SERIOUSNESS OF OFFENCE IN BIBLICAL LAW

'The semiotics of biblical law can no longer be ignored.'
Bernard Jackson

The case-studies disclose that biblical law discriminates between the seriousness of different offences and between the seriousness of committing the same offence in different ways. They also show that judgments of seriousness involve a moral evaluation. In the following discussion I will summarize the results of my investigation and its implications for the modern search for seriousness. Attention is drawn to comparative material from English law, insofar as this illuminates certain research findings concerning biblical law. The inclusion of such comparative material is not, of course, central for the purpose of the claims made in this book regarding seriousness of offence in biblical law. However, whilst it is beyond the remit of this book to attempt a systematic comparison, I hope that this may be an area for further research.

7.1. *The Praxis of Seriousness of Offence*

The results are consistent with the reconstruction of biblical legal praxis outlined in Chapter 1. The case-studies demonstrate the advantages of reading biblical law narratively, rather than semantically (see 7.1.1 below). They also have the cast of self-executing rules, defined in 1.1.5 above as rules formulated in such a way as to reduce the need for third-party adjudication (see 7.1.2 below).

7.1.1. *Use of Paradigm Cases*
Each of the case-studies demonstrates the value of a narrative, as opposed to a semantic, approach to biblical law. In Chapter 2 we saw that the phrases 'stubborn and rebellious' and 'a glutton and a drunkard' refer, not to a semantic definition, but to a narrative stereotype of deviant behaviour. Similarly, in Chapter 3, I proposed a narrative reading of the noun יכם

(Deut. 25.5, 7) and the verb יבם Deut. 25.5, 7). Instead of restricting it to the semantic meaning of 'her husband's brother' and '[to] perform the duty of a brother-in-law' respectively, I argued that the root יבם refers to a wider range of agnatic kin in one's own (and possibly the senior) generation. In this way, I argued, the levirate duty is not restricted to the brother-in-law alone. Support for this narrative approach was found in Genesis 38 and Ruth. In Chapter 4, I argued that the meaning of בתולה in Deut. 22.13-21 was best understood in narrative terms; viz. the בתולה (or 'marriageable girl') is one who has come of age but whose womb has not been opened by birth or miscarriage. The likelihood is that such a girl is also a virgin but this is not essential. I argued that, in the context of Deut. 22.13-21, the most important aspect of the stereotype is whether she has conceived and that the absence of בתולים was the typical proof of conception. In Chapter 5, I argued that the correlation between status, sin and sacrifice indicates the need to bring a sacrifice that is broadly in line with the offeror's status. For this reason, it does not matter that the priesthood is not formally mentioned as a separate category of offender in Lev. 4.1-35. Finally, in Chapter 6 I noted a convergence between the structure of Ezekiel 8 and the paradigm case of acting like an idolater in Exod. 20.3-6.

7.1.2. Self-Executing Rules

The results bear out the methodological assumption that biblical law was largely in the hands of the people and that its paradigms formed the basis of individual negotiation and settlement. Knowledge of the law and of legal reasoning was not restricted to cadres of professionals. Rather, all members of the community were encouraged to engage in it.

We saw in Chapter 2 that the stubborn and rebellious son is chastised by his parents but when his behaviour becomes too serious, he is handed over to the elders. The parents take the initiative in applying and executing the law. Similarly in Chapter 3, the legal process is initiated by the complainant (the widow) and not by officials. The dead brother's claim is in the hands of his widow throughout. She is the Crown Prosecution Service (CPS), Prosecutor and Executive all rolled into one. In Chapter 4, I suggested that the role of the בתולים is an example of an arbitrary evidence rule in which a particular concrete test (examining the שמלה) is conclusive of a wider issue (playing the harlot whilst betrothed). The advantage of such a test is that it can be applied by anyone. Chapter 5 is also consistent with the pattern of self-executing rules insofar as the means of discovery involves informal notification.

I noted in Chapter 1 that one motive for placing law in the hands of the people, rather than legal specialists, is the desire to avoid shame. In Chapters 2 and 3, strenuous efforts are made to avoid public shame. In Chapter 2, the parents try to deal with their son within the family. They go to court only as a last resort. In Chapter 3, the elders try to deflect the levir from the חליצה ceremony in the course of what seems to be a private meeting (Deut. 25.8).

I also noted that self-executing rules often contain an element of rough justice. In Chapter 4, the בתולים only prove that the girl was not pregnant at the time of the marriage. They do not prove that she wholly abstained from relations during the period of betrothal. This unfairness is the price that has to be paid for the benefit of resolving the case between the parties concerned.

Finally, I note that the punishment in Chapters 2, 3 and 4 is implemented and enforced by the community. The rebellious son and the rebellious daughter are stoned by the entire community (Deut. 21.21, 22.21). The levir's new name also requires community enforcement (Deut. 25.10), consistent with the practice of self-executing rules.

7.2. Values

The results indicate some of the values of seriousness of offence in biblical law. In Chapter 2 the underlying values are those of honouring parents and respect for the Land. The latter is shown by self-restraint (that is, by not behaving like a 'son of Belial'). Chapter 3 fuses these values (just family relationships and the Land) in the obligation to raise up a name for the dead brother. This reflects the value of continuing the lineage and of ensuring that the family property descends in the dead brother's line. Chapter 4 demonstrates the need for cultic integrity on the part of the priestly family. The priest's daughter is not to imitate pagan practices by engaging in cultic prostitution. It also underlines the importance of paternity. A husband had a right to be sure that the children born within the marriage were his. Chapter 5 demonstrates the value of maintaining the purity of the Temple, even in the face of inadvertent sins. This is because a polluted Temple would prompt the deity to leave his Sanctuary, occasioning national disaster. Finally, divine temple abandonment in Chapter 6 reflects the absolute value of aniconic worship in Israel.

7.3. *Elements of Seriousness*

The results indicate several elements of seriousness of offence. These include status, location and the type of relationship involved (see 7.3.1–7.3.3 below). This raises questions concerning the approach taken to seriousness in modern criminal law (see 7.3.4 below).

7.3.1. *Status*

We saw in Chapter 4 that the seriousness of an offence varied according to the social status of the offender. The priest's daughter is executed by means of burning whereas the commoner's daughter is put to death by means of stoning. We also saw that the seriousness of the commoner's daughter's offence depends on her status as a betrothed woman. Similarly, in Chapter 5 the seriousness of the offence varied according to whether the offender was a high priest, a נשיא or a commoner. Finally, we saw in Chapter 6 that the seriousness of the abominations relies, in part, on the fact that the idolaters comprise a social élite.

7.3.2. *Location*

We saw in Chapter 6 that location is a key factor in determining seriousness of offence. The worst abomination is the abomination that takes place between the portico and the altar in the inner court of the Jerusalem Temple before the eastern entrance. This concern for location is also apparent in Chapter 4. Either the offence of the priest's daughter takes place at the eastern entrance of the Tabernacle or else her position as a member of the priestly family means that the profane is geographically proximate to the holy.

7.3.3. *Type of Relationship*

Seriousness of offence also depends on the nature of the relationship involved. In Chapter 2, the seriousness of the offence reflects the importance that is attached in biblical law to the proper relationship of a son to his parents. In Chapter 3, seriousness derives from the obligation that a levir owes to his childless and deceased brother. In Chapter 4 the charge of harlotry brought against the priest's daughter echoes the theme of respect for parents in Chapter 2 and anticipates the theme of cultic purity in Chapters 5 and 6. The seriousness of her offence derives from the nature of her obligations, as a member of the priestly family, towards YHWH and her father. The seriousness of the offence of the commoner's daughter is expressed differently, but still in relational terms. Seriousness in her case derives from her obligation towards her fiancé not to engage in promiscuous behaviour. By contrast, similar behaviour on the part of an unbetrothed girl does not appear to be punished. Finally, in Chapter 6, seriousness stems from the obligation of the House of Israel and the elders of Israel to worship YHWH alone.

Evaluations of seriousness reflect the obligations of particular relationships. This is consistent with the observation that biblical justice is conceived in terms of relationships rather than abstract norms.[1] In contrast to modern seriousness studies,[2] it could be argued that the salience of seriousness in biblical law is not so much individual impact as relational impact. In other words, seriousness appears to be related, not so much to its impact upon an individual, but to the violation of a given relationship, whether within the family, or the community or towards YHWH. Certainly, Chapter 6 suggests that the most serious offences are those that impact upon Israel's relationship with YHWH.

The case-studies suggest that, unlike modern seriousness studies, the impact of the offence in biblical law is registered more widely than the immediate victims of the crime. All offences are regarded as crimes against YHWH, especially in Chapters 5 and 6. The threat posed to the wider community is a factor in Deut. 21.21 (Chapter 2), Deut. 22.21 (Chapter 4) and possibly also in Lev. 21.9 (Chapter 4), if the priest is disabled from performing his normal function. Offences are also regarded as serious if they violate the Land (Chapter 2) or arrangements for its division and inheritance (Chapter 3). By contrast, modern seriousness studies emphasize the effect of the crime upon the victim, almost to the extent that so-called 'victimless' crimes (e.g. narcotics, drunkenness) are not considered serious.[3] Indeed, some of the offences covered in our case-studies (dishonouring parents, prostitution, promiscuity and false worship) would probably today be classed as 'victimless' crimes.

7.4. *Performative Registers*

The results indicate a number of registers of seriousness of offence in biblical law (see 7.4.1–7.4.4 below). This raises questions concerning how seriousness is registered in modern criminal law (see 7.4.5 below).

1. See 1.5.2.
2. Such as those of M. O'Connell and A. Whelan, 'Taking Wrongs Seriously', *British Journal of Criminology* 36 (1996), pp. 299-318.
3. O'Connell and Whelan, 'Taking Wrongs Seriously'.

7.4.1. *Form of Penalty*

'Seriousness distance' refers to the gap between the most and the least serious offence items as measured by the form of the penalty. In our case-studies the most serious offence item is idolatry, whilst the least serious item is committing an inadvertent offence. This is communicated by the form of the punishment. This ranges all the way from national catastrophe for national idolatry to a sacrificial tariff for inadvertent offending. In between these two extremes, there are variations on the death penalty (the exemplary form of burning and the common form of stoning) and the use of a shaming ceremony. The form of the penalty registers the seriousness of the offence.

7.4.2. *Ritual Consequence*

The ritual consequence of an offence also functions as a register of seriousness. This is seen in Chapter 4 with regard to the behaviour of the priest's daughter. She is profaned and so is her priestly father. Ritual consequences register the seriousness of her offence. In Chapter 5, the seriousness of the offence is related to what part of the Sanctuary is defiled. The inadvertent sin of the high priest and the כל־עדת ישראל penetrates the Holy Place, whereas that of the נשיא and that of the common person is limited to the courtyard. This degree of spatial penetration is registered by the blood rite (seven times towards the veil or not), the cleansed object (whether the incense altar horns or the עלה altar horns) and whether the animal carcass is destroyed or eaten.

7.4.3. *Location*

The location of the punishment is significant in Chapter 4 (execution at the entrance to the father's house). It registers the seriousness of the offence by drawing attention to her betrothed status at the time of its commission.

7.4.4. *Jurisdiction*

The bringing of the case before different categories of people also functions as a register of seriousness. Chapter 2 differentiates between two spheres of legal jurisdiction: the family and the elders. These are distinguished by their powers of punishment, namely of corporal and capital punishment respectively. In Chapter 2, the public nature of the enquiry functions as a register of the seriousness of the offence. The offence must come before the elders. It is too serious to be dealt with by the parents alone. In Chapter 5 the matter falls within the jurisdiction of the priest. This reflects the special interest of the priesthood in cultic offences (cf.

2 Chron. 19.11), but it may also reflect the seriousness of the offence. This special interest may explain why Ezekiel is made a witness of Israel's idolatry in Chapter 6. As a priest, he is in a better position than a non-priest to appreciate the seriousness of this particular offence.

7.4.5. *Comparative Issues*
7.4.5.1. *Extending the Range of Registers*. The primary register in the modern criminal justice process is the type of punishment.[4] In modern law, seriousness distance extends from the maximum sentence of life imprisonment for the most serious crimes to a conditional discharge for the least serious. However, as a register of seriousness, type of punishment is a fairly blunt instrument in modern law. Fine defaulting and mass murder may both be dealt with by means of imprisonment. In such cases, seriousness is registered in terms of the length of imprisonment. But this is not a salient register for most lay people, or even for many judges.[5] Modern law lacks the range of expression that gives seriousness of offence in biblical law its semiotic valence, or semiotic power. This narrow range is at constant risk of shrinking further with the increasing reliance on imprisonment as the primary form of punishment.[6]

Recent studies suggest that seriousness is largely equated in the public mind with penal severity.[7] However, the idea that seriousness should be expressed exclusively in terms of punishment is itself a major limitation. Biblical law suggests that responses to moral wrongdoing need not take the form only of penal sanctions. The need to develop other registers is increasingly recognized by penal philosophers.[8] Reflection on the form of

---

4. There are, of course, other registers. One example is the jury verdict of 'guilty' or 'not guilty'. A jury may think that a person is guilty of the offence as charged but may not think that the charge is sufficiently serious (e.g. marijuana possession) or, if it is, think that it should not have been brought against this particular defendant (e.g. a charge of grievous bodily harm that was committed in response to provocation). In such cases, a verdict of 'not guilty' amounts to a statement by the jury, in the only way that they are able to express it, that the charge is not sufficiently serious to warrant a conviction. However, since juries are only used in a small minority of cases, this is not an important register of seriousness.

5. C. Fitzmaurice and K. Pease, *The Psychology of Judicial Sentencing* (Manchester: Manchester University Press, 1986), pp. 104-15.

6. The number of people (male and female) imprisoned in England and Wales was 66,026 as of 1 June 2001 (Prison Population and Accommodation Briefing, H.M. Prison Service), an increase of over 40 per cent since 1992.

7. O'Connell and Whelan, 'Taking Wrongs Seriously', p. 306.

8. J. Kleinig, 'Punishment and Moral Seriousness', *Israel Law Review* 25 (1991),

punishment in biblical law and what it communicates about the seriousness of the offence may assist the contemporary search for alternatives to custody.[9]

7.4.5.2. *Jurisdiction*

Modern law is familiar with the use of different jurisdictions, with different powers of punishment, to communicate seriousness. Indeed, the cut-off point between a Magistrates' Court and the Crown Court (which can, of course, impose a higher tariff) is arguably one of the main registers of seriousness in the criminal justice process. Even so, the use of different jurisdictions in biblical law to communicate different senses of seriousness suggests that there is room for greater diversity of authority in modern law. We should not assume that the State is always the most appropriate agent for punishment.[10] The criminal justice system, it can be argued, has too wide a spectrum of behaviour to deal with. This is a limiting factor in terms of the semiotics of seriousness. If the same system deals with trivial matters that are not regarded as morally very bad, this will affect the sense produced by the treatment of the non-trivial.

7.5. *Descriptive Registers*

In addition to describing these performative registers, the results also indicate a range of descriptive registers of seriousness of offence in biblical law. In Chapters 2 and 4 the stated purpose of the punishment is a register of seriousness. In both Deut. 21.21 and Deut. 22.21, the purpose of the punishment is said to be expiatory. This signifies that the entire community is in danger and that communal action is needed to purify the city and the people of Israel. Further descriptive registers include the use of public-example formulae (Deut. 21.21), the purpose of the sanction (Deut. 21.21, Deut. 22.21) and whether it is a repeat offence (Deut. 21.18, 21.21, 25.8, Lev. 21.9). Some of the descriptive registers have a strongly affective aspect, eliciting strong feelings of aversion concerning the offence, for

---

pp. 401-421 (412) suggests an increased role for public criticism. Wrongdoers should be censured or reproved for their moral infractions.

9. One 'register' that stands out when we juxtapose the concerns of the ancient and the modern world is that of 'shame'. Not only did shame play a crucial role in biblical society, but its revival as a penal sanction is urged by some modern criminologists, e.g. Braithwaite, *Crime, Shame and Reintegration*; 'Shame and Modernity'.

10. Cf. Kleinig, 'Moral Seriousness', p. 420.

example, the use of נבלה (Deut. 22.13-21) and the description of the idols as תועבות (Ezek. 8.6, 13, 15 and 17).

This range of descriptive registers illustrates the biblical practice of communicating the seriousness of the offence to as wide an audience as possible in as many different ways as possible. By contrast, modern law assumes that statutes are written for legal specialists and not for the general public. This limits the communication of legal values. There is not the same expectation as under biblical law that legal values will have an impact on the general public. The range of descriptive registers available in biblical law raises the question of how to maximize the communication of legal values in modern society. One possible method is the 'two-document' solution in which one statute is written for lawyers and another is written for the general public. One might expect the latter document to have some impact on the public. In some cases it may even be desirable to present modern laws for particular groups within society, such as children. This might help to extend the potential audience for legal values in modern law.

7.6. Communicating Legal Values

The case-studies indicate some of the techniques used to communicate underlying values of seriousness. These include direct sense perception (see 7.6.1 below) and emotions (see 7.6.2 below). This in turn raises questions concerning how seriousness is expressed in modern criminal law (see 7.6.3 below).

7.6.1. Direct Sense Perception
Immediate sense perception is the primary means of sense-construction. I shall concentrate on two main types of sense-perception and communication; the visual and the aural.

7.6.1.1. *Visual.* Vision is pre-eminent among the senses and hence visual images are powerful determinants of legal sense construction. Particular privilege is attached to the visual form of perception in biblical law.[11] In Chapter 2, the behaviour of the 'glutton and a drunkard' is conceived in stereotypical visual categories. In Chapters 2 and 4, the execution of the offenders takes place in full public view. The shaming ceremony in Chapter 3 may or may not occur in public, but either way it is a visually striking

---

11. E.g. Exod. 20.18. See B.S. Jackson, 'Envisaging Law', *International Journal for the Semiotics of Law* 21, pp. 311-44 (313-14).

performance. Chapter 4 shows a preference for visually salient forms of evidence with the display of the שִׂמְלָה whilst in Chapter 5 the seriousness of the pollution, and hence the offence, is visibly demonstrated by the application of blood on certain objects. Chapter 6 also stresses the power of the visual (it is, after all, a vision). The prophet is repeatedly asked whether or not he sees the abominations ('do you *see*?... Go in and *see*' etc.; Ezek. 8.6, 9 my italics). Visual direct sense perception of either the offence, the punishment or both is an important aspect of communicating the seriousness of the offence.

7.6.1.2. *Aural.* The aural communication of legal values through popular debate and discussion (e.g. Deut. 6.6-7) is integral to the narrative approach set out in Chapter 1. Legal values may also be transmitted aurally through the public reading of the law (e.g. 2 Chron. 17.7-9, Neh. 8.1-8). Indeed, the texts in Chapters 2, 3 and 4 (Deut. 21.18-21, Deut. 25.5-10 and Deut. 22.13-21) are examples of preached law (Deut. 1.5). The same chapters also hint at the role played by local gossip (the publicly known behaviour of the rebellious son [Deut. 21.20], the levir going about in Israel under a new name [Deut. 25.10] and the husband who brings out an evil name against his wife [Deut. 22.14]).

Variety in the identity of the speaker is of particular significance to the semiotician.[12] In Chapter 2, the behaviour of the stubborn and rebellious son is described in an aurally arresting way. Firstly, the narrator tells us that the son is stubborn and rebellious (Deut. 21.18) and then the characters within the story do, in the form of an explicit speech-act (Deut. 21.20).[13] This means that the facts of the case are repeated, but in the words of someone else. The repetition in Deut. 21.20 is designed to stick in the minds of the hearers. It is more direct in the first person than in the third person (a principle well-known to modern advertisers).[14] Other examples of narration and explicit speech-act using first- and second-person forms are found in Chapters 3 and 4. In Chapter 3 the woman is to appear before the elders in the gate 'and say, "My husband's brother refuses to perpetuate his brother's name in Israel; he will not perform the duty of a husband's brother to me"' (Deut. 25.7). Again, in Chapter 4 the husband lays charges against his wife, 'saying, "I took this woman, and when I came near her, I

12. Jackson, 'Semiotic Questions', p. 10.
13. In addition, the speech-act itself makes the son's behaviour more vivid, an effect that would be lost if the text was, for example, to read 'The parents should say'.
14. See Jackson, *Making Sense in Law*, pp. 54-55.

did not find in her the tokens of virginity"' (Deut. 21.14). As in Deut. 21.18-21, the distinctive feature is the direct quote by which the accusation is made. It is a vivid mode of formulation that goes beyond the standard casuistic sense and impresses upon its hearers the 'seriousness' of the offence.

7.6.1.3. *Immediacy and Extent.* Immediate sense perception, whether visual or aural, makes assumptions about the directness of the communication and the extent of the audience. In Chapters 2, 3 and 5 the perception is conveyed directly to the following groups: the elders, the parties to the case and any onlookers. We saw in Chapter 3 that the extent of the audience in Deut. 25.5-10 is not clear, but in Chapters 2 and 4, at any rate, the audience potentially includes the whole town. In Chapter 5 the immediacy of the communication and the extent of the audience depend on the seriousness of the offence and the nature of the register that is used. In the case of the sin of the high priest and the כל־עדת ישראל, only other priests would have a clear view of the application of the blood on the curtain and on the incense altar. However, if we take a different register such as the fate of the carcass (see 5.3.4 above), the potential audience is far greater. This is because of the greater publicity that is given to carrying the cadaver outside the camp. In Chapter 6, the immediacy of the sense perception is restricted to the prophet Ezekiel.

7.6.2. *Affective Aspect*
Biblical law shows a strongly affective aspect. It has emotive force, evoking feelings of one kind or another. As we saw in Chapter 1, questions of attitude, motive and disposition towards *torah* are at least as important as the rules themselves. This may be one reason why direct sense perception is important in biblical law. How we perceive things by our senses partly determines how they make us feel (cf. Exod. 20.18-20). This is relevant when we consider seriousness of offence in biblical law because seriousness, by definition, expresses things that people feel strongly about. Thus, whilst all judgments involve an emotional component (cf. Freudian psychoanalysis which asserts that the id always makes a contribution to the sense-making exercise),[15] such modalities are bound to be especially prominent in evaluations of seriousness. Examining how the legal values that underlie seriousness of offence in biblical law are communicated

---

15. Jackson, *Making Sense in Law*, pp. 273-85.

requires us to consider how the Bible generates the emotions that are associated with seriousness. The case-studies suggest several ways in which emotions and their expression shape the biblical understanding of seriousness.

7.6.2.1. *Direct Sense Perception.* As already suggested, direct sense perception has an important part to play in generating emotions. The 'men of the city' who take part in the offenders' stoning in Chapters 2 and 4 experience and express the seriousness of committing a capital offence. In Chapter 3, feelings of shame are generated in the levir by the dominant and atypical behaviour of the woman. In Chapter 5, the sight of the butchered animal and the administration of blood communicates the seriousness of inadvertent offending. This is reinforced by the sense of touch, specifically the offenders' act of pressing their hand upon the animal's head (Lev. 4.4, 15, 24, 29 and 33). The importance of direct sense perception in generating emotions is also seen in Chapter 6. Sight and smell are important in communicating to Ezekiel the horror and nausea associated with idolatry. Indeed, that of which Ezekiel has direct sense perception (seeing abominations in the Temple) is made the basis of a moral extension (Israel has committed the worst sin possible under the covenant). The movement from what can be seen and smelt to a more abstract characterization is based on the experience of sight and smell.

7.6.2.2. *Stereotypical Visual Images.* Visual stereotypes are an important means of generating emotions. This is because they constitute a form of internalized social knowledge that is very often deployed without conscious thought. In Chapter 3, the חליצה ceremony concludes with a barefoot man, summoning up the stereotypical image of a person who is vulnerable and defenceless. These are exactly the emotions that are associated with shame. The חליצה ceremony thus creates feelings of shame, not only in the levir but also in the onlookers.

7.6.2.3. *Strong Language.* Emotions are sometimes generated because of their association with particular words. Strong language shocks. Examples may include the charge of being 'a glutton and a drunkard' in Chapter 2, the use of נבלה, with its connotations, in Chapter 4 and the designation תועבה in Chapter 6.

7.6.2.4. *Relational Context.* There is more emotion in criticizing someone for breaking a law in the context of a direct interpersonal relationship than exists in a formal statement of the offence. For example, a standard rule of social etiquette is the statement, 'it is rude to interrupt people'. But to ask someone to 'stop interrupting' injects an emotional element that goes with the criticism. There is more feeling in the criticism that arises from the relationship than there is in the mere statement of the rule. This is inevitable. Norms are inherently less emotional because they are not a function of direct personal relationships. In this regard it is important to note that biblical law is given in the context of a pre-existing relationship between YHWH and Israel (cf. Exod. 20.3: 'I am the LORD your God, who brought you out of Egypt, out of the house of bondage'). This relational context makes seriousness of offence inherently affective. It means that law-breaking is not about breaking a rule, it is about offending a person, namely YHWH. The offence is serious because it is personalized: it is a personal offence against a personal God.

Chapters 2, 3 and 4 contain texts from the preached law of Deuteronomy (Deut. 21.18-21, 22.13-21 and 25.5-10) whose hortative introduction (Deut. 1.6–4.43) makes it clear that breaking the law means breaching the covenant relationship. Likewise in Chapter 5 the seriousness of inadvertent sin is reinforced by the awareness of YHWH's presence at the Sanctuary. This is signalled by the repeated use of 'before the LORD' in Lev. 4.4, 6, 7, 15, 17, 18 and 24. The relational context of seriousness is also important in Chapter 6 which is not surprising because, as we have seen, idolatry is presented as the relational offence *par excellence*.[16] The prophet repeatedly brings home the directness of the relationship that is being violated. The charges themselves are brought in the context of a relationship between YHWH and the prophet. Ezekiel is led around Jerusalem by a divine figure who personally shows him what is wrong. Rhetorically speaking, this is much stronger than a formal charge of law-breaking. We are made to feel about the offence in the same way that YHWH feels about it. The relational setting generates strong emotions and communicates a sense of seriousness.

7.6.3. *Comparative Issues*
7.6.3.1. *Direct Sense Perception.* Modern law is familiar with the biblical emphasis upon vision as a means of communicating legal values. Jackson provides a number of illustrations of the potency of visual images in the modern legal system.[17] Concerning the aural sense, the act of sentencing in

---

16. See 6.4.3 above.
17. Jackson, 'Envisaging Law', pp. 318-26.

which the judge may directly address the defendant can sometimes be significant, especially to the person being punished. Thus, whilst judges may give defendants an absolute discharge they may also, in addressing them, give them a real 'dressing-down'. However, its importance as a means of communicating seriousness is probably limited. Outside interest usually falls on the defendant's sentence rather than that what the judge said to the defendant in passing sentence.

7.6.3.2. Reintegrating Law and Social Feeling. Modern law is a matter of linguistic proposition. Legal statutes are abstracted from the facts of particular cases and from the emotions of particular people in that situation. Yet psychoanalysis suggests that in making sense of law we cannot completely separate the emotional from the cognitive.[18] If correct, it follows that the more conceptual and abstract our language becomes, the more we distance ourselves from our emotions. By contrast the language of biblical law is, as we have seen, less abstract and more concrete than modern law. On the basis of form alone, we might hypothesize that biblical law is closer to how people really think about justice, crime and punishment than modern law. There may be lessons to learn from the presentation of biblical law if we want the criminal justice process to get in better 'touch' with ordinary people.

Biblical law uses emotions to shape its understanding of seriousness. This raises the question whether we have institutionally approved ways of channelling similar emotions within our legal system.[19] In the future, greater efficacy in communicating seriousness of offence may depend on a better integration within the legal system of cognition and emotion. One way of achieving this may be through the use of narrative rules rather than abstract concepts, whilst another might be by a greater focus on the relationships that have been violated by the offence.

---

18. Jackson, *Making Sense in Law*, pp. 273-85.

19. B. Hanson, *Application of Rules in New Situations: A Hermeneutical Study* (Lund: Gleerup, 1977) suggests that rules may be used in six different ways. They may be 'archivative' (storing up past values for the future), used in argumentation to provide reasons for actions, designed to initiate action, to awaken emotions or to pose perspectives on relationships, and finally, they may be used to express ideals. By contrast, positivist legal philosophy conceives of legal rules primarily in terms of the act-initiating function with perhaps subsidiary attention to the use of legal rules in argumentation and in setting up ideals, but with very little regard to the archivative, emotion-awakening or perspective-posing functions, Jackson, 'Ceremonial and the Judicial', p. 29.

7.7. Harmfulness and Wrongfulness

Broadly speaking, there are two types of judgment that may be made when evaluating the seriousness of a crime: namely, the factual and the normative. A factual response evaluates the degree of damage ('how much harm was done by the offence?'). Here, seriousness equals harmfulness. A normative response evaluates the degree of moral culpability or blameworthiness involved ('how culpable is the offender?'). This involves a number of factors, including intent and premeditation. Here, seriousness equals wrongfulness. Thus, some offences are regarded as more wrong than harmful (e.g. stealing a bicycle from a drive) whilst others are seen as more harmful than wrong (e.g. a teenager hitting an old woman in the street). It is a debatable question whether respondents determine seriousness entirely by harmfulness, entirely by wrongfulness, or by some combination of the two. It is also possible that respondents alternate between wrongfulness and harmfulness, depending on which of the two attributes is greater for any particular crime.

7.7.1. Harmfulness and Wrongfulness in Modern Studies

Recent research in seriousness studies has tried to address separately concepts of harm and culpability. One study found that harmfulness and wrongfulness are distinct dimensions but that these dimensions were given different weight by different people in different circumstances.[20] Whether harmfulness or wrongfulness prevails depends on what is commonly viewed as the most striking feature of the crime. If this is correct, it suggests that respondents do not use both harmfulness and wrongfulness in judging seriousness.[21] Rather, they choose one criterion or the other, depending on which of the two is greater for any particular crime. Warr distinguishes several categories of offence, one in which offences are perceived to be more

---

20. M. Warr, 'What is the Perceived Seriousness of Crimes?', *Criminology* 27 (1989), pp. 795-821. Warr's finding applies to those whom he terms 'discriminators', that is, those who see differences in the moral gravity of offences. This is as opposed to 'nondiscriminators' who refuse to discriminate between the relative wrongfulness of offences. By contrast, such respondents appear to rely solely on harmfulness in judging seriousness. If Warr is correct, much of the individual variability in seriousness ratings is attributable to variation across individuals in the perceived 'harmfulness' and 'wrongfulness' of crimes. These two dimensions help to explain differences in seriousness ratings, not only from one crime to the next, but also among individuals, Warr, 'Perceived Seriousness of Crimes', pp. 816-17.

21. Warr, 'Perceived Seriousness of Crimes', p. 809.

'wrong' than 'harmful' (e.g. dole fraud) and another where offences are perceived to be more 'harmful' than 'wrong' (e.g. killing a pedestrian whilst speeding).[22] His findings suggest that conventional classes of crime (personal, property, public order) systematically differ on these two dimensions.

We may draw the following, preliminary, conclusions. Firstly, seriousness is a complex variable that reflects the relative weight given to the wrongfulness and harmfulness of an offence. Secondly, factual and normative mechanisms of evaluating seriousness appear to be held differentially by different respondents. Thirdly, the principal, or most striking, feature of a crime appears to determine public perceptions of its seriousness.

7.7.2. *Perceptions of Seriousness*

Meaning is not universal in any society but is contingent upon the sense-creating conventions of a variety of semiotic groups.[23] 'Semiotic groups' are social and/or professional groups that are distinguished one from another by the often overlapping, but still distinct, systems of signification operating within them.[24] The modern criminal justice process is essentially a composite of semiotic groups. It is an aggregated growth of microsystems, each with its own characteristic language norms and subculture. This means that in modern discussions of seriousness, we cannot assume that the meaning of a particular offence or punishment is necessarily the same for everyone who has contact with the legal process. Empirical research confirms that different semiotic groups perceive the seriousness of an offence and the seriousness of its penalty differently.

Although some researchers report no significant effects upon crime seriousness ratings when results are divided according to particular categories,[25] other researchers have found variations among sub-groups. Sparks *et al.* found a positive relationship between age and seriousness perceptions,[26] whilst Rose and Prell found that social class had a significant

---

22. Warr, 'Perceived Seriousness of Crimes', p. 805.
23. Jackson, 'Anchored Narratives', p. 43.
24. Jackson, 'Anchored Narratives', pp. 32-33.
25. P.H. Rossi and J.P. Henry, 'Seriousness: A Measure for all Purposes?', in M.W. Klein *et al.* (eds.), *Handbook of Criminal Justice Evaluation* (Beverly Hills: Sage, 1980), pp. 489-505 and Cullen, *et al.* 'Seriousness of Crime', pp. 83-102 report no effect for age, sex, race and educational attainment among their samples, whilst O'Connell and Whelan, 'Taking Wrongs Seriously', p. 312 found no significant effect for class.
26. Richard Sparks *et al.*, *Surveying Victims* (London: Wiley, 1977).

effect, although the relationship varied from offence to offence.[27] Gender is also important. Rose and Prell found that women tended to be significantly more punitive than men towards child-beaters, bigamists, forgers and drunk-drivers but not towards offenders who have committed assault, bribery, arson or theft.[28] O'Connell and Whelan found that men attributed to mugging, burglary and dole fraud a relatively higher rank of seriousness than women.[29] Respondents from rural areas are more inclined to deal harshly with those convicted of arson or of cutting electric or telephone lines than those from urban areas.[30] Variations also exist between criminal justice professionals and lay people. Compared to the police, the public tends to perceive offences as more serious[31] whilst McCleary *et al.* found that lawyers tend to be more reliant than the public on legalistic conceptions of seriousness (e.g. for lawyers, victim harm was a less important dimension).[32]

A number of studies have examined variations in the perceived seriousness of different kinds of offences. They show that some offences are perceived differently by different semiotic groups. These include certain crimes of violence, prison violence, sex offences, drug offences, property crimes and traffic offences.

Walker and Marsh found significant differences in disapproval for violent crime among certain groups.[33] For example, younger working-class men and women were least censorious when presented with a story of an ex-boxer who accepted a challenge to fight outside a pub with another man. Older working-class women were the most tolerant of the husband who assaulted his wife because she spent all day 'gossiping' and did not clean the house or prepare dinner. Other studies suggest similar variations of class and gender. Walker found that people of higher social class tend to perceive violent offences as significantly more serious than those of

---

27. A.M. Rose and E.A. Prell, 'Does the Punishment Fit the Crime? A Study in Social Valuation', *AJS* 61 (1955), pp. 247-59.

28. Rose and Prell, 'Does the Punishment Fit The Crime?'

29. O'Connell and Whelan, 'Taking Wrongs Seriously', p. 314.

30. Rose and Prell, 'Does the Punishment Fit The Crime?', p. 259.

31. M. Levi and S. Jones 'Public and Police Perceptions of Crime Seriousness in England and Wales', *British Journal of Criminology* 25 (1985), pp. 234-50.

32. R. McCleary *et al.*, 'Effects of Legal Education and Work Experience on Perceptions of Crime Seriousness', *Social Problems* 28 (1981), pp. 276-89.

33. N. Walker and C. Marsh, 'Do Sentences Affect Public Disapproval?', *British Journal of Criminology* 24 (1984), pp. 27-48.

lower social class.[34] The 1992 British Crime Survey found that female victims of home-based and domestic violence regarded it as more serious than male victims. By contrast, the figures for work-based and pub and club violence were the same for both male and female victims.[35] Braswell and Miller found that, among prison staff, crimes committed by an inmate against a member of the prison staff were regarded as significantly more serious than crimes committed against another inmate.[36] Violence against inmates (except murder but including rape and felonious assault) was not considered serious. This may reflect general societal attitudes in which 'prison violence' is not regarded as seriously as 'street violence' because it is seen as a part of prison life and punishment for offenders. Main *et al.* found that women rate different drug offences (e.g. ecstasy, drink, glue-sniffing, heroin) as being more serious than do men.[37] O'Connell and Whelan found that as people become more educated, they tend to regard marijuana sale as less serious.[38] Sparks *et al.* reported that lower social class respondents tended to view property crime as more serious.[39] Consistent with this, Walker and Marsh found that younger middle-class men and women were more tolerant than others about the offence of vandalizing a telephone box.[40] Walker and Marsh found that working-class respondents (with the exception of older women) were more tolerant of the decision not to use a seat-belt than other groups.[41] Finally, Corbett and Simon found that the public rate the seriousness of traffic offences higher in absolute terms than do the police.[42]

---

34. M.A. Walker, 'Measuring the Seriousness of Crimes', *British Journal of Criminology* 18 (1978), pp. 348-64.

35. P. Mayhew *et al.*, The *1992 British Crime Survey* (Home Office Research Study 132; London: HMSO, 1992), p. 94.

36. M.C. Braswell and L.S. Miller 'The Seriousness of Inmate Induced Prison Violence', *Journal of Criminal Justice* 17 (1989), pp. 47-53 (51).

37. D.J. Main *et al.*, 'Law and Psychology in the Perception of Crime Seriousness: Towards a Joint Approach', in Graham Davies *et al.*, *Psychology, Law and Criminal Justice* (New York: W. de Gruyter, 1996), pp. 401-406, cf. O'Connell and Whelan, 'Taking Wrongs Seriously', p. 314.

38. O'Connell and Whelan, 'Taking Wrongs Seriously', p. 312.

39. Sparks *et al.*, *Surveying Victims*.

40. Walker and Marsh, 'Public Disapproval'.

41. Walker and Marsh, 'Public Disapproval'.

42. C. Corbett and F. Simon, 'Police and Public Perceptions of the Seriousness of Traffic Offences', *British Journal of Criminology* 31 (1991), pp. 153-64 (163).

Different semiotic groups also perceive variations in the seriousness of punishment. In general terms, offenders (for whom punishment is a real and unpleasant experience) perceive punishment as more severe than do police officers (for whom sanctions are usually intended for others).[43] Specifically, the relative seriousness of different kinds of penalties varies between different groups. Sebba and Nathan found that American prisoners gave relatively high scores in terms of imprisonment equivalents to long probation orders.[44] Among prisoners, a probation order of ten years' duration was the equivalent of between twelve months' and eighteen months' imprisonment, whereas for the other two groups (probation officers and students), it was only thought equivalent to between six and twelve months' imprisonment. This probably reflects their first-hand experience of probation orders as burdensome. At the lower end of the scale, only prisoners regarded a fine of $250 as more severe than a one-month prison sentence. They also regarded a $100 fine as more severe than one year's probation. This perception probably reflects prisoners' poorer economic circumstances. The salience of the death penalty also varies. Sebba and Nathan also found that, of all groups, prisoners were the most opposed to the use of capital punishment whereas the police were the group most in favour.[45] Prisoners were more likely to respond emotionally to the death penalty, whereas the police were more likely to regard the death penalty unemotionally as an instrument of penal policy.[46] Consequently, punishment is perceived and experienced differently by different groups.

7.7.3. *Wrongfulness in Chapters 2 to 6*

The results of our case-studies suggest that seriousness of offence in biblical law is primarily defined in terms of wrongfulness rather than harmfulness. We saw in Chapter 2 that a key element of the seriousness of the rebellious son is his violation of the Fifth Commandment. This is primarily a matter of wrongfulness, not harmfulness. The Israelites are commanded to 'purge the evil' from their midst which, again, is a normative rather than a factual judgment. Likewise, in Chapter 3, the levir's refusal to perform his obligation cannot be defined primarily in terms of harm. As in Chapter 2, the normative command is given to 'purge the evil' from their midst.

---

43. L. Sebba and G. Nathan, 'Further Explorations in the Scaling of Penalties', *British Journal of Criminology* 23 (1984), pp. 221-47.
   44. Sebba and Nathan, 'Scaling of Penalties', p. 234.
   45. Sebba and Nathan, 'Scaling of Penalties', p. 225.
   46. Sebba and Nathan, 'Scaling of Penalties', p. 239.

His offence consists in a normative wrong against his dead brother. In Chapter 4 the harmfulness of the priest's daughter is clearly stated: she profanes herself and her father. However, this is offset by the statement of wrongfulness: she 'played the harlot'. As we saw, the seriousness of her offence lies in the violation of Israel's cultic distinctiveness. This is primarily a matter of wrongfulness and not of harmfulness. Likewise, in the case of the commoner's daughter, the statement that 'she has wrought folly in Israel by playing the harlot in her father's house' characterizes the offence as one of wrongfulness and not of harmfulness. Again, in Chapter 5 whilst inadvertent sin does result in harm (because it pollutes the Sanctuary), the offence itself is not defined primarily in terms of harmfulness. Rather, it is primarily seen as a matter of wrongfulness. This is underlined in two ways. Firstly, only Lev. 4.3-12 (the case of the high priest) draws attention to the consequence of inadvertent sin. Lev. 4.3 refers to his bringing guilt upon the people (Lev. 4.3) which is primarily a matter of wrongfulness and not of harmfulness. Secondly, in the case of the other parties, attention is drawn to the fact that they are guilty before YHWH (Lev. 4.13, 22 and 27) and need to be forgiven (Lev. 4.20, 26, 31 and 35). Once again, the defining feature is wrongfulness and not harmfulness. Finally, in Chapter 6 the harmfulness of the offence is made clear by the departure of the *Shekhinah* and its consequences. However, the harmfulness of the offence is not emphasized. The account of the destruction of Jerusalem, for example, is remarkably restrained, taking place out of vision (Ezek. 9.7-11). Stress is placed upon the wrongfulness of idolatry and not simply its harmfulness.

7.7.4. *Relationship between Wrongfulness and Harmfulness*

The results show that there is a causal relationship between wrongfulness and harmfulness. Each of the above offences leads to harm, including that against parents and the community (Chapter 2), the dead brother and his patrimony (Chapter 3), the priestly father of the cult prostitute (Chapter 4), the husband of the promiscuous fiancée (Chapter 4), the Temple (Chapter 6) and the House of Judah (Chapter 6). However, we have seen that whilst harmfulness is a feature of biblical seriousness, it does not appear to be the primary feature. Rather, seriousness of offence in biblical law is cast primarily in terms of wrongfulness. Harmfulness is simply the consequence of wrongfulness. Harm is defined in terms of wrong.

By contrast, the results of modern seriousness studies suggest that wrong is defined in terms of harm. Therefore, if an offence does not appear to result in measurable harm, it is not regarded as being wrong or serious. This may explain why biblical law rates the seriousness of rebelling against parents very highly, but the results of modern seriousness studies rate the repeated refusal to obey parents 128th out of 140 possible offences.[47] The idea that harm is consequent upon wrong is consistent with the idea that Israel's suzerain is also the Creator of the whole earth. To break the law is not only to offend against YHWH but also to offend against Israel's highest welfare (cf. Deut. 28). The vital correspondence between obedience and welfare means that wrongfulness entails a corresponding measure of harmfulness. It also suggests that dimensions of wrongfulness and harmfulness are more integrated in biblical law than they are in modern conceptions of seriousness.

7.8. *Character*

Seriousness of offence raises deep philosophical and anthropological questions concerning the link between a person's deeds and his or her reputation. Several of the case-studies (Chapters 2, 3 and 4) suggest that seriousness of offence in biblical law is related to some inherent quality or ontology of the individual. In Chapter 2 the son is accused of being stubborn and rebellious and a glutton and a drunkard. The charge relates to a narrative stereotype and it stigmatizes his character. He is not punished simply for what he has done, but for who he is. This is also apparent in Chapter 3. The חליצה ceremony does more than penalize an offence. It passes judgment on the levir's character by changing his name. This is because of the close relationship between name and character in biblical thought.[48] In addition, his new name ('family of the unsandalled one') can be read either pragmatically or syntactically. Pragmatically, it can be read as a description of something that has been done to him ('the house of him who has had his sandal removed'). But syntactically, the Hebrew can express a continuing state ('the house of the person who is in the condition of having had his sandal removed'). The syntactic reading adds further weight to the idea that the punishment in Deut. 25.10 is related to character. The same relationship between seriousness and character is also found in Chapter 4 in respect of the commoner's daughter. The husband gives his wife an 'evil name' (Deut. 22.14). Her reputation is the point at issue in the subsequent judgment (Deut. 22.15-21). If the husband is proved wrong

---

47. Cullen *et al.*, 'Seriousness of Crime', p. 91.
48. See 3.4.4, above.

he is punished for impugning her character (Deut. 25.19). If he is correct, she is punished, not simply because of what she has done, but because of what she is revealed to be (Deut. 25.21).

The case-studies also suggest that repeat offending is a mediating construct between character and seriousness, viz. whether the offence is a repeat offence or a one-off offence. Single acts do not necessarily indicate dispositions.[49] Repeat offending justifies making the inference from an act to a disposition. In Chapter 2, the offence of the stubborn and rebellious son is described in terms of repeat offending. This is implicit not only in his stubborn, and hence repeated, failure to obey his parents, but also in an established pattern of deviance ('he is a glutton and a drunkard'). In Chapter 3, we can be quite sure that the woman does not appear before the elders on the basis of a single refusal. Her complaint that the levir refuses to sire an heir implies a repeated refusal. Indeed, he 'insists' on refusing when brought before the elders (Deut. 25.8). In Chapter 4, the daughters are accused of being prostitutes which implies repeated behaviour. The girl in Deut. 22.13-21 is convicted if she is found to be pregnant, as opposed to having simply lost her virginity. The use of a pregnancy test assumes that the typical case is that of promiscuity, and therefore of repeat offending.

We do not have to conclude that punishment in biblical law is always related either to character or to deeds. It is a matter of investigation in each case. But the fact that there are some examples where character is emphasized more than the deed (as in Chapters 2, 3 and 4) indicate that this may have been an important element in the seriousness of an offence in biblical law. It is sufficient to say that in biblical law, judgment is passed on the character of the person to a greater extent than in modern criminal law. In modern law, only the deed is criminalized and character is only a matter of mitigation.[50] Under section 66(6) of the Criminal Justice Act 1993 judges are allowed to take an offender's previous offending history into account in determining the seriousness of the offence. This may or may not involve behaviour that is similar to the charge on which the offender is convicted. However, the language of section 66(6) is, conceptually at least, act-oriented rather than person-oriented. The interest is in the offender's previous record, not his or her character as such.

---

49. M.D. Bayles, 'Character, Purpose, and Criminal Responsibility', *Law and Philosophy* 1 (1982), pp. 5-20 (8).

50. E.g. *Attorney-General's References Nos. 3, 4 and 5 of 1992 (Stephen Boyd and others)* (1993) 14 Cr. App. R. (S.), pp. 191-95.

This may perhaps be the main difference between biblical and modern conceptions of punishment. There is a contrast between the person-oriented punishment of biblical times and the act-oriented punishment of modern law. Biblical law is interested in character and it directs punishment against the character of the offender. Or, to put it another way, it holds offenders responsible for the moral choices they make that mould their character.[51] Modern law, at least in theory, looks at the seriousness of the offence itself and is not interested in the character of the offender.[52] Some penal philosophers and criminologists have recently reasserted the nexus of punishment and moral dereliction, arguing that character should play an increased role in modern criminal law.[53] In practice, it may be argued that all punishment makes intimations concerning a person's character. This is because, in punishing, there is an implicit or explicit denunciation or condemnation of the punishee who is deemed to have acted in a morally discreditable manner. Some aspect of his character is called into question.[54]

7.9. *Semiotic Groups*

We saw in Chapter 1 that meaning-making varies with the sense-creating conventions of different semiotic groups. We saw that different groups inside and outside the criminal justice process perceive the meaning of a particular offence or punishment differently. This creates the hypothesis that seriousness of offence in biblical law was also perceived differently by different semiotic groups in biblical society. Of course, if the case-studies are wholly a product of their writers, it is possible that none of the

---

51. Cf. E.L. Pincoffs, 'Legal Responsibility and Moral Character', *Wayne Law Review* 19 (1973), pp. 905-23.

52. Although Bayles, 'Character', argues that a Humean view of criminal responsibility is compatible with current criminal law. In the Humean view, blame and punishment are meted out, not directly for acts, but for character traits, where 'character traits' refers to any socially desirable or undesirable disposition of a person. This is compatible with *mens rea* and with the distinction between acting purposely, knowingly, recklessly and negligently, Bayles, 'Character', pp. 8-11. He argues that it is also compatible with the law of attempts and abandonment, whilst also providing a rationale for the conviction and punishment of impossible attempts as well as providing the broad outlines of a basis for the excuse of mistake, Bayles, 'Character', pp. 14-15. It may also help to explain the requirement of 'reasonableness' in defences of mistake of law, Bayles, 'Character', pp. 16-17.

53. Bayles, 'Character'.

54. Kleinig, 'Moral Seriousness', p. 403.

promulgators' ideas of seriousness are referable to their society at all, let alone to particular semiotic groups. As with the Essene community of the Dead Sea Scrolls period, it is possible that the values expressed in these texts are at odds with their social milieux. Ultimately, we have no way of discerning to what extent the ideas of seriousness that we have been considering were shared across ancient Israelite society. However, it is plausible to suggest that some ideas were closer to dominant social values than to others. It may be that those aspects of the values of the criminal law that are related to deep theological claims, either to the covenantal relationship or to the people's relationship to the land, may have been more removed than those values that were more 'populist'. As in modern times, some cases or evaluations of 'seriousness' have a more general appeal than others.

It is plausible to suggest that biblical law took some account of different semiotic groups in biblical society. That is to say, the same text may have been directed at different audiences. It communicated different messages at levels that were appropriate to each group.[55] Certainly, the idea that more than one level of meaning attaches to legal rules is old and is expressed very directly by Aquinas.[56] It may help to explain why multiple understandings are given to a single commandment (e.g. the Sabbath is variously explained as *imitatio Dei* [Gen. 2.1-3], the sign of the Sinaitic covenant [Exod. 31.12-17], a humanitarian institution [Deut. 5.14] and a memorial to the Exodus [Deut. 5.15]). In modern law, judges frequently address remarks in their judgments concerning seriousness both to the assembled court *and* to the Court of Appeal. Consequently, there may have been different levels of communicable seriousness. Some aspects of seriousness may not have been equally intelligible to everyone and certain beliefs about seriousness may have operated in some social circumstances more than in others. A semiotic approach to seriousness requires us to ask of each case-study: what kind of audience would be expected to know about what levels of seriousness?

7.9.1. *Perceptions of Seriousness of Offence*
The possibility that perceptions of seriousness differ according to semiotic groups compels us to look more closely at the pragmatics of seriousness in biblical law (viz. how the text might have been used). Since we are dealing with moral messages and with different ways of signifying moral values, it

---

55. Jackson, 'Ideas of Law', pp. 198-99 using the example of Exod. 21.2-6.
56. Jackson, 'Ideas of Law', p. 260.

is important to take into account the sender and the receiver. Key questions include: who says what to whom in what context, and what makes the communication effective?

7.9.1.1. Semiotic Groups in Chapters 2, 3 and 4. As already noted, the Deuteronomic texts in Chapters 2, 3 and 4 are presented as an oral address by Moses to the people (Deut. 1.1-5). They assume an ordinary, popular audience. This is reinforced by the content of the case-studies. Deut. 21.18-21 and Deut. 22.13-21 deal with situations that are common to all (viz. the relationship between parents and children). Likewise, the case envisaged in Deut. 25.5-10 could potentially affect any brother. Consequently, it is not hard for the hearers to identify with the seriousness of the offence at an emotional level.

However, this does not exclude the possibility of there being other communicable levels of seriousness. We have no way of knowing what constituted popular language, but it is possible that terms such as נבלה, in Chapter 4, had a specialist meaning (see 4.6 above). Certainly, literary characteristics of the law that go beyond the functional import of the individual rules presuppose a level of literacy that would not have been shared by all. At the very least, the existence of a chiasmus in Deut. 21.13-29, for example, presupposes an additional, more literary audience than the hearers of the individual laws. Each punishment in Chapters 2, 3 and 4 takes the form of a ceremony that has strong visual images. There is the stoning at the city gate; the highly theatrical sandal-removing ceremony and the stoning of the daughter at the door of the father's house. It may be that the visual sense is the most popular and effective means of conveying a message of seriousness. It signifies values at a more popular level, compared perhaps to a more abstract categorization such as נבלה. Biblical law constructs and appropriates judicial conventions to form a visual idiom that is meaningful to the widest possible population.

7.9.1.2. Semiotic Groups in Chapter 5. The text in Chapter 5 is also presented as an address by Moses to the Israelite people (Lev. 4.1-2), albeit to a different generation and in a different setting. The main difference, in semiotic terms, is that in Chapter 5 Moses relays the words of YHWH to the people ('The LORD spoke to Moses, saying: Speak to the Israelite people thus', Lev. 4.1-2 [JPS]). However, in Chapters 2, 3 and 4, Moses' address to the people is made on his own behalf ('These are the words that Moses spoke to all Israel', Deut. 1.1). Moses is not presented in these chapters as YHWH's mouthpiece in quite the same way.

The addressees are 'all Israel' (Deut. 1.1) or 'the Israelites' (Deut. 1.3). But it is possible that the text may also have been communicated to a narrower semiotic group, such as the priesthood. Certainly, the priesthood forms a highly distinctive semiotic group within Israel that is consistent with their status as the guardians of Israel's cultic identity. The use of priestly ritual and language in Leviticus 4, together with the fact that seriousness consists in harm to the Temple, suggests a level of communicable seriousness that is directed at the priesthood. I noted in Chapter 1 that some offences (e.g. domestic violence, sexual offences) are particularly salient for certain semiotic groups (female victims and women, respectively). In the same way, we might posit that the seriousness of certain offences in biblical law are more salient to certain groups than to others. Thus we might expect the priesthood to be particularly sensitive to the seriousness of polluting the Sanctuary. Indeed, a comparison between Lev. 21.9, Leviticus 4 and Ezekiel 8 suggests that a concern for social status and location may reflect an appropriately priestly conception of seriousness.

7.9.1.3. Semiotic Groups in Chapter 6. In Chapter 6 the role of semiotic groups is important in understanding how seriousness of offence is constructed and communicated in Ezekiel 8. This text involves a number of different senders and receivers. Firstly, YHWH addresses the prophet directly about the abominations in the Temple. This is consistent with the idea in 7.9.1.1 above that the priesthood is a distinct semiotic group that was particularly sensitive to the seriousness of polluting the Sanctuary. Secondly, Ezekiel tells 'the exiles all the things that the LORD had shown me' (Ezek. 11.25, JPS). This act of telling begins, necessarily, with the elders of Judah who were sitting before the prophet when 'the hand of the LORD God' fell upon him (Ezek. 8.1). The elders have a special reason for being able to identify with the seriousness of the offence because, as we saw in Chapter 6, the involvement of the elders played an important role in accounting for the gravity of the offence. The line of communication, from priest to elders to people, runs through those who can identify most closely with the seriousness of the offence. To conclude, it appears from each of the case-studies that the salience of seriousness is related to an identification with the offence by different semiotic groups. This is consistent with the findings of modern seriousness studies.

7.9.2. Perceptions of Seriousness of Punishment
We saw in Chapter 1 that perceptions of seriousness of offence vary according to perceptions of the seriousness of the penalty. The modern

'twin-track' approach to penal policy makes a clear distinction between custodial and non-custodial sentences. This bifurcation establishes the greater severity of imprisonment as a form of punishment. But it also makes it harder for receivers to agree on the relative leniency of non-custodial penalties.[57] These appear to be regarded as 'much of a muchness'. By contrast, as we saw at 7.4.1–7.4.5 above, biblical society has a wider range of penalties and communicatory strategies. Because the seriousness distance between different sanctions is greater, it is easier to generate a consensus as to relative severity and leniency. The results of the case-studies indicate that capital punishment is worse than the חליצה ceremony (in the sense of loss of life rather than loss of name), which in turn is worse than the חטאת ritual (loss of animal). The semiotic power of the different sanctions ensures greater differentiation than is possible today among, for example, non-custodial penalties.

But although we may assume that there was greater consensus in biblical society concerning the *overall* ranking of punishment, it is likely that different semiotic groups regarded the *relative* severity of each punishment differently. In other words, some groups may have perceived the ritual sacrifice, for example, or the act of stoning more seriously than others. We saw in 7.7.2 that modern perceptions of severity depend to some extent on the degree of contact the parties have with the penal process, either as professionals or as recipients of punishment. It also depends on whether certain groups identified with the person being punished or not. Studies show that groups such as criminology students, who had greater empathy with prisoners, were more likely to perceive punishments as severe than those who had not.[58] With this is mind it is extremely likely that perceptions of the seriousness of punishment varied across and within towns in ancient Israel. Towns that rarely witnessed capital punishment would regard it more seriously than towns where it was carried out more frequently. It is also likely that, in many cases, the receivers of punishment perceive it more seriously than those who are performing it. We might also reason that those who participated in the stoning of offenders (i.e., the men of the

---

57. Walker and Marsh, 'Public Disapproval', p. 31 invited a sample to rank punishments in order from the 'toughest' to the 'mildest'. For the great majority of subjects, a prison sentence was 'toughest', but unanimity decreased when it involved ranking the following (fine, community service, probation and suspended sentence). Walker and Marsh concluded that no measure in the present court's repertoire stands for leniency in everyone's eyes.

58. Sebba and Nathan, 'Scaling of Penalties', p. 233.

town, Deut. 21.21, Deut. 22.21) may have regarded it less seriously than those who did not, because of their involvement. Likewise, the priesthood may have regarded the חטאת ritual less seriously than the laity. Like the police who, in modern seriousness studies, are somewhat hardened to penal concepts, the priesthood may attach less weight to ritual sanctions because it is the coin in which they deal daily.

Chapter 8

CONCLUSION

Biblical law shows a conception of seriousness of offence. It discriminates between the seriousness of different offences. It also discriminates between the relative seriousness of the same offence when it is committed by different people and when it is performed in different ways. The presentation of seriousness of offence in biblical law in this book reflects the core beliefs and underlying values that are preserved in six selected texts. How far these results hold true for other texts that are drawn from different periods of Israel's history is undetermined. These underlying values of seriousness are expressed through a wide variety of descriptive and performative registers. A range of communicatory strategies disseminate an understanding of seriousness of offence to different semiotic groups. The findings present a remarkably coherent picture. Elements include status, location and the type of relationship involved. The concern for status and location in several texts may reflect a particularly priestly understanding of seriousness. To what extent this interest in status and location as aspects of seriousness is present in other literary genres (such as Wisdom, for example) is a matter for further investigation. Evaluating the question of seriousness of offence in biblical law as a matter of cultural semiotics helps to ensure that our methodological presuppositions approximate, so far as possible, to biblical legal praxis. The study demonstrates the value of a semiotic approach to biblical law by providing further examples of paradigm cases. It also has a number of implications for the modern search for seriousness. In particular, it suggests that a better method for measuring seriousness is by presenting respondents with paradigm cases. It also underlines the need to develop a wider and more appropriate range of penal and non-penal registers with which to communicate a sense of seriousness. This would assist in shaping societal consensus concerning the relative harmfulness and wrongfulness of different crimes.

BIBLIOGRAPHY

Ackerman, S., 'A *Marzeah* in Ezekiel 8.7-13?', *HTR* 82 (1989), pp. 267-81.
Allott, P.J., *Eunomia* (Oxford: Oxford University Press, 1990).
Alster, B., 'Tammuz', in K. van der Toorn *et al.* (eds.), *Dictionary of Deities and Demons in the Bible* (Leiden: E.J. Brill, 1995), pp. 1567-79.
Andersen, F.I., 'Israelite Kinship Terminology and Social Structure', *BT* 20 (1969), pp. 29-39.
Andersen, F.I., and D.N. Freedman, *Hosea* (AB; New York: Doubleday, 1980).
Anderson, G.A., *Sacrifices and Offerings in Ancient Israel: Studies in their Social and Political Importance* (Atlanta: Scholars Press, 1987).
—'Sacrifice and Sacrificial Offerings', in *ABD*, V, pp. 870-86.
André, 'טמא', *TDOT* (1980), pp. 330-42.
Ashworth, A., *Sentencing in the 80's and 90's: The Struggle for Power* (Eighth Eve Saville Memorial Lecture, 21 May 1997; London: Institute for the Study and Treatment of Delinquency).
Ashworth, A., and M. Hough, 'Sentencing and the Climate of Opinion' *Criminal Law Review* (1996), pp. 776-87.
Ashworth, A., and A. von Hirsch, 'Recognising Elephants: The Problem of the Custody Threshold', *Criminal Law Review* (1997), pp. 187-99.
Bailey, K.E., and W.L. Holladay, 'The "Young Camel" and "Wild Ass" in Jer. 2.23-25', *VT* 18 (1968), pp. 256-60.
Bailey, S.J., 'Hebrew Law and its Influence on the Law of England', *Law Quarterly Review* 47 (1931), pp. 533-35.
Bal, M., *Death and Dissymmetry: The Politics of Coherence in the Book of Judges* (Chicago: University of Chicago Press, 1988).
Barr, J., *The Semantics of Biblical Language* (Oxford: Oxford University Press, 1978 [1961]).
Barton, J., 'Ethics in Isaiah of Jerusalem', *JTS* 32 (1981), pp. 1-18.
—*Ethics and the Old Testament* (London: SCM Press, 1998).
Bayles, M.D., 'Character, Purpose, and Criminal Responsibility', *Law and Philosophy* 1 (1982), pp. 5-20.
Beattie, D.R.G., 'The Book of Ruth as Evidence for Israelite Legal Practice', *VT* 24 (1974), pp. 251-67.
Bechtel, L.M., 'Shame as a Sanction of Social Control in Biblical Israel: Judicial, Political and Social Shaming', *JSOT* 49 (1991), pp. 47-76.
—'The Perception of Shame within the Divine–Human Relationship in Biblical Israel', in L.M. Hopfe, *Uncovering Ancient Stones: Essays in Memory of H. Neil Richardson* (Winona Lake, IN: Eisenbrauns, 1994), pp. 79-92.
Belkin, S., 'Levirate and Agnate Marriage in Rabbinic and Cognate Literature', *JQR* 60 (1969), pp. 275-329.
Bellefontaine, E., 'Deuteronomy 21.18-21: Reviewing the Case of the Rebellious Son', *JSOT* 13 (1979), pp. 13-31

Ben-Amos, D., 'Comments on Robert C. Culley's "Five Tales of Punishment in the Book of Numbers"', in S. Niditch (ed.), *Text and Tradition: The Hebrew Bible and Folklore* (Atlanta: Scholars Press, 1990), pp. 35-45.
Benjamin, D.C., *Deuteronomy and City Life* (New York: University Press of America, 1983).
Binger, T., *Goddesses in Ugarit, Israel and the Old Testament* (JSOTSup, 232; Sheffield: Sheffield Academic Press, 1997).
Biran, A., 'Dan', in E. Stern *et al.* (eds.), *The New Encyclopaedia of the Holy Land* (London: Simon & Schuster, 1993), pp. 323-32.
Bird, P.A., 'Images of Women in the Old Testament', in N.K. Gottwald (ed.), *The Bible and Liberation* (Maryknoll, NY: Orbis Books, 1983), pp. 252-88.
—'The Harlot as Heroine', *Semeia* 46 (1989), pp. 119-39.
—'To Play the Harlot', in Peggy L. Day (ed.), *Gender and Difference in Ancient Israel* (Philadelphia: Fortress Press, 1989), pp. 75-94.
—*Missing Persons and Mistaken Identities: Women and Gender in Ancient Israel* (Philadelphia: Fortress Press, 1997).
Blank, S.B., 'The Death of Zechariah in Rabbinic Literature', *HUCA* 12-13 (1938), pp. 327-46.
Bledstein, A.J., 'Female Companionships: If the Book of Ruth Were Written by a Woman', in A. Brenner (ed.), *A Feminist Companion to Ruth* (Sheffield: Sheffield Academic Press, 1993), pp. 116-33.
Blenkinsopp, J., *Wisdom and Law in the Old Testament: The Ordering of Life in Israel and Early Judaism* (Oxford: Oxford University Press, 1983).
Block, D.I., *The Book of Ezekiel* (Grand Rapids: Eerdmans, 1997).
Bockmuehl, M., 'Natural Law in Second Temple Judaism', *VT* 45 (1995), pp. 1-44.
Bonar, A.A., *A Commentary on Leviticus* (London: Banner of Truth, 1972 [1846]).
Boose, L.E. 'The Father's House and the Daughter in It', in L.E. Boose and B.S. Flowers (eds.), *Daughters and Fathers* (London: The Johns Hopkins University Press, 1989), pp. 19-74.
Braithwaite, J., *Crime, Shame and Reintegration* (Cambridge: Cambridge University Press, 1989).
—'Shame and Modernity', *BCJ* 33 (1993), pp. 1-18.
Braswell, M.C., and L.S. Miller, 'The Seriousness of Inmate Induced Prison Violence', *Journal of Criminal Justice* 17 (1989), pp. 47-53.
Brenner, A., 'Female Prostitution', in *The Israelite Woman: Social Role and Literary Type in Biblical Narrative* (Sheffield: Sheffield Academic Press, 1985), pp. 78-83.
Brichto, H.C., 'Kin, Cult, Land and Afterlife—A Biblical Complex', *HUCA* 44 (1973), pp. 1-54.
Brin, G., 'The Formula "If He Shall Not (Do)"' and the Problem of Sanctions in Biblical Law', in David P. Wright *et al.* (eds.), *Pomegranates and Golden Bells: Studies in Biblical, Jewish and Near Eastern Ritual, Law and Literature in Honour of Jacob Milgrom* (Winona Lake, IN: Eisenbrauns, 1995), pp. 341-61.
Brooks, B.A., 'Fertility Cult Functionaries in the Old Testament', *JBL* 60 (1941), pp. 227-53.
Brown, C., *Miracles and the Critical Mind* (Grand Rapids: Eerdmans, 1984).
Buckland, W.W., *A Textbook of Roman Law from Augustus to Justinian* (ed. P. Stein; Cambridge: Cambridge University Press, 1966).
Budd, P.J., *Numbers* (Waco, TX: Word Books, 1984).
—*Leviticus* (Grand Rapids: Eerdmans, 1996).
Burrows, M., 'Levirate Marriage in Israel', *JBL* 59 (1940), pp. 23-33.
—'The Ancient Oriental Background of Hebrew Levirate Marriage', *BASOR* 77 (1940), pp. 2-15.

Bush, G., *Notes on Leviticus* (Minneapolis: James & Klock, 1976 [1852]).
Calvin, J., *Commentary on the Old Testament: Ezekiel, Daniel* (Grand Rapids: Baker Book House, 1979 [1565]).
Carley, K.W., *Ezekiel Among the Prophets* (London: SCM Press, 1975).
Carmichael, C.M., *The Laws of Deuteronomy* (London: Cornell University Press, 1974).
—'A Ceremonial Crux: Removing a Man's Sandal as a Female Gesture of Contempt', *JBL* 96 (1977), pp. 321-36.
—*Women, Law and the Genesis Traditions* (Edinburgh: Edinburgh University Press, 1979).
—'"Treading" in the Book of Ruth', *ZAW* 92 (1980), pp. 248-66.
—'Uncovering a Major Source of Mosaic Law: The Evidence of Deut. 21.15-22.5', *JBL* 101 (1982), pp. 505-20.
—*Law and Narrative in the Bible: The Evidence of the Deuteronomic Laws and the Decalogue* (Ithaca, NY: Cornell University Press, 1985).
—'Laws of Leviticus 19', *HTR* 87 (1994), pp. 239-50.
—'Forbidden Mixtures in Deuteronomy 22.9-11 and Leviticus 19.19', *VT* 45 (1995), pp. 433-48.
Clements, R.E. (ed.), *The World of Ancient Israel: Sociological, Anthropological and Political Perspectives* (Cambridge: Cambridge University Press, 1989).
Clifford, R.J. *The Cosmic Mountain in Canaan and the Old Testament* (Cambridge, MA: Harvard University Press, 1972).
Clines, D.J.A., 'X, X *Ben* Y, *Ben* Y: Personal Names in Hebrew Narrative Style', *VT* 22 (1972), pp. 266-87.
Coats, G.W., *Rebellion in the Wilderness: The Murmuring Motif in the Wilderness Traditions of the Old Testament* (Nashville: Abingdon Press, 1968).
Cogan, M., *Imperialism and Religion: Assyria, Judah and Israel in the Eighth and Seventh Centuries BCE* (SBLMS, 19; Missoula, MT: 1974).
Cohn, H.H., 'The Penology of the Talmud', *ILR* 5 (1970), pp. 53-74.
—'Rebellious Son', in *EncJud* (Jerusalem: Keler), XIII, p. 1604.
Collins, O.E., 'The Stem *znh* and Prostitution in the Hebrew Bible' (Unpublished PhD dissertation, Brandeis University, 1977).
Cooke, G.A., *The Book of Ezekiel* (Edinburgh: T. & T. Clark, 1936).
Corbett, C., and F. Simon, 'Police and Public Perceptions of the Seriousness of Traffic Offences', *British Journal of Criminology* 31 (1991), pp. 153-64.
Craigie, P.C., *The Book of Deuteronomy* (Grand Rapids: Eerdmans, 1976).
—'Deuteronomy and Ugaritic Studies', in D.L. Christensen (ed.), *A Song of Power and the Power of Song* (Winona Lake, IN: Eisenbrauns, 1993), pp. 109-22.
Crüsemann, F., *The Torah: Theology and Social History of Old Testament Law* (trans. A.W. Mahnke; Edinburgh: T. & T. Clark, 1996).
Crystal, D., *The Cambridge Encyclopaedia of Language* (Cambridge: Cambridge University Press, 1991).
Cullen, F.T., *et al.*, 'The Seriousness of Crime Revisited', *Criminology* 20 (1982), pp. 83-102.
Dahood, M., *Psalms I (1–50)* (New York: Doubleday, 1966).
Daube, D., *Studies in Biblical Law* (Cambridge: Cambridge University Press, 1947).
—'*Consortium* in Roman and Hebrew Law' *Juridical Review* 62 (1950), pp. 71-91.
—'Concessions to Sinfulness in Jewish Law', *JJS* 10 (1959), pp. 1-13.
—'To Be Found Doing Wrong', *Studi in onore di Edoardo Volterra* 2 (1969), pp. 1-13.
—*The Duty of Procreation* (Edinburgh: Edinburgh University Press, 1977).
—'The Form is the Message', in *idem*, *Ancient Jewish Law* (Leiden: E.J. Brill, 1981), pp. 71-129.

—'Shame Culture in Luke', in M.D. Hooker and S.G. Wilson (eds.), *Paul and Paulinism: Essays in Honour of C.K. Barrett* (London: SPCK, 1982), pp. 355-72.
Davies, D.S., *The Bible in English Law* (London: Jewish Historical Society of England, 1954).
Davies, E.W., 'Inheritance Rights and the Hebrew Levirate Marriage: Part 1', *VT* 31 (1981), pp. 138-44.
—'Inheritance Rights and the Hebrew Levirate Marriage: Part 2', *VT* 31 (1981), pp. 257-68.
—'Ethics of the Hebrew Bible: The Problem of Methodology', *Semeia* 66 (1994), pp. 43-53.
—*Numbers* (Grand Rapids: Eerdmans, 1995).
Day, P.L., 'Why is Anat a Warrior and Hunter?', in D. Jobling *et al.* (eds.), *The Bible and the Politics of Exegesis: Essays in Honour of Norman K. Gottwald on his Sixty-Fifth Birthday* (Cleveland, OH: The Pilgrim Press, 1991), pp. 141-46.
Dempster, S., 'The Deuteronomic Formula *Ki Yimmase* in the Light of Biblical and Ancient Near Eastern Law', *RB* 91 (1984), pp. 188-211.
Dever, W.G., 'Gezer', in Ephraim Stern *et al.* (eds.), *The New Encyclopaedia of the Holy Land* (London: Simon & Schuster, 1993), pp. 496-506.
De Ward, E.F., 'Mourning Customs in 1, 2 Samuel (Part I)' *JJS* 23 (1972), pp. 1-27.
—'Mourning Customs in 1, 2 Samuel (Part II)' *JJS* 23 (1972), pp. 145-166.
Dillard, R., 'Joel', in Thomas Edward McComiskey (ed.), *The Minor Prophets: An Exegetical and Expository Commentary*. I. *Hosea, Joel and Amos* (Grand Rapids: Baker Book House, 1992), pp. 1-237.
Dommershausen, W., חלל, in *TDOT*, IV, pp. 409-17.
Dostoevsky, F., *The House of the Dead* (New York: Macmillan, 1982).
Douglas, M., 'Atonement in Leviticus', *JSQ* 1 (1993), pp. 109-30.
—'The Glorious Book of Numbers', *JSQ* 1 (1993), pp. 193-216.
—'Poetic Structure in Leviticus', in David P. Wright *et al.* (eds.), *Pomegranates and Golden Bells: Studies in Biblical, Jewish and Near Eastern Ritual, Law and Literature in Honour of Jacob Milgrom* (Winona Lake, IN: Eisenbrauns, 1995), pp. 239-56.
—*Leviticus as Literature* (Oxford: Oxford University Press, 2000).
Driver, S.R., *A Critical and Exegetical Commentary on Deuteronomy* (Edinburgh: T. & T. Clark, 1895).
Duguid, I.M., *Ezekiel and the Leaders of Israel* (VTSup, 56; Leiden: E.J. Brill, 1994).
Dunbar, I., and A. Langdon, *Tough on Justice: Sentencing and Penal Policies in the 1990s* (London: Blackstone, 1998).
Dunnill, J., *Covenant and Sacrifice in the Letter to the Hebrews* (Cambridge: Cambridge University Press, 1992).
Durham III, A.M., 'Public Opinion Regarding Sentences for Crime: Does it Exist?' *Journal of Criminal Justice* 21 (1993), pp. 1-11.
Dworkin, R., *Taking Rights Seriously* (London: Duckworth, 1978).
Eichler, B.L., 'Literary Structure in the Laws of Eshnunna', in F. Rochberg-Halton (ed.), *Language, Literature and History: Philological and Historical Studies Presented to Erica Reiner* (New Haven: American Oriental Society, 1987), pp. 71-84.
Eissfeldt, O., 'Renaming in the Old Testament', in P. R. Ackroyd and B. Lindars (eds.), *Words and Meanings: Essays Presented to D.W. Thomas* (Cambridge: Cambridge University Press, 1968), pp. 69-79.
English, F., 'Shame and Social Control', *TA* 5 (1975), pp. 24-28.
Epperlein, T., and B.C., Nienstedt, 'Re-examining the use of Seriousness Weights in an Index of Crime', *Journal of Criminal Justice* 17 (1989), pp. 343-60.
Erlandsson, S., 'Zanah', in *TDOT*, IV, pp. 99-104.

Fairman, H.W., 'Worship and Festivals in an Egyptian Temple', *BJRL* 37 (1954), pp. 165-203.
Fass, D.E., 'The Symbolic Uses of North', *Judaism* 148 (1988), pp. 465-73.
Faulkner, D., 'All Flaws and Disorder', *The Guardian*, 11 November 1993.
Faur, J., 'The Biblical Idea of Idolatry', *JQR* 69 (1978), pp. 1-15.
Fields, W.W., '"Everyone will be salted with fire" (Mark 9.49)', *GTJ* 6 (1985), pp. 299-304.
—*Sodom and Gomorrah* (JSOTSup, 231; Sheffield: Sheffield Academic Press, 1997).
Finkelstein, J.J., 'Sex Offences in Sumerian Law' *JAOS* 86 (1966), pp. 355-72.
—'The Ox That Gored', *Transactions of the American Philosophical Society* 71 (1981), pp. 3-89.
Fishbane, M., *Biblical Interpretation in Ancient Israel* (Oxford: Clarendon Press, 1985).
Fisher, E.J., 'Cultic Prostitution in the Ancient Near East?: A reassessment', *BTB* 6 (1976), pp. 225-36.
Fitzmaurice, C., and K. Pease, *The Psychology of Judicial Sentencing* (Manchester: Manchester University Press, 1986).
Flanagan, J.W., 'Chiefs in Israel', *JSOT* 20 (1981), pp. 47-73.
Fleishman, J., 'Father's Authority to Prostitute his Daughter in Mesopotamian and Biblical Law' (Paper delivered at 1998 Conference of the Jewish Law Association in Ramat Rahel, Israel).
Fleming, D.E., *The Installation of Baal's High Priestess at Emar* (Harvard Semitic Studies, 42; Atlanta: Scholars Press, 1992).
France, R.T., *The Gospel according to Matthew* (Leicester: Inter-Varsity Press, 1985).
Frazer, Sir J.G., *Folk-lore in the Old Testament: Studies in Comparative Religion, Legend and Law* (London: Macmillan, 1923).
Freedman, D.N., 'The Book of Ezekiel', *Int* 8 (1954), pp. 446-71.
Freedy, K.S., and D.B. Redford, 'The Dates in Ezekiel in Relation to Biblical, Babylonian and Egyptian Sources', *JAOS* 90 (1970), pp. 462-85.
Frishtik, M., 'Physical Violence by Parents against their Children in Jewish History and Jewish Law', *JLA* 10 (1992), pp. 79-97.
Frost, S.B., 'The Memorial of the Childless Man', *Int* 26 (1972), pp. 437-50.
Frymer-Kensky, T., 'Pollution, Purification and Purgation in Biblical Israel', in C.L. Meyers and M. O'Connor (eds.), *The Word of the Lord Shall Go Forth* (Winona Lake, IN: Eisenbrauns, 1983), pp. 399-414.
—*In the Wake of the Goddesses* (New York: The Free Press, 1992).
—'Virginity in the Bible', in V.H. Matthews *et al.* (eds.), *Gender and Law in the Hebrew Bible and the Ancient Near East* (JSOTSup, 262; Sheffield: Sheffield Academic Press, 1998), pp. 79-96.
Gaballa, G.A., *The Memphite Tomb-Chapel of Mose [Text and Translations]* (Warminster: Aris & Phillips, 1977).
Garland, D., *Punishment and Modern Society: A Study in Social Theory* (Chicago: University of Chicago Press, 1990).
Garrett, K.A., and P.H. Rossi, 'Judging the Seriousness of Child Abuse', *Medical Anthropology* 2 (1978), pp. 1-48.
Gaster, T.H., 'Ezekiel and the Mysteries', *JBL* 60 (1941), pp. 289-310.
—'Belial', in C. Roth (ed.), *EncJud* (Jerusalem: Keter, 1971), IV, pp. 428-29.
Giovannini, M.J., 'Female Chastity Codes in the Circum-Mediterranean: Comparative Perspectives', in D.D. Gilmore (ed.), *Honour and Shame and the Unity of the Mediterranean* (Washington DC: American Anthropological Association, 1987), pp. 61-74.
Goodman, L.E., 'The Biblical Laws of Diet and Sex', in B.S. Jackson (ed.), *Jewish Law Association Studies II* (Atlanta: Scholars Press, 1986), pp. 17-57.

Gorman, F.H., Jr, *The Ideology of Ritual* (JSOTSup, 91; Sheffield: JSOT Press, 1990).
—*Leviticus: Divine Presence and Community* (Grand Rapids: Eerdmans, 1997).
Greenberg, M., 'Some Postulates of Biblical Criminal Law', in Menahem Haran (ed.), *Yehezkel Kaufmann Jubilee Volume* (Jerusalem: Magnes Press, 1960), pp. 5-28.
—'Prolegomenon to *Pseudo-Ezekiel and the Original Prophecy*', in C.C. Torrey, *Pseudo-Ezekiel and the Original Prophecy* (New York: Ktav Publishing, 1970 [1930]), pp. i-xxix.
—*Ezekiel: 1–20* (New York: Doubleday, 1983).
Greenspahn, F.E., *When Brothers Dwell Together: The Pre-eminence of Younger Siblings in the Hebrew Bible* (Oxford: Oxford University Press, 1994).
Gruber, M.I., *The Motherhood of God and Other Studies* (Atlanta: Scholars Press, 1992).
Gurney, O.R., 'Tammuz Reconsidered: Some Recent Developments', *JSS* 7 (1962), pp. 147-60.
Hagedorn, A.C. 'Guarding the Parents' Honour—Deuteronomy 21. 18-21', *JSOT* 88 (2000), pp. 101-21.
Halbertal, M., and A. Margalit, *Idolatry* (trans. N. Goldblum; Cambridge, MA: Harvard University Press, 1992).
Hallo, W.W., 'The Slandered Bride', in *Studies Presented to A. Leo Oppenheim* (Chicago: University of Chicago Press, 1964), pp. 95-105.
—'Biblical Abominations and Sumerian Taboos', *JQR* 76 (1985), pp. 21-40.
Halperin, D.J., *Seeking Ezekiel* (Pennsylvania: Pennsylvania State University Press, 1993).
Hamilton, V.P., *Handbook on the Pentateuch* (Grand Rapids: Baker Book House, 1982).
—*The Book of Genesis Chapters 1–17.* (Grand Rapids: Eerdmans, 1990).
Hanson, B., *Application of Rules in New Situations: A Hermeneutical Study* (Lund: Gleerup, 1977).
Harrelson, W., *The Ten Commandments and Human Rights* (Philadelphia: Fortress Press, 1980).
Harris, W.V., 'The Roman Father's Power of Life and Death', in R.S. Bagnall and W.V. Harris, *Studies in Roman Law in Memory of A. Arthur Schiller* (Leiden: E.J. Brill, 1986), pp. 81-95.
Harrison, R.K., *Leviticus: An Introduction and Commentary* (Leicester: InterVarsity Press, 1980).
Hart, H.L.A., 'Prolegomenon to the Principles of Punishment', in *Punishment and Responsibility* (Oxford: Clarendon Press, 1968), pp. 1-27.
Hartley, J.E., *Leviticus* (Dallas: Word Books, 1992).
Herntrich., 'The Old Testament Term משפט', in *TDNT*, III, pp. 923-33.
Hess, R.S., *Studies in the Personal Names of Genesis 1–11* (Neukirchen-Vluyn: Neukirchener Verlag, 1993).
Hillers, D.R., 'Analyzing the Abominable: Our Understanding of Canaanite Religion', *JQR* 75 (1985), pp. 253-69.
Hirsch, S.R., *The Pentateuch Volume 3: Leviticus (Part 1)* (trans. Isaac Levy; Gateshead: Judaica Press, 1989 [1837]).
—*The Pentateuch Volume 5: Deuteronomy* (trans. Isaac Levy; Gateshead: Judaica Press, 1989 [1837]).
Hoffman, P.B., and P.L. Hardyman, 'Crime Seriousness Scales: Public Perception and Feedback to Criminal Justice Policymakers', *Journal of Criminal Justice* 14 (1986), pp. 413-31.
Home Office, *Crime, Justice and Protecting the Public* (Cm. 965; London: HMSO, 1990).
Hugenberger, G.P., *Marriage as a Covenant* (Leiden: E.J. Brill, 1994).

Humbert, P. 'Le substantif *tôʿēḇah* et la verbe *tʿb* dans l'Ancien Testament', *ZAW* 72 (1960), pp. 217-37.
Hurowitz, V., *I Have Built You an Exalted House* (JSOTSup, 115; Sheffield: Sheffield Academic Press, 1992).
Hurvitz, A., *A Linguistic Study of the Relationship between the Priestly Source and the Book of Ezekiel* (Paris: Gabalda, 1982).
Jackson, Bernard S., 'Reflections on Biblical Criminal Law' *JJS* 24 (1973), pp. 29-37.
—'Liability for Animals in Scottish Legal Literature' *The Irish Jurist* 10 (1975), pp. 334-351.
—'Susanna and the Singular History of Singular Witnesses', in W. de Vos *et al.* (eds.), *Acta Juridica: Studies in Honour of Ben Beinart* (Cape Town: Juta & Co., 1977), II, pp. 37-54.
—'Travels and Travails of the Goring Ox', in Y. Avishur and J. Blau (eds.), *Studies in Bible and the Ancient Near East* (Jerusalem: Rubinstein, 1978), pp. 41-56.
—'The Ceremonial and the Judicial: Biblical Law as Sign and Symbol', *JSOT* 30 (1984), pp. 25-50.
—'Some Semiotic Questions for Biblical Law', in A.M. Fuss (ed.), *Jewish Law Association Studies III: The Oxford Conference Volume* (Atlanta: Scholars Press, 1987), pp. 1-25.
—*Law, Fact and Narrative Coherence* (Liverpool: Deborah Charles Publications, 1988).
—'Ideas of Law and Legal Administration: A Semiotic Approach', in R.E. Clements (ed.), *The World of Ancient Israel: Sociological, Anthropological and Political Perspectives* (Cambridge: Cambridge University Press, 1989), pp. 185-202.
—'Legalism and Spirituality', in Edwin B. Firmage, Bernard G. Weiss and John W. Welch (eds.), *Religion and Law: Biblical-Judaic and Islamic Perspectives* (Winona Lake, IN: Eisenbrauns, 1990), pp. 243-61.
—'Practical Wisdom and Literary Artifice in the Covenant Code', in B.S. Jackson and S.M. Passamaneck (eds.), *Jewish Law Association Studies VI: The Jerusalem 1990 Conference Volume* (Atlanta: Scholars Press, 1992), pp. 65-92.
—'Envisaging Law', *International Journal for the Semiotics of Law* 21 (1994), pp. 311-334.
—*Making Sense in Law* (Liverpool: Deborah Charles Publications, 1995).
—'The Literary Presentation of Multiculturalism in Early Biblical Law', *International Journal for the Semiotics of Law* 23 (1995), pp. 181-206.
—'Anchored Narratives and the Interface of Law, Psychology and Semiotics', *Legal and Criminological Psychology* 1 (1996), pp. 17-45.
—*Making Sense in Jurisprudence* (Liverpool: Deborah Charles Publications, 1996).
—'An Aye for an I?: The Semiotics of Lex Talionis in the Bible', in W. Pencak and J. Ralph Lindgren (eds.), *Semiotics and the Human Sciences: New Directions—Essays in Honor of Roberta Kevelson* (New York and Bern: Peter Lang, 1997), pp. 127-49.
—*Studies in the Semiotics of Biblical Law* (JSOTSup, 314; Sheffield: Sheffield Academic Press, 2000).
Jacobsen, T., 'Toward the Image of Tammuz', in William L. Moran (ed.), *Toward the Image of Tammuz and Other Essays on Mesopotamian History and Culture* (Cambridge, MA: Harvard University Press, 1970), pp. 73-103.
Jenson, P.P., *Graduated Holiness* (JSOTSup, 106; Sheffield: JSOT Press, 1992).
Joosten, J., *People and Land in the Holiness Code* (Leiden: E.J. Brill, 1996).
Kaiser, Walter C., Jr, 'The Weightier and Lighter Matters of the Law: Moses, Jesus and Paul', in Gerald F. Hawthorne (ed.), *Current Issues in Biblical and Patristic Interpretation* (Grand Rapids: Eerdmans, 1975).
—*Toward Old Testament Ethics* (Grand Rapids: Eerdmans, 1983).
Katsh, A.I., *The Biblical Heritage of American Democracy* (New York: Ktav, 1977).

Kaufman, S.A., 'The Structure of the Deuteronomic Law', *Maarav* 1 (1979), pp. 105-58.
Kee, H.C., 'Jesus: "A Glutton and a Drunkard"', *NTS* 42 (1996), pp. 374-93.
Keil, C.F., and F. Delitzsch, *Leviticus* (Grand Rapids: Eerdmans, 1976 [1876]).
Kellerman, D., אשם, in *TDOT*, I, pp. 429-37.
Kiuchi, N., *The Purification Offering in the Priestly Literature* (JSOTSup, 36; Sheffield: JSOT Press, 1987).
Klawans, J., 'The Impurity of Immorality in Ancient Judaism', *JJS* 48 (1997), pp. 1-16.
Klein, R.W., *1 Samuel* (Waco, TX: Word Books, 1983).
Kleinig, J., 'Punishment and Moral Seriousness', *Israel Law Review* 25 (1991), pp. 401-21.
Knohl, I., 'The Sin Offering in the 'Holiness School' (Numbers 15.22-31)', in G.A. Anderson and S.M. Olyan (eds.), *Priesthood and Cult in Ancient Israel* (JSOTSup, 125; Sheffield: Sheffield Academic Press, 1991), pp. 192-203.
Koch, K., חטא, in *TDOT*, IV, pp. 309-19.
Köhler, Ludwig, *Hebrew Man* (London: SCM Press, 1956).
Kruger, P.A., 'Symbolic Acts Relating to Old Testament Treaties and Relationships', *Journal for Semitics* 2 (1990), pp. 156-70.
Kruger, Paul A., 'The Removal of the Sandal in Deuteronomy XXV 9: "A Rite of Passage"?', *VT* 46 (1996), pp. 534-38.
Laffey, A.L., *Wives, Harlots and Concubines: The Old Testament in Feminist Perspective* (Philadelphia: Fortress Press, 1988).
Laski, H.J., *The Rise of European Liberalism* (London: Unwin Books, 1962).
Lee, R.W., *The Elements of Roman Law* (London: Sweet & Maxwell, 1956).
Leeb, Carolyn S., *Away from the Father's House: The Social Location of na'ar and na'arah in Ancient Israel* (JSOTSup, 301; Sheffield: Sheffield Academic Press, 2000).
Leggett, D.A., *The Levirate and Go'el Institutions in the Old Testament: With Special Attention to the Book of Ruth* (New Jersey: Mack, 1974).
Levi, M., and S. Jones, 'Public and Police Perceptions of Crime Seriousness in England and Wales', *British Journal of Criminology* 25 (1985), pp. 234-50.
Levine, B.A., *In the Presence of the LORD: A Study of Cult and Some Cultic Terms in Ancient Israel* (Leiden: E.J. Brill, 1974).
Levine, B., *Leviticus* (Philadelphia: Jewish Publication Society of America, 1989).
Levine, E., 'On Intra-Familial Institutions of the Bible', *Bib.* 57 (1976), pp. 554-59.
Levinson, B.M., 'Calum M. Carmichael's Approach to the Laws of Deuteronomy', *HTR* 83 (1990), pp. 227-57.
Lewis, C.S., *Surprised by Joy* (London: Geoffrey Bles, 1955), p. 181.
Lim Teng Kok, J., *The Sin of Moses and the Staff of God* (Assen: Van Gorcum, 1997).
Lipiński, E., 'Shemesh' שמש, in Karel van der Toorn *et al.* (eds.), *Dictionary of Deities and Demons in the Bible* (Leiden: E.J. Brill, 1995), pp. 1445-52.
Loader, J.A., 'Of Barley, Bulls, Land and Levirate', in F. Garcia Martinez *et al.* (eds.), *Studies in Deuteronomy* (Leiden: E.J. Brill, 1994), pp. 123-38.
Locher, C., *Die Ehre einer Frau in Israel* (Göttingen: Vandenhock & Ruprecht, 1986).
Lundquist, J.M., 'What is a Temple? A Preliminary Typology', in H.B. Hoffman *et al.* (eds.), *The Quest for the Kingdom of God* (Winona Lake, IN: Eisenbrauns, 1983), pp. 205-19.
McCarthy, C., *The Tiqqune Sopherim* (Göttingen: Vandenhoeck & Ruprecht, 1981).
McCarthy, D.J., 'Notes on the Love of God in Deuteronomy and the Father-Son Relationship between Yahweh and Israel', *CBQ* 27 (1965), pp. 144-47.
McCleary, R., *et al.*, 'Effects of Legal Education and Work Experience on Perceptions of Crime Seriousness', *Social Problems* 28 (1981), pp. 276-89.

McComiskey, T.E., 'Hosea', in Thomas Edward McComiskey (ed.), *The Minor Prophets: An Exegetical and Expository Commentary*. I. *Hosea, Joel and Amos* (Grand Rapids: Baker Book House, 1992), pp. 1-237
McConville, J.G., *Grace in the End* (Carlisle: The Paternoster Press, 1993).
McCurley, F.R., *Ancient Myths and Biblical Faith* (Philadelphia: Fortress Press, 1983).
Maag, V., 'Belija'al im Alten Testament', *TZ* 21 (1965), pp. 287-99.
MacIntyre, A., *Whose Justice? Which Rationality?* (Trowbridge: Duckworth, 1988).
Magistrates' Association, *Sentencing Guidelines 1992* (The Magistrates' Association, 1992).
Main, D.J., *et al.*, 'Law and Psychology in the Perception of Crime Seriousness: Towards a Joint Approach', in Graham Davies *et al.*, *Psychology, Law and Criminal Justice* (New York: W. de Gruyter, 1996), pp. 401-406.
Malinowski, B., *Crime and Custom in Savage Society* (London: Routledge, 1966).
Mann, T.W., 'Passover: The Time of Our Lives', *Int* 50 (1996), pp. 240-50.
Martin, D.B., 'Heterosexism and the Interpretation of Romans 1.18-32', *BibInt* 3 (1995), pp. 332-45.
Matthews, V.H., 'Entrance Ways and Threshing Floors: Legally Significant Sites in the Ancient Near East', *Fides et Historia* 19 (1987), pp. 25-40.
—'The Anthropology of Clothing in the Joseph Narrative', *JSOT* 65 (1995), pp. 25-36.
—'Honor and Shame in Gender-Related Legal Situations in the Hebrew Bible', in V.H. Matthews *et al.* (eds.), *Gender and Law in the Hebrew Bible and the Ancient Near East* (JSOTSup, 262; Sheffield: Sheffield Academic Press, 1998), pp. 97-112.
Matthews, V.H., and D.C. Benjamin, *Social World of Ancient Israel, 1250–586 BCE* (Peabody, MA: Hendrickson, 1993).
May, H.G., 'The Departure of the Glory of Yahweh', *JBL* 56 (1937), pp. 309-21.
Mayhew, P., *et al.*, The *1992 British Crime Survey* (Home Office Research Study 132; London: HMSO, 1992).
Melnyk, J.L.R., 'When Israel Was a Child: Ancient Near Eastern Adoption Formulas and the Relationship between God and Israel', in M. Patrick Graham *et al.*, *History and Interpretation* (JSOTSup, 173; Sheffield: Sheffield Academic Press, 1993), pp. 245-59.
Mendelsohn, I., 'The Family in the Ancient Near East', *BA* 11 (1948), pp. 24-40.
—'On the Preferential Status of the Eldest Son', *BASOR* 156 (1959), pp. 38-40.
Mendelsohn, S., *The Criminal Jurisprudence of the Jews* (New York: Sepher-Hermon Press, 1991 [1890]).
Meyers, C.L., 'The Roots of Restriction: Women in Early Israel', in Norman K. Gottwald (ed.), *The Bible and Liberation* (Maryknoll, NY: Orbis Books, 1983), pp. 289-306.
Milgrom, J., 'The Cultic שגגה and its Influence in Psalms and Job', *JQR* 58 (1967), pp. 115-25.
—'The Shared Custody of the Tabernacle and a Hittite Analogy', *JAOS* 90 (1970), pp. 204-209.
—'A Prolegomenon to *Leviticus* 17.11', *JBL* 90 (1971), pp. 149-56.
—'Sin-offering or Purification-offering?', *VT* 21 (1971), pp. 237-39.
—'First-born', in Keith Crim *et al.* (eds.), *Illustrated Bible Dictionary: Supplementary Volume* (Nashville: Abingdon Press, 1976), pp. 337-38.
—'Israel's Sanctuary: The Priestly *Picture of Dorian Gray*', *RB* 83 (1976), pp. 390-99.
—'Review of *Sühne als Heilsgeschehen*', *JBL* 104 (1985), pp. 302-304.
—*Numbers* (Philadelphia: Jewish Publication Society, 1990).
—*Leviticus 1–16* (New York: Doubleday, 1991).
Miller, P., 'The Place of the Decalogue in the Old Testament and its Law', *Int* 43 (1989), pp. 229-42.
Montaigne, M. de., *Essais livre second* (Paris: Fernand Rockes, 1931 [1613]).

Moore, M., *Foundations of Liberalism* (Oxford: Clarendon Press, 1993).
Morgernstern, J., 'The Gates of Righteousness', *HUCA* 6 (1929), pp. 1-37.
Motyer, J.A., *The Prophecy of Isaiah* (Leicester: InterVarsity Press, 1993).
—'Name', in J.D. Douglas *et al.* (eds.), *New Bible Dictionary* (London: InterVarsity Press, 3rd edn, 1996), pp. 799-802.
Mullins, P.O.C., 'The Status of Women in Family Life: A Comparative Study of Old Testament Times', *Milltown Studies* 41 (1998), pp. 51-81.
Neufeld, D., 'Eating, Ecstasy and Exorcism (Mark 3.21)', *BTB* 26 (1996), pp. 152-62.
Neufeld, E., *Ancient Hebrew Marriage Laws* (London: Longmans, Green & Co., 1944).
Nicholas, B., *An Introduction to Roman Law* (Oxford: Clarendon Press, 1962).
Niditch, S., 'The Wronged Woman Righted: An Analysis of Genesis 38', *HTR* 72 (1979), pp. 144-49.
Niehaus, J.J., 'Amos', in T.E. McComiskey (ed.), *The Minor Prophets: An Exegetical and Expository Commentary*. I. *Hosea, Joel and Amos* (Grand Rapids: Baker Book House, 1992), pp. 315-494.
—*God at Sinai: Covenant and Theophany in the Bible and Ancient Near East* (Carlisle: Paternoster Press, 1995).
Noonan, J.T., Jr, 'The Muzzled Ox', *JQR* 70 (1979), pp. 172-75.
Oboler, R.S., 'Nandi Widows', in Betty Potash (ed.), *Widows in African Societies* (Stanford: Stanford University Press, 1986), pp. 66-83.
O'Connell, M., and A. Whelan, 'Taking Wrongs Seriously', *British Journal of Criminology* 36 (1996), pp. 299-318.
Oden, R.A., Jr, *The Bible Without Theology: The Theological Tradition and Alternatives to it* (San Francisco: Harper & Row, 1987), pp. 131-53.
Ollenburger, B.C., *Zion, the City of the Great King* (JSOTSup, 41; Sheffield: JSOT Press, 1987).
Olson, D.T., *Deuteronomy and the Death of Moses* (Minneapolis: Fortress Press, 1994).
Olyan, S.M., 'Honour, Shame and Covenant Relations in Ancient Israel and its Environment', *JBL* 115 (1996), pp. 201-18.
Otto, E., 'False Weights in the Scales of Biblical Justice? Different Views of Women from Patriarchal Hierarchy to Religious Equality in the Book of Deuteronomy', in V.H. Matthews *et al.* (eds.), *Gender and Law in the Hebrew Bible and the Ancient Near East* (JSOTSup, 262; Sheffield: Sheffield Academic Press, 1998), pp. 128-46.
Ottosson, M., *Temples and Cult Places in Palestine* (Uppsala: Acta Universitatis Upsaliensis, 1980).
Patai, R., *The Hebrew Goddess* (Detroit: Wayne State University Press, 1990).
Patrick, D., *Old Testament Law* (London: SCM Press, 1985).
Payne, L., *The Broken Image* (Eastbourne: Kingsway, 1988).
Pedersen, J., *Israel: Its Life and Culture* (2 vols.; London: Oxford University Press, 1959).
Phillips, A., *Ancient Israel's Criminal Law* (Oxford: Basil Blackwell, 1970).
—'Nebalah—a Term for Serious Disorderly and Unruly Conduct', *VT* 25 (1975), pp. 237-42.
Pickett, W.H., 'The Meaning and Function of *T'b/To'evah* in the Hebrew Bible' (PhD thesis submitted to Hebrew Union College, Cincinnati, 1985).
Pincoffs, E.L., 'Legal Responsibility and Moral Character', *Wayne Law Review* 19 (1973), pp. 905-23.
Plaskow, J., *Standing again at Sinai: Judaism from a Feminist Perspective* (Harper: San Francisco, 1991).

Potash, B., 'Wives of the Grave: Widows in a Rural Luo Community', in B. Potash (ed.), *Widows in African Societies* (Stanford: Stanford University Press, 1986), pp. 44-65.
Poythress, V.S., *The Shadow of Christ in the Law of Moses* (Phillipsburg, NJ: P & R Publishing, 1991).
Pressler, C., *The View of Women Found in the Deuteronomic Family Laws* (New York: W. de Gruyter, 1993).
—'Sexual Violence and Deuteronomic Law', in A. Brenner (ed.), *A Feminist Companion to Exodus to Deuteronomy* (Sheffield: Sheffield Academic Press, 1994), pp. 102-12.
Preuss, ערי, in *TDOT*, IV, pp. 143-62.
Pritchard, J.B. (ed.), *Ancient Near Eastern Texts* (Princeton: Princeton University Press, 1950).
Prouser, O.H., 'Clothes Maketh the Man', *BR* 14 (1998), pp. 22-27.
Pursiful, D.J., *The Cultic Motif in the Spirituality of the Book of Hebrews* (Lewiston, NY: Mellen Biblical Press, 1993).
Rankin, O.S., 'Name', in A. Richardson (ed.), *A Theological Word Book of the Bible* (London: SCM Press, 1967), pp. 157-58.
Rattray, S., 'Marriage Rules, Kinship Terms and Family Structure in the Bible', in *Society of Biblical Literature 1987 Seminar Papers* (Society of Biblical Literature, 1987), pp. 537-44.
Rendtorff, R., *Die Gesetze in der Priesterschrift* (Göttingen: Vandenhoeck & Ruprecht, 1954).
Ringgren, H., בער, in *TDOT*, II, pp. 201-205.
Rofé, A., 'Methodological Aspects of the Study of Biblical Law', in B.S. Jackson (ed.), *Jewish Law Association Studies II: The Jerusalem Conference Volume* (Atlanta: Scholars Press, 1986), pp. 1-16.
Rogerson, J.W., *Anthropology and the Old Testament* (Oxford: Basil Blackwell, 1978).
Rose, A.M., and E.A. Prell, 'Does the Punishment Fit the Crime? A Study in Social Valuation', *AJS* 61 (1955), pp. 247-59.
Ross, Allen P., שם, *NIDOTE*, pp. 147-51.
Rossi, P.H., and J.P. Henry, 'Seriousness: A Measure for all Purposes?', in M.W. Klein *et al.* (eds.), *Handbook of Criminal Justice Evaluation* (Beverly Hills: Sage, 1980), pp. 489-505.
Rotenberg, M., and B.L. Diamond, 'The Biblical Conception of Psychopathy: The Law of the Stubborn and Rebellious Son', *JBS* 7 (1971), pp. 29-38.
Roth, Martha T., *Law Collections from Mesopotamia and Asia Minor* (Atlanta: Scholars Press, 2nd edn, 1997).
Rowley, H.H., 'The Marriage of Ruth', *HTR* 40 (1947), pp. 77-99.
Rushdoony, R.J., *The Institutes of Biblical Law* (Craig Press: Presbyterian and Reformed Publishing Co., 1973).
Ruppert, סרר, in *ThWAT*, V, pp. 957-63.
Saller, R.P., *Patriarchy, Property and Death in the Roman Family* (Cambridge: Cambridge University Press, 1994).
Sasson, J.M., *Ruth* (Sheffield: Sheffield Academic Press, 1995).
Schmitt, J.J., 'The Gender of Ancient Israel', *JSOT* 26 (1983), pp. 115-25.
—'Virgin', in *ABD*, VI, pp. 853-54.
Schulz, F., *Principles of Roman Law* (Oxford: Clarendon Press, 1936).
Schwartz, B.J., 'The Bearing of Sin in the Priestly Literature', in David P. Wright *et al.* (eds.), *Pomegranates and Golden Bells: Studies in Biblical, Jewish and Near Eastern Ritual, Law and Literature in Honour of Jacob Milgrom* (Winona Lake, IN: Eisenbrauns, 1995), pp. 3-21.

Sebba, L., and G. Nathan, 'Further Explorations in the Scaling of Penalties', *British Journal of Criminology* 23 (1984), pp. 221-47.
Seidl, שגה/שגג, in *ThWAT*, VII, pp. 1058-65.
Simkins, R., *Creator and Creation: Nature in the Worldview of Ancient Israel* (Peabody, MA: Hendrickson, 1994).
Smedes, L., *Shame and Grace: Healing the Shame We Don't Deserve* (London: Triangle, 1993).
Smith, M., 'The Veracity of Ezekiel, the Sins of Manasseh, and Jeremiah 44.18', *ZAW* 87 (1975), pp. 11-16.
Snaith, N.H., 'The Daughters of Zelophehad', *VT* 16 (1966), pp. 124-27.
Sparks, R., *et al.*, *Surveying Victims* (London: Wiley, 1977).
Speiser, E.A., 'Of Shoes and Shekels', *BASOR* 77 (1940), pp. 15-20.
—'Background and Function of the Biblical Nasi', *CBQ* 25 (1963), pp. 111-17.
Stacey, W.D., *Prophetic Drama in the Old Testament* (London: Epworth Press, 1990).
Stager, L.E., 'The Archaeology of the Family in Ancient Israel', *BASOR* 260 (1985), pp. 1-36.
Sterring, A., 1994. 'The Will of the Daughters', in A. Brenner (ed.), *A Feminist Companion to Exodus to Deuteronomy* (Sheffield: Sheffield Academic Press, 1994), pp. 88-99.
Stone, K., *Sex, Honor, and Power in the Deuteronomistic History*. (JSOTSup, 234; Sheffield: Sheffield Academic Press, 1996).
Stulman, L., 'Sex and Familial Crimes in the D Code: A Witness to Mores in Transition', *JSOT* 53 (1992), pp. 47-63.
Sudnow, D., 'Normal Crimes: Sociological Features of the Penal Code in a Public Defender Office', *Social Problems* 12 (1965), pp. 255-76.
Taylor, J.G., *Yahweh and the Sun* (JSOTSup, 111; Sheffield: Sheffield Academic Press, 1993).
Terence, *Heauton Timorumenos in The Comedies* (trans. Betty Radice; London: Penguin Books, 1965), l. 77.
Thompson, R.J., 'Sacrifice and Offering: I. In the Old Testament', in *IBD*, III, pp. 1358-66.
Thompson, T., and D. Thompson, 'Some Legal Problems in the Book of Ruth', *VT* 18 (1968), pp. 79-99.
Tigay, J.H., 'Examination of the Accused Bride in 4Q159: Forensic Medicine at Qumran', *JANESCU* 22 (1993), pp. 129-34.
—*Deuteronomy* (Philadelphia: Jewish Publication Society of America, 1996).
Toeg, A., 'A Halakhic Midrash in Num. XV.22-31', *Tarbiz* 43 (1973) I-II (Summary), pp. 1-20.
Torczyner, H., 'Semel Ha-qin'ah Ha-Maqneh', *JBL* 65 (1946), pp. 293-302.
Torrey, C.C., *Pseudo-Ezekiel and the Original Prophecy* (New York: Ktav Publishing, 1970 [1930]).
Ushedo, B., 'Forensic Narration in the Book of Ruth', *Scripture Bulletin* 28 (1998), pp. 28-40.
Van den Boom, G.P.F., '*Wd-ryt* and Justice at the Gate', *JNES* 44 (1985), pp. 1-25.
Van der Toorn, K., 'The Significance of the Veil in the Ancient Near East', in David P. Wright *et al.* (eds.), *Pomegranates and Golden Bells: Studies in Biblical, Jewish and Near Eastern Ritual, Law and Literature in Honour of Jacob Milgrom* (Winona Lake, IN: Eisenbrauns, 1995), pp. 327-39.
Vendler, Z., 'Verbs and Times', *Philosophical Review* 66 (1957), pp. 143-60.
Viberg, A., *Symbols of Law* (Stockholm: Almquistse Wiksell, 1992).
Von Hirsch, A., 'Proportionality in the Philosophy of Punishment: From "Why Punish?" to "How Much?"', *Criminal Law Forum* 1 (2) (1990), pp. 259-90.
—'The Politics of "Just Deserts"' *Canadian Journal of Criminology* 32 (1990), pp. 397-413.

Von Hirsch, A., and N. Jareborg, 'Gauging Criminal Harm: A Living-Standard Analysis', *Oxford Journal of Legal Studies* 11 (1991), pp. 1-38.
Wadsworth, T., 'Is There a Hebrew Word for Virgin? *Bethulah* in the Old Testament', *ResQ* 23 (1980), pp. 161-71.
Walker, D.M., *The Oxford Companion to Law* (Oxford: Clarendon Press, 1980).
Walker, M.A., 'Measuring the Seriousness of Crimes', *British Journal of Criminology* 18 (1978), pp. 348-64.
Walker, N., and C. Marsh, 'Do Sentences Affect Public Disapproval?', *British Journal of Criminology* 24 (1984), pp. 27-48.
Walker, N., *Why Punish?* (Oxford: Oxford University Press, 1991).
Warr, M., 'What is the Perceived Seriousness of Crimes?', *Criminology* 27 (1989), pp. 795-821.
Washington, H.C., '"Lest He Die in the Battle and Another Man Take Her": Violence and the Construction of Gender in the Laws of Deuteronomy 20-22', in V.H. Matthews *et al.* (eds.), *Gender and Law in the Hebrew Bible and the Ancient Near East* (JSOTSup, 262; Sheffield: Sheffield Academic Press, 1998), pp. 185-213.
Watts, J.W., 'Public Readings and Pentateuchal Law', *VT* 45 (1995), pp. 540-57.
—'Rhetorical Strategy in the Composition of the Pentateuch', *JSOT* 68 (1995), pp. 3-22.
Weiner, H.M., 'The Arrangement of Deuteronomy XII–XXVI' in H. Loewe (ed.), *Posthumous Essays* (London: Oxford University Press, 1932), pp. 26-36.
Weinfeld, M., *Deuteronomy and the Deuteronomic School* (Oxford: Clarendon Press, 1972).
Wenham, G.J., 'Deuteronomy and the Central Sanctuary', *TynBul* 22 (1971), pp. 103-18.
—'*Betulah*: A Girl of Marriageable Age', *VT* 22 (1972), pp. 326-48.
—*Leviticus* (Grand Rapids: Eerdmans, 1979).
—*Numbers* (Leicester: InterVarsity Press, 1981).
—*Genesis 1–15* (Dallas: Word Books, 1987).
—'The Gap between Law and Ethics in the Bible', *JJS* 48 (1997), pp. 17-29.
Wenham, Gordon J., and J.G. McConville, 'Drafting Techniques in some Deuteronomic Laws', *VT* 30 (1980), pp. 248-52.
Westbrook, R., 'The Law of the Biblical Levirate', in R. Westbrook, *Property and the Family in Biblical Law* (JSOTSup, 113; JSOT Press: Sheffield, 1991), pp. 69-89.
Westenholz, J.G., 'Tamar, *qedesa*, *qadistu* and Sacred Prostitution in Mesopotamia', *HTR* 82 (1989), pp. 245-65.
Wiggins, S.A., 'Yahweh: The God of Sun', *JSOT* 71 (1996), pp. 89-106.
Wiseman, D.J., 'Rahab of Jericho', *TynBul* 14 (1964), pp. 8-11.
—'Law and Order in Old Testament Times', *VE* 8 (1973), pp. 5-21.
Wittgenstein, L., *Philosophical Investigations* (trans. G.E.M. Anscombe; Oxford: Blackwell, 1958).
Wright, C.J.H., 'The Israelite Household and the Decalogue: The Social Background and Significance of Some Commandments', *TynBul* 30 (1979), pp. 101-24.
—'Family', in *ABD*, II, pp. 761-69.
—*Deuteronomy* (Peabody, MA: Hendrickson, 1996).
Wright, D.P., 'The Spectrum of Priestly Impurity', in G.A. Anderson and S.M. Olyan (eds.), *Priesthood and Cult in Ancient Israel* (JSOTSup, 125; Sheffield: Sheffield Academic Press, 1991), pp. 150-81.
Wright, G.E., 'Israelite Daily Life', *BA* 18 (1955), pp. 50-79.
Wright, N.T., 1993. *The New Testament and the People of God: Christian Origins and the Question of God*, I (London: SPCK, 2nd edn, 1993).

Yamauchi, E.M., 'Cultic Prostitution', in H.A. Hoffner, Jr (ed.), *Orient and Occident* (Neukirchen–Vluyn: Neukirchener Verlag, 1973), pp. 213-22.
Yaron, R., 'Biblical law: Prolegomena', in B.S. Jackson (ed.), *Jewish Law in Legal History and the Modern World* (Jewish Law Annual Supplement, 2; Leiden: E.J. Brill, 1980), pp. 27-44.
Yeats, W.B., *Selected Poetry* (ed. A. Norman Jaffares; London: Macmillan, 1962).
Zimmerli, W., *Ezekiel I: A Commentary on the Book of the Prophet Ezekiel Chapters 1–24* (trans. R.E. Clements; Philadelphia: Fortress Press, 1979).
Zimmermann, F., 'Folk Etymology of Biblical Names', in *Volume du congrès* (VTSup, 15; Leiden: E.J. Brill, 1966), pp. 311-26.
Zohar, N., 'Repentance and Purification: The Significance and Semantics of חטאת in the Pentateuch', *JBL* 107 (1988), pp. 609-18.

INDEXES

INDEX OF REFERENCES

OLD TESTAMENT

Genesis						
				109, 226	16.9	169
1.11	116	38.2-5	94		16.10	169, 170
1.28	104	38.7-9	85		17	74
2.1-3	248	38.8-11	94, 96, 97		17.1	169
2.7	109	38.8-10	91, 98		20.1-17	199
2.19-20	115	38.8-9	109		20.2-3	200
2.24	93	38.8	85, 97, 98		20.2	63, 200,
6.13	213	38.9	87, 94, 97,			202, 203
7.1-23	213		109, 114		20.3-6	200-203,
11.1-9	119	38.11	100			226
11.4	119	38.12-19	102		20.3	199, 201,
11.9	119	38.13-26	98			205, 237
12	116	38.14	154		20.4-6	200
15.9	175	38.24	123, 125,		20.4-5	197, 198
17.5	115, 117,		144		20.4	197, 201
	118	38.26	98, 100		20.5	190, 197,
17.15	117	43.12	161			201
22.17	109	48.6	86		20.8-11	60
24.16	140	49.4	128		20.12	59-61, 63,
25.30	117	49.10	223			71, 74
27.36	118	50.10	144		20.13-17	201
29.31–30.24	223				20.18-21	199
30.1	103	*Exodus*			20.18-20	235
32.28	117, 118	1.1-4	223		20.18	233
34.7	136	4.22-23	62		20.22-23	199
34.12	152	12.3	168		21	173
34.25-26	136	12.6	170		21.4-6	113
35.10	118	12.26-27	61		21.4	113
35.11	109	12.47	168		21.5-6	113
35.22	128	13.14-15	61		21.12-19	173
37.3	150	16.1-3	169		21.15	59, 63, 70
37.31-33	152	16.1	169		21.17	59, 63
38	96, 99,	16.2	169		21.19	152
	100, 102,	16.3	49		21.20-21	173

21.22	18	34.15-16	202	4.16-18	160		
21.23	22	34.22	195	4.16-17	177		
21.26-27	173	34.29	195	4.17	160, 237		
21.28-35	173	35.1	169, 170	4.18	160, 165, 182, 237		
21.28	173	35.4	169, 170				
21.29	173	35.20	169, 170	4.20	158, 244		
21.30	22	39.2-7	176	4.21	160, 182-84		
21.31	173	39.22-26	176				
21.32	173	40.20	211	4.22-35	183		
21.33-35	173			4.22-26	160, 167, 170, 171, 173, 177		
21.36	13	*Leviticus*					
22.2-3	14	1.3	177				
22.3	13	3.2	177	4.22-23	162, 163		
22.4	14, 152	4	33, 35, 158-64, 166, 172-77, 250	4.22	157, 158, 162, 166, 171, 244		
22.5	13, 32						
22.16-17	139, 145, 152			4.23-24	163		
23.16	195	4.1-35	157, 158, 160, 226	4.23	160, 175, 176		
23.20	50						
23.21	50	4.1-2	249	4.24-25	160		
24.9-11	194, 206	4.2	157, 163	4.24	236, 237		
25.16	211	4.3-12	160, 166, 167, 173, 244	4.25	160, 165, 182		
25.21	211						
25.40	212			4.26	158, 244		
26.31	222	4.3	166, 167, 172, 244	4.27-35	160, 172, 173, 177		
26.33	177						
27.9-19	177	4.4	160, 175, 176, 236, 237	4.27-31	158, 167, 172, 173		
27.16	222						
28.1	167			4.27-28	162, 163		
28.3	167	4.5-7	160	4.27	157, 158, 166, 172, 244		
28.6-12	176	4.5-6	177				
28.15-30	176	4.6	160, 237				
28.31-42	176	4.7	160, 165, 182, 237	4.28	160, 173, 175, 176		
28.31-35	176						
29.1	167	4.11-12	160, 182	4.29	236		
29.4	177	4.12	182-84	4.30	160, 165, 182		
29.32	177	4.13-21	158, 160, 168, 170, 173				
29.37	182			4.31	158, 244		
29.42	177			4.32-35	172, 173		
30.10	182	4.13-14	162, 163	4.32	160, 173, 175, 176		
30.22-33	166	4.13	157, 158, 162, 168-70, 244				
31.12-17	248			4.33	236		
31.14	127			4.34	160, 165, 182		
32	201	4.14	159, 160, 162, 175, 176				
32.6	132			4.35	158, 244		
32.17-19	53			5.1-13	157, 158, 183		
32.20	124	4.15	168, 236, 237				
34.14	190			5.2	172		

Leviticus (cont.)		20.9	59, 63	11.1-3	117
5.6-13	175	20.21	102	11.1	124
5.7	175	21	126	11.34	117
5.9	158	21.1-9	128, 132	12.14	114
5.11	175	21.1	132	13.1-15	171
5.12	158	21.4	126	13.26–14.10	170
5.15	161	21.5-6	124	13.26	169, 170
6.30	182	21.5	132	14	170
8.12	166	21.6	128	14.1-45	42
8.30	166	21.7	148	14.5	170
9.24	124	21.8	127	14.7	169, 170
10.2	124	21.9	33, 35, 121, 122, 124-29, 131-37, 155, 156, 206, 229, 232, 250	14.10	170
10.10-11	135, 168			14.11	74
10.10	126			14.29	170
10.16-20	183			14.33	129
10.17	183			15.22-31	158, 159
10.18	183			15.22-29	158, 159, 163
11.10-11	193				
12–15	164			15.22-26	158
12.6	177	21.10	166	15.22	163
14.10	175	21.12	127	15.24-29	158, 159
14.21-22	175	21.15	127	15.24	158
14.21	175	21.17-21	124	15.25	158, 169
15.31	165	22.12	74	15.26	158, 161
16.4	167	22.13	127	15.27-29	158, 161
16.7	177	22.14	161	15.27	158
16.16	165	22.15	127	15.29	158
16.23-24	167	22.32	127	15.30-31	158
16.32-34	177	23.40	196	15.30	158
17.7	129	24.18	22	15.39	129
18.1-30	132	27.1-8	175	16.2	171
18.16	102			16.3	117
18.21	127, 132	*Numbers*		16.35	124
19.2	133, 169	1.2-3	169	19.20	165
19.3	63	1.2	169	20	74
19.8	127	1.5-16	171	20.12	73, 74
19.26-31	134	1.16	171	20.13	117
19.26	134	3.3	166	20.29	144
19.27-28	124, 134	3.23	135	25.1-2	132
19.29	127-29, 133, 134, 147	3.29	135	25.1	129, 132
		3.30	171	25.6-8	132, 133
		3.32	171	26.63	88
		3.33	135	27.1-11	88
19.30	134	3.35	171	27.4	79, 85
19.31	134	3.38	135, 222	27.5	79
20.3	135, 165	5.11-31	155	27.7-11	93, 94
20.5-6	129	6.24-26	195	27.8-11	112
20.5	132	7.2	171	27.20	170
20.6	132	8.9	169		

Index of References

31.17	140	5.16	59, 61-63,	17.6-7	141
31.18	140		71	17.8-13	11, 13
31.21-23	124	5.31	103	17.12	37, 137
32.42	115	5.33	103	17.13	38
34.16-28	171	6–28	60	17.18-20	11
35.9-29	83	6.1	103	18.15-19	50
35.11	161	6.3	40, 103	19.11-12	83
35.24	168	6.6-7	234	19.13	37
36	88, 93	6.7	51	19.20	38
36.1	171	6.10-12	40	21.7	95
36.5-9	93	6.10	103	21.10-14	59, 144,
36.6-13	93	6.13	200		146, 151
36.6-9	94	6.18	103	21.10-13	61
36.13	88	6.20-24	61	21.11	144
		6.23	103	21.13-29	249
Deuteronomy		7.1	103	21.13	74, 144,
1	78	7.3-4	61		151
1.1-5	249	7.5	124	21.14	144, 235
1.1-2	40	7.12-16	78	21.15-23	73, 74
1.1	88, 103,	7.25	124	21.15-17	71, 74-76,
	249, 250	8.1	103		128
1.3	250	8.3	65	21.15	148
1.5	40, 234	8.5	62	21.16-17	148
1.6–4.43	237	8.12-14	65	21.16	75
1.6–4.40	76	9.6	40	21.17	95, 155
1.6–3.29	76	9.7	77	21.18-21	16, 31-33,
1.26	76	9.23-24	77		35, 37, 38,
1.31	62	10.1-5	211		40-42, 44-
1.34-41	76	11.14-16	65		50, 54-60,
1.43	77	11.19	51		63-68, 70-
2	106	11.21	78		79, 128,
4.1	77, 78	11.28	202		142, 234,
4.9-10	51, 62	12–26	60		235, 237,
4.9	61	12.3	104, 105,		249
4.15	199		124	21.18	37-39, 46,
4.16-19	198	13	67		48, 50, 56,
4.16	198	13.11	38		68-70, 76,
4.17-18	207	14.1	62		78, 232,
4.17	198	14.24-26	174		234
4.18	198	14.26	40	21.19	37, 56, 68,
4.19	194, 198	15.7-11	88		69, 76
4.24	124, 198	15.12-15	88	21.20	37-39, 46,
4.25-27	78	16–18	71		47, 50, 51,
4.40	62	16.18–18.22	60		53, 54, 58,
4.44–28.68	73, 76	16.18-20	12		59, 66,
5.12	60	17.1	204		68-71, 76,
5.14	248	17.3	194, 195		78, 234
5.15	248	17.5	142	21.21	37, 38,

Deuteronomy (cont.)			145, 147,			102, 112,
	137, 227,		153, 227,			226, 234
	229, 232,		229, 232,	25.8		79-81, 94,
	252		252			97, 227,
21.22-23	74, 75,	22.22	37, 137,			232, 246
	153		138, 147,	25.9-10		79, 92, 95,
21.23	75		151			99, 105,
22	144	22.23-27	138, 151			110, 112-
22.5	176, 204	22.23-24	138, 141,			14
22.6-7	61		142, 146,	25.9		81, 85, 89,
22.13-29	138, 139,		147, 149,			95, 102,
	141, 146,		154			105, 106,
	147, 150,	22.23	147			108, 109,
	154, 155	22.24	37, 137,			113
22.13-21	31, 33, 35,		138, 142	25.10		27, 79, 81,
	134, 137-	22.25-27	138, 146			105, 106,
	51, 154,	22.25	147			114-16,
	155, 226,	22.28-29	138, 153			118, 227,
	233, 234,	22.28	147			234, 245
	237, 246,	22.30	150	25.11-12		111
	249	23.1	150	25.11		111
22.13-19	71, 137,	23.17	135	25.12		111
	138, 141	24.5	150	25.19		246
22.13	108, 138,	24.7	37, 137	25.21		246
	143, 144,	25	110	27.15		193
	147, 148	25.4-12	109	27.16		59, 63
22.14	137, 149,	25.4	104	28		76, 245
	155, 234,	25.5-12	111	28.4-5		40
	245	25.5-10	31, 33, 35,	28.17-18		40
22.15-21	245		79, 83, 85,	28.26		123
22.16-17	153		87-91, 93-	28.39		40
22.16	153		104, 110,	29.22		124
22.17	140, 141,		111, 113,	30.15-20		76
	150, 151,		234, 235,	31.16		129
	153		237, 249	31.20		65
22.18-19	141, 151	25.5-7	89, 93, 95	31.27		77
22.19	74, 117,	25.5-6	84, 97	32.15		65
	148	25.5	90, 92,	32.45-47		73
22.20-21	121, 125,		94-97,	34.8		144
	134-39,		108, 226			
	141, 142,	25.6-7	85	*Joshua*		
	145-47,	25.6	81, 82,	2.15		192, 220
	154-56		86-89, 92,	4.6-7		61
22.20	137		102	4.21-23		61
22.21	37, 121,	25.7-10	94	6.24		124
	125, 132,	25.7	80, 82, 84,	7		122
	134-37,		85, 89, 90,	7.15		122, 136
	140, 142,		95-99,	7.24		123

7.25-26	122	4.9-10	85, 86	14.8-11	79
7.25	122, 123	4.10	86, 98, 99	15.30	113
7.26	153	4.12	98, 99	16	117
8.29	153	4.17	89	16.5	118
8.35	169	4.18-22	101	16.7-8	118
9.15	171	4.21	89	18.17	153
10.27	153	*1 Samuel*		20.1-22	57
11.6	124	1.16	56	20.1	57
11.9	124	1.22-25	56	20.8	176
13.21	171	1.22	56	24.9	62
20.3	161	2.12-17	55, 57		
22.14	171	2.12	56, 57, 68	*1 Kings*	
22.18	168	2.13-14	55	2.31-34	153
		2.15-16	55	3.9	12
Judges		2.15	55	3.28	12
1.14	112	2.16	56	5.11	117
2.17	129	2.17	55	6.29	212
6.32	117	2.22	56, 57	6.32	212
8.27	129	2.25	56	6.35	212
8.33	129	4.17	56	7.1-12	216
11.37-39	140	5.2-5	214	8	188, 196
12.1	123	5.4	214	8.2	196
17.2-3	112	5.5	214	8.9	213
18.27	124	6.14	175	8.10-13	188
19.22	57	7.3	200	8.14	169, 188
19.23-24	136	9.1	115	8.19	109
19.25-28	57	10.27	57	8.22	169
19.26-27	214	15.22	6	8.55	169
20.6	136	17.21	62	8.64	220
20.10	136	18.17-19	138	8.65	169
20.13	137	18.25	152, 153	11.26	115
20.46	136	18.26-27	138	11.38	85
21.19-21	56	18.30	117	13.1-31	123
		25.25	118	13.2	123
Ruth		31.11-13	123	13.22	123
1.2-4	101	31.13	123, 144	13.28	123
1.20	101			13.31	123
3.9	100	*2 Samuel*		14.11	123
4	96, 98, 99, 112	7.23	117	14.12	213
		7.27	85	14.17	213
4.1-12	81, 92, 96, 98, 101	13.12-13	136		
		13.12	136	*2 Kings*	
4.3	112	13.18	150, 176	1.10	124
4.6	94	13.28-29	136	1.12	124
4.7-8	110	14.1-20	79	1.14	124
4.7	109, 112, 113	14.4-11	102	4.10	192
		14.7	79	8.1-6	112

2 Kings (cont.)

10.8-9	214
11.19	217
16.14	220
18.13-16	175
21.3	194
21.5	192
21.24	172
22.3-20	207
22.10	207
22.11	207
22.12	207
23.1-25	207
23.5	194
23.6	123, 192
23.11	220
23.16	123
23.30	172
25.18	207
25.29	176

1 Chronicles

5.25	129
10.12	144
14.12	214
17.10	85
21.5	62
24.7-19	207

2 Chronicles

4.1	218
4.9	216
4.10	218
6.9	109
15.3	168
17.7-9	13, 234
19.4-11	11
19.6-7	11, 12
19.7	12
19.8	12
19.9-11	12
19.9	12
19.11	168, 231
21.11	129
21.13	129
26.19	193
33.7	192
33.15	192

Ezra

2.61-62	93
2.62	94
7.11	168
9.2	61
10.2	61

Nehemiah

7.63-64	93
7.64	94
8.1-8	234
8.2	168
9.24-26	65
9.26-29	49
9.26	43, 49
9.29	43, 49

Esther

6.11	105

Job

12.16	161
29.18	109
30.8	117
30.10	114
42.15	112

Psalms

18.5	57
19.13	198
21.10	103
25.13	103
26.5	169
27.5	187
29.3	188
29.10	188
41.5	104
50.3	124
51.16-19	6
66.10	124
69.36	103
73.27	129
78.8	49
78.14	195
78.40	48
78.69	212
80.1	211
89.39-45	187
89.39-40	113
89.39	128
95.7-11	49
99.1	211
106.7	48
106.28	133
106.39	129
109.13	85
113.9	85
115.5-6	206
118.25	196
128.3	103
128.6	103
133.1	90
135.16	206

Proverbs

1.7	12
1.8	61
3.1	61
4.2	61
6.20	61
7.1	61
13.19-22	66
17.3	124
17.21	136
20.1	161
22.1	116
23.19-22	54, 55
23.19	54
23.20	51, 54
23.21	54
23.22	54
23.35	54
25.7-10	14, 80
28.7	51, 54, 56
31.1	61

Ecclesiastes

6.10	104
7.1	116

Isaiah

1.2-3	63
1.11-17	6

Index of References

1.25	124	29.21-23	136	8.1–11.24	216
14.22	85	29.23	136	8.1-18	186
20.2-4	113	32.33	197	8.1	190, 191,
20.2	109	36.10-12	207		210, 250
22.16	123	36.10	220	8.3-18	188
23.9	128	36.12	220	8.3-16	197
30.1	48	36.25	220	8.3-13	216
30.9	48	39.14	207	8.3-6	192, 221
31.9	124	44.4	189	8.3-5	221
43.22-24	6	44.15	169	8.3	192, 198,
47.1-3	151				206, 210,
50.6	114	*Lamentations*			213-15,
56.4	85	2.2	128		217-21
56.5	85			8.4	188, 210
56.9	53	*Ezekiel*		8.5-18	187
56.10	53	1.1–3.15	188	8.5-13	197
56.11	53	1.1-3	207	8.5-6	206
56.12	53	1.1-2	191	8.5	190, 192,
57.3	132	1.2-3	190		198, 205,
57.5-9	132	1.3	206, 223		210, 214,
60.6	57	1.4	188		217-19
63.10	48	1.13	188	8.6	186, 189,
65.2	43, 47	1.24	188		201, 205,
66.15-16	124	1.26	188		210, 215,
66.22	104	2.3-8	190		216, 233,
		3.7	190		234
Jeremiah		4.1–5.4	210	8.7-10	210
1.1	207	4.3	210	8.7	213-15,
1.13-14	192	5.5	189, 211		217, 219,
1.18	172	5.8-9	189		220
2.23	57	5.11	135	8.9	193, 201,
2.25	113	6	190		205, 210,
2.27	197	7.21	188		234
3.19	72	7.23-24	188	8.10-12	193
5.4-5	186	7.26	168	8.10	193, 198,
5.5	168	7.27	172		202, 210,
5.20	49	8	33, 35,		219
5.23	43, 49		186, 188,	8.11	190, 193,
6.27-30	124		190, 191,		197, 202,
6.28	43, 47		193, 194,		205-207,
8.19	211		196-98,		220
15.19	52		202, 205,	8.12	191, 201,
16.4	123		206, 208,		205, 206
18.18	168		210, 215,	8.13	189, 201,
20.3	118		217-19,		205, 215,
26.24	207		221-23,		216, 219,
29.3	207		226, 250		233

Ezekiel (cont.)		10.6-7	216	4.13-14	132
8.14-16	197	10.6	198	4.13	132
8.14-15	193	10.7	216	4.14	132
8.14	197, 206,	10.18	186, 187	4.16	43, 47
	210, 213-	10.19	210	4.17-18	53
	17, 220,	11.23	186, 187,	6.6	6
	221		210	7.15	48
8.15	189, 193,	11.25	250	8.12	11
	201, 205,	14.1-8	208	10.8	211
	215, 216,	16	190		
	221, 222,	16.40	169	*Joel*	
	233	16.62-63	202	1.5	53
8.16-18	196	19.18	188	2.15-16	169
8.16	193, 194,	20	208	2.17	221
	196-98,	20.3-6	188		
	203, 206,	20.18	48	*Amos*	
	207, 210,	20.21	43, 48	1.4	124
	214-17,	22.17-22	124	1.7	124
	221	23	190	1.10	124
8.17-18	216	23.46-47	169	1.12	124
8.17	189, 197,	24.9-10	188	1.14	124
	198, 205,	34.24	171	2.1	123
	208, 210,	36.20	127	2.2	124
	216, 233	36.21	127	2.5	124
8.18	196, 205	38.12	212	5.21-24	6
9–11	187	40–48	208, 209	6.12	63
9	190	40–46	217	8.6	113
9.1–11.25	191	43.1	223		
9.1-11	213	43.2	223	*Micah*	
9.1	221	43.4	223	6.6-8	6
9.2	221	43.8	217		
9.3	186, 187	44.24	209	*Nahum*	
9.4	190	45.16	172	3.4-7	136
9.5-7	190	45.22	172	3.4	132, 136
9.5	207	48	86	3.6	136
9.6	206, 207,	48.1-29	86		
	221	48.1	86	*Habakkuk*	
9.7-11	244			2.15	54
9.9	191	*Hosea*			
9.11	216	1.2	148, 202	*Zephaniah*	
10	209	2.5-12	136	3.1-2	43, 48
10.2	198, 216	2.5-10	202	3.2	48
10.3	217, 218	2.5	136		
10.4-5	186	2.12	149	*Haggai*	
10.4	186, 187,	4.6	168	2	172
	195	4.10	131	2.4	172
10.5	217, 218	4.11	53		

Index of References

Zechariah	
7.11	43, 47
13.9	124

Malachi	
2.7	168
3.2	124

Apocrypha

Wisdom of Solomon	
14.27	198

Ecclesiasticus	
5.6	161
7.28	63
10.5	161
44.9	79
44.14	79

NEW TESTAMENT

Matthew	
4.10	200
9.13	6
11.16-17	66
11.18-19	66
11.19	65
12.7	6
12.14	67
12.24-28	67
15.4	59
23.13-36	210
23.35–24.2	209
23.35	209
23.37-38	209
24.1-3	208
24.2	210
24.3	210
27.46	xi

Mark	
3.20	67
3.21	67
3.22-30	67
3.22	67
3.35	96
7.10	59
12.28-34	6

Luke	
7.31-32	66
7.33-34	66
7.34	65
10.30-37	168
11.14-20	67
12.48	208
15.2	67
15.11-32	67

John	
1.42	115

Romans	
1.25	198

1 Corinthians	
6.9-10	72

2 Corinthians	
5.21	xi

Galatians	
5.19-21	72

Ephesians	
6.2	61

Hebrews	
3.7-19	49

1 Peter	
4.3	55
4.17	208

Revelation	
18.7-9	124

Pseudepigrapha

T. Levi	
19.1	57

Mishnah

Abod. Zar.	
12a	204

Ḥul.	
5a	198

Hor.	
8a	198

Kel.	
1.9	221

Neg.	
12.4	212

Qid.	
1.27d	6

Sanh.	
7.2	124
8.2	55
8.5	43
52a	128
71a	41, 42
72a	43
74a	198
90a	198

Suk.	
5.4	196

Talmuds

b. Sanh.	
72a	43

b. Yeb.	
24a	95

j. Yeb.	
4.12	87
13a	107

Midrash
Lam. R.
25   210

Num. R.
9.24   53

Philo
Sobr.
1.4   53
1.18 58
1.19 58
8.27 53

Classical
Justinian's *Code*
9.15.1 68
9.17.1 68

Collatio Legum
4.8   68

Justinian's *Digest*
28.2.11 68
48.8.2   68

Ancient Near Eastern Lawcodes
CE
25   153

Code of Hammurabi
160   153

Hittite Laws
29   153
166 154

Laws of Eshnunna
16   90

Laws of Hummarabi
21   154
25   154
196 173
198 173
256 154

Middle Assyrian Laws
A.14   139
A. 40-41 151
B. 2   90
B. 3   90

INDEX OF AUTHORS

Ackerman, S. 193, 217, 223
Allott, P.J. 2, 5
Alster, B. 193, 194
Anderson, F.I. 96, 117, 132
Anderson, G.A. 174, 175
André, 211
Ashworth, A. 3

Bailey, K.E. 57, 58
Bailey, S.J. 5
Bal, M. 125
Barr, J. 46
Barton, J. 33, 186
Bayles, M.D. 246, 247
Beattie, D.R.G. 99, 101
Bechtel, L.M. 80, 81, 105, 106, 112, 114, 187, 202
Belkin, S. 83, 101, 108
Bellefontaine, E. 39, 44, 45
Ben-Amos, D. 116
Benjamin, D.C. 8, 39, 49, 71, 72, 74, 75, 77, 82, 86, 97, 98, 106, 108, 175
Binger, T. 131
Biran, A. 80
Bird, P.A. 61, 129-31, 150, 175
Blank, S.B. 209
Bledstein, A.J. 99
Blenkinsopp, J. 54
Block, D.I. 187, 215, 218
Bockmuehl, M. 63
Bonar, A.A. 167
Boose, L.E. 92, 139, 152
Braithwaite, J. 81, 105, 232
Braswell, M.C. 242
Brenner, A. 130
Brichto, H.C. 16, 38, 39, 55, 85, 89, 108, 124
Brin, G. 97

Brooks, B.A. 130
Brown, C. 67
Buckland, W.W. 68
Budd, P.J. 159, 164, 166, 179, 183
Burrows, M. 87, 99, 104, 110
Bush, G. 172, 177

Calvin, J. 205, 216
Carmichael, C.M. 25, 38, 59, 63, 101, 104, 107, 109, 110, 114
Clements, R.E. 8
Clifford, R.J. 212
Clines, D.J.A. 57, 58
Coats, G.W. 49, 50
Cogan, M. 194
Cohn, H.H. 43, 123
Collins, O.E. 127, 135, 136, 142, 145
Cooke, G.A. 191, 215
Corbett, C. 242
Craigie, P.C. 62, 97, 142
Crüsemann, F. 11
Crystal, D. 8
Cullen, F.T. 2, 240, 245

Dahood, M. 198
Daube, D. 60, 61, 80, 90, 104, 106, 107, 114, 118, 119
Davies, D.S. 5
Davies, E.W. 87, 90, 91, 97, 106, 107, 158, 159, 175
Day, P.L. 143
De Ward, E.F. 153, 203
Delitzsch, F. 167
Dempster, S. 80, 106, 107
Dever, W.G. 80
Diamond, B.L. 43, 45, 54
Dillard, R. 53
Dommershausen, W. 127, 128

Dostoevsky, F. x
Douglas, M. 164-66, 176
Driver, S.R. 136
Duguid, I.M. 171, 172, 208, 209, 215, 217
Dunbar, I. 7
Dunnill, J. 184
Dworkin, R. 19

Eichler, B.L. 14, 15
Eissfeldt, O. 117
Eliot, T.S. 157
English, F. 107
Erlandsson, S. 129

Fairman, H.W. 205
Fass, D.E. 210
Faulkner, D. x
Faur, J. 206
Finkelstein, J.J. 21, 24, 142
Fishbane, M. 158, 163
Fisher, E.J. 130
Fitzmaurice, C. 231
Flanagan, J.W. 171
Fleishman, J. 133
Fleming, D.E. 176
France, R.T. 66
Frazer, Sir J.G. 5
Freedman, D.N. 132, 191
Freedy, K.S. 191
Frishtik, M. 68
Frost, S.B. 102, 123
Fry, C. 10
Frymer-Kensky, T. 131, 137, 139, 142, 145, 146, 148, 165

Gaballa, G.A. 116
Garland, D. 34
Gaster, T.H. 195
Giovannini, M.J. 146
Gorman, F.H. Jr. 157, 166, 184
Greenberg, M. 21-24, 186, 190, 220
Greenspahn, F.E. 91, 94, 100
Gruber, M.I. 131, 143
Gurney, O.R. 193

Hagedorn, A.C. 41, 46
Halbertal, M. 202, 205

Hallo, W.W. 142, 189
Halperin, D.J. 192, 207, 215
Hamilton, V.P. 42, 109
Hanson, B. 238
Hardyman, P.L. 2
Harrelson, W. 62, 63
Harris, W.V. 69
Harrison, R.K. 164
Hart, H.L.A. 2
Hartley, J.E. 124, 164, 165
Henry, J.P. 240
Herntrich, 12
Hess, R.S. 116
Hillers, D.R. 130
Hirsch, S.R. 41, 47, 51, 86, 107
Hoffman, P.B. 2
Holladay, W.L. 57, 58
Hough, M. 3
Hugenburger, G.P. 140, 145
Humbert, P. 189
Hurowitz, V. 212, 214
Hurvitz, A. 193

Jackson, B.S. 5, 10-24, 26, 29-32, 63, 95, 152, 190, 199-201, 203, 204, 225, 233-35, 237, 238, 240, 248
Jacobsen, T. 193, 194, 203
Jareborg, N. 7
Jenson, P.P. 122, 126, 127, 174, 177, 211, 218, 222
Jones, S. 241
Joosten, J. 127

Kaiser, W.C. Jr. 6
Katsh, A.I. 44
Kaufman, S.A. 59, 60
Kee, H.C. 67
Keil, C.F. 167
Kellerman, D. 167
Kiuchi, N. 161, 163, 164, 179, 183, 184
Klawans, J. 135
Klein, R.W. 56
Kleinig, J. 231, 232, 247
Knohl, I. 159, 164
Köhler, L. 136
Kruger, P.A. 26, 108

Laffey, A.L. 140

Index of Authors

Langdon, A. 7
Laski, H.J. 3
Lee, R.W. 69
Leeb, C.S. 139, 142
Leggett, D.A. 91
Levi, M. 241
Levine, B.A. 163-65, 174, 182
Levine, E. 89
Levinson, B.M. 25, 110
Lewis, C.S. ix
Lim Teng Kok, J. 74
Lipinski, E. 194, 195
Loader, J.A. 111
Locher, C. 139
Lundquist, J.M. 212

Maag, V. 57
McCarthy, C. 205
McCarthy, D.J. 62
McCleary, R. 241
McComiskey, T.E. 149
McConville, J.G. 59, 88, 103, 138
McCurley, F.R. 211, 212
MacIntyre, A. 4
Main, D.J. 242
Malinowski, B. 82
Margalit, A. 202, 205
Marsh, C. 241, 242, 251
Martin, D.B. 52
Matthews, V.H. 8, 70, 99, 107, 139, 140, 145, 175, 176, 213, 214
May, H.G. 195
Mayhew, P. 242
Melnyk, J.L.R. 72, 73
Mendelsohn, I. 106, 155
Mendelsohn, S. 1
Meyers, C.L. 150
Milgrom, J. 74, 155, 159, 161-67, 171, 172, 177, 179, 182-84, 223
Miller, L.S. 242
Miller, P. 59, 60, 63, 201
Montaigne, M. de 1
Moore, M. 4, 5
Morgernstern, J. 195
Motyer, J.A. 53, 105
Mullins, P.O.C. 137

Nathan, G. 243, 251

Neufeld, D. 64-66
Neufeld, E. 84, 89, 95, 97, 98, 100
Nicholas, B. 68, 69
Niehaus, J.J. 124, 187, 188, 195, 214
Noonan, J.T. Jr. 104

O'Connell, M. 229, 231, 240-42
Oboler, R.S. 95
Oden, R.A. Jr. 130, 131
Ollenburger, B.C. 187, 211
Olson, D.T. 59, 60, 70, 71
Olyan, S.M. 27, 60, 80, 81, 106
Otto, E. 112, 141
Ottosson, M. 216

Patai, R. 186
Patrick, D. 70
Payne, L. 121
Pease, K. 231
Pedersen, J. 104, 136
Phillips, A. 61, 136, 142
Pickett, W.H. 189
Pincoffs, E.L. 247
Plaskow, J. 137, 155
Potash, B. 89, 95
Poythress, V.S. 61, 198
Prell, E.A. 240, 241
Pressler, C. 112, 137, 138, 140, 142, 146, 148, 151
Preuss, 103
Pritchard, J.B. 15
Prouser, O.H. 176
Pursiful, D.J. 167

Rankin, O.S. 117
Rattray, S. 118
Redford, D.B. 191
Rendtorff, R. 158
Ringgren, H. 37
Rofé, A. 137, 139
Rogerson, J.W. 8
Rose, A.M. 240, 241
Ross, A.P. 84
Rossi, P.H. 240
Rotenburg, M. 43, 45, 54
Roth, M.T. 139, 148, 151, 153, 154, 173
Rowley, H.H. 87, 91, 99, 191
Ruppert, 47, 48

Rushdoony, R.J. 44

Saller, R.P. 68, 69
Sasson, J.M. 86, 90, 91, 98, 99, 101, 103, 108, 112, 145
Schmitt, J.J. 62, 143
Schulz, F. 68
Schwartz, B.J. 164
Sebba, L. 243, 251
Seidl, 161
Shakespeare, W. 37
Simkins, R. 28
Simon, F. 242
Smedes, L. 105, 106
Smith, M. 191
Snaith, N.H. 97
Sparks, R. 240, 242
Speiser, E.A. 107, 171
Stacey, W.D. 191
Stager, L.E. 142
Sterring, A. 93
Stone, K. 139, 145, 147, 149
Stulman, L. 64
Sudnow, D. 17

Taylor, J.G. 195, 196
Terence, ix
Thompson, D. 99, 100, 112
Thompson, R.J. 176
Thompson, T. 99, 100, 112
Tigay, J.H. 76, 87, 89, 97, 98, 111, 139, 141, 146, 152
Toeg, A. 159
Torczyner, H. 192

Ushedo, B. 221

Van den Boom, G.P.F. 214
Van der Toorn, K. 150, 151
Viberg, A. 26, 29, 87, 107
Von Hirsch, A. 3, 7

Wadsworth, T. 139, 141, 147
Walker, D.M. 5
Walker, M.A. 242
Walker, N. 34, 241, 242, 251
Warr, M. 239, 240
Washington, H.C. 144
Watts, J.W. 146, 201
Weiner, H.M. 75
Weinfeld, M. 13
Wenham, G.J. 59, 86, 87, 119, 138-40, 143-45, 148, 150, 162, 164, 169, 170, 175
Westbrook, R. 84, 90, 97, 107, 108, 112
Westenholz, J.G. 130, 131
Whelan, A. 229, 231, 240-42
Wiggins, S.A. 195
Wiseman, D.J. 105
Wittgenstein, L. 58
Wright, C.J.H. 43, 49, 60-62, 67, 71, 142, 197
Wright, D.P. 157, 165
Wright, G.E. 192
Wright, N.T. 28

Yamauchi, E.M. 130
Yaron, R. 17
Yeats, W.B. 213

Zimmerli, W. 192, 193, 205, 206, 215-17
Zimmermann, F. 105, 117
Zohar, N. 164

JOURNAL FOR THE STUDY OF THE OLD TESTAMENT
SUPPLEMENT SERIES

198 T.J. Meadowcroft, *Aramaic Daniel and Greek Daniel: A Literary Comparison*
199 J.H. Eaton, *Psalms of the Way and the Kingdom: A Conference with the Commentators*
200 M. Daniel Carroll R., David J.A. Clines and Philip R. Davies (eds.), *The Bible in Human Society: Essays in Honour of John Rogerson*
201 John W. Rogerson, *The Bible and Criticism in Victorian Britain: Profiles of F.D. Maurice and William Robertson Smith*
202 Nanette Stahl, *Law and Liminality in the Bible*
203 Jill M. Munro, *Spikenard and Saffron: The Imagery of the Song of Songs*
204 Philip R. Davies, *Whose Bible Is It Anyway?*
205 David J.A. Clines, *Interested Parties: The Ideology of Writers and Readers of the Hebrew Bible*
206 Møgens Müller, *The First Bible of the Church: A Plea for the Septuagint*
207 John W. Rogerson, Margaret Davies and M. Daniel Carroll R. (eds.), *The Bible in Ethics: The Second Sheffield Colloquium*
208 Beverly J. Stratton, *Out of Eden: Reading, Rhetoric, and Ideology in Genesis 2–3*
209 Patricia Dutcher-Walls, *Narrative Art, Political Rhetoric: The Case of Athaliah and Joash*
210 Jacques Berlinerblau, *The Vow and the 'Popular Religious Groups' of Ancient Israel: A Philological and Sociological Inquiry*
211 Brian E. Kelly, *Retribution and Eschatology in Chronicles*
212 Yvonne Sherwood, *The Prostitute and the Prophet: Hosea's Marriage in Literary-Theoretical Perspective*
213 Yair Hoffman, *A Blemished Perfection: The Book of Job in Context*
214 Roy F. Melugin and Marvin A. Sweeney (eds.), *New Visions of Isaiah*
215 J. Cheryl Exum, *Plotted, Shot and Painted: Cultural Representations of Biblical Women*
216 Judith E. McKinlay, *Gendering Wisdom the Host: Biblical Invitations to Eat and Drink*
217 Jerome F.D. Creach, *Yahweh as Refuge and the Editing of the Hebrew Psalter*
218 Harry P. Nasuti, *Defining the Sacred Songs: Genre, Tradition, and the Post-Critical Interpretation of the Psalms*
219 Gerald Morris, *Prophecy, Poetry and Hosea*
220 Raymond F. Person, Jr, *In Conversation with Jonah: Conversation Analysis, Literary Criticism, and the Book of Jonah*
221 Gillian Keys, *The Wages of Sin: A Reappraisal of the 'Succession Narrative'*
222 R.N. Whybray, *Reading the Psalms as a Book*
223 Scott B. Noegel, *Janus Parallelism in the Book of Job*
224 Paul J. Kissling, *Reliable Characters in the Primary History: Profiles of Moses, Joshua, Elijah and Elisha*

225 Richard D. Weis and David M. Carr (eds.), *A Gift of God in Due Season: Essays on Scripture and Community in Honor of James A. Sanders*
226 Lori L. Rowlett, *Joshua and the Rhetoric of Violence: A New Historicist Analysis*
227 John F.A. Sawyer (ed.), *Reading Leviticus: Responses to Mary Douglas*
228 Volkmar Fritz and Philip R. Davies (eds.), *The Origins of the Ancient Israelite States*
229 Stephen Breck Reid (ed.), *Prophets and Paradigms: Essays in Honor of Gene M. Tucker*
230 Kevin J. Cathcart and Michael Maher (eds.), *Targumic and Cognate Studies: Essays in Honour of Martin McNamara*
231 Weston W. Fields, *Sodom and Gomorrah: History and Motif in Biblical Narrative*
232 Tilde Binger, *Asherah: Goddesses in Ugarit, Israel and the Old Testament*
233 Michael D. Goulder, *The Psalms of Asaph and the Pentateuch: Studies in the Psalter, III*
234 Ken Stone, *Sex, Honor, and Power in the Deuteronomistic History*
235 James W. Watts and Paul House (eds.), *Forming Prophetic Literature: Essays on Isaiah and the Twelve in Honor of John D.W. Watts*
236 Thomas M. Bolin, *Freedom beyond Forgiveness: The Book of Jonah Re-examined*
237 Neil Asher Silberman and David B. Small (eds.), *The Archaeology of Israel: Constructing the Past, Interpreting the Present*
238 M. Patrick Graham, Kenneth G. Hoglund and Steven L. McKenzie (eds.), *The Chronicler as Historian*
239 Mark S. Smith, *The Pilgrimage Pattern in Exodus*
240 Eugene E. Carpenter (ed.), *A Biblical Itinerary: In Search of Method, Form and Content. Essays in Honor of George W. Coats*
241 Robert Karl Gnuse, *No Other Gods: Emergent Monotheism in Israel*
242 K.L. Noll, *The Faces of David*
243 Henning Graf Reventlow (ed.), *Eschatology in the Bible and in Jewish and Christian Tradition*
244 Walter E. Aufrecht, Neil A. Mirau and Steven W. Gauley (eds.), *Urbanism in Antiquity: From Mesopotamia to Crete*
245 Lester L. Grabbe (ed.), *Can a 'History of Israel' Be Written?*
246 Gillian M. Bediako, *Primal Religion and the Bible: William Robertson Smith and his Heritage*
247 Nathan Klaus, *Pivot Patterns in the Former Prophets*
248 Etienne Nodet, *A Search for the Origins of Judaism: From Joshua to the Mishnah*
249 William Paul Griffin, *The God of the Prophets: An Analysis of Divine Action*
250 Josette Elayi and Jean Sapin, *Beyond the River: New Perspectives on Trans-euphratene*
251 Flemming A.J. Nielsen, *The Tragedy in History: Herodotus and the Deuteronomistic History*

252 David C. Mitchell, *The Message of the Psalter: An Eschatological Programme in the Book of Psalms*
253 William Johnstone, *1 and 2 Chronicles, Volume 1: 1 Chronicles 1–2 Chronicles 9: Israel's Place among the Nations*
254 William Johnstone, *1 and 2 Chronicles, Volume 2: 2 Chronicles 10–36: Guilt and Atonement*
255 Larry L. Lyke, *King David with the Wise Woman of Tekoa: The Resonance of Tradition in Parabolic Narrative*
256 Roland Meynet, *Rhetorical Analysis: An Introduction to Biblical Rhetoric*
257 Philip R. Davies and David J.A. Clines (eds.), *The World of Genesis: Persons, Places, Perspectives*
258 Michael D. Goulder, *The Psalms of the Return (Book V, Psalms 107–150): Studies in the Psalter, IV*
259 Allen Rosengren Petersen, *The Royal God: Enthronement Festivals in Ancient Israel and Ugarit?*
260 A.R. Pete Diamond, Kathleen M. O'Connor and Louis Stulman (eds.), *Troubling Jeremiah*
261 Othmar Keel, *Goddesses and Trees, New Moon and Yahweh: Ancient Near Eastern Art and the Hebrew Bible*
262 Victor H. Matthews, Bernard M. Levinson and Tikva Frymer-Kensky (eds.), *Gender and Law in the Hebrew Bible and the Ancient Near East*
263 M. Patrick Graham and Steven L. McKenzie, *The Chronicler as Author: Studies in Text and Texture*
264 Donald F. Murray, *Divine Prerogative and Royal Pretension: Pragmatics, Poetics, and Polemics in a Narrative Sequence about David (2 Samuel 5.17–7.29)*
265 John Day, *Yahweh and the Gods and Goddesses of Canaan*
266 J. Cheryl Exum and Stephen D. Moore (eds.), *Biblical Studies/Cultural Studies: The Third Sheffield Colloquium*
267 Patrick D. Miller, Jr, *Israelite Religion and Biblical Theology: Collected Essays*
268 Linda S. Schearing and Steven L. McKenzie (eds.), *Those Elusive Deuteronomists: 'Pandeuteronomism' and Scholarship in the Nineties*
269 David J.A. Clines and Stephen D. Moore (eds.), *Auguries: The Jubilee Volume of the Sheffield Department of Biblical Studies*
270 John Day (ed.), *King and Messiah in Israel and the Ancient Near East: Proceedings of the Oxford Old Testament Seminar*
271 Wonsuk Ma, *Until the Spirit Comes: The Spirit of God in the Book of Isaiah*
272 James Richard Linville, *Israel in the Book of Kings: The Past as a Project of Social Identity*
273 Meir Lubetski, Claire Gottlieb and Sharon Keller (eds.), *Boundaries of the Ancient Near Eastern World: A Tribute to Cyrus H. Gordon*
274 Martin J. Buss, *Biblical Form Criticism in its Context*
275 William Johnstone, *Chronicles and Exodus: An Analogy and its Application*
276 Raz Kletter, *Economic Keystones: The Weight System of the Kingdom of Judah*
277 Augustine Pagolu, *The Religion of the Patriarchs*

278 Lester L. Grabbe (ed.), *Leading Captivity Captive: 'The Exile' as History and Ideology*
279 Kari Latvus, *God, Anger and Ideology: The Anger of God in Joshua and Judges in Relation to Deuteronomy and the Priestly Writings*
280 Eric S. Christianson, *A Time to Tell: Narrative Strategies in Ecclesiastes*
281 Peter D. Miscall, *Isaiah 34–35: A Nightmare/A Dream*
282 Joan E. Cook, *Hannah's Desire, God's Design: Early Interpretations in the Story of Hannah*
283 Kelvin Friebel, *Jeremiah's and Ezekiel's Sign-Acts: Rhetorical Nonverbal Communication*
284 M. Patrick Graham, Rick R. Marrs and Steven L. McKenzie (eds.), *Worship and the Hebrew Bible: Essays in Honor of John T. Willis*
285 Paolo Sacchi, *History of the Second Temple*
286 Wesley J. Bergen, *Elisha and the End of Prophetism*
287 Anne Fitzpatrick-McKinley, *The Transformation of Torah from Scribal Advice to Law*
288 Diana Lipton, *Revisions of the Night: Politics and Promises in the Patriarchal Dreams of Genesis*
289 Jože Krašovec (ed.), *The Interpretation of the Bible: The International Symposium in Slovenia*
290 Frederick H. Cryer and Thomas L. Thompson (eds.), *Qumran between the Old and New Testaments*
291 Christine Schams, *Jewish Scribes in the Second-Temple Period*
292 David J.A. Clines, *On the Way to the Postmodern: Old Testament Essays, 1967–1998 Volume 1*
293 David J.A. Clines, *On the Way to the Postmodern: Old Testament Essays, 1967–1998 Volume 2*
294 Charles E. Carter, *The Emergence of Yehud in the Persian Period: A Social and Demographic Study*
295 Jean-Marc Heimerdinger, *Topic, Focus and Foreground in Ancient Hebrew Narratives*
296 Mark Cameron Love, *The Evasive Text: Zechariah 1–8 and the Frustrated Reader*
297 Paul S. Ash, *David, Solomon and Egypt: A Reassessment*
298 John D. Baildam, *Paradisal Love: Johann Gottfried Herder and the Song of Songs*
299 M. Daniel Carroll R., *Rethinking Contexts, Rereading Texts: Contributions from the Social Sciences to Biblical Interpretation*
300 Edward Ball (ed.), *In Search of True Wisdom: Essays in Old Testament Interpretation in Honour of Ronald E. Clements*
301 Carolyn S. Leeb, *Away from the Father's House: The Social Location of na'ar and na'arah in Ancient Israel*
302 Xuan Huong Thi Pham, *Mourning in the Ancient Near East and the Hebrew Bible*

303 Ingrid Hjelm, *The Samaritans and Early Judaism: A Literary Analysis*
304 Wolter H. Rose, *Zemah and Zerubbabel: Messianic Expectations in the Early Postexilic Period*
305 Jo Bailey Wells, *God's Holy People: A Theme in Biblical Theology*
306 Albert de Pury, Thomas Römer and Jean-Daniel Macchi (eds.), *Israel Constructs its History: Deuteronomistic Historiography in Recent Research*
307 Robert L. Cole, *The Shape and Message of Book III (Psalms 73–89)*
308 Yiu-Wing Fung, *Victim and Victimizer: Joseph's Interpretation of his Destiny*
309 George Aichele (ed.), *Culture, Entertainment and the Bible*
310 Esther Fuchs, *Sexual Politics in the Biblical Narrative: Reading the Hebrew Bible as a Woman*
311 Gregory Glazov, *The Bridling of the Tongue and the Opening of the Mouth in Biblical Prophecy*
312 Francis Landy, *Beauty and the Enigma: And Other Essays on the Hebrew Bible*
313 Martin O'Kane (ed.), *Borders, Boundaries and the Bible*
314 Bernard S. Jackson, *Studies in the Semiotics of Biblical Law*
315 Paul R. Williamson, *Abraham, Israel and the Nations: The Patriarchal Promise and its Covenantal Development in Genesis*
316 Dominic Rudman, *Determinism in the Book of Ecclesiastes*
317 Lester L. Grabbe (ed.), *Did Moses Speak Attic? Jewish Historiography and Scripture in the Hellenistic Period*
318 David A. Baer, *When We All Go Home: Translation and Theology in LXX 56–66*
319 Henning Graf Reventlow and Yair Hoffman (eds.), *Creation in Jewish and Christian Tradition*
320 Claudia V. Camp, *Wise, Strange and Holy: The Strange Woman and the Making of the Bible*
321 Varese Layzer, *Signs of Weakness: Juxtaposing Irish Tales and the Bible*
322 Mignon R. Jacobs, *The Conceptual Coherence of the Book of Micah*
323 Martin Ravndal Hauge, *The Descent from the Mountain: Narrative Patterns in Exodus 19–40*
324 P.M. Michèle Daviau, John W. Wevers and Michael Weigl (eds.), *The World of the Aramaeans: Studies in Honour of Paul-Eugène Dion*, Volume 1
325 P.M. Michèle Daviau, John W. Wevers and Michael Weigl (eds.), *The World of the Aramaeans: Studies in Honour of Paul-Eugène Dion*, Volume 2
326 P.M. Michèle Daviau, John W. Wevers and Michael Weigl (eds.), *The World of the Aramaeans: Studies in Honour of Paul-Eugène Dion*, Volume 3
327 Gary D. Salyer, *Vain Rhetoric: Private Insight and Public Debate in Ecclesiastes*
328 James M. Trotter, *Reading Hosea in Achaemenid Yehud*
329 Wolfgang Bluedorn, *Yahweh Verus Baalism: A Theological Reading of the Gideon-Abimelech Narrative*
330 Lester L. Grabbe and Robert D. Haak (eds.), *'Every City shall be Forsaken': Urbanism and Prophecy in Ancient Israel and the Near East*
331 Amihai Mazar (ed.), with the assistance of Ginny Mathias, *Studies in the Archaeology of the Iron Age in Israel and Jordan*

332 Robert J.V. Hiebert, Claude E. Cox and Peter J. Gentry (eds.), *The Old Greek Psalter: Studies in Honour of Albert Pietersma*
333 Ada Rapoport-Albert and Gillian Greenberg (eds.), *Biblical Hebrew, Biblical Texts: Essays in Memory of Michael P. Weitzman*
334 Ken Stone (ed.), *Queer Commentary and the Hebrew Bible*
335 James K. Bruckner, *Implied Law in the Abrahamic Narrative: A Literary and Theological Analysis*
336 Stephen L. Cook, Corrine L. Patton and James W. Watts (eds.), *The Whirlwind: Essays on Job, Hermeneutics and Theology in Memory of Jane Morse*
337 Joyce Rilett Wood, *Amos in Song and Book Culture*
338 Alice A. Keefe, *Woman's Body and the Social Body in Hosea 1–2*
339 Sarah Nicholson, *Three Faces of Saul: An Intertextual Approach to Biblical Tragedy*
340 Philip R. Davies and John M. Halligan (eds.), *Second Temple Studies III: Studies in Politics, Class and Material Culture*
341 Mark W. Chavalas and K. Lawson Younger Jr (eds.), *Mesopotamia and the Bible*
343 J. Andrew Dearman and M. Patrick Graham (eds.), *The Land that I Will Show You: Essays on the History and Archaeology of the Ancient Near East in Honor of J. Maxwell Miller*
345 Jan-Wim Wesselius, *The Origin of the History of Israel: Herodotus' Histories as Blueprint for the First Books of the Bible*
346 Johanna Stiebert, *The Construction of Shame in the Hebrew Bible: The Prophetic Contribution*
347 Andrew G. Shead, *The Open Book and the Sealed Book: Jeremiah 32 in its Hebrew and Greek Recensions*
348 Alastair G. Hunter and Phillip R. Davies, *Sense and Sensitivity: Essays on Reading the Bible in Memory of Robert Carroll*
350 David Janzen, *Witch-hunts, Purity and Social Boundaries: The Expulsion of the Foreign Women in Ezra 9–10*
351 Roland Boer (ed.), *Tracking the 'Tribes of Yahweh': On the Trail of a Classic*
352 William John Lyons, *Canon and Exegesis: Canonical Praxis and the Sodom Narrative*
353 Athalya Brenner and Jan Willem van Henten (eds.), *Bible Translation on the Threshold of the Twenty-First Century: Authority, Reception, Culture and Religion*
354 Susan Gillingham, *The Image, the Depths and the Surface: Multivalent Approaches to Biblical Study*
356 Carole Fontaine, *Smooth Words: Women, Proverbs and Performance in Biblical Wisdom*
357 Carleen Mandolfo, *God in the Dock: Dialogic Tension in the Psalms of Lament*
359 David M. Gunn and Paula N. McNutt, *'Imagining' Biblical Worlds: Studies in Spatial, Social and Historical Constructs in Honor of James W. Flanagan*
361 Franz V. Greifenhagen, *Egypt on the Pentateuch's Ideological Map: Constructing Biblical Israel's Identity*
364 Jonathan P. Burnside, *The Signs of Sin: Seriousness of Offence in Biblical Law*